REFORGING THE GREAT CHAIN OF BEING

SYNTHESE HISTORICAL LIBRARY

TEXTS AND STUDIES IN THE HISTORY OF

LOGIC AND PHILOSOPHY

VOLUME 20

REFORGING THE GREAT CHAIN OF BEING

Studies of the History of Modal Theories

Edited by

SIMO KNUUTTILA

University of Helsinki, Dept. of Philosophy, Helsinki, Finland

D. REIDEL PUBLISHING COMPANY

DORDRECHT : HOLLAND / BOSTON : U.S.A.

LONDON : ENGLAND

Library of Congress Cataloging in Publication Data

CIP

Main entry under title:

Reforging the great chain of being.

(Synthese historical library ; v. 20)
Includes bibliographies.
1.   Modality (Logic)—Addresses, essays, lectures.   2.   Modality
(Theory of knowledge)—Addresses, essays, lectures.   I.   Knuuttila,
Simo, 1946–   II.   Series.
BC199.M6R36   160   80–19869
ISBN 90–277–1125–9

Published by D. Reidel Publishing Company,
P.O. Box 17, 3300 AA Dordrecht, Holland.

Sold and distributed in the U.S.A. and Canada
by Kluwer Boston Inc.,
190 Old Derby Street, Hingham, MA 02043, U.S.A.

In all other countries, sold and distributed
by Kluwer Academic Publishers Group,
P.O. Box 322, 3300 AH Dordrecht, Holland.

D. Reidel Publishing Company is a member of the Kluwer Group.

Printed in The Netherlands

TABLE OF CONTENTS

INTRODUCTION

A sports reporter might say that in a competition all the participants realize their potentialities or possibilities. When an athlete performs far below his usual standard, it can be said that it was possible for him to do better. But the idea of fair play requires that this use of 'possible' refers to another competition. It is presumed that the best athlete wins and that no real possibility of doing better is left unrealized in a competition. Here we have a use of language, a language game, in which modal notions are used so as to imply that if something is possible, it is realized. This idea does not belong to the general presuppositions of current ordinary usage. It is, nevertheless, not difficult to find other similar examples outside of the language of sports. It may be that such a use of modal notions is sometimes calculated to express that in the context in question there are no real alternative courses of events in contradistinction to other cases in which some possible alternatives remain unrealized.

Even though modal notions are currently interpreted without the presupposition that each genuine possibility should be realized at some moment of the actual history, there are contemporary philosophical models of modalities which incorporate this presupposition. In his book *Untersuchungen über den Modalkalkül* (Anton Hain, Meisenheim am Glan 1952, pp. 16–36), Oscar Becker presents a statistical interpretation of modal calculi. The basic definitions are as follows:

(1) $\quad \Box p = (x)P(x) \equiv \sim(Ex)\sim P(x)$

(2) $\quad \sim\Diamond p = \sim(Ex)P(x) \equiv (x)\sim P(x)$

(3) $\quad \Diamond p = (Ex)P(x) \equiv \sim(x)\sim P(x)$

(4) $\quad \sim\Box p = \sim(x)P(x) \equiv (Ex)\sim P(x)$

($\Box$ stands for necessity, $\Diamond$ for possibility). In this interpretation it is presupposed that there is a variable element in modal propositions. 'Necessity' and 'possibility' are captured by the universal operator and the existential operator, respectively. They operate on propositional functions, of which those are necessarily true that are satisfied by all values of the bound variable 'x'. Those propositional functions are possible that are satisfied by some value

vii

S. Knuuttila (ed.), *Reforging the Great Chain of Being*, vii–xiv.
Copyright © 1980 *by D. Reidel Publishing Company.*

of 'x'. If the bound variable 'x' ranges over moments of time, then we have the presupposition mentioned.

According to Becker, this is one possible way of understanding the statistical interpretation of modal notions, and he refers to the following passage in Kant: "The Schema of possibility . . . . is the determination of the representation of a thing at any time whatsoever. The schema of reality is the existence at a given time. The schema of necessity is the existence of an object at all times." (Immanuel Kant, *Critique of Pure Reason*, transl. by F. Max Müller, Doubleday, Garden City, N.Y. 1966, p. 125).

This is not the only explication Becker offers to his statistical interpretation of modal calculi. But on this interpretation modal notions are reduced to extensional terms, and hence similar ideas were not uncommon among the logical positivists. (For some examples see H. Poser, 'Das Scheitern des logischen Positivismus an modaltheoretischen Problemen', *Studium Generale* 24 (1971), pp. 1522–1535).

Other examples of this line of thought can be easily found in the works of Bertrand Russell. In 'The Philosophy of Logical Atomism' (1918) he writes: "One may call a propositional function necessary when it is always true; possible, when it is sometimes true; impossible, when it is never true." (See Bertrand Russell, *Logic and Knowledge. Essays 1901–1950*, edited by R. C. Marsh, Allen & Unwin, London 1956, p. 231). Russell says that he gets the notion of existence out of the notion of sometimes "which is the same as the notion of possible". So by saying that unicorns exist one means that "*x* is a unicorn" is possible i.e., there is at least one value of *x* for which this is true. If there is no such value, then the propositional function is impossible. (*Op. cit.* pp. 231–233). It is then contended that ordinary uses of the word 'possible' are derived from the idea that a propositional function is possible, when there are cases in which it is true. This is elucidated by discussing the (rather ambiguous) sentence "It is possible it may rain to-morrow". According to Russell this means that "It will rain to-morrow" belongs to "the class of propositions 'It rains at time *t*', where *t* is different times. We mean partly that we do not know whether it will rain or whether it will not, but also that that is the sort of proposition that is quite apt to be true, that it is a value of a propositional function of which we know some value to be true." (*Op. cit.* pp. 254–255. For Russell's views, see also G. H. von Wright, 'Diachronic and Synchronic Modalities', *Teorama* IX (1979), pp. 231–245.)

It is easy to see why Russell must say that modal notions are attributes of propositional functions and not of propositions. He trusts in the analogy between modal notions and those expressing historical frequency without considering the idea of alternatives of a temporally definite case. On his interpretation the statistically understood modal notions refer to realization in the actual history, and when temporally definite events or propositions are discussed, they as such seem to have no modal status.

It is typical that in the above quotation the focus of attention is changed from the temporally definite proposition to a form where there is a blank to be filled by a temporal specification. It is clear that the alleged possibility of the latter, i.e. the fact that it is true for some moments of time, does not say anything about the possibilities at the moment to which the original proposition refers. Contrary to what Russell says, it does not appear to be typical for the contemporary understanding of possibility that it refers to types of states of affairs exemplified in the actual history. The current ordinary understanding of modality is rather codified, for instance, in what is generally known as possible worlds semantics. According to it the logic of modal notions can be spelled out only by considering several possible worlds and their relations to each other at the same time. For example, $\Diamond p$ is true in the actual world if there is a possible world in which p is true. There is no demand that the possible world in which p holds true should sometime be actual in the real history. (See, e.g., Jaakko Hintikka, *Models for Modalities*, D. Reidel, Dordrecht 1969). Although there are in contemporary philosophy approaches to the logic of modal notions analogous to those mentioned above, they have mainly lost their attraction as theories about modality. It is widely thought that when modal notions are reduced to extensional terms which classify events of the actual history, the resulting idiom does not speak about modality at all.

Be this as it may, it seems to be a historical fact that certain kinds of reductionistic statistical interpretations of modal terms enjoyed a prominent status among the presuppositions of Western thought from Aristotle until the late thirteenth century. This was realized by C. S. Peirce, who wrote in his article 'Modality' for Baldwin's *Dictionary of Philosophy and Psychology* (MacMillan, Gloucester, Mass. 1901) as follows: "The simplest account of modality is the scholastic, according to which the necessary (or impossible) proposition is a sort of universal proposition; the possible (or contingent, in the sense of not necessary) proposition, a sort of particular proposition. That is to assert 'A must be true' is to assert not only that A is true but that all propositions analogous to A are true; and to assert 'A may be true' is to assert only that some proposition analogous to A is true. If it be asked what is there meant by analogous propositions, the answer is − all those of a certain class which the conveniences of reasoning establish."

I don't comment here on Peirce's own interpretation of "the scholastic account of modality"; it is not scholastic. But it is interesting that he refers to the scholastic theory in which 'necessity' and 'possibility' were defined in terms of "true in every case" and "true in some cases", respectively.

In 1936 Arthur O. Lovejoy published his William James Lectures delivered at Harvard University in 1933 under the title *The Great Chain of Being: A Study of the History of an Idea*, (Harvard University Press, Cambridge, Mass. 1936). In this famous study of the history of certain concepts much attention is paid to the so-called Principle of Plenitude, according to which no genuine possibility remains unrealized. Lovejoy treats this principle merely as a corollary to the idea of the Great Chain of Being, *i.e.*, the idea that the selection of different kinds of individuals as are exemplified in actuality is the fullest possible one. Following his general methodological guidelines, he also argues that the Principle of Plenitude is a perennial idea which different thinkers have built into their systems in different ways. In fact the Principle of Plenitude, when it is understood as a certain kind of relation between possibility and actuality, can have many various roles in philosophical argumentation. It is, e.g., contained in reductionistic statistical modal theories described above. It can be shown that Lovejoy's reliance on the assumption of 'unit ideas' prevented him from realizing the variety of ways in which this alleged 'unit idea' figures in the history of Western thought.

The methodological shortcomings of Lovejoy's attempt are pointed out in Jaakko Hintikka's essay 'Gaps in the Great Chain of Being: An Exercise in the Methodology of the History of Ideas' (below pp. 1–17). It serves as a general introduction to the topics of this book. Hintikka calls attention to different traditions and lines of thought which in fact imply the Principle of Plenitude but which were not dealt with in Lovejoy's study. If the Principle is understood as a possible ingredient of a theory of modal notions, we can use it as a theoretical concept in the study of the history of modal notions. Then we will find instances of it as more as less explicit parts of various doctrines in the history of thought. Many different starting points may yield the same opinion that each possibility must ultimately bear fruit.

Perhaps the most important single mistake in Lovejoy's book is his claim that the Principle of Plenitude was explicitly denied by Aristotle. This view also made him blind to certain peculiarities of the interpretation of modal notions in the Aristotelian tradition. In his many studies on Aristotle's theory of modality Hintikka has maintained that the principle is in fact included in all of Aristotle's modal paradigms. Some of his evidence against Lovejoy's view of Aristotle is collected in the article 'Aristotle on the Realization of Possibilities in Time' included in this volume (pp. 57–72).

In his book Lovejoy referred to certain passages in which Aristotle seems to maintain that some possibilities can remain unrealized. This could be called the Principle of Scarcity. In his interpretation Hintikka maintains that Scarcity does not pertain to total possibilities in Aristotle. It is trivially true that there are all sorts of unrealized potentialities according to Aristotle. For instance, he distinguishes what might be called active potencies from passive ones. If the former is an efficient cause and the latter a material cause, it is of course possible that in an individual case the material cause is actual but that the efficient cause is not present. In this sense there can be unrealized partial potentialities or partial possibilities. But because neither sort of potentiality alone can initiate a change or motion, a partial possibility cannot be actualized in so far it is only a partial possibility. Because a partial possibility cannot, as such, be actualized, it cannot be a genuine possibility according to Aristotle. In his paper 'Aristotle and the Priority of Actuality' R. M. Dancy discusses the respective roles of the Principles of Plenitude and Scarcity in Aristotle's metaphysics (pp. 73–115). He shows that, in the argument for the priority of actuality on which the doctrine of the eternity of the world is based, Aristotle uses both the Principle of Plenitude as well as the Principle of Scarcity. They do not contradict each other in Aristotle, Dancy argues, for all that Scarcity tells us is that a potentiality need not, at any given time, be actualized. Plenitude tells us that every possibility must sooner or later be realized. In this form both principles go together with the statistical interpretation of modal notions.

In both of the works mentioned Hintikka doubts Lovejoy's claim that Plato adopted the Principle of Plenitude without qualifications. Many other scholars have also been skeptical about this view of Lovejoy's. In his paper 'Empty Forms in Plato' Michael Rohr discusses the alleged counter-evidence, especially the opinion according to which Plato thought that there are empty forms (pp. 19–56). Rohr argues that in Plato there are no forms which have only the forms themselves as instances, i.e., that there is no form which is never instantiated by any particulars. Although some forms may be temporally empty, all forms have as many instances as they can. His careful argumentation lends interesting support to Lovejoy's somewhat sketchy thesis and offers challenges to further studies of Plato's modal ideas.

Aristotle regarded the typical form of singular declarative statements as temporally unqualified. Hintikka has maintained that the statistical model of modality in Aristotle is connected with his preference for this type of sentences, which contain a reference to the time of utterance as a part of their meaning. On the statistical interpretation of modality in Aristotle, necessary statements are identified with those that are true whenever uttered, possible statements with those that are sometimes true, and impossible ones with those that are never true. In my paper 'Time and Modality in Scholasticism' I explain how this model was introduced into scholastic thought and how it was used in it (pp. 163–257). In particular, I discuss certain common types of argument in which the Principle of Plenitude in its Aristotelian form is employed. I also mention some early deviations from the acceptance of this principle in medieval thought. In the latter part of my paper I claim that an important change in the history of modal theories took place in the beginning of the fourteenth century. In Duns Scotus the meaning of modal notions is connected with the idea of considering different alternative states of affairs at the same time. In the late medieval modal theory, to be seen already in Duns Scotus' thought, the domain of possibility is accepted as an a priori area of conceptual consistency. It is then divided into different classes of compossible states of affairs of which the actual world is one. Of logical possibilities some are mere conceptual possibilities and some are real alternatives of the actual world. The Principle of Plenitude does not hold of either group of possibilities.

The Principle of Plenitude was usually not accepted in the Middle Ages without qualification, because it was thought to restrict God's power and freedom. As I argue in my paper, this did not belie the widespread acceptance of a statistical interpretation of natural possibilities in early medieval thought. However, Eileen Serene argues in her paper 'Anselm's Modal Conceptions' that the Principle of Plenitude is not present in Anselm's modal theory (pp. 117–162). Anselm's treatment of modal notions is an early example of a theory in which the Principle of Plenitude is ignored. (There is some evidence that certain Stoic philosophers may have denied the principle; for a recent discussion of some examples see D. E. Hahm, *The Origins of Stoic Cosmology*, Ohio State University Press, Columbus, Ohio 1977, pp. 103–107, 260–266.) It is also interesting that Anselm's modal theory seems to have nothing in common with the ideas of the modern modal theory developed in the early fourteenth century. Anselm's theory of modal notions proper is as reductionistic as the statistical ones are. As Serene points out, the literal sense of necessity is constraint or force and the literal sense of possibility is capacity or potency. Serene shows that Anselm in fact becomes involved in many difficulties when he tries to interpret different uses of modal notions with the help of those basic notions. Perhaps the most interesting of those problems are formulated in Anselm's late works. He was, e.g., worried about cases in which a possibility-predicate is ascribed to a nonexistent subject. In her paper

Serene tries to construct Anselm's solution which is not to be found in the texts known to us.

The fourteenth century modal theory mentioned above has some striking similarities with Leibniz's theory of modality discussed by Hintikka in his paper 'Leibniz on Plenitude, Relations, and "the Reign of Law" ' (pp. 259–286). Leibniz's theory of complex predicates, his idea of individuals reflecting the whole universe, and certain other doctrines treated in the article can be understood as attempts to answer some of the philosophical problems connected with the principal idea according to which the domain of possibility is structured by sets of relational compossibilities. Although Leibniz's modal theory may be in many ways objectionable, Hintikka shows in his paper how the new way of treating modality originated in the fourteenth century is interwoven with the development of the idea of mathematical law of nature in early modern science and with the development of the concepts of relation and function.

Traditional presuppositions did not, however, disappear as soon as the new ideas were introduced. Hintikka refers to Hobbes, Descartes, and Spinoza, all of whom accepted at least partially the idea that genuine possibilities cannot remain unrealized forever. Lovejoy presents a vivid picture of the popularity of this idea in the early modern period. In their joint paper Hintikka and Heikki Kannisto discuss Immanuel Kant's attitude toward the Principle of Plenitude (pp. 287–308). In the first period of his thought Kant accepted the principle in a traditional way for natural possibilities and denied it with respect to God's possibilities in a good scholastic manner. In his early critical philosophy Kant denies the principle, but ironically enough his theory of the categories of human perception and thought lead him to accept a view very similar to that of Thomas Aquinas. According to Thomas there are unrealized Divine possibilities, but it does not belong to the epistemic capacities of men to know what those unrealized possibilities are. Similarly, in Kant, the noumenal possibilities which might overthrow the Principle of Plenitude are beyond the realm of human understanding. For phenomenal possibilities (possibilities of experience), Kant came back to something close to the acceptance of the principle.

The many-faceted role of the Principle of Plenitude in Leibniz and Kant is spelled out more fully in the two papers just mentioned. They illustrate vividly its connection with a large number of other important philosophical ideas. These connections make the Principle of Plenitude an exceptionally useful focal point of a close study of the history of ideas. In spite of its methodological shortcomings and historical mistakes Lovejoy's *The Great*

Chain of Being is a success because of its author's realization of the uses of this focal point. So it is proper, if not to re-forge literally the Great Chain of Being itself, at least to re-evaluate and to reconstruct the argument of *The Great Chain of Being*.

Jaakko Hintikka's 'Gaps in the Great Chain of Being: An Exercise in the Methodology of the History of Ideas' originally appeared in the *Proceedings and Addresses of the Americal Philosophical Association*, Vol. XLIX (1976), pp. 22–38. It has been revised for publication. 'Aristotle on the Realization of Possibilities in Time' appeared as the fifth chapter of Hintikka's book *Time and Necessity: Studies in Aristotle's Theory of Modality*, Clarendon Press, Oxford 1973. Hintikka's 'Leibniz on Plenitude, Relations, and "the Reign of Law"' appeared in Harry G. Frankfurt (ed.), *Leibniz: A Collection of Critical Essays* (Modern Studies in Philosophy), Doubleday, Garden City, N.Y. 1972, pp. 155–190. The joint paper by Jaakko Hintikka and Heikki Kannisto has been published in *Philosophic Exchange*, Vol. 2 (1976), pp. 69–85. These papers are reprinted here without major changes. An abstract from Michael Rohr's *Empty Forms in Plato* appeared in *Archiv für Geschichte der Philosophie* **60** (1978), pp. 268–283. These papers are reprinted with the permissions of the relevant authors, publishers, and editors. The permissions are gratefully acknowledged.

SIMO KNUUTTILA

JAAKKO HINTIKKA

GAPS IN THE GREAT CHAIN OF BEING: AN EXERCISE IN THE METHODOLOGY OF THE HISTORY OF IDEAS*

For some historians, to understand everything is to pardon everything. For others, like Lord Acton, history is not only a judge, but a hanging judge. But when everything is said and done — and read and understood — surely the most appropriate key for the music of Clio, the Muse of History, is irony. Any such irony can scarcely be sharper than the one created by a juxtaposition of the following two quotes. (I call your attention especially to the italicized sentences and to their role in the overall argument. These italics are all mine.)

We find in nature things that are possible to be and not to be, since they are found to be generated, and to be corrupted, and consequently, it is possible for them to be and not to be. But it is impossible for them always to exist, for *that which can not-be at some time is not*. Therefore, if everything can not-be, then at one time there was nothing in existence. Now if this were true, even now there would be nothing is existence, because that which does exist begins to exist only through something already existing. Therefore, if at one time nothing was in existence, it would have been impossible for anything to have begun to exist; and thus even now nothing would be in existence — which is absurd. Therefore, not all things are merely possible, but there must exist something the existence of which is necessary.

I esteem Mr. Descartes almost as much as one can esteem any man, and, though there are among his opinions some which seem false to me, and even dangerous, this does not keep me from saying that we owe nearly as much to Galileo and to him in philosophical matters as we owe to the whole of antiquity. At present I recall only one of the . . . dangerous propositions. It occurs in the *Principles of Philosophy*, Part III, Article 47, in the following words:

> And, after all, it makes very little difference what we assume in this respect, because it must later be changed in accordance with the laws of nature. Hardly anything can be assumed from which the same effects cannot be derived, though perhaps with greater trouble. For, due to these laws, *matter takes on, successively, all the forms it is capable*. Therefore if we considered these forms in order, we could eventually arrive at that one which is our present world, so that in this respect no false hypothesis can lead us into error.

I do not believe that a more dangerous proposition than this could be formulated. For if matter takes on, successively, all possible forms, it follows that nothing can be imagined so absurd, so bizzare, so contrary to what we call justice, that it would not have happened and will not some day happen. These are precisely the opinions which Spinoza

1

S. Knuuttila (ed.), Reforging the Great Chain of Being, 1–17.
Copyright © 1980 by D. Reidel Publishing Company.

has expounded more clearly, namely, that justice, beauty, and order are relative to us but that the perfection of God consists in the magnitude of his activity by virtue of which *nothing is possible or conceivable which he does not actually produce*. These are also the opinions Mr. Hobbes, who asserts that *everything that is possible is either past or present or future*, and that there will be no place for trust in providence if God produces everything and makes no choice among possible beings . . . . In my opinion, this is the 'first falsehood' and the basis of atheistic philosophy, though it always seems to say the most beautiful things about God. (Translated by Loemker.)

The former passage is from the famous *tertia via*, the third proof for God's existence in the *Summa theologiae* of St. Thomas Aquinas. The second one is from a letter by Leibniz to Philipp, dated in January 1680. The greatest common denominator of the subject matter of the two quotes is the assumption that whatever *can* happen, *will* happen in the long run, i.e., that no genuine possibility can remain unfulfilled through an infinity of time. The history of this assumption is to lode from which I shall mine the materials for this talk.

Aquinas announces a version of this principle and goes on to appeal to it when he says that if all things existed contingently (merely possibly), there needs would have been a time when nothing was in existence. Leibniz finds the same assumption expressed in so many words by Messrs. Descartes, Spinoza, and Hobbes.

The most obvious aspect of the irony present here is that the very same assumption which served as the cornerstone of one of the main proofs of God's existence in St. Thomas was branded by Leibniz with most uncharacteristic vehemence "the first falsehood and the basis of atheistic philosophy". An explanation of this complete reversal of attitude is in order, for it is as dramatic a change as one can find in the whole history of ideas. Some ingredients of an explanation will be offered later in this essay.

Meanwhile, it is salutary to note that the irony here is not only or even mostly on Baron von Leibniz or on the good friar Thomas. The irony is also and primarily on historians of ideas. Practicing philosophers less knowledgeable than Leibniz are not the only ones who would have been surprised by the long-term history of the ideas they are trafficking in. Professional historians of human thought have seldom followed the genealogy of our ideas far enough or systematically enough to be exempt from similar surprises.

However, the irony here is far subtler than a simple oversight. One of the rare ideas of clearly definable import whose career has in fact been followed through the whole history of Western thought is precisely the assumption I am now examining. The assumption that all possibilities are realized is one of the two ideas whose development is studied in Arthur O. Lovejoy's classical work *The Great Chain of Being*.[1] This book has probably been the most influential single work in the history of ideas in the United States during the last half century. Even though its author was a professional philosopher, the influence of his book nevertheless seems to have been stronger among literary scholars than among historians, and stronger among historians than among philosophers. In view of the relatively intense attention which has thus been devoted to the idea here considered, to the idea that all possibilities are eventually realized, it is doubly ironic that Lovejoy's account of the history of this idea is seriously defective, not just in its details but also in some of its main outlines.

And when we realize the reasons for the shortcomings of Lovejoy's narrative, they press the irony even further. The principle or assumption in question was Lovejoy's prize specimen of one of the most important types of ideas that historians of ideas are supposed to study. It was his paradigm case of what he called *unit ideas*. According to Lovejoy, historians of ideas are especially concerned with the manifestations of such specific unit ideas. My first main thesis to-night is that even though the eventual realization of each possibility is perhaps as close to a unit idea as we can hope to get in history, in the last analysis *it is not a unit idea*.

This conclusion casts serious doubts on Lovejoy's whole methodology. For the strategy of Lovejoy's theory and practice of the history of ideas was, to use his own expression, a "quest of the unit ideas" which in different combinations make up different thinkers' systems. These unit ideas are the proper study of historians of the kind he wanted to exemplify himself. Lovejoy says in the very beginning of *The Great Chain of Being* that the history of ideas "is differentiated primarily by the character of the units with which it concerns itself". These units are of course just Lovejoy's unit ideas. Hence to question the existence of genuine unit ideas is to question one of the main theoretical assumptions on which Lovejoy's whole enterprise is based.

Since the interest and importance of Lovejoy's books and essays is nevertheless unmistakable, we are led to ask where the true reasons for this interest lies. If even the theme of Lovejoy's famous book on *The Great Chain of Being* is not a unit idea, where does the charm and the relevance of his enterprise come from?

But what are the infelicities of Lovejoy's book that I alleged it to contain? Perhaps the most conspicuous of them is that the assumption we are discussing has more interpretations and more variants than he recognizes. It is again more than a little surprising that a philosopher and historian who elsewhere[2]

distinguishes from each other over a hundred different shades of meaning of
the terms 'nature' and 'natural' should have failed to distinguish between the
clearly different applications that can be given to the assumption that all
possibilities are realized. This nevertheless is what happened, it seems to me.
Even Lovejoy's terminology is affected by this failure. He calls the assumption under scrutiny "the Principle of Plenitude". Since it does not seem to
have possessed a handy name at any other time of its many-splendored
history, I shall in the sequel use this label myself. However, we must realize
that it is a highly misleading term in that it emphasizes too much one kind of
application of the underlying idea. In dubbing the assumption that all genuine
possibilities are eventually exemplified in actuality "the Principle of Plenitude" Lovejoy was clearly thinking of possibilities of different kinds of
individuals, such as species and genera. What the principle says then is that
the selection of such kinds of entities as are actually realized is the fullest
possible one: it comprises all that there could possibly be. The selection of
specimens for the zoo that this universe of ours can be thought of as being
is as fully representative of possible species and genera as Noah's ark was
reputed to have been of the actually existing ones: nothing is left out. If this
is what one has in mind, then it might seem natural indeed to call the idea
we are discussing the Principle of Plenitude. It is in this direction that we find
the connecting link between the Principle of Plenitude and the idea signalled
by the title of Lovejoy's famous book. Conversely, in so far as the Principle
fails in the domain just delineated, the result is an equal number of gaps in
the Great Chain of Being.

However, this is not the only way in which the assumption may be applied,
for it can also be applied for instance to *particular* individuals and *particular*
events (as distinguished from *kinds* thereof) or to possible sequences of
events. Then the appropriateness of the term becomes much less obvious. In
the sequel we shall uncover even more striking reasons for being dissatisfied
with Lovejoy's term. However, I shall still take the liberty of using it in what
follows, albeit as a *terminus technicus* only.

It is worth noting that the distinctions just made are absolutely crucial for
the implications of the Principle. If all possible species are always realized, we
have a doctrine of the permanence of species. If all potential kinds of beings
will sooner or later emerge when the time proceeds from some starting-point
on, we have a doctrine of infinite evolution. But if all possibilities concerning
particular events are actualized, one easily lands in hard determinism. These
different consequences are not always separated sharply enough from each
other by Lovejoy.

Nor is the distinction between the different senses of the Principle of Plenitude of a terminological and systematic interest only. It is directly relevant to the history of the principle, including our initial quotes from Aquinas and Leibniz. In fact, the whole spectacular disagreement between Leibniz and Descartes which my second initial quote exhibits might seem to boil down to a difference in the field of application they assigned to the Principle. One of the most remarkable things about the Principle is the drastic consequences of trying to assume it in connection with possible sequences of events.[3] Since exceptions to each putative natural law are at least conceptually possible, and since the Principle says that these possibilities will be realized, any and every alleged law of nature will sooner or later be overthrown. No wonder Leibniz was upset by the loss of order and beauty which seems to result from the Principle of Plenitude.

This seeming conclusion rests on presuppositions which are less than self-evident. However, these weaknesses of Leibniz' (partly tacit) line of thought are quite as interesting historically as its strengths. First of all, inferring an actual exception to a law of nature from the conceivability of such exceptions seems to stretch the Principle of Plenitude close to a breakdown point in that it involves thinking of the possibilities the Principle traffics in as logical or conceptual possibilities. The legitimacy of so doing is not obvious, and will be commented on later.

Second, it is not obvious that Leibniz is not stacking his deck of modalities rather too favorably to himself in concentrating his attention on possible sequences of states. It is clear enough to us that he is so focusing his attention although it may not have been equally clear to Leibniz himself. In the very passage I quoted Leibniz refers to what is "contrary to justice". Now justice is primarily a matter of sequences of events, of actions in their relationship to subsequent rewards and punishments. Hence Leibniz' concern is certainly with longer or shorter segments of the history of events as distinguished from temporal cross-sections of such histories. But such contemporaneous states of affairs are just what Descartes is in so many words talking about in my Leibnitian quote within quotes. He is discussing the different configurations or 'forms' which matter can assume. Conversely, Descartes is not countenancing exceptions to laws of nature, but is rather taking the laws for granted and asking what follows from them concerning the possible configurations which the material world can exhibit. In sum, Leibniz and Descartes are talking about different things. Leibniz is envisaging the Principle of Plenitude as being applied to possible sequences of events, whereas Descartes is thinking of it as dealing with possible states of affairs. This contrast illustrates one line of large-scale historical development, which incidentally illuminates the contrast between Aquinas and Leibniz which my initial quotes also exemplified. It also illustrates the variety of different conceptions — well, different *ideas*, to use the magic word — which are combined in the seductively simple formula I am calling the Principle of Plenitude.

We might express the point I am trying to make by saying that the Principle of Plenitude is not *one* idea, but a conglomeration of several interrelated ideas. For this reason alone, the Principle is not a 'unit idea' in Lovejoy's own sense, even though he labels it one.

But the history of the Principle of Plenitude is not made deceptively subtle just by its having several different kinds of applications and hence several different variants. That the Principle is not *one* idea but several is only one reason why it fails to be a unit idea. The Principle fails to be an atom-like unit also because its implications are not independent of its conceptual and theoretical environment. This allegedly unit-like building-block as it were changes its shape under the pressure of the rest of the structure into which it is being built.

This observation has striking implication for the appropriateness of the very term "the Principle of Plenitude". This thesis is only an ontological balance sheet, not an entry into one column rather than into another. It does not assert the plenitude of actual realizations, but only an equation between possibilities and their realizations. It is as much or as little a Principle of the Paucity of Possibilities as a Principle of Plenitude of their Realizations. No plenitude of any sort can be extracted from the Principle except in conjunction with a sufficiently strong assumption concerning the richness of the range of possibilities whose eventual realization is asserted by the Principle. Hence Lovejoy's term "the Principle of Plenitude" is a misnomer in a double sense. What it refers to is neither *the* Principle of Plenitude, nor the Principle of *Plenitude*.

To put the same point in different terms, the reason why a thinker adopts the so-called Principle of Plenitude may be his belief in the richness of the real world. But it may also be his narrow view of the hidden possibilities that lurk behind the ontological backdrop of our actual world, hoping to enter the limelight of actuality.

Again, the significance of this observation extends far beyond terminological and systematic questions. It is directly relevant to the history of the Principle. Among many other things, it is one of the features in the background of the adoption of the Principle by several major thinkers of Antiquity and early as well as high Middle Ages. It is also one of the most important clues to the gradual abandonment of the Principle in the late medieval and early modern period.

It is one of the flaws of Lovejoy's unit-idea approach that it leads him to neglect this facet of the saga of the Principle of Plenitude. It is for instance symptomatic that in dealing with the Renaissance period Lovejoy's main attention is attuned to the widening of people's ideas about the actual universe, that is, to the broadening of the sphere of actualizations. But this pertains only to one half of the equation that is the so-called Principle of Plenitude. It is a much more striking observation than any of Lovejoy's to point out that in spite of this tremendous expansion of the intellectual boundaries of the actual world relatively few thinkers — typically exceedingly wild thinkers in the stamp of Giordano Bruno — could accept the Principle of Plenitude, that is, could find enough actual realizations to match the realm of possibilities. For many thinkers, apparently for the great majority, possibilities had multiplied even faster than their presumed realizations.

This widening of realm of possibilities is one of the most interesting overall features of the history of Western thought which is made clearer to us by a study of the Principle of Plenitude. This change is not confined to the Renaissance period, but was firmly launched already in the midst of the Middle Ages.[4] Even though the aetiology and the precise chronology of this deep change largely remain to be studied, there is among the *cognoscenti* no doubt any longer of its importance not only for the history of philosophy but also for the history of science, history of theology, and general intellectual history. Thus e.g. John Murdoch has emphasized the importance in the history of science of this widening of the realm of possibilities which served "to push the examination of questions beyond the confines of the physical possibilities licit within Aristotelian natural philosophy into the broader field of what was logically possible".[5] The only thing to be added here is that the distinction between logical and physical possibilities was not initially available to the medievals but evolved in the course of the very process I am describing. Earlier we saw that Leibniz was still ready to apply the Principle of Plenitude to what is imaginable, i.e., to logical or conceptual possibilities, at least for polemical purposes.

This change is not always easy to recognize or to comment on directly. I doubt that the medieval thinkers themselves were fully aware of the process. Often their attitude is betrayed only or primarily by the difficulty which the widening of the range of possibilities imposed on their attempts to retain the respectable Aristotelian Principle of Plenitude. Late medieval thought (together with its aftereffects) is therefore one of the most important areas where the Principle can be expected to serve as a most sensitive intellectual barometer. It is for instance unmistakable that the gradual widening of what counts as possible is one of the explanations of the ironic contrast between the respective attitudes of Aquinas and of Leibniz to the Principle of Plenitude.

But the dependence of the Principle of Plenitude on the range of one's presupposed possibilities is not the only way in which the Principle interacts with other important ideas. There are several other concepts and assumptions in the context of which the Principle of Plenitude has actually occurred in the course of the history of thought. Lovejoy considers relatively few of these contexts of ideas, mainly such ideas as creation and evolution. The Principle of Plenitude is according to him "a single specific proposition or 'principle' " and "an attempted answer to *a* philosophical question which it was natural for man to ask" (my italic). We have already seen that the Principle is scarcely a single proposition and that it is not really so specific, either. It will now turn out, furthermore, that the famous Principle can be an answer to many different questions. If one considers the Principle only in the context of ideas of creation and divine generosity which is supposed to grant the gift of existence to as many beings as possible, one might expect that Plato should subscribe to the Principle but Aristotle not. And this is indeed what Lovejoy claims. In reality, however, this is dead wrong. I have shown earlier (see especially Chapter 5 of *Time and Necessity*[6]) that Aristotle accepted the Principle, argued for it, and used it in his philosophy. Furthermore, it has been argued by Maula that Plato never embraced the Principle as an unqualified philosophical thesis.[7]

And the reasons for Lovejoy's mistakes lie – especially in Aristotle's case – precisely in a one-side view of the conceptual neighborhood of the Principle of Plenitude. In a topical perspective it is even a little surprising that a practicing philosopher like Lovejoy should underestimate the logical and ontological significance of the Principle of Plenitude which after all ties together time and modality in a most dramatic way, perhaps even allowing for a reduction of modal notions to temporal ones. I have elsewhere analyzed Aristotle's reasons for adopting the Principle.[8] They are too complex to allow for a brief summary, but they certainly include such conceptions as the role of this actual sequence of 'nows' as the only forum on which a possibility can prove its mettle, the relationships between the concepts of time and truth, etc., that is, conceptions of metaphysical, epistemological, and logical rather than theological, aesthetic, or moral nature. Perhaps the most important single reason for philosophers within the Aristotelian tradition to adopt the

Principle was the assumption that one could characterize modalities in what I have ventured to call statistical terms. Possible is according to this model what happens sometimes, necessary is what happens always, and so on. These characterizations were in turn made possible by the fact that Aristotle considered temporally indefinite sentences (e.g., 'now' sentences) as paradigmatically typical vehicles of thought and communication. A failure to appreciate this type of conceptual environment of the Principle of Plenitude in Aristotle and in other important Western thinkers was undoubtedly instrumental in leading Lovejoy astray.

Ongoing work by an associate of mine, Simo Knuuttila,[9] has amply shown that all the main conceptual peculiarities concerning time, truth, the Principle of Plenitude, and so on, that I have sought to attribute to Aristotle and laboriously argued for in terms of the fine print of Aristotelian texts are present explicitly and overwhelmingly clearly in the Aristotelians of the high middle ages, especially of the all-important thirteenth century. Their conceptual motivation also seems to have been similar to Aristotle's, among other things vis-à-vis the role of the statistical model of modalities as a source of the Principle of Plenitude. Even though all this is not even indirect evidence concerning Aristotle, it at least shows the tremendous historical interest of my still disputed interpretations. It is especially interesting to see how medieval attempts to apply the statistical paradigm to temporally determinate propositions (particular future events) frequently landed them precisely in the same deterministic difficulties as Aristotle had been discussing in the form of his famous sea-fight problem according to my interpretation of this famous Aristotelian argument.[10]

Nor are the Aristotelians an extreme instance of the kind of conceptual company which the Principle of Plenitude has sometimes kept but which is largely overlooked by Lovejoy. In the famous Master Argument of Diodorus Cronus the Principle appears as a conclusion of an allegedly logical (conceptual) argument.[10] Even though further metaphysical premises are likely to have been involved, we have here a far cry from the idea of creator's generosity which Lovejoy emphasizes.

Instead of a logical motivation the Principle has sometimes been offered an epistemological one. It is not hard to see how such a motivation might come about. One of the first possibilities of arguing for the Principle of Plenitude that is likely to occur to a modern philosopher is what is known as the Paradigm Case Argument. I cannot now discuss this dubious argument beyond reminding you what it amounts to in the case at hand. Its relevant import can perhaps best be expressed in the form of the rhetorical question:

How else can a possibility prove its mettle – its reality – except by being realized in time? Hence it may be expected that the same or essentially similar reason for the Principle should be found in the course of its checkered history. In my own case at least, this expectation turned out to be justified only after several years. According to Simo Knuuttila, the most prominent victim of the Paradigm Case Argument in the history of the Principle of Plenitude is St. Thomas Aquinas. According to him, all our 'true' concepts are forged by *intellectus agens* from forms which our *intellectus possibilis* receives from external reality. In order for us to receive 'true' concepts, they must therefore already be exemplified in antecedent reality. All humanly conceivable possibilities must therefore be instantiated in the external world. Thus a kind of empiricist epistemology leads Aquinas to the adoption of the Principle of Plenitude for humanly conceivable possibilities, if not for the Divine ones. The motivation of the Principle, in brief, can thus also be an epistemological one.

Lest it be suspected that I am exclusively interested in a long forgotten past, let me mention an especially amusing occurrence of a version of the Principle of Plenitude in a somewhat more recent history. You are all familiar with G. E. Moore's famous criticism of the so-called Naturalistic Fallacy in the beginning of his *Principia Ethica* (The University Press, Cambridge, 1956, first edition 1903). But what is the logical gist of this famous fallacy? What Moore says is the following. "It may be true that all things which are good are *also* something else . . . . But far too many philosophers have thought that when they named those other properties they were actually defining good; that these properties, in fact, are not 'other', but absolutely and entirely the same with goodness." In other words, one commits the Naturalistic Fallacy if one raises a property (or a complex of properties) which *always* accompanied goodness to the status of a necessary mark of goodness in the strong sense of a *defining* mark. Since one form of the Principle of Plenitude says, when contraposited, that whatever happens *always*, happens *necessarily*, the target of Moore's criticism, the assumption he labels 'Naturalistic Fallacy', can be interpreted as a version of the Principle – a very strong version in that it asserts that whatever things are not definitionally connected will sometimes occur separately. Moore's point is seen even more clearly from what he says in the chapter on metaphysical ethics later in the *Principia Ethica*. For instance, on p. 124 we read: "But philosophers suppose that the reason why we cannot take goodness up and move it about is not that it is a different *kind* of object from any which can be moved about, but only that it *necessarily* exists together with anything with which it does exist." (Italics in the original.) A closely related version of Moore's criticism of the Principle of Plenitude is his famous 'Open Question Argument'.

Hence every moral philosopher who had discussed the Naturalistic Fallacy or the Open Question Argument has *ipso facto* considered the Principle of Plenitude in one of its many forms. Nor is this the only inroad the Principle has made into twentieth-century philosophy.

Among the neighbor ideas which interact with the Principle of Plenitude and on which the Principle can shed indirect light are its own presuppositions. There are certain thinkers whose attitude to the Principle of Plenitude is especially elusive. One of them is Descartes. For this reason, the justifiability of Leibniz' violent attack on him is difficult to assess, even though there is no doubt whatsoever that Leibniz was aiming at something important and fundamental in Descartes' thought.[11] Another case in point is Kant. *Prima facie*, Kant might seem easier to pigeonhole in his relation to the Principle than, e.g., Descartes. In a separate paper (written jointly with Heikki Kannisto and reprinted below in the present volume) I have shown that in Kant we find a double change. The first change was from an early dogmatic acceptance of the Principle of Plenitude to a sharp rejection of it. This change was connected with the role which for a while was played in Kant's thinking by the contrast between the intelligible world and the sensible world. The possibilities present in the former just cannot all be accommodated within the confines of the latter.

However, the crucial development in Kant's subsequent thought was the limitation of the legitimate uses of human understanding to possible experience, excluding the intelligible world of things considered in themselves. This restricted realm of experiential possibilities was narrow enough to enable Kant to return to a qualified form of the Principle of Plenitude. (Contemporary philosophers of logic will undoubtedly recognize the interest of the Kantian move, which parallels the recommendations of some of us for a way out of the semantical problems which Quine has found in the uses of modal concepts like possibility.[12]) This double movement in Kant's thought which first led him to a rejection and then later to a readoption of the Principle seems to have been overlooked by most historians.

What is even more striking, however, is the difficulty of pinning the Kant of his mature, critical period down for an outright unqualified affirmation of the Principle. This difficulty is far greater than what is entailed by Kant's notorious obscurity. It seems to me that the true explanation lies in the fact that according to Kant the limitation of the range of possible experience is in the last analysis accomplished by ourselves, through the way we structure and synthesize our experience. Even though this is not done by each of us individually but only through the workings of our shared human nature, in some sense the limitations could in principle be different – or be altogether absent.

It should be clear what this implies for the Principle of Plenitude. The Principle says of possibilities within a certain range that they are all realized in time. It makes clear sense only in so far as this range is antecedently specified independently of all questions which would already pertain to the realization of possibilities. Now for Kant (during his mature 'critical' period) this is not the case. The very range of experiential possibilities was seen to have been defined by what we do ourselves. If we had synthesized our experience differently, a different range of possible experiences would have resulted. Crudely expressed, it is possible for possible experience to have been different from what it is for us.

If so, it is no wonder that Kant's mature attitude to the Principle of Plenitude is somewhat ambivalent. The reason lies in the failure of one of the presuppositions of the Principle, viz. the failure of there being an independently defined range of possibilities.

What makes this dialectic of Kant's attitude to the Principle of Plenitude historically poignant is its similarity to several earlier thinkers' difficulties with the nature of Divine possibilities vis-à-vis the Principle of Plenitude. Descartes may be the sharpest example of this, but he certainly is not the only one. The Cartesian God is supposed to have freely decided even what counts and what does not count as being logically possible. Even the laws of logic are at His mercy. Consequently, even if all logical possibilities that we humans can comprehend (the medievals would have said *in statu viae*) should be realized *apud* Descartes, there are certain humanly incomprehensible possibilities which are not. But their nature is bound to be quite as mysterious as the Kantian world of things-in-themselves. In general, a comparison between Descartes and Kant offers to us a nice instance of Kantian humanism – or Kantian *hubris*. Superficial differences apart, a Kantian man is with respect to the Principle of Plenitude in the same ambivalent position as a Cartesian God. Both have created the relevant range of possibilities themselves, thereby also bringing the ambivalence upon themselves.

Out of this variety of historical stories a couple of important methodological morals can be extracted. They concern my initial query about the interest and importance of the history of ideas in the teeth of Lovejoy's failure to explain or even to describe the true nature of the enterprise. Bluntly and uncompromisingly put, the morals we have reached concern the reasons why specific particular ideas like the eventual realization of each possibility are worth studying in intellectual history. We have seen that the reason is not the one Lovejoy assumed. It is not that such conceptions are 'unit ideas' in the sense of building blocks out of which we can as it were reassemble conceptual and intellectual history. There just are no such unit ideas. Even Lovejoy's own prime example is not one. The real reasons why ideas are such ideal focal points for an intellectual and philosophical historian are far subtler – and far deeper. One of them is ultimately based on the fact that all of the most general conceptions and assumptions of a thinker are rarely formulated by him explicitly. They have to be inferred from their indirect effects, from their joint implications together with other ideas. These consequences have of course to be explicit in order to be ascertainable at all. And the clearer and sharper the connection between these explicit consequences and their hidden premises is, the better they reflect their holder's tacit presuppositions.

To find a simple illustration of this point, I only have to recall the background of the Principle of Plenitude in Aristotle. The Stagirite never *says* that each possibility must be a possibility concerning this particular world history of ours. Nor does he ever quite say that there are no possible worlds altogether different from our actual world history. Both important presuppositions will have to be gathered from their consequences, for instance just from the way they encourage him to uphold the Principle of Plenitude.

And there is a plenitude of similar examples. Late medieval thinkers did not put to themselves or to each other the proposition, "Let's consider a new, wider range of possibilities". Rather, they did this largely unwittingly, because of pressures and insights of which they were not fully aware. Hence their in effect saying so can only be inferred from the tensions between this wider conception of possibility and the Principle of Plenitude, together with other similar indirect evidence. (The more possibilities there are, the harder it becomes to maintain that they all are realized or will be realized.)

Likewise Leibniz only hints at the premium he is putting on laws governing sequences of successive events in contrast to questions concerning the selection of different kinds of individuals or of different kinds of events actually exemplified in the world. In order to consolidate these hints, we need precisely the kind of evidence Leibniz' pronouncements on the Principle of Plenitude amount to. Furthermore, this evidence we can come by only by sharpening our topical, conceptual insights. In the present instance, one of the relevant insights concerns the implications of applying the Principle of Plenitude to sequences of events rather than individual events or states of affairs.

This kind of interaction of different ideas is what lends to clearly formulated assumptions like the so-called Principle of Plenitude one of their most important roles in the history of ideas. The Principle is not independent of the surrounding ideas. It can serve as a mirror in which these other presuppositions can be seen, often including implicitly held ones. This mirror is made sharp by the conceptual specificity of the Principle. But this specificity is not unproblematic. The specificity is what a philosopher *qua* philosopher can, and must, bring about through his analyses and syntheses.

Here we in fact have another major reason for the fascination and relevance of the history of ideas. It is also a reason for us philosophers to occupy ourselves with the subject. If all that is involved in the history of ideas were the isolation of unit ideas and the tracing of them throughout history, philosophers *qua* philosophers could not hope to contribute very much to the enterprise. However, it is in the teasing out of hidden ambiguities and in the discovery and clarification of the frequently surprising interrelations of different ideas that professional philosophers can come into their own. It is thus in connection with those very phenomena which Lovejoy partly overlooks that his colleagues can make a contribution to the field he helped to found. At the same time, these phenomena, especially the subtle interdependencies of different ideas, go a long way toward explaining the significance of an analytical study of the history of ideas.

I cannot resist the temptation of giving you a modest example of the power of sharper conceptual insights to illuminate historical material. An entry to the problem I have in mind is offered by Aristotle's statement of his attitude to his "ancestors and forerunners" in *Metaphysics* λ 8. 1074a38–b14. It reads in part:

> But if one were to separate the first point from these additions and take it alone . . . and reflect that, while probably *each art and each science has often been developed as far as possible* and has again perished, those opinions, with others, have been preserved with the present like the relics of an ancient treasure. It is only in this way that we can explain the opinions of our ancestors and forerunners. (My italics, needless to say.)

A similar point is found in Aristotle's *Politics* VII 10. 1329b25–35.

These words might seem merely to reflect Aristotle's reverent attitude to the wisdom of the ancients, and they have usually been understood as being just such a pious formula. At best a question has been raised concerning the cultural determinants of this attitude. However, once we recognize the core of Aristotle's statement as a direct corollary to the Principle of Plenitude, as an application of the Principle to certain human possibilities (arts and sciences), Aristotle's words suddenly assume a much sharper systematic import.

Instead of an expression of elevated sentiments, we have in front of us a sharp, specific application of Aristotle's logico-metaphysical theory to the philosophy of history. And once we see this, we can likewise see what connects Aristotle's statement with a large number of other things in Aristotle and elsewhere in the history of the philosophy of history.

For one thing, we can see how very closely Aristotle's statement is related to his tantalizing technique of philosophical argumentation in that he tries to extract his own views from those of his predecessors — or to read his views back into theirs, as some uncharitable historians have suggested. Now we can see that Aristotle's procedure is not fortuitous, not a mere expositional trick. Since Aristotle's own metaphysical principles imply that every possible truth has been discovered sometime in the endless past, we certainly ought not to be surprised if he is seriously trying to find the truth about some particular problem he is discussing by sifting the opinions of his predecessors on it: he believes that the truth is somewhere among those opinions.

We can now also understand better a number of pronouncements in the history of the philosophy of history similar to Aristotle's. (Here are two: Dante, *On Monarchy*, in Ralph Lerner and Muhsin Mahdi, *Medieval Political Philosophy: A Sourcebook*, The Free Press, Glencoe, Ill. 1963, pp. 422–423; Kant, *Idee zu einer allgemeinen Geschichte*, Academy Edition of Kant's works, Vol. 8, Berlin 1912, pp. 18–19.) One dimension of special interest here is brought out by Aristotle's original formulation. If the Principle of Plenitude holds and if the past is infinite, there just cannot be any genuine novelties in the world. Hence philosophers' ideas of such subjects as novelty, invention, artistic creation, and progress are apt to be affected by their acceptance of the Principle of Plenitude, especially in conjunction with an assumption of the infinity of the past. These potential implications of the Principle are as important as any in the whole history of philosophy.

The links between such applications of the Principle in the history of philosophy are likewise interesting. In their different contexts, the several affirmations of the Principle are not only connected horizontally through a departmental tradition among philosophers of history. They usually have also vertical links to epistemological and metaphysical doctrines of the same thinker and through them connections with an intricate network of other ideas.

All these insights are ultimately prompted by the simple conceptual recognition of the import of Aristotle's pronouncement as being an application of the Principle of Plenitude.

Thus the source of the importance of the Principle of Plenitude is different from Lovejoy's 'unit idea' idea. The Principle is truly a gem of an idea, not because of its alleged resistance to the pressure of other ideas, but because of its capacity to reflect brilliantly the light of others. And this reflective capacity need not be an original property of the Principle but a result of the way we philosophers have managed to cut it so as to increase its sparkle. The intended object lesson of my talk is to suggest that this is what we ought to be looking forward to in intellectual and conceptual history in general: not to unit ideas but to ideas that can accurately reflect different thinkers' outlook. And these reflections are the sharper the clearer we are ourselves about the logical relationships between different assumptions and the more perceptive we are about the conceptual issues involved. It is in the sharpening of these conceptual mirrors and lenses that we philosophers can render a service also to our non-philosophical colleagues, in particular, to our brethren laboring in the vineyards of historical research. Metaphorically speaking, we ought to consider our task the same as the *métier* of the great philosopher whose tercentennial we shall be celebrating next year: [13] the grinding of lenses.

Florida State University

NOTES

* Originally delivered as Professor Hintikka's Presidential Address at the Fiftieth Annual Meeting of the American Philosophical Association, Pacific Division, in Berkeley, Calif., March 26, 1976.
[1] Harvard University Press, Cambridge, Mass. 1936.
[2] See G. Boas and A. O. Lovejoy, *Primitivism and Related Ideas in Antiquity*, John Hopkins University Press, Baltimore 1935.
[3] Cf. my paper 'Leibniz on Plenitude, Relations, and "the Reign of Law" ', reprinted in this volume, pp. 259–286.
[4] It is not a continuous linear change, either. Duns Scotus was freer from the fetters of the Principle than most renaissance philosophers, and the revival of Aristotelianism in the seventeenth century academic philosophy seems to have encouraged thinkers to adopt the Principle of Plenitude in some form or other.
[5] See John Murdoch, 'Philosophy and the Enterprise of Science in the Later Middle Ages', in Yehuda Elkana, (ed.), *The Interaction Between Science and Philosophy*, Humanities Press, New York 1974, pp. 51–74.
[6] *Time and Necessity. Studies in Aristotle's Theory of Modality*, Clarendon Press, Oxford 1973; partially reprinted in this volume, pp. 57–72.
[7] See his paper 'Plato on Plenitude' in *Ajatus* 29 (1967), 12–50. (Even though Maula fails to mention it, much of that paper was written by me.) Recently, Michael D. Rohr has argued for the contrary conclusion, as witnessed by his contribution to the present volume. In spite of his learned and able arguments, I remain critical of Lovejoy's bland

attribution of the Principle of Plenitude to Plato. Even if Rohr is right, Lovejoy is over-simplifying Plato's position, especially the role of the demiurge.

[8] See *Time and Necessity* and cf. *Aristotle on Modality and Determinism*, North-Holland, Amsterdam 1977.

[9] See his contribution to the present volume and the further references given there.

[10] Cf. *Time and Necessity*, last chapter, and the literature referred to there.

[11] The role of the 'statistical' model of modal and epistemic concepts in Descartes has recently been pointed out by John Etchemendy (forthcoming).

[12] Cf. my 'Quine on Quantifying In' in *The Intentions of Intentionality*, D. Reidel, Dordrecht 1975.

[13] I.e., in the year 1977.

MICHAEL DAVID ROHR

EMPTY FORMS IN PLATO

I

Aristotle tells us that Plato claimed that the Forms are separate from
and prior to particulars (e.g. *Metaphysics* M4.1078b30–32, 9.1086b1–2,
Z6.1031b11–15), and later scholars have usually agreed with Aristotle.[1]
Unfortunately, there is no agreement about what Plato's claim amounts
to. In this article, I examine and refute one proposed interpretation of
Plato's thesis. According to this interpretation, the separation and priority
of the Forms consisted, for Plato, in the propositions that (A) there can be,
and in fact are, Forms which have no instances, but (B) there cannot be
things which are *F* ('*F*' a general term) if there is no Form of *F*ness. I shall
concentrate on (A) throughout and eliminate (B) only in passing. In outline,
my course will be this: In the remainder of Section I, I distinguish different
versions of (A); in Sections II–IV, I show the falsity of the Empty Forms
Thesis (hereafter, 'EFT'), i.e. the thesis that Plato accepted (A). In Section II,
I show conditionally that EFT is false for an important subclass of Forms;
in Section III, that it is unconditionally false for all Forms that can have
particulars as instances; and in Section IV, that there are no Forms other
than those discussed in Section III.

Here are some statements of EFT:

For Plato nothing could exist in space and time with a definite character, *F*, if there
did not exist a corresponding [Form] ϕ, while the converse would not be true at all:
the existence of a specific Form, say of a *chiliagon*, would of itself not offer the
slightest assurance of its physical instantiation; not only the Form of the Ideal City
(*R.* 592AB), but infinitely many other Forms as well exist which have been uninstantiated since time began and may so remain for ever in Plato's universe.[2]

To say that a form is 'separate' is to say that there can be a form without there being
particulars which exemplify it.[3]

Well, what does Plato mean by saying that forms exist apart from particulars, that the
form of justice, for example, exists apart from just individuals? He must have meant
at least that the form of justice is something which would exist even if there were no
just individuals.[4]

19

S. Knuuttila (ed.), Reforging the Great Chain of Being, 19–56.
Copyright © 1980 *by D. Reidel Publishing Company.*

Assertions of EFT are not very common; neither are rejections of it or alternatives to it. This is because most writers on the Theory of Forms, unlike the three quoted above, offer *no* clear expression of what they take separation and the ontological priority of Forms to consist in. Nonetheless, EFT has been questioned[5] and even explicitly rejected:

> . . . to every Idea there correspond 'many' objects participating in the Idea. Hence, according to Plato, there are no Ideas in which no objects participate or which have empty classes for their extensions. The conscious recognition of empty concepts and empty classes is the result of a logical sophistication at which the Greek philosophers of Plato's time had obviously not yet arrived.[6]

Before considering the evidence for and against EFT, some clarifications are necessary. First of all, what sort of instances are denied by (A)? One simple formulation of (A) is

(A1)   Some Form *F*ness is such that nothing is *F*.

On one standard account of Plato's Theory of Forms, however, (A1) will not do, because Plato held

(SP)   Every Form *F*ness is such that *F*ness is itself *F*.[7]

I find this standard account convincing; but whether or not it is correct, our formulation of (A) should be compatible with attributing (SP) to Plato. Let us try

(A2)   Some Form *F*ness is such that at most *F*ness is F.

This still won't do, however. (A2)'s falsity might not impair the priority of the Forms if the other *F* things were all Forms too; e.g., if the only other stable things (besides Stability) were Forms, EFT might still be tenable.[8] We should therefore restrict the second quantifier in (A) to concrete particulars (that are not Forms):

(A3)   Some Form *F*ness is such that no *particular* is *F*.

(I use throughout 'particular' for "concrete particular that is not a Form" and 'empty' for "not instantiated by any particular".)

Secondly, just as temporary vacuousness of a name or definite description raises no serious semantic problems, so temporary emptiness of a Form raises no serious metaphysical problems. 'Plato' is unproblematically a name of Plato, and "the first baby born on the moon" a definite description for the first baby born on the moon, despite the current vacuousness of both terms. Likewise, *Tyrannosaurus rex* is the species of various dinosaurs, all now dead, just as 'Hittites' is a name of a number of humans, all now dead. I see no reason why Plato might not have supposed that *being a Form of*, like *being a name of*, holds retrospectively or prospectively.[9] Wedberg is wrong if he means (p. 20 above) that no Greek before Plato could conceive of *temporarily* empty concepts; already in 409 B.C. Sophocles could say: "Holiness does not die with the men that die. Whether they live or die, it cannot perish".[10]

Vlastos alleges only temporary actual emptiness as supported by Plato's text but is clearly more interested in the possible permanent emptiness he supposed to follow from it; likewise, Faris clearly means "no just individuals *ever*". I shall follow them in concentrating mainly on permanent or eternal emptiness; since the Forms are timeless, one should suppose only this sort relevant to them anyway. Where evidence of temporary emptiness crops up, though, I shall notice it. So far, then, the view I take EFT to attribute to Plato is

(A4)   Some Form *F*ness is such that no particular is *ever F*.

Next, we must consider whether to regard emptiness of *some* Forms ((A1)–(A4)) as sufficient for the ontological priority of the Forms or to require the stronger

(A5)   *Every* Form *F*ness is such that no particular is ever *F*.

If we decide to adopt a modalized version of EFT, we must likewise distinguish between these two formulations:

(A6)   Some Form *F*ness is such that possibly no particular is ever *F*.

(A7)   Every Form *F*ness is such that possibly no particular is ever *F*.

(A4) and (A6) (with (B)) would account for the priority of the *realm* of Forms, though not for the priority of *each* Form to the particulars instantiating it. (A5) sounds implausible but is a consequence of a popular view of instantiation rejected under (4) in Section II. (A7) seems to be what Faris, Hardie, and Vlastos are after and is the strongest plausible version of (A). If (A4) is ultimately the version we must consider, it will be because we have been driven back to it by the failure of the other, stronger candidates.

Finally, we must consider modalities in their own right. If a text in Plato explicitly shows that a certain Form is actually empty, we may conclude that it's possibly empty but probably not that it's necessarily empty; while if he says that a certain Form has an instance, we usually can't conclude that it couldn't have been empty. Here, then, we must be careful about what modalities we use in our conclusions. If, on the other hand, we *prove*, from basic general principles of Plato's metaphysics, that Forms of a certain class are all empty, then we are in a position, due to the way in which we arrived at the proposition, to strengthen its modality and say that they *must* be empty; similarly, if we prove that no Form of a certain class is empty, appealing to fundamental Platonic doctrines, then we may assert that it's impossible that those Forms should exist without particular instances. Since this last situation will be the one we find ourselves in, the distinction between modalities will not concern us greatly.

II

Vlastos, unlike most who attribute empty Forms to Plato, cites a text as evidence:

> I understand, he [Glaucon] said, you mean in the city which we were founding and described, our city of words, for I do not believe it exists anywhere on earth.
> Perhaps, I [Socrates] said, it is a model laid up in heaven, for him who wishes to look upon, and as he looks, set up the government of his soul. It makes no difference whether it exists anywhere or will exist.[11]

Plato does seem to be intimating here that the model described has no copies in this world and may never have any, and Vlastos's reference to this model as a Form is surely correct. Verbal reminiscences suggest that Plato is here reminding us of an earlier passage in *Republic* 5 which seems to provide evidence for the stronger claim that it may not even be *possible* for the Form in question to have instances. The speakers are again Socrates and Glaucon:

> Well then, do we not also say that we were making a model of a good city in our argument? — Certainly.
> Do you think our discussion less worthwhile if we cannot prove that it is possible to found a city such as we described? — Not at all.
> And indeed, I said, that is the truth.[12]

These passages constitute a prima facie case for versions (A4) and (A7) of EFT. To launch my refutation of EFT, it will be instructive to consider why they cannot be used as Vlastos would use them. I shall present four reasons in order of increasing importance.

(1) It is Glaucon, not Socrates, who denies the existence of an ideal city (592a11–b1); Socrates merely points out that the question of the existence (592b3–4) or provable possibility (472e3–6) of such a city is irrelevant to his present purposes. He does *not* assert that there isn't or hasn't been such a city, or even that he doesn't know that there is or has been one or can't prove it.[13] Elsewhere, he rejects the accusation of wishful thinking or proposing Utopias[14] (5.450d1–2, 456b12, 6.499c4–5, 7.540d1–2) and insists on the possibility of his ideal city[15] and its institutions (5.456c4–8, 473c2–4, 6.499a11–c3, d4–5, 7.540d3); long ago or far away, he tells Glaucon, it may well have existed or even now exist (6.499c7–d4). Having found such hints, we should not be surprised to find him later assuring us that it has in fact existed; and so we do.

At the beginning of the *Timaeus*, Socrates recapitulates to Critias and others an account of the ideal state which he had expressed to them the day before (17c1–19b2) and expresses a desire to hear a narrative in which a city such as he has described reveals its virtues by its actions in time of war (19b3–20c3). Critias responds that the great Solon had once learned from an Egyptian priest that Athens had been, nine thousand years earlier, just such a city, had manifested its power in an apocalyptic war, and had thereafter been reduced to savagery by floods and earthquakes (20d7–25e2). He continues:

When you were speaking yesterday about your state and its citizens, I recalled this story and I was surprised to notice in how many[16] points your account exactly agreed, by some miraculous chance, with Solon's . . . [Having recalled Solon's story exactly,] I am ready now, Socrates, to tell the story, not in summary, but in full detail as I heard it. We will transfer the state you described yesterday and its citizens from story to history; we will take the city to be Athens and say that your imaginary citizens are those actual historical ancestors of ours, whom the priest spoke of. They will fit perfectly, and there will be no inconsistency[17] in declaring them to be the real men of those ancient times.[18]

Socrates endorses the historicity of Critias' account, remarking that "its connection with the goddess makes it specially appropriate to her festival today; and it is surely a great point that it is no fiction, but genuine history".[19] In the brief sketch of antediluvian Athens that Critias gives after Timaeus' great discourse, he reassures his auditors that the guardian class of those real archaic Athenians "followed *all* the practices we spoke of yesterday when we talked of those feigned guardians" (*Critias* 110d3–4).

The relevance of all this is of course that the ideal city which Socrates recalls in the *Timaeus* and which ancient Athens is asserted to have exemplified perfectly is identical with the ideal city described in the *Republic*. The institutions and practices match exactly,[20] there are many verbal reminiscences and parallels,[21] and the passages where Socrates requests a narrative and Critias assures him of the correspondence between history and his construction seem to respond to the passages in the *Republic* whose evidential force we are now considering.[22] If we take Plato as his word, he has assured us that the Form mentioned at *Republic* 9.592ab as perhaps uninstantiated was in fact instantiated many years ago by a city and its citizens – namely, Athens.[23] This objection to Vlastos is not conclusive, however, since it is not certain, despite the avowals of truthfulness, just how far Plato believed the history he recounts through Critias to have foundation in fact; the Atlantis story has seemed to most to be mere fable.[24] Less problematic instances of the Form in question would be welcome.

(2) Vlastos calls his purported example of an empty Form "the Form of the Ideal City",[25] but this is misleading. Throughout most of the *Republic* and the rest of the Platonic corpus, the Form in question goes by the simple name 'Justice' or 'the just itself'. Plato describes a completely just man and a completely just city, but these descriptions are accounts not of two distinct Forms but of ways in which a man and a city respectively may be "in no way different from that Justice itself but in every way such as Justice is" (*Republic* 5.472b8–c1; see all of 472b3–e9). The account of the just city is introduced in the *Republic because* a just city will be made just by exemplifying the same Form as a just man; the Form of Justice is the same in men and souls and cities and anything else that 'does its own'.[26] Hence, in neither passage does Plato suggest that any Form is uninstantiated. At most, he says that Justice is or might be uninstantiated, permanently or temporarily, *by a city*; a just man can instantiate the model of a just city even if no city does, as the main passage we've been judging shows (*Republic* 9.592b2–4).

Are there, then, or have there been any things other than cities which Plato regarded as just? We know, of course, that Plato thought that Socrates was extremely just (*Phaedo* 118a17, cf. *Epistles* 7.324e2); but he thought that other men were just too (*Phaedo* 82a10–b3, 89e7–90a10), for instance his dear friend Dion of Syracuse (*Epistles* 7.336a8–b1) and even himself (e.g. *Epistles* 7.329a7–b1, 330c3–8). He even thought that there are just beasts (*Republic* 10.620d2–5). Hence, the alleged evidence for the actual emptiness of this Form is without force. Still, the same passages might be taken to support the *possible* emptiness of Justice. Moreover, showing Justice to have instances does nothing to show that there is not some other Form that is actually or possibly empty. Two further objections of a more general nature will eliminate the first of these difficulties and partially remedy the second.

(3) The third reason why the *Republic* passages cannot support EFT has been stated succinctly by R. E. Allen:

> . . . the evidence cited to show that [EFT] was Plato's view is drawn, not from texts implying lack of exemplification, but deficiency of exemplification. Plato may well have thought, as a matter of economy in the universe, that the existence of a Form implies the existence of instances of it, that Forms, so to speak, have existential import; this is, of course, a far cry from saying that the existence of a Form implies that this or that shall be an instance of it. *Republic*, V, 471c–472e, (cf. IX, 592a–b), has been cited as evidence for empty essences; it is in fact evidence that essences such as justice are only deficiently realized.[27]

Allen is here largely, though not entirely, correct; in fact, as I showed in presenting the first two objections, the texts don't *imply* deficiency of exemplification, since Plato there leaves it open, and elsewhere suggests, that the account of the ideal state may be and has been exactly realized by some city and the Form of Justice it renders exemplified by particulars other than cities. Still, deficiency of exemplification clearly comes up in the earlier *Republic* passage. He does there distinguish between exemplifying Justice exactly and exemplifying it only approximately (472b7–d2, paralleled by 473a5–b2), and it is only the former whose possibility Plato regards as problematic. He seems to suppose that various human beings, maybe cities too, are just, even very just, but perhaps none can be *perfectly* just. More precisely, Plato is here *prepared to find* that no just particular is "in no way different from Justice itself and such as Justice is in every respect" (472b8–c1), but rather that at best particulars come close to being such as Justice is, i.e. are deficiently just. Since none of this goes to show that no particulars are just or exemplify any other Form, or even that Plato thought it *possible* that no particulars are just, the *Republic* passages are useless for proving any version of EFT. Still, we've so far done nothing to show that EFT must be false. A yet deeper account is needed.

(4) This deeper account may be found by considering what the deficiency of exemplification mentioned under objection (3) consists in. An older account maintained that a thing x deficiently exemplifies a Form Fness just in case x is not exactly F, not fully F, not, in short, F, but only approximately F. When x is deficiently F, x strives to be F and approaches being F but never in fact gets there; 'deficiently' works like 'almost' and 'nearly', or like 'spuriously' and 'speciously', to negate the adjective following. On this account, the claim that all particulars are at most deficiently what they are, which is at least suggested by *Republic* 5.471–473, would entail that

no particular ever is, strictly speaking, equal, for example,[28] or just, thus establishing (A5) (cf. p. 21 above). Hence, if this interpretation were correct, objection (3) would not be effective against Vlastos, since what is almost but not quite just isn't just, period, and so will not count against the emptiness of the Form of Justice. Socrates actually would be prepared to find that no particular city or man is just.

Fortunately, this older interpretation of the deficiency of exemplification by particulars is not correct, and an adequate alternative has been developed which does not have these unpleasant consequences.[29] According to this account, x deficiently exemplifies the Form Fness just in case x exemplifies Fness and also exemplifies the opposite Form un$F$ness. In such cases, one can correctly say that x is F and also that x is not F and (since x, being F, is the kind of thing that *can* be F) that x is un$F$. These apparently self-contradictory conditions for deficient exemplification we see to be consistent when we recognize that Plato regards exemplification of Forms like Justice by concrete particulars as always in some way relative. Thus a thing may be F in one respect, un$F$ in another; F in relation to one thing, un$F$ in relation to a different thing; F in one place, un$F$ in another; F under one description or qua being a thing of one kind, un$F$ under another description or qua being a thing of a distinct kind. Henry is handsome compared to King Kong but ugly compared to Apollo; Algernon is a large mouse but a small mammal; my armchair is elegant in my livingroom but ostentatious in yours; my abode is one apartment but many rooms.[30] Or so says Plato.[31] What general principle applying to all particulars underlies these examples? Using 'F' as a schematic relative predicate, we may proceed thus. First and obviously,

(D1a)   Every particular that is F is also possibly un$F$,

since it could be un$F$ relative to something other than what it's F relative to, and also

(D1b)   Every particular that is un$F$ is also possibly F

for the same reason. But we can attribute to Plato a stronger position. We should not, of course, attribute to him the view that

(D2)   Every particular is both F and un$F$

or even the view that

(D3)   Every particular is possibly both F and un$F$,

since there are particulars y and characters G such that y does not fall within the range of possible instances of G: a stone which is deficiently equal is not even deficiently courageous – it is neither brave nor unbrave (rash or cowardly). What we can attribute to Plato, though, is this:

(D4)   Every particular which is either F or un$F$ is both F and un$F$.[32]

I shall examine only one unambiguous passage that supports the attribution of (D4) to Plato, *Republic* 5.478e7–479d3.[33] Socrates there imagines himself addressing a Foe of the Forms thus:

"My dear sir, of all those many beautiful things, is there one which will not also appear ugly? And is there one of those just things which will not also appear unjust? And of pious things, one that will not appear impious? . . . What about the many things that are double? Are they any less half than double? . . . So with things big and small, light and heavy, does any of the things we call them apply to them any more than its opposite? . . . Is then each of the many things, more than it is not, that which anyone might call it?" (479a5–8, b3–4, 6–7, 9–10)

Here "that which anyone might call it" (479b10) and "any of the things we call them" (479b6–7) must refer just to relative characteristics, not to any feature introduced by a general term, as is shown by the examples adduced and by *Republic* 7.523a10–524d6[34] and other passages that distinguish disputables from decidables.[35] Thus restricted, the conclusion at 479b9–10 is clearly equivalent to (D4) and not merely (D1) or (D5). Furthermore, Plato's Theory of Forms requires the full strength of (D4). Forms of relatives are needed to serve as paradigms, cognitively and hence semantically and ethically. No particular can serve, since any particular which is F is also not F, so we cannot rely on it to tell what being F is.[36] Hence, if even one particular were F without also being un$F$ or un$F$ without also being F, that particular could function as a paradigm of Fness or of un$F$ness, cognitively, semantically, and ethically, even if it were both G and un$G$ for some or even every other relative character G.[37] In such a case, there would be no need for a Form of Fness. Hence, (D4) is needed to guarantee the full range of Forms of relatives to Plato.

But if (D4) is true, then every Form is exemplified which meets these two conditions: (i) It is the Form of some relative character F. (ii) There is at least one particular which is possibly F. The Form of Justice meets these conditions: (i) Particulars can be only relatively just (e.g. *Phaedo* 89e7–90a10), and (ii) there are particulars which are possibly just (e.g. men). Hence, Justice is not and cannot be empty, so long as there are men or animals or cities. More generally, the ethical and quantitative Forms of the *Phaedo*, *Symposium*, and *Republic*, being all Forms of relative characteristics, are, far from being empty, all instantiated by as many particulars as possible. This does not, however, show that no Forms can be empty. Three points must be dealt with before we may conclusively reject EFT. First, not every Form meets condition (i) above. Second, though there must be just men if there are men, we have as yet no reason to believe that there *must* be men; more generally, we have offered no ground for thinking that there must be particulars of the various sorts to which relative characters may attach, and so that every Form of a relative characteristic *must* have instances. Third, for all I have shown, there may be Forms, whether of relative characters or not, which cannot apply to *any* kind of particular, but only to Forms; such Forms would be necessarily empty, verifying (A4) (p. 21 above). I shall devote the remainder of this article to closing these loopholes.

III

Plato was well aware that, to put it crudely, there are things such that there aren't any of them. It doesn't follow that he thought that there are any uninstantiated Forms of kinds of things. There aren't any goatstags (*Republic* 6.488a6); but we shouldn't infer that the Form of Goatstag is uninstantiated, since according to Plato there is no such Form.

It will immediately be objected that Plato is committed to the existence of such a Form by a general principle which guarantees the existence of a Form corresponding to every general word; since 'goatstag' is a general word, there must be for Plato a Form of Goatstag. It is alleged that Plato states this principle — the One Over Many Principle — at *Republic* 10.596a6–7; here are two typical formulations of what Plato is supposed to say there: "Plato did in truth believe in an Idea answering to every common name . . . ."[38] "There can be no shadow of doubt that at the time when Plato wrote that one sentence, though not necessarily for the rest of his life, he thought of the world of Ideas as co-extensive with language . . . . Nothing that Plato himself wrote after the *Parmenides* gainsays that conclusion."[39] What these claims (especially the latter) suggest is that Plato believed that there is a one-one correspondence of general terms and Forms; hence, a Form of Goatstag. But these claims are mistaken all the way around. First, what Plato actually says is this: "We are wont to *posit* some one Form for each *many* to which we give the same name" (*Republic* 10.596a6–7). The correspondence holds primarily between the many particulars and the Form they instantiate; any correspondence between name and Form will be derivative. No provision is made for inferring or positing a Form in cases where the name is vacuous,

i.e. not given to a many.[40] The same conclusion is derivable from statements of this principle elsewhere in the *Republic* (6.507b2–8) and later
(*Parmenides* 132a2–4, d9–e5). The function of the name is just to enable
us to pick out the many to which the Form is to correspond, the same
function which is alternatively fulfilled by the likeness condition at *Parmenides* 132d9–e5. Second, as A.C. Lloyd has pointed out,[41] Plato only
licenses *positing* a Form when the conditions are met (τίθεσθαι *Republic*
10.596a7, τιθέντες 6.507b7); it is left open by the Principle that the hypothesis may have to be withdrawn. Plato is quite explicit that the existence
or even applicability of a general term is *not* a sufficient condition for the
existence of a corresponding Form at *Statesman* 262a–263b (see especially
262d4–e3), an application of *Phaedrus* 265e1–266b1.[42] Very roughly,
what is necessary and sufficient is that the hypothesized Form apply to a
group of things which have a common ordered nature which explains their
behavior and has a place in the maximally coherent and rational explanatory
system of such natures. More will be said on this matter later on.[43]

Since this restriction on the One Over Many Principle is often neglected,
I should like to point out its application in a passage not usually connected
with the Theory of Forms. This is Plato's account of smells at *Timaeus*
66d1–67a6. He says there:

In the case of the faculty residing in the nostrils, there are no Forms. For a smell is
always a half-formed thing, and no form of elementary particles has the proportions
necessary for having an odor. (66d1–4)

His claim is not that there are no differences in smell – that things don't
smell different – but that smells don't fall into natural kinds, since there
are no common natures of a rationally accountable kind (i.e., describable
in terms of uniform elementary geometrical structure) which explain similarities and differences in smell.[44] Thus, though there are varieties ποικίλματα
67a1) of smell, these don't constitute a number of distinct simple Forms –
infimae species – to which collection could be applied (67a1–2), so that the
dichotomy of smells he recognizes he does not call *Forms* of smell (67a2–3).
Does this case provide a counter-exemple to the unrestricted One Over Many
Principle? At first it seems not, since Plato says that the varieties of smell
are nameless (67a1). If by this he means that we have no names for talking
about smells, he is of course mistaken, about Greek as well as English. He
himself mentions the pleasant and the unpleasant (67a3; remember that
for Plato adjectives are as much names as nouns); and Aristotle provides
many more in his chapters on smell, *De Anima* B9 and *De Sensu* 5: foul

and fragrant (421b22f, 444a18), sweet* and bitter* (421a27, 443b9), pungent*, astringent* and putrid (443b10f), harsh*, sharp* and oily* (421a30). Why then does Plato call smells nameless? His point is probably that smells have no names *of their own*; the names we use for smells are borrowed from names of flavors (those marked with '*' above, according to Aristotle, *DA* 421a26–b3, cf. *DS* 443b7–12) or from terms we use for describing material objects that have smells (e.g. 'putrid', used primarily for fish etc., secondarily for the odors they give off).[45] Thus Aristotle, who insists against Plato that there are species of smell (*DS* 443b17–18), says that a large class of them "are divided into as many species as there are different tastes" (*DS* 444a6–7).[46] If this is Plato's point at *Timaeus* 67a1, then this passage does provide a counterexample to the unrestricted One Over Many Principle, since each variety of smell, e.g. the pungent, will be a class of smells called by the same name to which no Form corresponds.[47] There are, therefore, no positive grounds in Plato's theory which commit him to Forms corresponding to empty terms like 'goatstag'.[48]

So far my claim is the negative one that Plato is uncommitted to uninstantiated nonrelative Forms applicable to particulars. It is, of course, possible that when Plato mentioned goatstags in the *Republic*, the question, whether there are any such uninstantiated Forms, had just not occurred to him. Later, though, it did occur to him, and he committed himself to an answer: (*P*) there are no uninstantiated nonrelative Forms of natural kinds of particulars. This claim has been defended by Arthur O. Lovejoy in his magisterial history of the Principle of Plenitude on the basis of Plato's argument at *Timaeus* 29d7–31a1.[49] Unfortunately, Lovejoy's account of that argument is wrong about both its reasoning and its conclusion. I will therefore expose and remedy Lovejoy's errors to justify attributing (*P*) to Plato.[50]

First, I shall lay out Plato's argument at *Timaeus* 29d7–31a1; since a complete analysis of the passage is not to our purpose, I shall omit premisses and supporting citations where they are obvious or irrelevant.

(1)   The Demiurge was (perfectly) good (29e1).

(2)   Whatever is (perfectly) good is not jealous of anything (29e1–2).

It follows from (1) and (2) (and obvious further premisses) that

(3)   The Demiurge wished what existed to be as good (and so as well off) as it could be (29e2–3,[51] 30a2–3, 6–7).

It follows from (3) and some fundamental principles of Plato's axiology and the Theory of Forms which we cannot, despite their great interest, here go into that

(4)   The Demiurge wished what existed to be the best kind of thing it could be, i.e. to instantiate the best and most perfect natural kind Form it could instantiate (30a6–7).

(5)   The best and most perfect natural kind Form instantiable by what existed was the Form of (the genus) Living Creature, because that Form (a) has soul and intelligence (30b1–3) and (b) contains all subgenera and species of living creatures as parts (30c4–8).

(6)   What existed was the preexisting sensible stuff in disorderly motion (30a3–5; cf. 52d–53b, 69b).

It follows from (4), (5), and (6) that

(7)   The Demiurge wished the preexisting sensible stuff to instantiate the Form of Living Creature.

Given the view of instantiation Plato holds in the *Timaeus* and some obvious premisses about the connection between desire and action, (7) leads to

(8)   The Demiurge made the preexisting sensible stuff to be as like the Form of Living Creature as possible.

Combining (8) with (5), Plato concludes that

(9)   The Demiurge made the Universe to (a) have soul and intellect as well as body (by (5a): 30b7–9) and (b) contain living creatures of *all* species and genera (by (5b): 30d1–31a1).[52]

Given that the world has stayed and will stay as it then was (37c6–38c3), we may conclude from (9b) that (P') there are no uninstantiated Forms of kinds (genera and species) of living creatures.

We are now in a position to expose Lovejoy's errors. First, he claims that the Demiurge creates instances of all Forms because he is not jealous of them (the *instances*) and so wishes to share with them existence (which is a good).[53] This cannot be right. When the Demiurge wished "that all

things should come as near as possible to being like him" (29e3) and was
not jealous of anything, his benevolence and potential jealousy could then
have had as object only those things which he then believed did exist or
would exist; for though the objects of feelings of benevolence or jealousy
need not ever actually exist, the subject of these feelings must *believe* the
objects to exist then or at some relevant time in the past or future.[54] But
if one believes both that a thing will come to exist and that it will come to
exist only if one brings it into existence, one cannot deliberate about or
choose whether to bring it into existence.[55] Hence, the Demiurge's
deliberations cannot have been motivated by benevolence towards "the
sensible counterparts of every one of the Ideas", whose existence (he knew)
depended on the results of his deliberation and consequent action, but only
towards sensible stuff in disorderly motion; and this was the object of his
benevolent activity. Hence, all that *immediately* follows from 29d7–e3
(= (1)–(3)) is not that all Forms had instances, or even all Forms of living
creatures, but merely that the best Form instantiable by sensible stuff had
an instance.

Second, this best Form of the visible turns out (5) to be the generic
Form of Living Creature. According to Plato, what follows from its best
possible instantiation is that all Forms of subgenera and species of living
creatures have instances as well, i.e. (P'). His actual argument commits him
(9b) to no more than that explicitly. Lovejoy acknowledges in passing
that "in the *Timaeus*, it is true, Plato speaks chiefly of 'living things' or
'animals' "[56] but elsewhere entirely ignores this and throughout interprets
Plato's argument at 29d7–31a1 as having (P), not (P'), as its conclusion.[57]
There is therefore a serious gap between Plato's explicit argument as laid
out in (1)–(9) above and the conclusion (P) which Lovejoy attributes to it.
Since I too wish to claim that Plato held (P) and not merely (P'), I must
rescue Lovejoy by showing that (a) an extension to all Forms of natural
kinds instantiable by particulars is implicit in Plato's actual line of argument
and (b) Plato himself extended his claim beyond the restriction to kinds
of living creatures (as at 30d1, 39e3–9, 92c5–6) to all kinds of particulars.

(a) The Universe contains things other than living creatures: the natural
parts and components of living creatures, i.e. the elements, various organic
parts, and also, since the Universe is itself a living creature, the components
of a universe – mountains, rivers, and so on. But we know that its contents
are those not merely of a universe, but of the best possible universe. Now
just as the perfection of the Universe is constituted in part by its containing
all the species of living creature there are (5b), i.e. by the completeness of

its contents ("for no copy of that which is incomplete can ever be good", 30c5), by parity of reasoning it must make use of all possible kinds of constituents of a living creature (a living universe) if it is to have the completeness required for being the best possible universe; for the Form it's a copy of is *in every way* complete (30d2). Furthermore, Plato would be committed, by denying this, to the implausible view that some possible component of a living creature is not a component of any possible *kind* of living creature, since if it were, it would be realized when that kind of living creature was realized.

Why then does Plato talk here only of kinds of living creatures, and not of kinds of parts of living creatures — limbs, lakes, and so on? The reason is, I think, that in this part of the dialogue, at the outset of the main body of Timaeus' discourse, Plato is interested almost entirely in soul-making and the operations of soul, and in body-making primarily only to mention how the functioning of the body serves or affects the operation of the soul (cf. 46c7–47a1); it is only in the latter part of Timaeus' discourse (47e3ff) that the corporeal components of living creatures are treated in their own right. When, in the first part, corporeal components are discussed, just such considerations of plenitude as I have outlined in the preceeding paragraph are applied to these components (32c5–33b1).

(b) Having seen that the unrestricted requirement of a plenitude of Forms (*P*) is implicit in the reasoning underlying Plato's adoption of the explicitly stated restricted requirement (*P'*), we may now notice outcroppings of the unrestricted requirement from time to time in Timaeus' speech. First, a specific case: the elementary bodies. (I shall omit all except strictly relevant detail.) The Demiurge must make (masses of) exactly four kinds of primary bodies, fire, air, water, and earth. (Why bodies? And why four kinds? See 31b4–32b8.) The requirement of excellence (53d7–e2, 4–8) demands that the elementary bodies be regular polyhedra; the four regular polyhedra He chooses are the tetrahedron (pyramid) for fire, the hexahedron (cube) for earth, the octohedron for air, and the icosahedron for water (55d8, 56b4–6). There is, besides these four, one more kind of regular polyhedron, the dodecahedron. Now Plato might just have said, or implied by silence, "The dodecahedron is uninstantiated as a component of the Universe." But the requirement of a plenitude of Forms makes this unthinkable, for *no* possible component may go unused; so he says instead, "There still remained one construction, the fifth; and the god used it for the whole, making a pattern of animal figures thereon" (55c4–6). But perhaps, you object, Plato just thought the whole *was* a dodecahedron, so that as it fortunately turned out, all five kinds of possible components got instantiated. I reply as follows. First, the impression 55c4–6 makes is that the dodecahedron's being left over imposes a *requirement* (of reason) on the Demiurge – as Cornford puts it (without further explanation), "there remains the fifth regular solid, the dodecahedron, for which some use *must* be found."[58] And second, the whole, according to Plato, is *not* a dodecahedron; its shape is "the figure that comprehends in itself all the figures there are . . . rounded and spherical, equidistant every way from center to extremity" (33b3–5; see all of 33b2–c1 and also 58a4–6). Plato was quite willing to contradict himself, or at least seem to,[59] in order to comply with the unrestricted principle of plenitude of Forms.[60]

Here we have seen (*P*) at work in a particular case. Its general applicability is shown in Plato's discussion of the characterlessness of the Receptacle (50d4–51b2). The Receptacle must not have a character of its own (i.e. not instantiate some one Form everywhere and always, as well as others here and there at various time), because it must be fit to receive, since it *does* receive, *all* Forms. His statements of the main premiss of his argument are repeatedly given this universal assertoric formulation (50d4–5: "if there is to be an impress presenting all diversities of aspect"; 50e5: the Receptacle is "that which receives in itself all kinds"; 51a1–3: the Receptacle "is going duly to receive over the whole of itself often likenesses of all the eternal things"[61]) because a premiss with a universal quantifier over Forms is needed to yield his universal conclusion that the Receptacle "must in itself be free of all Forms" (50e4, 51a3). If all the likenesses it receives are of only some but not all of the Forms, this is no reason why the Receptacle should not have a character of its own which is incompatible only with those Forms it won't receive likenesses of.[62]

The evidence is now sufficient[63] that for Plato in the *Timaeus*, the truth of (*P*) is a requirement of reason in accordance with basic principles of goodness and perfection. Since these are the principles which ground the existence of the Forms themselves, the existence of sensible and concrete instances of all Forms is as deeply rooted in Plato's thought as that of the Forms they instantiate.[64] *We* may properly speak of the necessity of (*P*), though Plato himself would not, [64a] since for him, necessity is what is required or imposed not by reason but by the irrational aspect of the world. All this, of course, is contingent upon there actually existing a sensible given which the Demiurge is required by reason to make into the best and so fullest possible universe. But the existence of a perceptible world is just what Plato does regard as necessary – eternally yet unaccountably ineluctable.

Not all Forms of nonrelative characters of particulars fall within the scope of the previous line of argument; Forms of the various kinds of artifacts remain. That there are Forms of artifacts in Plato's ontology has been adequately proved elsewhere; Ross's discussion[65] seems to me right on every point relevant to the present issue. He shows that Plato asserted the existence of Forms of artifacts and regarded the existence of artifacts as natural and required by rational principles of excellence, just like that of the works of nature (i.e. the Demiurge), "since they are products of mind in accordance with sound reasoning" (*Laws* 890d7). It follows from man's rational nature to make tools and pass laws, as it follows from a plant's nature to flower, and both are in accordance with goodness. Hence beds, like stars and unlike barbarians, form a natural class; and the existence of beds, like that of stars, is a requirement of reason.

I. M. Crombie has, however, raised the difficulty, whether the line of argument just presented can be extended to "forms of misbegotten products such as nuclear weapons."[66]

... the distinction between nuclear weapons and things which are not nuclear weapons is not an arbitrary distinction like that between Greeks and barbarians, but a distinction which we have to draw in accordance with the method of classifying things which is acceptable to reason. This does not mean that it is desirable that nuclear weapons should exist ....[67]

Clearly, the existence of a 'natural' kind of artifact the existence of instances of which is or would be undesirable seems to break that link which allowed us to extend to the existence of tables the same necessity which we earlier accorded to the existence of horses. (Crombie merely offers this as a problem and regards it as quite possible that Plato did not notice this difficulty and so did really suppose that every Form is instantiated, that "ordered and consistent patterns of behaviour are not to be found except where reason has imposed them, and that therefore there exist no common natures of a determinate kind except those of things whose existence reason sees to be desirable."[68] He later attributes to Plato, without any reservations, warnings, or exceptions, a 'principle of impartiality' equivalent to an unrestricted principle of plenitude of Forms.[69]) My solution is this: Plato thought the existence of evils such as nuclear weapons, diseases, and the like to be (a) insofar as evil, necessary, and (b) insofar as not evil, desirable. (b) All such artifacts are to be functionally defined, i.e. conceived as something which operates to achieve some good; and it is to this conceived goodness that they owe their existence as a natural expression of man's rationality (cf. *Republic* 10.601d4–6). (a) Insofar as their actual operation achieves not good but evil, this is due to (i) inevitable human ignorance and (equivalently, Plato would say) (ii) the basic imperfection of physical exemplification and embodiment, whereby everything good must also be its contrary.[70] Thus the difficulty is dispelled.

We may thus unconditionally adopt the result of Section II, that there are not, and cannot be, empty Forms of relative characteristics of particulars, the complementary conclusion of this section, that there are not, and cannot be, empty Forms of nonrelative characteristics of particulars — natural kinds, artifacts, and their features — either. It is of course *permanent* emptiness that is here denied to Forms of particulars. If we take the creation story of the *Timaeus* literally, then the Forms existed before their instances, at least in most cases;[71] and Plato's views on reincarnation *may* entail that all species of animals other than gods and humans will become extinct when all human souls have escaped the cycle of rebirth.[72] If we take Timaeus' account not literally,[73] but as a presentation in mythical form of what the Universe has been like throughout an infinite past and will be like forevermore, then Plato's view, like Aristotle's,[74] will be that for every Form, there has been no time before which that Form had always lacked instances. In either case, there are, *sub specie aeternitatis*, no empty Forms, and cannot be any, so that the ontological priority of the Forms cannot consist in every Form's possible emptiness. One gap in my argument remains, however. My claim must as yet be restricted to Forms of characteristics or kinds of particulars. It has thus far been left open whether there are Forms which are uninstantiated by particulars because they are Forms of characteristics which only Forms can have. Were this the case, the world of Forms would be independent of and prior to the world of particulars in that there could be a world of Forms, namely of Forms of Form-characteristics, all instantiated, but only by Forms, and so no world of particulars at all. Are there, then, any Forms which *cannot* have concrete instances?

IV

That Forms can have Forms among their instances is clear from a number of passages in both the middle and late dialogues. A large number of scholars have thought that, at least during his middle period, Plato believed that every Form is an instance of itself.[75] At least some certainly are, e.g. Beauty.[76] Forms are also instantiated by Forms other than themselves. All the Forms are just (*Republic* 6.500c3–4), holy (*Phaedrus* 250a4), stable (250c3, *Phaedo* 78d1–9, *Republic* 6.500c2–3, *Sophist* 248a11–13)[77] realities (*Phaedrus*

247e2–3, *Republic* 6.507b7, 511e3, 7.519b4). But are there any Forms, these or others, which are instantiated *only* by Forms?

One of Aristotle's attacks on the Theory of Forms may be read as ascribing an affirmative answer to Plato. According to this criticism (which I shall call the Superduplication Objection), the Theory is grotesquely uneconomical, for it tries to account for the kinds of things by more than doubling their number:

> ... it's almost as if a man wished to count certain things, and while they were few thought he would not be able to count them, but made more of them and then counted them; for the Forms are, one may say, *more numerous than* the particular sensible groups .... For to each there answers an entity which has the same name and exists apart from the substances, and so also in the case of all other groups there is a one over many, whether the many are the things here *or the eternal things*.

The passage quoted is *Metaphysics* M4.1078b34–1079a4; this is a later version of A9.990b2–8, which differs verbally from it in a few respects, the only one of any importance being that where the later version has "one may say, more numerous than", the earlier version has "practically equal to – or not less than –".[78] Two main points in the interpretation of these passages must be established.

First, Aristotle must be talking about *groups* or *kinds* of particular sensible things throughout these passages, and not about individual particular sensible things themselves, if his argument is to be taken literally and have any force. (a) The correspondence between Forms and things here is made to depend explicitly on the application of the One Over Many Principle, which provides a mapping of 'homonymous' or similar *groups* of particulars into the Forms. The suggestion that there might be Forms of individual particulars has not yet surfaced[79] and constitutes a new and separate objection to the Theory of Forms when it does,[80] so it's groups that Forms answer to and hence (at least) duplicate. (b) Counting particulars is out of the question, since there are infinitely many of them (only finitely many of each sort at a given time, of course, since the Universe is finite, but the human race, for example, is eternal, and so there have been and will be infinitely many human beings (cf. *Physics* Γ6–7, esp. 6.206b13–14)), and so there can't be more Forms of particulars than particulars, so far as Aristotle is concerned. (c) Aristotle is contrasting the Platonists' view with his own, according to which the object of scientific investigation is an Aristotelian universal, a one holding of many but not separate from and over them (cf. *Posterior Analytics* A11.77a5–9, 22.83a33–35). He takes the existence of these universals as a matter of fact, and criticizes Plato for superfluously adding duplicates of *these* to his ontology. My claim that he is comparing the number of Forms with the number of natural *classes* of particulars is rejected by both Ross and Cherniss.[81] But their alternative, that the number of Forms is compared with the number of individual particulars, requires that what Aristotle says "is not to be taken very strictly", and we must regard him as "speaking very roughly" (Ross); Cherniss acknowledges points (a) and (b) above when he notes that "neither the ἴσα of A nor the πλείω of M can be taken quite strictly, since there could be no way of calculating the relative number of ideas and individual sensibles". My account will allow Aristotle to be speaking with care and exactitude.

Second, we need to see why Aristotle amended 'equal' to 'not less than' (990b4–5) and later made the point of the amendment explicit (and his objection sharper) by substituting 'more' (1078b36). Application of the One Over Many Principle to all natural groups of particulars will produce Forms only equal in number to the kinds of particulars. Where do the extra Forms come from? Is Aristotle appealing to Forms not generable by the One Over Many Principle, e.g. Forms of Goatstag and Centaur? No; it explicitly rests solely on the One Over Many Principle in both *A* and *M*. The one clue we have is the final phrase of the objection: "whether the many are the things here or the eternal things" (καὶ ἐπὶ τοῖσδε καὶ επὶ τοῖς ἀιδίοις 990b8, 1079a4). What are "the eternal things"? Ross says that Aristotle is here referring to the eternal sensibles: "τοῖς ἀιδίοις is in 991a9 expanded into τοῖς ἀιδίοις τῶν αἰσθητῶν, i.e. the heavenly bodies".[82] This interpretation would help us justify "more numerous than" (1078b36) if Aristotle were supplementing the 'Object of Thought' Argument with the One Over Many Principle; for then, in addition to the Forms of kinds of *perishable* particulars yielded by the former argument, there would be *more* Forms provided by the supplement, namely Forms of kinds of *imperishable* particulars. But even this case more favorable to Ross's interpretation would not provide a total number of Forms greater than the total number of classes of sensible particulars, which was the desired result. And of course the 'Object of Thought' Argument plays no role at all in the Superduplication Objection; only the One Over Many Principle does, and there is no philosophically significant difference at all between the way the One Over Many Principle applies to groups of perishable particulars – men, shuttles, or equals – and the way it applies to groups of eternal particulars – stars or planets. Hence there would be no point in distinguishing eternal from perishable particulars in the Superduplication Objection. Further, the contrast at 990b8 is not made in exactly the same way as that at 991a9, cited by Ross as a parallel. The latter explicitly contrasts two kinds of particulars; the former merely contrasts 'things here' with 'eternal things'. The trouble with interpreting 990b8 as a way of contrasting heavenly bodies with sublunary things is that at least one important sublunary thing ('thing here') is eternal, namely the Earth (*Timaeus* 40b8–c3 with 41a7–b6; *De Caelo* B3.286a13–22 and B14), so that the required opposition is not forthcoming.

The whole Superduplication Objection makes good sense, however, if 'the eternal things' are Forms and the 'things here' are particulars.[83] Aristotle's argument will then be this: In addition to all the Forms yielded by applying the One Over Many Principle to all the natural groups of particulars, the Platonists are committed to yet *more* Forms, namely those yielded by applying the One Over Many Principle to those natural groups having as members only (some or all of the) Forms derived earlier (and Forms derived now as well; the definition of such second-order Forms will often be unavoidably impredicative). These latter groups will have only Forms as members because no particular can share the name which makes the group and the Form over it homonymous. On the interpretation suggested, the number of Forms will be greater than the number of natural classes of particulars, just as Aristotle says, since the One Over Many Principle will provide a one-one mapping of groups of particulars onto only a proper subset of the set of Forms and, since there are only finitely many Forms (a requirement of their ultimate knowability), no other mapping can do better. The Theory of Forms not only duplicates all natural kinds of particulars, it can't stop there; the uncontrollably incestuous One Over Many Principle, as in some creation myth, bears progeny of its own offspring and so brings forth monsters (Hesiod *Theogony* 126–128 + 147–153). This interpretation makes the Superduplication Objection both strict and valid and seems therefore to be the most satisfactory.

If the interpretation just presented is correct, it shows that Aristotle thought that the Theory of Forms requires the existence of Forms which have, and must have, only Forms as instances. It does not show that Plato recognized or accepted any such implication, or even that Aristotle thought he did, merely that Aristotle thought that he ought to recognize and accept it. Actual attribution of the view to Plato should await the discovery of some definite examples of Forms which have only Forms as instances. That no such examples are to be found is the gravest objection to this last defense of EFT and so counts against the effectiveness of the Superduplication Objection as well.

Cherniss has a suggestion as to what these Form-generated Forms might be: "Aristotle points out that the relationship of ἓν ἐπὶ πολλῶν exists among

the ideas as well as in the case of phenomena, so that, besides the ideas of
sensible substances and of the qualities etc. exhibited by those substances,
there must be other ideas which are the 'genera' of those ideas (cf. 991a29–
31)".[84] What Aristotle says at 991a29–31 is this: "Again, the Forms are
patterns not only of sensible things, but of Forms themselves *also*; i.e. the
genus, as genus of various species, will be so; therefore the same thing will be
pattern and copy". But a genus of various species, though a Form which has
Forms as instances, does not have *only* Forms as instances. Cows and dogs,
like Cow and Dog, instantiate Animal. All particulars will fall under a genus
which fall under the species-Forms which fall under it, and so it will already
have been yielded by the One Over Many Principle applied to the natural
group of particulars of that genus. Hence it will not be one of the Forms by
which the set of Forms outnumbers the set of natural groups of particulars.
So Cherniss's candidates for the class of Form-generated Forms fail.

But surely, you may say, 990b8 = 1079a4 itself provides us with (so to
speak) the ideal candidate; one group containing only eternal things must be
the class of eternal things. Doesn't the Form of Eternity have only Forms as
instances? Plato is sometimes taken to be saying just this in a famous passage
in the *Timaeus*:

When the father who had begotten it saw it set in motion and alive, a shrine brought into
being for the everlasting (ἀϊδίων) gods, he rejoiced and being well pleased he took
thought to make it yet more like its pattern. So as that pattern is the Living Creature
that is for ever existent (ζῷον ἀϊδιον ὄν), he sought to make this Universe also like it,
so far as might be, in that respect. Now the nature of that Living Creature was eternal
(αἰώνιος), and this character it was impossible to confer in full completeness (παντελῶς)
on the generated thing. But he took thought to make, as it were, a moving likeness of
eternity (αἰῶνος); and, at the same time that he ordered the Heaven, he made, of eternity (αἰῶνος) that abides in unity, an everlasting (αἰώνιον) likeness moving according to
number – that to which we have given the name Time. (*Timaeus* 37c6–d7)

Taylor summarizes thus: "He could not make it, like its model, eternal
(ἀϊδιος) (since nothing sensible can be so), but he made it as nearly eternal as
he could".[85] But in fact Plato says something quite contrary to this. Particulars can't have eternity completely (37d3–4) or perfectly, i.e. they can't
have it in the way that Forms have it, but they can and do have it. The situation is the same as with other relative characteristics of sensible particulars;
the particular doesn't manage to be *perfectly* eternally what it is because
there are some things it is but not eternally, though there are others it eternally is, whereas a Form is perfectly eternal because *everything* it is it eternally is. The stars are eternally stars and so are "eternal divine existent living

creatures abiding always the same" (*Timaeus* 40b5–6), though they are only intermittently, not eternally, overhead; whereas the Form of Star is eternally everything it is. Taylor and Cherniss have mistakenly adopted the older interpretation of defective instantiation rejected in Section II(4) above (pp. 25–27); in Plato's real view, Forms and particulars share eternity just as they share justice.[86] Nor should the reader suspect that there might be a Form of Perfect Eternity instantiable by Forms only. Such a Form would be utterly redundant in Plato's theory. That a given Form is perfectly eternal is already completely explained by its exemplifying the Form of Eternity perfectly; there is nothing further to be accounted for by exemplification of a Form of Perfect Eternity. So Plato nowhere makes the move from instantiating the Form of *F*ness perfectly to instantiating the Form of Perfect *F*ness.[87] Furthermore, Forms of Perfect Justice, etc., in addition to the Forms of Justice, etc., would have enabled Aristotle to strengthen 'more' to 'twice as many' in the Superduplication Objection; but he is everywhere silent concerning any such move in the Platonic theory. In the case at hand, Plato never to my knowledge explicitly mentions even a plain Form of Eternity, though as we've seen he could have done so consistently with the thesis of this paper. This candidate for the role of Form uninstantiable by particulars therefore fails completely. But there are further candidates carrying impressive credentials, so we cannot give up the search yet.

Plato often contrasts Forms and particulars as characterized by stability and flux respectively (e.g. *Phaedo* 78d1–79a11, among many well-known passages). Some scholars have claimed that, at least in the middle period dialogues, just as the Forms are totally stable, so sensible particulars are totally in flux and lacking in all stability.[88] If these scholars are right, then the Form of Stability will be a Form having only Forms as instances. But they are not right. Stability and change, like justice and injustice, are relative characteristics, and so a particular can exhibit both at once by changing in one respect while remaining stable in another respect. It follows that *both* characteristics must belong to every particular, by (D4) in section II(4) above (p. 27).[89] If particulars were in total flux, they would be perfect instances of motion, and so no Form of Motion would be needed as a paradigm. But as Plato never tires of telling us, no particular is a perfect instance of any of its characteristics. The stability of particulars comes out very clearly in the argument for the complexity of the soul at *Republic* 4.436b8ff, especially at 436c9–d1, describing a man who is at rest in respect of one part of himself and in motion in respect of another part of himself at the same time, and at 436d5–e4, similarly describing spinning tops as both standing still and moving simultaneously.[90] Again, Plato's argument at *Phaedo* 80c2–d4 requires that the stability attributed to mummies, bones, and sinews[91] be the same kind of stability attributed to souls in the immortality thesis (e.g. at 79e3–5) and so to Forms (80b2–3); the difference is only that mummies, bones, and sinews have it in some respects and for a long time, Forms have it always in all respects, while souls have it always in some respects (e.g. being a soul) and gain it in all respects permanently when they take up residence in Hades.[92] The argument of *Phaedo* 80c2–d4 is of course invalid,[93] but this is no reason to suppose that Plato didn't believe its premisses or think that they provide some support for the immortality thesis.[94] Even in the *Timaeus*, where the evidence for extreme (nonsensical) Heracliteanism has seemed to many to be strongest,[95] many particulars are asserted to be stable, even eternally so, in certain respects, e.g. the Universe and the gods (heavenly bodies) in respect of being the kind of living creatures they are (*Timaeus* 41a7–b6; cf. *Laws* 10.904ab) and in respect of some species of locomotion (40b2–4). The thesis of continual change, whatever it amounts to, is restricted to the manifestation of Forms of the elements and opposites by regions of space and is not extended to every sort of Form (*Timaeus* 49b7–50a4) or to particulars that move in space. It is therefore not incompatible with (D4) when the latter is applied, as we have been doing, to particulars. I conclude that both the relativity of stability and the explicit wording of several Platonic texts require that the Form of Rest be exemplified by particulars; this candidate too has failed to qualify.

Another obvious candidate is the Form of Being or Reality (οὐσία), since Plato often characterizes the Forms/particulars distinction as one between things that are but don't become and things that become but never are (e.g. *Timaeus* 26d6–28a1, among many well-known passages). The reader should quickly see that this candidate must fail for the same reason as the last. For Plato, Being, like Stability and Eternity, is an incomplete characteristic of particulars (likewise Not-Being and hence also Coming-to-Be and Ceasing-to-Be); '*x* is' is short for '*x* is *F*', and more significantly '*x* is and is not' is short for '*x* is *F* and is not *F*' (as at *Republic* 5.477a–479d)[96] or (in late dialogues) '*x* is *F* and is not *G*' (as at *Sophist* 256e5–6, 259b5–6, 263b11–12).[97] In the middle period dialogues, Being is distinctive of the Forms as against the particulars not because only the Forms have Being but because only the Forms have Being only;[98] in the particulars always, but in the Forms never, is Being contaminated by Not-Being. In short, to think that only Forms have Being is to be led astray by the false theory of deficient exemplification rejected in Section II(4). It is in the way sketched out just above that we should understand *Timaeus* 27d6–28a1 cited above (and so take the amplification of ὂν δὲ οὐδέποτε 28a1 into ὄντως δὲ οὐδέποτε ὄν 28a3–4 as expressing Plato's meaning more precisely) and such oft-cited earlier passages as *Phaedo* 77a3–4, 78d1–e4, 92d9. It is unnecessary for me to argue here for the interpretation of Plato's theory of Being here employed; it is an application of an important achievement of recent scholarship.[99] Its significant result is that we can regard Plato's use of εἶναι, ὄν, and οὐσία when talking about particulars as not mere slips or loose talk but exactly what he meant. Hence, the Form of Being too turns out not to be the exclusive possession of the Forms.

One more desperate try: surely a Form of Formhood, the Itself Itself, would have only Forms as instances, and surely Plato recognized such a Form when he singles out the Forms as the things we call 'Itself' (*Phaedo* 75d2, cf. 78d3–4).[100] It is only natural to take this Form to be the Form of Perfection, i.e. of Being Perfectly *F*.[101] The argument of Section II(4) so often appealed to above shows that no particular could be among the instances of such a Form. But is there a Form of Formhood in Plato? One obstacle to his having recognized such a Form must fail: Plato is quite willing to countenance the existence, applicability, and of course self-applicability of transcendental or categoreal Forms. The clearest examples are the Very Important Kinds of the *Sophist*, Being, Stability, Change, Sameness, and Otherness (254b–259b), most of which made an appearance in earlier dialogues (e.g. *Republic* and *Timaeus*). Still, applying the One Over Many Principle here is not troublefree. In Plato's Greek as in English, 'Itself', like 'what is', is correctly applied to many things other than Forms, and Plato so uses it, applying it to immanent characters (*Phaedo* 103b4–5)[102] and even to sensible particulars (*Republic* 7.532a3–5).[103] As the two passages just cited show, a thing is called even 'the *F* itself' relatively, so that any *F* thing can be called 'the *F* itself' in an appropriate context. Of course, the Form of *F*ness is *always* the *F* itself; but this fact is not sufficient to mark off a class to which Plato may apply the One Over Many Principle. In one passage, Plato or a contemporary Platonist[104] does mention αὐτὸ ταὐτό (*Alcibiades I* 129b1); but he is there talking about a man's own self, his soul (130c3, 5–6), and not what we have been searching for, a Form of Forms.[105] There is, of course, one Form which makes all the Forms to be what they are, namely the Form of the Good (*Republic* 6.509b6–10); but this Form is not possessed by or a cause of Forms only, since it is shared by and a cause of particulars as well (as is implied by *Republic* 10.601d4–6 and *Timaeus* 29d7–31b3; cf. p. 34 above). I conclude that either the proposed interpretation of the Superduplication Objection is wrong or the Objection itself doesn't hit its target.There are *no* Forms which have only Forms as instances.

Sections II through IV taken together show that there is no Form, whether of a relative character, a natural kind, an artifact, or any other sort of thing, which never has any particulars as instances, and that, though some may be temporarily empty, all Forms have as many instances as they can — infinitely many, in fact. The separation and ontological priority of the realm of Forms cannot, therefore, consist in the possible or actual emptiness of any Form. What it does consist in, must be the subject of another essay.

Rutgers University,
Newark College of Arts and Sciences

NOTES

[1] Cf. Harold Cherniss, *Aristotle's Criticism of Plato and the Academy*, Johns Hopkins Press, Baltimore 1944, pp. 206–211.
[2] Gregory Vlastos, 'Reasons and Causes in the *Phaedo*', *Philosophical Review* 78 (1969), p. 301, reprinted in Vlastos (ed.), *Plato I*, Anchor Books, Garden City, New York 1970, p. 142, and Vlastos, *Platonic Studies*, Princeton University Press, Princeton 1973, p. 86.
[3] W. F. R. Hardie, *A Study in Plato*, Oxford University Press, Oxford 1936, p. 73.
[4] J. A. Faris, *Plato's Theory of Forms and Cantor's Theory of Sets*, The Queen's University, Belfast 1968, p. 11. This account of separation underlies Russell Dancy's objection to Owen's interpretation of *Categories* 2.1a24–25 in Dancy, 'On Some of Aristotle's First Thoughts about Substances', *Philosophical Review* 84 (1975), pp. 345–347. EFT is defended at length by Erkka Maula, 'On Plato and Plenitude', *Ajatus* 29 (1967), pp. 12–50; cf. note 64a below.
[5] R. E. Allen, *Plato's 'Euthyphro' and the Earlier Theory of Forms*, Humanities Press, New York 1970, p. 132n3, quoted p. 25 below.
[6] Anders Wedberg, *Plato's Philosophy of Mathematics*, Almqvist & Wiksell, Stockholm 1955, p. 33; also in Vlastos (ed.), *Plato I*, pp. 36f. EFT has also been rejected by Arthur O. Lovejoy, *The Great Chain of Being*, Harvard University Press, Cambridge, Mass. 1936, pp. 45–55; see Section III below.
[7] The Self-Predication Assumption, first so-called by Vlastos, 'The Third Man Argument in the *Parmenides*', *Philosophical Review* 63 (1954), p. 324, reprinted in R. E. Allen (ed.), *Studies in Plato's Metaphysics*, Humanities Press, New York 1965, p. 236; he credits its isolation to A. E. Taylor, 'Parmenides, Zeno, and Socrates', *Proceedings of the Aristotelian Society* 16 (1915–6), pp. 250, 253, reprinted at Taylor, *Philosophical Studies*, Macmillan, London 1934, pp. 46, 49.
[8] I exclude from discussion the supposed mathematicals which Aristotle attributes to Plato and which some have found in the *Republic* and elsewhere and the immanent characters of *Phaedo* 102d, 103b and *Parmenides* 130b. The former I'm doubtful of; the latter exist only if immanent in a particular that's an instance of a Form and so are ignorable.

[9] No difficulty is raised in the *Cratylus* or elsewhere about names of the perished (e.g. Astyanax 392b), and Socrates considers past or future instantiation as good as present in countering accusations of talking about daydreams (*Republic* 6.499a11–d6).

[10] *Philoctetes* 1443–1444, trans. David Grene. Pearson's Oxford text is οὐ γὰρ ηὐσέβεια συνθνῄσκει βροτοῖς· κἂν ζῶσι κἂν θάνωσω, οὐκ ἀπόλλυται.

[11] *Republic* 9.592a10–b4. All *Republic* translations herein are based on those of G. M. A. Grube, Hackett Publishing Co., Indianapolis 1974.

[12] *Republic* 5.472d9–e6. All of 471c4–473b3 is of this nature and should be compared with the passage in Book 9.

[13] What is called 'the truth' at 472e6 is not that it is impossible to prove it possible to found an ideal city, but that such lack of proof would be irrelevant if a fact.

[14] An accusation which would have consigned Socrates' scheme to the class of utopian wishes being aired around the dramatic date of the *Republic*; see Friedrich Solmsen, *Intellectual Experiments of the Greek Enlightenment*, Princeton University Press, Princeton 1975, pp. 66–79. Socrates' proposals could easily have sounded like such Euripidean speculations as those at *Hippolytus* 916–20, *Medea* 214–65 and 1081–9, and *Protesilaus* fr. 653.

[15] Which is not at all meant to be a city in the sky, but in Greece (5.470e4–6), though of course it can be barbarian as well (6.499c9).

[16] Critias says 'in how many' rather than 'how in all' not because there was disagreement in some points but because he had not yet taken the trouble to recollect exactly all the points of Solon's story; having done so, he in effect corrects (26cd) 'many' to 'all'.

[17] By 'no inconsistency', Plato means not that the supposition that the ancient Athenians exemplified the ideal state is logically consistent but that there's no inconsistency between Solon's historical account and Socrates' theoretical one.

[18] *Timaeus* 25e2–5, 26c6–d5. All *Timaeus* translations herein are based on those of F. M. Cornford.

[19] *Timaeus* 26e3–5. Socrates' ἀληθινόν (26e4) echoes and acknowledges Critias' ἀληθῶς at 21a3.

[20] See the very thorough discussion by H. Herter, 'Urathen der Idealstaat', *Palingenesia* 4 (1969), pp. 112–132. Herter (p. 117n35) follows H. D. Rankin, 'Plato's Eugenic εὐφημία and ἀπόθεσις in *Republic*, Book V', *Hermes* 93 (1965), pp. 407–420, in finding a discrepancy between *Timaeus* 19a1–2 and *Republic* 5.459de, 406c, 461ac; I have space here only to say that I think Rankin's arguments can be shown to fail, but a minor discrepancy of the sort alleged could not in any case cast doubt on the obvious fact that Plato *intended* an exact correspondence.

[21] Cf. G. E. L. Owen, 'The Place of the *Timaeus* in Plato's Dialogues', in R. E. Allen (ed.), *Studies in Plato's Metaphysics*, p. 330n1.

[22] Cf. e.g. *Timaeus* 19b4–c1 with *Republic* 5.472d4–7 or *Timaeus* 26c8–d1, e4–5 with *Republic* 9.592a11–b1, 6.501e4–5.

[23] We should expect it to have been instantiated *sometime* by Athens, according to Plato, since he tells us that each city "has adopted every type of political system" at some time or other (*Laws* 3.676c1–2).

[24] Vlastos has argued convincingly that the history of the genesis of the world-order recounted through Timaeus is meant by Plato as verisimilar, not fictional; he just *might* have attributed the same order of truthfulness to Critias' tale. See 'The Disorderly

Motion in the *Timaeus*', in R. E. Allen (ed.), *Studies in Plato's Metaphysics*, pp. 380–383, and 'Creation in the *Timaeus*: Is It a Fiction?' in Allen, pp. 401–419; cf. *Republic* 2.382c10–d3.

[25] Vlastos, 'Reasons and Causes', p. 301/142/86, quoted on p. 19.

[26] A commonplace of Platonic doctrine; cf. *Republic* 2.368d2–369a4, 4.435a5–b3, 441d5–7, 442d7–9, 443b4–6, *Meno* 72a6–d1. Plato speaks most often of just men, but of just souls occasionally, e.g. *Republic* 10.620d, *Sophist* 247ab.

[27] R. E. Allen, *Plato's 'Euthyphro' and the Earlier Theory of Forms*, p. 132n3.

[28] 'No two sensible things, such as sticks or stones, are ever equal', J. E. Raven, *Plato's Thought in the Making*, Cambridge University Press, Cambridge 1965, p. 81.

[29] The fundamentals of the adequate alternative were presented by G. E. L. Owen, 'A Proof in the *peri ideōn*', *Journal of Hellenic Studies* 77 (1957), pp. 108–110, reprinted in R. E. Allen (ed.), *Studies in Plato's Metaphysics*, pp. 305–309, and elaborated in connection with other Platonic doctrines by Colin Strang, 'Plato and the Third Man', *Proceedings of the Aristotelian Society Supplementary* 37 (1963), pp. 158–162, reprinted in Vlastos (ed.), *Plato I*, pp. 194–198, and by Gregory Vlastos, 'Degrees of Reality in Plato', Renford Bambrough (ed.), *New Essays on Plato and Aristotle*, The Humanities Press, New York 1965, pp. 1–17, reprinted in Vlastos, *Platonic Studies*, pp. 58–73. (It is not clear that Vlastos actually adopts the interpretation I here follow, since he apparently rejects it in his review of Crombie at *Philosophical Review* 75 (1966), pp. 529–530, reprinted in Vlastos, *Platonic Studies*, pp. 377–378.) An extensive exposition and defense of the alternative account is given by Alexander Nehamas, 'Plato on the Imperfection of the Sensible World', *American Philosophical Quarterly* 12 (1975), pp. 105–117.

[30] Cf. *Hippias Major* 289a2–d5, 290b2–291a2, *Alcibiades I* 115b1–116a9, *Parmenides* 129c4–d2. Further examples may be found in Vlastos, 'Degrees of Reality in Plato', pp. 6/63, 10–15/66–72.

[31] He does not retract this doctrine at *Philebus* 51c1–52a4, where a careful reading shows that by καλὰ καθ᾽ αὑτά in contrast with πρός τι καλά Plato means to rule out only certain sorts of relativity, i.e. relativity to the needs and desires of the beholder and in general relativity to the context of perception; cf. J. C. B. Gosling, trans., *Plato's Philebus*, Oxford University Press, Oxford 1975, pp. 121–122 on 51c6. There is no suggestion in the text that such beautiful things can't be compared with each other in respect of pleasantness in virtue of e.g. how *long* they cause pleasure, and so also in respect of beauty, which here is more or less equated with pleasantness.

[32] (D4) is used to explicate deficiency of exemplification by Alexander Nehamas, 'Predication and Forms of Opposites in the *Phaedo*', *Review of Metaphysics* 26 (1973), pp. 467, 473.

[33] For further evidence, consult again Vlastos, 'Degrees of Reality in Plato', pp. 6/63, 10–15/66–72, and also Nehamas, 'Predication and Forms of Opposites', pp. 463–473. I say unambiguous because, unlike some other relevant passages, it does not allow of being interpreted as supporting merely the thesis that (D5) for every particular x there is *some* character F such that x is both F and un$F$.

[34] See the discussion by Nehamas, 'Predication and Forms of Opposites', pp. 467–468. I do not wish to commit myself to the stronger view that in the *Phaedo* and *Republic* 1–9, Plato did not yet recognize Forms of substances, qualities, shapes, colors, etc., but only Forms of relative qualities and quantities, as maintained in 1879 by Sir James

George Frazer, *The Growth of Plato's Ideal Theory*, Russell & Russell, New York 1967, pp. 39, 48–51, 57–60, 68, 70, 74–77, 110. (The same view is attributed to A. A. Krohn, *Der Platonische Staat*, R. Muhlmann, Halle 1876), p. 96, by J. Adam (ed.), *The REPUBLIC of Plato*, 2 Vols., Cambridge University Press, Cambridge 1902, note on 476a2; but I have not been able to check his reference.) Recently, it has been maintained by Nehamas in the article just cited and attacked by Robert Bolton, 'Plato's Distinction between Being and Becoming', *Review of Metaphysics* 29 (1975), pp. 79–80. In my view, the bee example at *Meno* 72b1–c5 shows a propensity to think about natural kinds and ethical characters similarly.

[35] See Strang, 'Plato and the Third Man', pp. 158–161/194–195.

[36] See Owen, 'A Proof in the *peri ideōn*', pp. 110–111/309–312; Strang, 'Plato and the Third Man., pp. 161–162/197–198; Vlastos, 'Degress of Reality in Plato', *passim*. More oldfashioned interpreters of Plato put the same point in their own way: ". . . to measure individuals against one another is to succumb to relativism": Harold Cherniss, 'The Philosophical Economy of the Theory of Ideas', *American Journal of Philology* 57 (1936), p. 447, reprinted in Allen (ed.), *Studies in Plato's Metaphysics*, p. 3, and Vlastos (ed.), *Plato I*, p. 18.

[37] It has been alleged by some (e.g. Terrence Irwin, in a paper he once presented) that it is universals (characters, types) which Plato says are both *F* and un*F*, not particulars. Very briefly, (a) Plato's argument requires *everything* except Forms to be imperfect, (b) the way in which such universals are both *F* and un*F* must infect any particulars they attach to (as at *Hippias Major* 289a2–d5), and (c) it's three *particular* fingers (οὗτοι τρεῖς δάπτυλοι *Republic* 7.523c4–5) about which sense gives contradictory reports at *Republic* 7.523e3ff.

[38] W. D. Ross, *Plato's Theory of Ideas*, Oxford University Press, Oxford 1951, p. 79.

[39] J. E. Raven, *Plato's Thought in the Making*, pp. 186, 211.

[40] Wedberg (quoted on p. 20 above) is mistaken in claiming that Plato here *rejects* (A4); a Form is posited for each many, but he doesn't assert the converse.

[41] A. C. Lloyd, 'Plato's Description of Division', in R. E. Allen (ed.), *Studies in Plato's Metaphysics*, p. 221n1.

[42] Hence Plato rejects thesis (B) on page 19 above.

[43] I am indebted, here and in later discussions, to I. M. Crombie, *An Examination of Plato's Doctrines*, 2 Vols., Routledge & Kegan Paul, London 1962–1963, Vol. II, Chapter 2.

[44] A. E. Taylor, *A Commentary on Plato's Timaeus*, Oxford University Press, Oxford 1928, p. 471, says that εἶδος "has the old geometrical significance 'regular figure'," rather than 'species' or 'Form', in both 66d2 and d3. I admit that it is unusual for Plato to use a technical term in two different ways in two consecutive lines, but (a) in the *Timaeus*, Forms (species) of smells would be kinds of geometrical figures if there were any, and (b) when 66d2 is more fully expressed at 67a2, εἶδος clearly has the unrestricted significance 'natural kind'.

[45] Foul and fragrant, pleasant and unpleasant require another account. Most likely they are accidents, not species, of smell, and "express only our likes and dislikes"; cf. F. M. Cornford, *Plato's Cosmology*, The Liberal Arts Press, New York 1957, p. 272.

[46] Cf. Theophrastus *de sensibus* 90 at H. Diels (ed.), *Doxographi Graeci*, 4th ed., Walter de Gruyter & Co., Berlin 1965, p. 526.23–24.

[47] Plato's Theory of Forms thus resembles most closely not Russell's Platonism of *The

Problems of Philosophy, William & Norgate, London 1912, Chapter 9, but the scientific realist theory of properties set forth independently by Hilary Putnam, 'On Properties', in Nicholas Rescher (ed.), *Essays in Honor of Carl G. Hempel*, Humanities Press, New York 1970, pp. 235–254, and D. M. Armstrong, 'Toward a Theory of Properties', *Philosophy* 50 (1975), pp. 145–155.

[48] It is worth noting, though unnecessary to my argument, that the correspondence between names and Forms may fail in the other direction. There are Forms that have no names corresponding to them, e.g. the nameless Forms of air (*Timaeus* 58d3) and water (60a3) in Plato's theory of the elements; and there are Forms which have two (or more) names corresponding to them, e.g. the Form of the Ideal Constitution at *Republic* 4.445d3–6, which is called kingship or aristocracy depending upon a quite accidental feature. This last Form, we saw earlier, also bears the name 'Justice'.

[49] Lovejoy, *The Great Chain of Being*, pp. 45–52.

[50] Lovejoy, *The Great Chain of Being*, p. 339n35 (to p. 51), cites other passages (*Timaeus* 39e, 42e, 51a, 92c) as further evidence. Of these, all but 51a support at most (*P'*) below; and he gives no account at all of 51a, which presents an argument very different from that of 29d–31a. I examine 51a and its context on p. 34 below.

[51] As like to himself as possible *in respect of being good*, the only feature of the Demiurge so far mentioned (29a3, 5–6, e1 (= (1))) and the shared feature elsewhere inferred. Since it is a possible object of jealousy, being good must here at least *entail* being well off, and for Plato in fact coincides with it.

[52] Hence Plato's blunder in copying the plenitude of the Form of Living Creature is different from that claimed by David Keyt, 'The Mad Craftsman of the *Timaeus*', *Philosophical Review* 80 (1971), pp. 233–234. Plato treats plenitude as a proper attribute of the Form of Living Creature in *selecting* that Form for copying (5), and so *must* copy that feature if his imposing that Form on the preexisting sensible stuff is to achieve its point at all. Plato's blunder here therefore comes at an earlier stage than in the two other cases of copying ideal attributes of Forms (31a2–5, 37c6–38c3) Keyt analyzes.

[53] "The 'best soul' could begrudge existence to nothing that could conceivably possess it, and 'desired that all things should be as like himself as they could be'. 'All things' here could consistently mean for Plato nothing less than the sensible counterparts of every one of the Ideas . . . ." Lovejoy, *The Great Chain of Being*, p. 50.

[54] This principle applies to a number of other feelings as well, e.g. compassion, love, hatred, anger, shame, indignation, envy, pride, pity; it does not, however, apply to fear or hope. In the present case, the relevant time is the future, since the Demiurge knows that 'all things' do not yet exist.

[55] This claim is closely related to proposition (A) in Carl Ginet, 'Can the Will Be Caused?', *Philosophical Review* 71 (1962), pp. 49–55.

[56] Lovejoy, *The Great Chain of Being*, p. 50.

[57] As in the quotation in note 53 above.

[58] Cornford, *Plato's Cosmology*, p. 218 (italics mine). Likewise, "he *has to* find a different use for the fifth": Taylor, *Commentary on Plato's Timaeus*, p. 377 (italics mine).

[59] I say 'or seem to' because a case *might* be made (though, I think, a bad one) that Plato may have thought that he could reconcile the two accounts he gives of the shape of the whole. In such a reconciliation, the whole would be a sphere made out of a dodecahedron (Cornford, *Plato's Cosmology*, p. 219) or a sphere divided into twelve

pentagonal regions and thus 'near enough to' a dodecahedron (Taylor, *Commentary on Plato's Timaeus*, p. 377) or dodecahedral in having its outer surface composed of a fifth, dodecahedral, elementary body (cf. W. K. C. Guthrie, *A History of Greek Philosophy*, Cambridge University Press, Cambridge 1967, I, pp. 270–271). None of these proposals in fact reconciles the two accounts; 55c does nothing to suggest that using the dodecahedron for the whole is anything different from making the whole a regular dodecahedron. As to what Plato might have thought, evidence is reviewed and hypotheses offered by Daniel Wyttenbach, *Platonis Phaedon*, Apud Haakios et Honkoopios, Lugduni-Batavorum 1810, pp. 304–306; John Burnet, *Early Greek Philosophy*, 4th ed., Meridian Books, Cleveland 1957, pp. 293–295, and *Plato's Phaedo*, Oxford University Press, Oxford 1911, pp. 131–132; Cornford, *Plato's Cosmology*, pp. 218–221; and Guthrie, *History*, I, pp. 268–273.

60 The account of this passage in Crombie, *An Examination of Plato's Doctrines*, II, p. 225, gets things backwards. He says, "the Craftsman had in fact no choice of which set of regular solids to create as elements; there had to be four of them, and of the five possibles one was already booked." But that's not what Plato says at 55c. The dodecahedron is left over – it's fifth, not first (and of course it's the sphere that was already booked). Even on Crombie' account, of course, the fact that a shape was already booked for one job would be no objection to using it as one of four for another job unless it were forbidden to leave any of the five over, so the passage would still be evidence for (*P*).

61 τῶν πάντων ἀεί τε ὄντων. I follow the MSS. with Burnet at 51a1 (though the conjectures of Stallbaum and Cook Wilson in his apparatus would make no difference) and reject Cornford's suggestion (*Plato's Cosmology*, p. 186n2) and the anonymous emendation listed by Burnet and supported by Taylor, *Commentary on Plato's Timaeus*, p. 329. If either were right, I could not use this passage as evidence. But the logic of Plato's argument requires πάντων rather than πάντα or νοητῶν (or in addition to the latter), as I'm about to show.

62 This is not quite right. To rule out the Receptacle's having a character of its own, we needn't say that it receives likenesses of all the Forms but only of all of a set of Forms such that any character of its own that the Receptacle might have would be incompatible with at least one member of that set. There is, however, no hint of this weaker and more complex premiss in the text or in Cornford's emendation. Nor does it need saying here, as Cornford would have it say, that the Receptacle will receive all the likenesses of Forms, the consequences of which were drawn at an earlier stage of the discussion (49a–50c).

One more objection to the evidential value of 50d4–51b2 needs to be cleared away. It might be claimed that by 'all' in the cited statements of his premiss, Plato means not all Forms in general but merely all Forms of the four elementary bodies (regular polyhedra), so that there is no commitment to the instantiation of Forms of Mountain, Blood, Gold, etc. I reply: (a) His argument requires that he be talking about *all* forms; a character for the Receptacle compatible with all four primary shapes would not be ruled out by a restricted premiss. (All four shapes can be imposed on gold, for example, as 50a5–7 implies, cf. also 50d8–51a1.) (b) He makes it quite clear that his argument extends not only to the four elements but to all their compounds and components as well (51a6). A later passage makes clear that *all* the varieties of the elementary bodies are instantiated too, since all possible components of the varieties (various sizes of triangles)

50 MICHAEL DAVID ROHR

are available (see 57c8–d3), from which an infinite variety of compounds are forth-coming (57d3–5).

[63] For external evidence that Plato rejected empty natural kind Forms (like the Form of Goatstag), see Aristotle *Post. An.* 92b4–8 (cf. R. Bolton, 'Essentialism and Semantic Theory in Aristotle', *Philosophical Review* 85 (1976), p. 516) and *On Ideas* fr. 3 Ross (cf. note 80 below).

[64] I take this to be part of what Plato is getting at in his notoriously obscure remarks about the Form of Good in *Republic* 6–7, esp. 6.509b6–10. Cf. Crombie, *Examination of Plato's Doctrines*, I, pp. 111–127, and II, pp. 153–156, 171–182.

[64a] Cf. Erkka Maula, 'On Plato and Plenitude', *Ajatus* 29 (1967), p. 32 and p. 49n33. Maula's defense of EFT, the most extensive in print, deserves a footnote of its own. His general line of attack on (P) consists in claiming that the non-omnipotence of the Demiurge and resistance of his material, and the consequent imperfection of the physical world, entail that "not all Forms are realized in the world of sensible particulars" (Maula, p. 12; cf. p. 22). But none of the evidence Maula cites for various incapacities or short-comings of the Demiurge, his materials, or his works does anything at all to show that among these shortcomings is the actual or possible emptiness of any Form, but only that the created world does not exemplify those Forms it does exemplify as perfectly as its model, the realm of Forms, does, a proposition quite compatible with the plenitude of Forms (P). This imperfect exemplification is to be understood as in Section II(4) (pp. 25–28 above) and so counts in favor of plenitude insofar as it has any bearing on it at all. Maula suggests four examples of unrealized Forms: (1) Destruction (φθορά, p. 47n22); (2) kinds of immortal terrestrial animals (pp. 16, 27, citing *Timaeus* 41c); (3) the Ideal State (p. 35); (4) Eternity (p. 26). On (1): Maula is not sure that there is such a Form which fails to be exemplified in the destruction of the world (pp. 13, 32f, citing *Timaeus* 41ab). But there is, and it has plenty of instances, even the world itself. It's the Form of Ceasing-to-Be, and the world does cease to be various things, though, of course, it never ceases to be the world (cf. pp. 40f and 42f below). On (2): Maula finally decides that these unmade immortal terrestrial animals would probably be of the same species as the mortal ones that were made (pp. 33, 36, 39, 41f), undermining their status as counterexamples to (P') (p. 31 above) and (P). On my own reading of *Timaeus* 41c2–3, the Demiurge says that if he made the rest of the animals, they'd be *gods* and so *not* of kinds not yet realized, as (P') requires (thus 41b5–c2). Plato agrees with Aristotle that the mortal and the immortal differ in kind (*Metaphysics* I10.1058b26–1059a10). On (3): For the evidence from the *Republic* Maula cites (p. 17), see Section II (pp. 22–28 above). The passages he cites from the *Laws* (712a, 739de, 875cd) imply not that no city has exemplified the first-best society (cf. 676c1–2), but rather that a prudent legis-lator without autocratic power (739a3–6, alluding to *Republic* 540e5–541a7) will choose to bring about the second-best society because it runs less risk of degenerating into the worst (cf. 875b1–c3 with 715d1–6). On (4): I treat Eternity in Section IV (pp. 40f below). Maula also claims Aristotelian evidence for EFT: "In Book Delta of the *Metaphysics* he ascribes to Plato the view that Forms are prior to things in an 'ontological' sense of priority, *i.e.* in a sense in which 'A is prior to B' is tantamount to 'A can exist without B, but not *vice versa*'" (Maula, p. 35). But Aristotle in his chapter on priority (Δ11) says merely that Plato distinguished this kind of priority and tells us nothing about what Plato applied it to (1019a2–4); and he nowhere else, to my

knowledge, takes the Platonic priority of Forms to entail EFT. I conclude that though Maula may have shown that some possibilities are unrealized according to Plato (e.g. p. 32f, citing *Timaeus* 41ab), he has done nothing to show that the emptiness of any Form is possible, much less actual.

[65] W. D. Ross, *Plato's Theory of Ideas*, pp. 171–175. Cf. also Harold Cherniss, *Aristotle's Criticism of Plato and the Academy*, p. 244.

[66] Crombie, *Examination of Plato's Doctrines*, II, p. 175.

[67] Crombie, *Examination of Plato's Doctrines*, II, p. 176.

[68] Crombie, *Examination of Plato's Doctrines*, II, p. 177.

[69] Crombie, *Examination of Plato's Doctrines*, II, pp. 212, 230.

[70] See Section I(4) above, pp. 26f. A similar solution applies to diseases, in themselves a good like other living kinds, e.g. lions, but relative to (e.g.) men an evil, also like lions. Cf. Harold Cherniss, 'The Sources of Evil According to Plato', *Proceedings of the American Philosophical Society* 98 (1954), pp. 26–27, reprinted in Gregory Vlastos (ed.), *Plato II*, Anchor Books, Garden City, New York 1971, pp. 252–253.

[71] The Forms of motion, fieriness, wateriness, airiness, and earthiness, and presumably also of hot, cold, wet, dry, light, dark, etc., *may* be eternally instantiated, having always appeared as traces in Space before the Demiurge began his work; cf. *Timaeus* 30a3–5, 52d4–53b4, and Vlastos, 'The Disorderly Motion in the *Timaeus*' and 'Creation in the *Timaeus*'.

[72] Besides the souls of gods, only human souls (*Timaeus* 41d4–42d2) and plant souls (77a3–c5) are separately created; all souls of lower animals are human souls reincarnated (91d6–92c3). (I take ὅς ποτε ἄνϑρωπος ἦν at *Phaedrus* 249b4–5 to be nonrestrictive.) *Timaeus* 42b3–d2 suggests to me that Plato expected ultimate permanent salvation for all human souls not permanently consigned to Tartarus (*Phaedo* 113e1–6).

[73] Cf. Cherniss, *Aristotle's Criticism of Plato and the Academy*, pp. 421ff and note 357.

[74] In the classic version of the Principle of Plenitude, every possibility (in this case every possible kind of thing) must, given an infinite stretch of time, be realized (as in Aquinas' Third Way, *Summa Theologiae*, 1a, 2, 3). But on the nonliteral reading of the *Timaeus*, prior to every past moment an infinite time has already elapsed. Since the human race has always existed, human beings have always already had an infinite time in which to develop the shuttle and tyranny; they may not have had shuttles and tyrannies continuously, but there's never been a time when they had not yet had them. (Hence Plato's remark that "time and again every city has adopted every type of constitution" (*Laws* 3.676c1–2).) Thus, we should recognize the historical occurrence of a version of plenitude intermediate between the 'all times' version and the 'some time, past, present or future' version distinguished by R. H. Kane, 'Nature, Plenitude and Sufficient Reason', *American Philosophical Quarterly* 13 (1976), p. 24; it was an "infinitely many times, past, present *and* future" version. Cf. also Jaakko Hintikka, *Time and Necessity*, Clarendon Press, Oxford 1973, Chapters V and VI.

[75] E.g. Vlastos, 'The Third Man Argument in the *Parmenides*', pp. 336f/248–250 (retracted in 'The Unity of the Virtues in the *Protagoras*', *Review of Metaphysics* 25 (1972), pp. 452–455, reprinted in Vlastos, *Platonic Studies*, pp. 259–262); Strang, 'Plato and the Third Man', pp. 151ff/187ff; G. E. L. Owen, 'Dialectic and Eristic in the Treatment of the Forms', in G. E. L. Owen (ed.), *Aristotle on Dialectic*, Oxford

University Press, Oxford 1968, pp. 111f; S. Marc Cohen, 'The Logic of the Third Man', *Philosophical Review* 80 (1971), pp. 464, 474. I think so too.

[76] *Symposium* 210e2–212a7; cf. Vlastos, 'The Unity of the Virtues in the *Protagoras*', pp. 455/262f.

[77] Plato uses a number of different words and phrases when he wants to mention or predicate stability (rest, changelessness); very frequently he uses some form of κατὰ ταὐτὰ ἀεὶ ἔχειν (holding always the same), but he also uses ἠρεμία, στάσις, ἀκινησία or their verbal or adjectival forms. The equivalence of these may be seen in a passage in the *Sophist* where a use of the first of these forms (248a12) is later picked up by τὸ ἠρεμοῦν (248d4), ἀκίνητον (249a10), and στάσεως (249c1).

[78] That M4 is later than A9 is argued by Werner Jaeger, *Aristotle: Fundamentals of the History of His Development*, trans. Richard Robinson, 2d ed., Oxford University Press, London 1962, pp. 171f. The change pointed out above falsifies Jaeger's claim that, excluding M4.1079b3–11, "their only difference lies in the systematic removal of the *first* person plural . . . ." One need not agree with Jaeger's explanation of the difference he mentions to reach his conclusion about relative dates; cf. Gilbert Ryle, 'Dialectic in the Academy', in G. E. L. Owen (ed.), *Aristotle on Dialectic*, p. 75. I discuss the difference he doesn't mention below.

[79] So Taylor, *Commentary on Plato's Timaeus*, p. 82.

[80] It's an objection to the 'Object of Thought' Argument (A9.990b14–15 = M4.1079a10–11), as Cherniss calls it, *Aristotle's Criticism of Plato and the Academy*, p. 272. The Platonists argue that since we still think about man when particular men perish, the object of our thought must be a separate Form not identical with any particular man. Aristotle objects that if the argument works, there will also be a Form of Socrates, since we think of him even when he no longer exists, and even a Form of Chimaera, since we think of chimaeras even when they don't exist (which is always). (This expansion of Aristotle's cryptic summary is drawn from Alexander's account of Aristotle's now lost treatise *On Ideas* (fr. 3 Ross; Alexander *Comm. in Met.* 81.25–82.7; Ross inexplicably omits Aristotle's objection from his Oxford text and translation of the fragment).) But the Platonists suppose there aren't any Forms of particulars like Socrates or of empty natural kinds like the chimaera. (This premiss, obviously required, is an application of 990b11 = 1079a7.) So such an argument can't establish that there are Forms even of the sort the Platonists want. Two points relevant to the thesis of this paper need to be made. (i) The 'Object of Thought' Argument doesn't say that the Form of Man *would* continue to exist even if *all* particular men *had* perished (though even this would be compatible with my thesis), but that it *does* continue to exist even though *various* particular men *do* perish. The circumstance in which the Form of Man goes on existing is one that actually occurs (μένει 81.27), and it never occurs that all particular men have perished. (ii) The implied Platonic rejection of a Form of Chimaera is strong further evidence for the conclusion of Section III. For further discussion of this argument, cf. W. D. Ross, *Aristotle's Metaphysics*, 2 Vols., Oxford University Press, Oxford 1924, I, p. 194; Cherniss, *Aristotle's Criticism*, pp. 229, 272–275; Paul Wilpert, *Zwei aristotelische Frühschriften*, Josef Habbel, Regensburg 1949, pp. 38–40, 71–72. Cherniss and Wilpert are fuzzy on (i); Ross gets it wrong.

[81] Ross, *Aristotle's Metaphysics*, I, p. 191 on 990b2; Cherniss, *Aristotle's Criticism*, p. 199n118. *Metaphysics* Z2.1028b19 is irrelevant for the reason given by Cherniss and because Aristotle's noncommittal exposition in Z2 is unlikely to mention what

is a harsh criticism in A9 and M4.

[82] Ross, *Aristotle's Metaphysics*, I, p. 191 on 990b8.

[83] Cherniss, *Aristotle's Criticism*, p. 199n117, presents evidence that 990b8 is a reasonable way for Aristotle to make this contrast.

[84] Cherniss, *Aristotle's Criticism*, p. 199n117.

[85] A. E. Taylor, *Plato: The Man and His Work*, Meridian Books, New York 1957, p. 446; also Cherniss, *Aristotle's Criticism*, p. 419n350.

[86] Fuller discussion of Plato's real view on this point may be found at G. E. L. Owen, 'Plato and Parmenides on the Timeless Present', *Monist* 50 (1966), pp. 333–334, reprinted at Alexander P. D. Mourelatos (ed.), *The Pre-Socratics*, Anchor Books, Garden City, New York 1974, pp. 286–287, and at Vlastos, 'Creation in the *Timaeus*', pp. 407–408.

[87] Owen, 'Plato and Parmenides', p. 333/286, claims that in *Timaeus* 38b8 Plato coins the word διαιώνιος for the notion of being perfectly eternal; were this so, Plato would there be making the move I deny he makes anywhere. But nothing in that passage or elsewhere *requires* that διαιώνιος at 38b8 mean anything different from ἀίδιος or αἰώνιος at 37d1–3; nothing even *suggests* that διαιώνιος is more than a stylistic variant of the other two, except that in this short passage it happens not to be applied to particulars.

[88] A recent example that discusses relevant earlier literature is Robert Bolton, 'Plato's Distinction between Being and Becoming', pp. 76–84.

[89] So J. B. Skemp, *Plato's Statesman*, Yale University Press, New Haven 1952, p. 73n2: "Of course physical objects can (and all do) exhibit both motion and rest at once. This is implied at *Politicus* 269d."

[90] The reader may object that Plato's assertion that in the case described at 436e4–6 the tops οὐδαμῇ ἑστάναι (436e6: "are in no wise at rest", Shorey translates) conflicts with (D4). But οὐδαμῇ here does not mean 'in no way' but only "in none of these ways", viz. the two ways just mentioned, κατὰ τὸ εὐθύ and κατὰ τὸ περιφερές. Each top may still be at rest in respect of e.g. its foot or its angle of inclination, as a precessing top usually is; and nothing in Plato's discussion requires any cases of total instability.

[91] Cf. esp. 80c5–6: "remains at it is for a very long time"; 80c9: "remains all but entire"; and the backward allusion at 86c7–8: "the physical remains of each body persist for a long time".

[92] This eventual exemption from (D4) constitutes the intermediate status which Plato often accords to the soul (e.g. at *Timaeus* 35a1–4). For similar remarks about stable traits of corpses and souls, see also *Gorgias* 524b2–d4.

[93] Cf. David Gallop, trans., *Plato's Phaedo*, Oxford University Press, Oxford 1975, pp. 142–143 on 80c2–d7.

[94] Plato elsewhere draws the body/Forms contrast so as to liken souls to Forms and thus show the immortal nature of souls; see e.g. *Republic* 10.611e2–3 and W. K. C. Guthrie, 'Plato's Views on the Nature of the Soul', in Vlastos (ed.), *Plato II*, pp. 232–233.

[95] E.g. Owen, 'The Place of the *Timaeus*', pp. 85–86/322–325.

[96] See Vlastos, 'Degrees of Reality in Plato', p. 6n4/63n21.

[97] See G. E. L. Owen, 'Plato on Not-Being', in Vlastos (ed.), *Plato I*, p. 259.

[98] We should similarly interpret the claims that eternity and stability are distinctive of the Forms (cf. pp. 40, 41 above).

54   MICHAEL DAVID ROHR

99 Cf. Owen, 'Plato on Not-Being', pp. 223–267, and the earlier work by various scholars he cites at pp. 223n1, 224n4.
100 I adopt Burnet's emendation of 75d2, followed by most recent translators but vigorously rejected by Gallop, *Plato's Phaedo*, p. 230n28. Unemended, the passage is at worst insufficient evidence for the proposal just rejected, the Form of Being as the exclusive as well as distinctive possession of the Forms.
101 Note that this suggestion does not commit us to the error warned against on p. 41 above of taking each Form to be or exemplify a Form of Perfect *F*ness; it merely acknowledges that in each case the Form of *F*ness is perfectly *F* and abstracts the character of being everything perfectly.
102 Cf. Vlastos, 'Reasons and Causes', p. 298n26/140n26/84n26.
103 Cf. Vlastos, 'Degrees of Reality in Plato', p. 5n4/62n17.
104 As Taylor remarks, *Plato*, p. 524n6, the allusions to Sparta's enormous wealth (*Alcibiades I* 122d3–123b1) would have been false before 404 B.C. (and so at the dramatic date of the dialogue before the start of the Archidamian War in 431 B.C.) and after Sparta's disastrous defeat at Leuctra in 371 B.C. So a date of composition during the first 16 years of the Academy (387–371 B.C.) and therefore a Platonic content are likely, whether the dialogue is authentic or by a student.
105 Only a Neoplatonic commentator would try to make a connection between this passage and Aristotle, *De Anima* Γ8.432a2 amount to anything.

BIBLIOGRAPHY

Adam, J. (ed.), *The Republic of Plato*, 2 Vols., Cambridge University Press, Cambridge 1902.
Allen, R. E., *Plato's 'Euthyphro' and the Earlier Theory of Forms*, Routledge & Kegan Paul, London, The Humanities Press, New York 1970.
Allen, R. E. (ed.), *Studies in Plato's Metaphysics*, Routledge & Kegan Paul, London, The Humanities Press, New York 1965.
Armstrong, D. M., 'Toward a Theory of Properties', *Philosophy* 50 (1975), 145–155.
Bolton, R., 'Essentialism and Semantic Theory in Aristotle', *Philosophical Review* 85 (1976), 514–544.
Bolton, R., 'Plato's Distinction between Being and Becoming', *Review of Metaphysics* 29 (1975), 66–95.
Burnet, J., *Early Greek Philosophy*, 4th ed., Meridian Books, Cleveland 1957.
Burnet, J., *Plato's Phaedo*, Oxford University Press, Oxford 1911.
Cherniss, H., *Aristotle's Criticism of Plato and the Academy*, Johns Hopkins Press, Baltimore 1944.
Cherniss, H., 'The Philosophical Economy of the Theory of Ideas', *American Journal of Philosophy* 57 (1936), 445–456, reprinted in R. E. Allen (ed.), *Studies in Plato's Metaphysics*, pp. 1–12, and G. Vlastos (ed.), *Plato I*, pp. 16–27.
Cherniss, H., 'The Sources of Evil According to Plato', *Proceedings of the American Philosophical Society* 98 (1954), 23–30, reprinted in G. Vlastos (ed.), *Plato I*, pp. 244–258.
Cohen, S. M., 'The Logic of the Third Man', *Philosophical Review* 80 (1971), 448–475.
Cornford, F. M., *Plato's Cosmology*, The Liberal Arts Press, New York 1957.

Crombie, I. M., *An Examination of Plato's Doctrines*, 2 Vols., Routledge & Kegan Paul, London, The Humanities Press, New York 1962–1963.

Dancy, R., 'On Some of Aristotle's First Thoughts about Substances', *Philosophical Review* 84 (1975), 338–373.

Diels, H. (ed.), *Doxographi Graeci*, 4th ed., Walter de Gruyter & Co., Berlin 1965.

Faris, J. A., *Plato's Theory of Forms and Cantor's Theory of Sets*, The Queen's University, Belfast 1968.

Frazer, J. G., *The Growth of Plato's Ideal Theory*, Russell & Russell, New York 1967.

Gallop, D. (transl.), *Plato's Phaedo*, Oxford University Press, Oxford 1975.

Ginet, C., 'Can the Will Be Caused?', *Philosophical Review* 71 (1962), 49–55.

Gosling, J. C. P. (transl.), *Plato's Philebus*, Oxford University Press, Oxford 1975.

Grube, G. M. A. (transl.), *Plato's Republic*, Hackett Publishing Co., Indianapolis 1974.

Guthrie, W. K. C., *A History of Greek Philosophy*, Cambridge University Press, Cambridge 1967.

Guthrie, W. K. C., 'Plato's Views on the Nature of the Soul', in G. Vlastos (ed.), *Plato II*, pp. 230–243.

Hardie, W. F. R., *A Study in Plato*, Oxford University Press, Oxford 1936.

Herter, H., 'Urathen der Idealstaat', *Palingenesia* 4 (1969), 108–134.

Hintikka, J., *Time and Necessity: Studies in Aristotle's Theory of Modality*, Oxford University Press, Oxford 1973.

Jaeger, W., *Aristotle: Fundamentals of the History of His Development*, transl. R. Robinson, 2d ed., Oxford University Press, London 1962.

Kane, R. H., 'Nature, Plenitude and Sufficient Reason', *American Philosophical Quarterly* 13 (1976), 23–31.

Keyt, D., 'The Mad Craftsman of the *Timaeus*', *Philosophical Review* 80 (1971), 230–235.

Krohn, A. A., *Der platonische Staat*, R. Muhlmann, Halle 1876.

Lloyd, A. C., 'Plato's Description of Division', in R. E. Allen (ed.), *Studies in Plato's Metaphysics*, pp. 219–230.

Lovejoy, A. O., *The Great Chain of Being*, Harvard University Press, Cambridge Mass. 1936.

Maula, E., 'On Plato and Plenitude', *Ajatus* 29 (1967), 12–50.

Nehamas, A., 'Plato on the Imperfection of the Sensible World', *American Philosophical Quarterly* 12 (1975), 105–117.

Nehamas, A., 'Predication and Forms of Opposites in the *Phaedo*', *Review of Metaphysics* 26 (1973), 461–491.

Owen, G. E. L., 'Dialectic and Eristic in the Treatment of the Forms', in G. E. L. Owen (ed.), *Aristotle on Dialectic*, pp. 103–125.

Owen, G. E. L., 'The Place of the *Timaeus* in Plato's Dialogues', *Classical Quarterly* 2 N.S. (1953), 79–95, reprinted in R. E. Allen (ed.), *Studies in Plato's Metaphysics*, pp. 313–338.

Owen, G. E. L., 'Plato on Not-Being', in G. Vlastos (ed.), *Plato I*, pp. 233–267.

Owen, G. E. L., 'Plato and Parmenides on the Timeless Present', *Monist* 50 (1966), 317–340, reprinted at A. P. D. Mourelatos (ed.), *The Pre-Socratics* (Modern Studies in Philosophy), Anchor Books, Doubleday, Garden City, New York 1974.

Owen, G. E. L., 'A Proof in the *peri ideōn*', *Journal of Hellenic Studies* 77 (1957), 103–111, reprinted in R. E. Allen (ed.), *Studies in Plato's Metaphysics*, pp. 293–312.

Owen, G. E. L. (ed.), *Aristotle on Dialectic: The Topics. Proceedings of the Third Symposium Aristotelicum*, Oxford University Press, Oxford 1968.

Putnam, H., 'On Properties', in N. Rescher (ed.), *Essays in Honor of Carl G. Hempel*, The Humanities Press, New York 1970, pp. 235–254.

Rankin, H. D., 'Plato's Eugenic εὐφημία and ἀπόθεσις in Republic, Book V', *Hermes* **93** (1965), 407–420.

Raven, J. E., *Plato's Thought in the Making*, Cambridge University Press, Cambridge 1965.

Ross, W. D., *Aristotle's Metaphysics*, 2 Vols., Oxford University Press, Oxford 1924.

Ross, W. D., *Plato's Theory of Ideas*, Oxford University Press, Oxford 1951.

Russell, B., *The Problems of Philosophy*, William & Norgate, London 1912.

Ryle, G., 'Dialectic in the Academy', in G. E. L. Owen (ed.), *Aristotle on Dialectic*, pp. 69–79.

Skemp, J. B. (transl.), *Plato's Statesman*, Yale University Press, New Haven 1952.

Solmsen, F., *Intellectual Experiments of the Greek Enlightenment*, Princeton University Press, Princeton 1975.

Strang, C., 'Plato and the Third Man', *Proceedings of the Aristotelian Society, Suppl.* **37** (1963), 147–164, reprinted in G. Vlastos (ed.), *Plato I*, pp. 184–200.

Taylor, A. E., *A Commentary on Plato's Timaeus*, Oxford University Press, Oxford 1928.

Taylor, A. E., 'Parmenides, Zeno, and Socrates', *Proceedings of the Aristotelian Society* **16** (1915–16), 234–289, reprinted A. E. Taylor, *Philosophical Studies*, Macmillan, London 1934.

Taylor, A. E., *Plato: The Man and His Work*, Meridian Books, New York 1957.

Vlastos, G., 'Creation in the Timaeus: Is it a Fiction?', in R. E. Allen (ed.), *Studies in Plato's Metaphysics*, pp. 401–419.

Vlastos, G., 'Degrees of Reality in Plato', in R. Bambrough (ed.), *New Essays on Plato and Aristotle*, Routledge & Kegan Paul, London, The Humanities Press, New York 1965, pp. 1–19, reprinted in G. Vlastos, *Platonic Studies*, pp. 58–75.

Vlastos, G., 'The Disorderly Motion in the Timaeus', *The Classical Quarterly* **33** (1939), 71–83, reprinted in R. E. Allen (ed.), *Studies in Plato's Metaphysics*, pp. 379–399.

Vlastos, G., *Platonic Studies*, Princeton University Press, Princeton 1973.

Vlastos, G., 'Reasons and Causes in the *Phaedo*', *Philosophical Review* **78** (1969), 291–325, reprinted in G. Vlastos (ed.), *Plato I*, pp. 132–166 and in *Platonic Studies*, pp. 76–110.

Vlastos, G., Review of I. M. Crombie, 'An Examination of Plato's Doctrines II', *Philosophical Review* **75** (1966), 526–530.

Vlastos, G., 'The Third Man Argument in the *Parmenides*', *Philosophical Review* **63** (1954), 319–349, reprinted in R. E. Allen (ed.), *Studies in Plato's Metaphysics*, pp. 231–263.

Vlastos, G., 'The Unity of Virtues in the *Protagoras*', *Review of Metaphysics* **25** (1972), 415–459, reprinted in *Platonic Studies*, pp. 221–269.

Vlastos, G. (ed.), *Plato I–II* (Modern Studies in Philosophy), Anchor Books, Doubleday, Garden City, New York 1970–71.

Wedberg, A., *Plato's Philosophy of Mathematics*, Almqvist & Wiksell, Stockholm 1955.

Wilpert, P., *Zwei aristotelische Frühschriften*, J. Habbel, Regensburg 1949.

Wyttenbach, D., *Platonis Phaedon*, Apud Haakios et Honkoopios, Lugduni-Batavorum 1810.

JAAKKO HINTIKKA

ARISTOTLE ON THE REALIZATION
OF POSSIBILITIES IN TIME

1. THE RELATION OF MODALITY TO TIME IN ARISTOTLE IS PROBLEMATIC

An attentive reader of the Aristotelian corpus can scarcely fail to notice that in certain respects the Stagirite used the *modal notions* of possibility and necessity in a manner different from our modern ways with them. A case in point is the relation of modality to time. That there is something not quite familiar about the way Aristotle was wont to operate with the concepts of necessity and possibility is already betrayed by his repeated statements to the effect that the past is necessary.[1] Natural though such statements sound, the sense of necessity involved here is not a familiar part of the conceptual repertoire of today's philosophers.

Another indication of a difference between Aristotle's modal notions and ours is the close connection that there is for him between necessary (apodeictic) truths and plain (assertoric) general truths, in short between necessity and universality. This is brought out strikingly by the role he ascribed to the assertoric syllogism as a vehicle of scientific demonstration. Since he also held that "the truth obtained by demonstrative knowledge will be necessary" (*An. Post.* I 4. 73ª21–4) and that "demonstrative knowledge must be knowledge of a necessary nexus, and therefore must clearly be obtained through a necessary middle term" (*An. Post.* I 6. 75ª12–14), an assertoric syllogism must clearly be capable of establishing necessity. On the other hand, Aristotle distinguished between assertoric (simple) and apodeictic (necessary) premisses and conclusions. Since even the assertoric syllogisms were seen to be capable of establishing necessary scientific truths, one may expect that they are somehow related to the apodeictic syllogisms in a closer manner than we are accustomed to.

2. THE REALIZATION OF POSSIBILITIES IN TIME

There is an assumption concerning the interrelations of time and modality which has undoubtedly played a much more important role in the history of Western thought — in the history of metaphysics, theology, logic, philosophy

S. Knuuttila (ed.), Reforging the Great Chain of Being, 57–72.
Copyright © 1980 *by D. Reidel Publishing Company.*

of nature, and even speculative poetry — than any other assumption concerning their relationships. This is the assumption that *all genuine possibilities*, or at least all possibilities of some central and important kind, *are actualized in time*. Any such possibility thus has been, is, or will be realized; it cannot remain unrealized through an infinite stretch of time; in a sense, everything possible will happen in the long run.

Obviously, this assumption admits of many variants, some of which will be distinguished from each other later in this chapter. For one thing, it is not clear what kind of possibility is intended in it. Possible events? Possible courses of events? Possible kinds of individuals? Possible individuals (particulars)? Some of these distinctions turn out to be crucial for the study of the later stages of the history of this principle.[2]

If the principle is applied to possible kinds of indiciduals, it says that *all* possible kinds of individuals are realized in the course of time — in that particular 'possible world' that is in fact actualized, as Leibniz would have said. In a sense, the assumption under consideration thus amounts to saying that the actual world is as full as it can be, that it is the fullest or most plentiful world possible. This has led Arthur O. Lovejoy to call the assumption 'the Principle of Plenitude'.[3] In the absence of any other convenient designation, I shall adopt this term, although it is important to realize that this locution can be highly misleading when used in contexts different from the rather limited one Lovejoy has primarily in mind. For us it will be a mere *terminus technicus*.

3. A PLENITUDE OF FORMULATIONS OF THE PRINCIPLE

In order to bring out some aspects of the role of the Principle of Plenitude, it may be useful to state some of its alternative formulations. The principle itself may (tentatively and approximately) be formulated as follows:

> each possibility is realized at some moment of time.

Later, we shall see that in order to catch Aristotle's intentions it must probably be expressed in a slightly qualified form

(T)   no unqualified possibility remains unactualized through an infinity of time.

Hence, if something can possibly exist, it sometimes will exist in fact. Hence the only things that *never* are, are the impossibilities. Thus we obtain the following variant of (T):

(T)$_1$ that which never is, is impossible.

By the same token, what never fails to be, cannot fail to be, that is, is necessarily:

(T)$_2$ what always is, is by necessity.

For some purposes, we might reformulate (T)$_2$ as follows:

what is eternal, is by necessity.

However, we are not entitled to mean by 'eternal' here anything more than omnitemporality. Hence if someone wants to make a distinction between what is omnitemporally and what is timelessly (eternally in *one* sense of the word), he cannot use this formulation.

In so far as we can disregard this point, however, it can be said that whoever adopts the Principle of Plenitude makes such attributions as 'eternal' and 'necessary' at least materially equivalent, and the same goes without qualifications for such attributes as 'necessary', 'imperishable', 'indestructible', 'omnitemporal', and 'always existing'.

As far as Aristotle is concerned, it is in fact the case that he did not distinguish 'eternal' and 'omnitemporal'. When he spoke of certain things being 'not in time', he made clear that he merely meant that they are not 'in the middle of time', so to speak, i.e. that their existence is not limited by the earlier and later moments of time. In other words, 'not being in time' was simply tantamount to 'omnitemporal'. (For evidence, see *Phys.* IV 12.)

For Aristotle what is contingently is not by necessity, and hence possibly is not. If this possibility is sometimes realized, the contingent cannot be eternal. Thus contraposition yields the following form of the principle:

(T)$_3$ nothing eternal is contingent.

By 'contingent' we mean here 'neither necessary nor impossible'.

It is clear that, with the exception of (T)$_3$, the implications we have formulated can be (on suitable assumptions accepted by Aristotle) strengthened into equivalences. The converse implications are in fact unproblematic, and also independent of the Principle of Plenitude. Hence they will not be discussed here.

It must be emphasized that the equivalence of the four forms of the principle listed above is not a projection of our latter-day logic back to Aristotle. On the contrary, all the assumptions that are needed to move from one to another are explicitly formulated by Aristotle in *De Int.* 12–13.[4] Moreover, Aristotle in fact used himself the resulting possibilities of reformulating the principle (T). He frequently operates with the other forms as well in a way which indicates that he identifies them with each other and with (T). Furthermore, he occasionally sketches arguments that relate some of the variants of the principle to each other. A case in point is found in *Met.* Θ 8. 1050^b6–24. Thus whatever evidence (or counter-evidence) there is for (or against) one vision of the Principle of Plenitude in Aristotle, is thus also evidence for (or against) all the others.

4. CONTRA LOVEJOY

Lovejoy tries to present some evidence against thinking that Aristotle subscribed to the Principle of Plenitude. He refers to two passages, and to two only, in support of his view. These are *Met. B* 6. 1003^a2 and Λ 6. 1071^b13–14. Lovejoy apparently does not realize, however, that both these passages are ambiguous. They are quoted by him as follows: '. . . it is not necessary that everything that is possible should exist in actuality'; '. . . it is possible for that which has a potency not to realize it'.

These may be construed in several ways. They are statements about the failure of a potentiality to be actualized. We have to ask: Do these equivocal statements pertain to *each* potency, or only to *some* potencies? Furthermore, we have to ask: Do they refer to a mere *temporary* failure of a potentiality to be actualized, or can the failure in question *last infinitely long*? According to the answers that are given to these questions we obtain four possible interpretations of Aristotle's thesis:

(a)   Some potentialities may *sometimes* fail to be actualized.
(b)   Some potentialities may fail to be actualized *ever*.
(a)'   Each potentiality may *sometimes* fail to be actualized.
(b)'   Each potentiality may fail to be actualized *ever*.

The text does not seem to allow a clear-cut decision between these readings. Hence the context will have to decide.

Of the interpretations listed, (a) and (a)' are compatible with the Principle of Plenitude in the form in which we are here considering it, and therefore fail to support Lovejoy's claim that Aristotle rejected the principle, whereas the readings (b) and (b)' contradict the principle. Hence we have to decide which of the two kinds Aristotle is presupposing.

There is no obvious way of excogitating Aristotle's meaning in *Met. B* 6. 1003ª2; and even if there were, it would not settle the question one way or the other, for Aristotle is in this passage formulating a problem rather than giving his own considered opinion.

Although the second passage quoted by Lovejoy is also quite terse, the context there makes his sense clear. A few lines later Aristotle writes: "Further, even if it (sc. a Platonic Form) acts, it will not be enough, if its essence is potency; for there will not be eternal movement, since that which is potentially may possibly not be" (*Met.* Λ 6. 1071ᵇ18–20; translation by Sir David Ross). The principle Aristotle is appealing to in the last clause is evidently the same he announced a few lines earlier in the passage Lovejoy quotes. The way he is using it here shows, first of all, that Aristotle is presupposing a sense of potentiality in which that which potentially is also potentially is not. In other words, Aristotle is using potentiality in the sense of two-way possibility (contingency); for him, the possibility (in the sense of contingency) of being entails the possibility of not being.

Aristotle is using the principle to argue that a Form that exists merely potentially cannot guarantee eternal movement because (being merely potential) it may fail to be actualized at some moment of time and hence incapable of supporting the movement at that time.Obviously, the formulations (b) and (b)′ are beside this avowed purpose of Aristotle's. (He is not claiming here that a potential form could *never* be a principle of motion.) Hence he does not deny the principle of plenitude in his argument, but rather assumes one of the weaker formulations (a)–(a)′.

Of the two remaining alternatives, (a) is clearly too weak to support Aristotle's argument. Aristotle wants to argue that if a Form is a mere potentiality, it may fail to exist. For this purpose, it does not suffice to assume that *some* potentialities may fail to exist, for those potentialities might then not include the forms. Hence Aristotle must assume (a)′ and not (a).

But even this is not enough for Aristotle's purposes. Even if it is true of each merely potential being that it *may* fail to exist at some moment of time, it may still *happen to* exist all through an eternity. Or, rather, it may so exist unless it is assumed that its possibility of not existing is at some time actualized. Now it is clear that Aristotle must make this assumption; for otherwise it might be alleged that the forms enjoy an accidental eternity, and hence can support eternal movement after all. (Such accidental eternity was perhaps ascribed to Plato's Forms in *Met. A* 9. 990ᵇ29–991ª7.) In other words, Aristotle is tacitly giving the principle he mentions the following strong sense:

(a)"   Each mere possibility (contingency) will in fact fail to be actualized
          at some moment of time.

This principle is an instance of the Principle of Plenitude; it says that the
possibility that each merely possible (potential) being has of not being cannot remain unactualized for an infinity of time. Hence we may turn the
tables against Lovejoy. Instead of demonstrating that Aristotle rejected the
Principle of Plenitude (in the form in which we have been discussing it),
the passage we have considered shows that Aristotle was in fact relying
on it.

5. OTHER APPARENT COUNTER-EVIDENCE

Apart from the evidence Lovejoy offers, there might seem to be passages and
whole theories in Aristotle that contradict the Principle of Plenitude. A case
in point is Aristotle's conception of infinity which is often formulated by
saying that according to the Stagirite infinity exists merely potentially – that
it is conceivable but never realized. In an earlier paper[5] I have shown that
Aristotle's real view is diametrically opposed to this popular view. According
to his most precise formulation, in the sense in which infinity is potential it is
also actual, and insofar as it is conceivable, it is also actually realized. Far from
constituting a counter-example to the Principle of Plenitude in Aristotle, his
theory of infinity relies on the principle. Another piece of apparent counter-
evidence is Aristotle's example in *De Interpretatione* 9: "For example, it is
possible for this cloak to be cut up, and yet it will not be cut up but will wear
out first." Here we in fact have a clear instance of possibility that according to
Aristotle will not be realized. It does not go to show that the principal forms
of the Principle of Plenitude cannot be attributed to Aristotle, however.
The possibility of a particular cloak's being cut up is a possibility concerning
an individual object, and not a possibility concerning kinds of individuals or
kinds of events. Nor does the unfulfilled possibility Aristotle mentions
remain unfulfilled through an infinity of time, for when the cloak wears out,
it goes out of existence, and no possibility can any longer be attributed to it.
Thus Aristotle's example does show that the 'genuine' possibilities which the
principle says are actualized do not for him include possibilities concerning
individual objects which only exist for a certain period of time. However,
it does not show that Aristotle did not believe in some other forms of the
principle which prima facie are much more plausible anyway.

A few further examples of apparently disconfirmatory evidence have to be disposed of. For instance, in a passage of *An. Post.* (see I 6. 75^{a}31–5), Aristotle says that accidental attributes (τὰ συμβεβηκότα) are not necessary, and if we draw a conclusion by their means, we therefore do not necessarily know why the conclusion is true; not even if the attributes belong always, but not *per se*, as in syllogisms through signs. Here Aristotle might seem to be denying (T)$_2$. However, this impression is rather misleading. First of all, it is not clear that Aristotle's statement is not counter-factual, for the optative εἴη scarcely commits Aristotle to holding that there *in fact* are cases of the kind he is describing. The only thing we can definitely extract from the passage is that even an attribute that always belongs to a subject is not necessarily *known* to do so, which of course does rule out that the attribute could belong (unknownst but) necessarily to the subject. In fact, the passage continues as follows (Oxford translation): ". . . for though the conclusion be actually essential, one will not know it as essential or know its reason". Hence, no exception to the Principle of Plenitude is being contemplated by Aristotle here.

Some editors and commentators have tried to find room in *Phys.* III 1. 200^{b}26 (and in *Met. K* 9. 1065^{b}5) for potentialities that are not actualized. As pointed out by Ross in his edition of the *Physics* (Clarendon Press, 1936, ad loc.), this does not have any support in the manuscripts of the *Physics*, in the best manuscripts of the *Metaphysics*, or in Alexander, Themistius, Porphyry, Philoponus, and Simplicius.

A counter-example to the principle of plenitude might seem to be offered by *Top.* IV 5. 126^{a}34 ff. Although too complicated to be analysed here, this passage does not contradict the principle.

A few other apparent counterexamples can be explained away in terms of Aristotle's distinction between absolute and relative necessity and possibility. A more difficult problem is presented by the mare's nest of perplexing arguments we find in *Met.* Θ 3–4. At times, Aristotle there seems to declare his adherence to the principle and yet he also very definitely wants to criticize the Megarians who do likewise. Since the interpretation of Aristotle's explicit statements *prima facie* favors the attribution of the Principle of Plenitude to him, the evaluation of his polemic against the Megarians depends very much of the overall interpretations of his theory of modality as compared with the views of the Megarians. I have argued elsewhere[6] that Aristotle's theory is compatible with the Principle of Plenitude. Indeed, it seems to me that rightly understood, *Met.* Θ 3–4 strongly supports my attribution of the Principle of Plenitude to Aristotle.

6. THE ROLE OF THE PRINCIPLE OF PLENITUDE AS A BRIDGE
BETWEEN TIME AND MODALITY

A word of warning seems to be in order here. However firmly Aristotle may
have believed in the Principle of Plenitude, it is very dubious whether he ever
considered it as giving us a definition of his concept of possibility. In other
words, however strongly he assumed that something is possible if and only if
it is sometimes the case, he did not on most occasions think of this as exhausting the meaning of assertions of possibility. Occasionally, he seems to
have been pushed to this by the intrinsic difficulties in his own conception
of possibility. (See, *e.g.*, the discussion of *Met.* 1047ª12–14 below). Furthermore, some of his occasional pronouncements point to this direction.

It is true that occasionally Aristotle seems to go as far as to be ready
to *define* certain particular modal expressions in temporal terms. A case in
point is found in *Top.* VI 6. 145ᵇ27 ff.: "Whenever, then, we say that a living
thing is now indestructible (ἄφθαρτον), we mean (τοῦτο λέγομεν) that it is at
present a living thing of such a kind as never to be destroyed." A closely
similar explanation of the meaning of ἄφθαρτον and ἀγένητον is given by
Aristotle in *De Caelo* I 12. 282ª27–30: "I use the words "ungenerated"
and 'indestructible' in their proper sense (τὰ κυρίως λεγόμενα), 'ungenerated'
for that which now is and could not at any previous moment of time have
been truly said not to be; 'indestructible' for that which now is and cannot at
any future time be truly said not to be."

Yet the general modal notions like possibility and necessity are apparently
never defined by Aristotle (unlike Diodorus Cronus) in purely temporal terms.

Defining necessity and possibility in temporal terms, using the formulations (T) and (T)₂ of the Principle of Plenitude (strengthened into equivalences) as a bridge between time and modality, would have meant for
Aristotle to base his modal notions entirely on what might be called a *statistical* model of modality: Something's being possible must be shown by its
sometimes happening, and what is always must be by necessity. Applications
of modal notions reduce in effect to comparisons of what happens at different
moments of time. Such a classificatory approach to modal concepts was not
foreign to Aristotle. A good illustration is offered by his distinction between
different subcases of contingency in *An. Pr.* I 13. 32ᵇ4–18. They include
what happens 'in most cases' (ὡς ἐπὶ τὸ πολύ), and what "inclines by nature
in the one way no more than in the opposite" (οὐδὲν μᾶλλον οὕτως πέφυκεν
ἢ ἐναντίως). Elsewhere Aristotle adds rare events to the list. It is extremely
natural to include necessary events into this statistical classification as events

that *always* happen, and impossible ones as those that *never* do. In fact, Aristotle seems to do this in the very passage mentioned, for in this context "falling short of being necessary" can scarcely mean anything but "falling short of always happening". If so the passage will parallel *Met. E* 2. 1026^{b}27–37. In any case, this is what the scholastics subsequently did in so many words. The sun rises necessarily, they said, 'ut semper'.[7] The same way of thinking was not far from Aristotle's mind, either, as shown by his acceptance of the Principle of Plenitude. I have in fact argued[8] that the statistical model can be said to have been one of the conceptual paradigms of Aristotle's theory of modality. It was not the only one, however, and hence did not quite yield to him *definitions* of the different modal notions.

7. CONFIRMING EVIDENCE

After all the apparent counter-examples have been refuted, it is in order to marshal the positive evidence for the attribution of the Principle of Plenitude to Aristotle, over and above the references already given.[9]

Here are some passages supporting the attribution: ". . . that which is capable of not existing is not eternal, as we had occasion to show in another context" (*Met. N* 2. 1088^{b}23–5). It is not clear what the address of Aristotle's reference is, although it illustrates the attention Aristotle paid to the principle. In any case, Aristotle offers a kind of proof for the principle in *De Caelo* I 12. 281^{a}28–282^{a}25. Here Aristotle is mainly concerned with the thesis (T), although occasional other versions come into play as well: "Anything then which always exists is absolutely imperishable" (*De Caelo* I 12. 281^{b}25). Here we have an instance of (T)$_2$. The same version is found in *De Gen. et Corr.* II 11. 338^{a}1–3: "Hence a thing is eternal if it is by necessity; and if it is eternal, it is by necessity. And if therefore the coming-to-be of a thing is necessary, its coming-to-be is eternal; and if eternal, necessary."

As to the version (T)$_3$, it is announced in so many words in *Met.* Θ 8. 1050^{b}7–8 and 20: "No eternal thing exists potentially" (ἔστι δ' οὐθὲν δυνάμει ἀίδιον); "Nor does eternal movement, if there be such, exist potentially" (οὐδὲ δὴ κίνησις, εἴ τίς ἐστιν ἀίδιος).

The form (T)$_1$ seems to make its appearance in *Met.* Θ 3. 1047^{a}12–14: τὸ δ' ἀδύνατον γενέσθαι ὁ λέγων ἢ εἶναι ἢ ἔσεσθαι ψεύσεται (τὸ γὰρ ἀδύνατον τοῦτο ἐσήμανεν) . . . Sir David Ross translates this: "He who says of that which is incapable of happening either that it is or that it will be will say what is untrue; for this is what incapacity means." Here Aristotle seems to go as far as to say that the Principle of Plenitude yields the very meaning of modal terms like 'impossible'. In this respect, however, the passage is perhaps somewhat inconclusive, for ἐσήμαινεν might possibly be a weak term here, to be translated in terms of 'indicating' rather than 'meaning'. In any case, the Principle of Plenitude *is* asserted here by Aristotle in no uncertain terms, barring of course the possibility that the quotation does not represent Aristotle's considered opinion. This lingering doubt will be dispelled later when we return to the interpretation of *Met*. Θ 3–4.

In *De Int*. 9. 18^{b}11–15 we find another passage which in its most literal sense agrees very well with the Principle of Plenitude, but whose interpretation is such a notorious mess that only an extended argument [10] can ascertain that it, like J. L. Austin, means what it says. Aristotle there infers "it *could* not not be so" from "it was *always* true to say that it is so or would be so" (my italics in both cases). Further evidence is found in a number of passages, for instance in *Top*. II 11. 115^{b}17–18 (what is destructible *haplōs* will be destroyed), *Phys*. III 4. 203^{b}30 (in the case of eternal things what may be is not different from what is), and *Phys*. IV 12. 221^{b}25–222^{a}9.

In some passages 'necessary' and 'always' are not in so many words asserted to be equivalent, but rather lumped together by Aristotle without explicit comment. Cases in point are the following: *Top*. II 6. 112^{b}1ff.; *De Gen. et Corr*. II 9. 335^{a}32–^{b}7; *De Part. An*. I 5. 644^{b}21–3; *Met. E* 2. 1026^{b}27–37; *Met. K* 8. 1064^{b}32ff. They support my ascription especially when combined with Aristotle's remarks in *An. Pr*. I 13. 32^{b}4ff. on the classification of events into necessary, general, indeterminate, and rare, and with *De Caelo* I 12.

In the absence of any counter-examples that would withstand critical scrutiny, we can safely ascribe the Principle of Plenitude to Aristotle.[11] His formulations suggest, moreover, that the version of the principle involved is just our (T), that is, the version that rules out an infinitely long frustration of a possibility. Even possibilities concerning individual objects fall within the scope of this principle, provided of course that the individual in question does not pass away, for there are in Aristotle's view no possibilities concerning non-existent particulars.

8. THE INTERPRETATION OF *METAPHYSICS* Θ 4

Very strong support for our ascription of the theses (T)–(T)$_3$ to Aristotle also seems to be forthcoming from *Met*. Θ 4. 1047^{b}3–6:

If what we have described is identical with the potential or convertible with it, evidently it cannot be true to say "this is possible but will not be", which would imply that things incapable of being would on this showing vanish.

The text reads:

εἰ δέ ἐστι τὸ εἰρημένον τὸ δυνατὸν ἢ ἀκολουθεῖ, φανερὸν ὅτι οὐκ ἐνδέχεται ἀληθὲς εἶναι τὸ εἰπεῖν ὅτι δυνατὸν μὲν τοδί, οὐκ ἔσται δέ, ὥστε τὰ ἀδύνατα εἶναι ταύτῃ διαφεύγειν.

The evidential value of this passage is not undisputed, however. It has been pointed out by G. E. L. Owen and by Martha Kneale that another reading of Aristotle's words is also possible here (private communications). We can "understand the ὥστε-clause (ὥστε with infinitive, not with indicative) in lines 5–6 as qualifying the preceding τὸ εἰπεῖν . . . οὐκ ἔσται δέ and not as stating a consequence that could be inferred from it. We then understand the sentence as follows: "It cannot be true to say that this is possible but will not happen and to say this *to such effect* that the existence of the impossible will escape us in this way" " (Martha Kneale, private communication).

Both the original quotation and Mrs. Kneale's translation are philologically possible. In order to use the evidence of *Met.* Θ 4. 1047^{b}3–6 for my purposes, I must hence rule out the latter reading. This can be done as follows. In the passage under consideration, Aristotle is warning us against a mistake. This mistake is different on the two different interpretations. On the former, Aristotle tells us that whatever is possible will be the case, i.e. he warns us against assuming that something is possible but will never be. On Mrs. Kneale's interpretation, Aristotle is allowing for a possibility never to be realized, as long as this assumption does not let the impossible escape us altogether – whatever that means.

The sequel shows which of these warnings Aristotle has in mind:

Suppose, for instance, that a man – one who did not take account of that which is incapable of being – were to say that the diagonal of the square is capable of being measured, but will not be measured, because a thing may well be capable of being or coming to be, and yet not be or be about to be. (1047^{b}6–9, Oxford translation.)

This shows quite clearly, it seems to me, that the mistake Aristotle is worried about is assuming that a possibility can remain for ever unrealized. (See especially the last clause of the quotation.) The reading he is presupposing is therefore the one originally given and not the one Mrs. Kneale is favouring.

It may be thought that this does not completely rule out Owen's and Mrs. Kneale's interpretation, if supplemented by the assumption that the mistake he is warning us against is "to suppose that *whenever* we can say 'It will never happen' we can also say 'It is possible' " (Mrs. Kneale). For several reasons this nevertheless cannot very well be what Aristotle means. For one thing, he is not envisaging a man who says that a diagonal can be measured because it never will be, but one who says that it can be measured and yet (μέντοι) will not be measured. For another, I do not see that a fallacious general inference from 'never' to 'possibly' is what Aristotle's alleged formula "to say that something is possible but will never be – and to say this to such effect that the existence of the impossible will escape us" can naturally express. This formula deals with one case only, not with the general fallacy – which Aristotle could have described much more simply anyway. A third reason is that a view as far off the mark as the fallacious inference in question is very unlikely to have merited Aristotle's explicit rejection. (There is no indication anywhere else in Aristotle that he was worried about this fallacy.) Furthermore, a separate analysis will show that there is nothing in *Met.* Θ 3 that commits him even to the view that sometimes a possibility can remain unrealized for ever so as to encourage the fallacy in question, contrary to what the critics of my interpretation seem to assume.

Hence it seems to me clear that the current reading of 1047^b3–6 with which I agree is correct. This means that this passage offers us strong evidence for Aristotle's adherence to the principle that each genuine possibility is sometimes realized.

9. PLENITUDE AND ARISTOTLE'S DEFINITION OF POSSIBILITY

If the reading favoured here is correct, further interesting conclusions will ensue. One fact that may have led interpreters astray is that Aristotle's example about the diagonal seems to involve a principle altogether different from the realization of all possibilities in time. What Aristotle argues for there is apparently not that each possibility *will be* realized, but that it *can be assumed to be realized* without implying any contradictions. What has been found strongly suggests that Aristotle is here assimilating the two principles together. (Note that Aristotle had just before appealed to the latter principle in *Met.* Θ 3. 1047^a24–9.) This observation is important for understanding his theory of modality in general. Aristotle's view is probably motivated by the idea that the only way in which we can think of a possibility to be realized is at some moment of time in our actual 'history of the world'. But if other things than those assumed actually take place at that moment, a contradiction does seem to result. Hence the second principle may seem to imply the first.[12]

Be this as it may, we can now see why Aristotle thought that a denial of his thesis of the realization of all possibilities in time would have lost sight of all instances of impossibility in a very strict sense of the phrase. Aristotle's very definition (working characterization) of possibility is as follows: "I use the terms 'possibly' and 'the possible' of that which is not necessary but, being assumed, results in nothing impossible" (*An. Pr.* I 13. 32^{a}18–20). Because of the assimilation of the two principles to each other, an unrealized possibility would have meant for Aristotle a possibility that cannot ever be assumed to be realized without running into impossibilities, and would therefore have involved the destruction of Aristotle's principal characterization of what is possible and (by implication) what is impossible. This would indeed involve losing sight of what is impossible and what is possible according to Aristotle's definition of these notions.

In fact, the above characterization of possibility is likely to be precisely the assumption Aristotle has in mind in the continuation of our quotations from *Met.* Θ 4:

But from the premises this necessarily follows, that if we actually supposed that which is not, but is capable of being, to be or to have come to be, there will be nothing impossible in this; but the result *will* be impossible, for the measuring of the diagonal is impossible. (1047^{b}9–13; Ross's italics)

The piece of reasoning is in precise agreement with *An. Pr.* I 13. 32^{a}18–20.

We can thus understand very well what Aristotle meant by 'the vanishing of the things that are incapable of being'. If we accept his characterization of possibility, as well as his assimilation of the two principles mentioned above to each other, possibilities can remain unrealized only at the expense of declaring a good number of impossibilities not to be impossible at all — perhaps all of them.

We can also now see, albeit only in its general features, another reason why Aristotle was tempted to assume the Principle of Plenitude, besides the ones mentioned above in Section 6. It was encouraged by Aristotle's way of understanding his own definition of possibility. The kind of assumption that a possibility is realized which was used in the definition meant for Aristotle assuming that it is realized at some moment of *our* time (the actual succession of 'nows'). This, for reasons that we can here only surmise, encouraged Aristotle to assume that every possibility *is in fact* realized in time.

10. CONSEQUENCES OF THE PRINCIPLE:
ARISTOTLE ON HIS PREDECESSORS

Aristotle's acceptance of the Principle of Plenitude was not without consequences for the rest of his philosophy. Here only one of them — a particularly important one — will be noted.

It has often been pointed out that Aristotle's attitude to his predecessors is unhistorical. He did not discuss their views as an antiquarian exercise, but as material from which he could extract his own position by means of critical and comparative analysis. As a consequence, he has been accused of reading his own problems and doctrines back to earlier philosophers.

No matter how these charges of unhistoricity against Aristotle's frequent historical surveys are to be judged, it must be emphasized that his attitude was not due to blind prejudice. The Principle of Plenitude gave Aristotle an important theoretical reason for his peculiar relation to his predecessors. If no possibility can remain unactualized for an infinity of time, every possible truth must presumably have been thought of some time or other. Hence a sufficiently comprehensive survey of the opinions of earlier thinkers will comprise each desired truth within its scope. The central problem thus lies in the sifting of the true opinions from the false ones rather than in the difficulty of discovering the truths in the first place; and, of course, also in collecting a large enough sample of well-established earlier opinions.

This rationale of Aristotle's method of discussion is explained in *Met.* Λ 8. 1074^{a}38–^{b}14. Especially instructive is the following passage:

But if one were to separate the first [original] point from these [later] additions and take it alone ... *and reflect that, while probably each art and each science has often been developed as far as possible and has again perished*, those opinions, with others, have been preserved until the present like relics of the ancient treasure. It is only in this way that we can explain the opinions of our ancestors and forerunners. (My italics, of course.)

In *Politics* VII 10. 1329^{b}25–35 Aristotle expresses a closely related idea as follows:

We must also believe that ... most other institutions ... have been invented in the course of years on a number of different occasions – indeed an infinite number .... We ought to take over and use what has already been adequately expressed before us, and confine ourselves to attempting to discover what has hitherto been omitted. (tr. Barker)

This passage is especially interesting in that it hints at the source of Aristotle's antiquarian interest which led him, *inter alia*, to compile the famous lost collection of constitutions. In this way, we begin to understand the relation of Aristotle's search for factual material to his theory of induction.

The same idea is expressed in *Politics* II 5. 1264ª1−5 as follows: "We are bound to pay some regard to the long past and the passage of years . . . . Almost everything has already been discovered, though some of the things discovered have not been coordinated, and some, though known, have not been put into practice" (tr. mostly Barker's). A similar point is made in *Meteor.* I 3. 339ᵇ27ff.

11. CONSEQUENCES OF THE PRINCIPLE: MODAL AND NON-MODAL LOGICS ARE INSEPARABLE

Another consequence of the Principle of Plenitude is that if there *can* be exceptions to a temporally unrestricted generalization, there *will in fact* be such exceptions. In other words, the only *true* unrestricted generalizations will be the necessary ones. Since Aristotle assumed that in syllogistic premisses one is quantifying over individuals past, present, and future without any temporal restrictions (see *An. Pr.* I 15. 34ᵇ7−11), this holds for the generalizations Aristotle dealt with in his syllogistic and also in his theory of science. Thus one of the puzzles mentioned in the beginning of this chapter receives a definitive explanation.

Indeed, we have a contrary problem in our hands. The outcome of our analysis is almost paradoxical. The very difference between assertoric and apodeictic generalizations seems to disappear for Aristotle. This is paradoxical, for Aristotle was the founder of modal logic. Furthermore, modal notions played a vitally important role in his philosophy. Yet for him, as for anyone who accepts the principle of plenitude, there should not be any sharp distinction between modal logic and plain syllogistic. In the last analysis, all modal statements should admit of reformulations in temporal (but otherwise wholly extensional) terms. On the contrary, the thinkers who (like some of the characteristically modern ones) reject the principle are the ones who might be expected to occupy themselves with modal logic and modal notions in general. For them, there can be a distinction between merely contingently true generalizations ('eternal accidents') and necessary ('lawlike') generalizations, as there cannot be for Aristotle. Yet the historical situation is to a large extent a mirror image of this legitimate expectation. There is something of a correlation between the demise of the principle and the decline of modal logic.

I do not have a simple answer to this problem. Maybe it is indicative of the deep tensions that seem to have been operative in Aristotle's thinking. He believed in indeterminism and in the special role of modal notions. Yet in his very own conceptual apparatus there were factors that tended to push him towards determinism and towards an extensional (tense-logical) reduction of modal notions to non-modal ones.

Florida State University

NOTES

[1] See, e.g., *Rhet.* III 17. 1418^{a}3–5; *Eth. Nic.* VI 2. 1139^{b}7–9; *De Caelo* I 12. 283^{b}13ff.

[2] See, e.g., my paper 'Leibniz on Plenitude, Relations, and the "Reign of Law" ', reprinted in this volume, pp. 259–286.

[3] Arthur O. Lovejoy, *The Great Chain of Being: a Study of the History of an Idea*, Harvard University Press, Cambridge, Mass., 1936.

[4] See my *Time and Necessity*, Clarendon Press, Oxford 1973, Chapter III.

[5] 'Aristotelian Infinity', *Philosophical Review* 75 (1966), pp. 197–212.

[6] See J. Hintikka *et al.*, *Aristotle on Modality and Determinism*, North-Holland, Amsterdam 1977, especially Section 17, and cf. *Time and Necessity*, pp. 161–162, 194–201.

[7] See Anneliese Maier, 'Notwendigkeit, Kontingenz und Zufall' in *Die Vorläufer Galieis im 14. Jahrhundert: Studien zur Naturphilosophie der Spätscholastik*, Edizioni di Storia e Letteratura, Rome 1949, pp. 219–50.

[8] See *Aristotle on Modality*, especially Section 4.

[9] The attribution of the principle of plenitude to Aristotle has been discussed (with reference to my earlier work) by C. J. F. Williams in 'Aristotle and Corruptibility', *Religious Studies* 1 (1965), 95–107, 203–15, especially 210–14. I am in several respects indebted to Williams's comments.

[10] See *Time and Necessity*, Chapter VIII, especially Section 8.

[11] For additional evidence, see *op. cit.*, Chapter VI.

[12] This suggestion has been elaborated in *Time and Necessity*, Chapter IX. Note that *De Caelo* I 11. 281^{a}5–7 shows clearly that the assumption which Aristotle took to give rise to impossibilities was that a commensurate diagonal should exist *at some particular moment of time*.

R. M. DANCY

ARISTOTLE AND THE PRIORITY OF ACTUALITY

1. MET. B 6. 1002^{b}32–1003^{a}5: A DILEMMA

Aristotle's book of metaphysical headaches, *Metaphysics* B, includes this dilemma (6. 1002^{b}32–1003^{a}5):[1]

Akin to this [viz., to the last problem Aristotle had dealt with[2]] is the problem whether the elements are [i.e., exist][3] potentially or in some other way. For if [they exist] in another way, there will be something else prior to the principles (for potentiality is prior to this sort of cause, but it is not necessary for everything potential to obtain in this way); but if the elements are potentially, it is possible that none of the things that are should be, for even what is not yet is capable of being, for that which is not comes-to-be, but none of what is incapable of being comes-to-be.

What does that mean?

Aristotle's question is whether the 'elements' ($\sigma\tauο\iota\chi\epsilon\tilde{\iota}α$, 1002^{b}33, 1003^{a}3), 'principles' ($\dot{\alpha}\rho\chi\alpha\dot{\iota}$, 1002^{b}34–1003^{a}1), or, perhaps, 'causes' (see '$\alpha\dot{\iota}\tau\dot{\iota}α$' in 1003^{a}1) exist potentially or 'in some other way' ($\tau\iota\nu$' $\ddot{\epsilon}\tau\epsilon\rhoο\nu$ $\tau\rhoό\piο\nu$, 1002^{b}33–34). This spectral 'other way' flits in and out of the subsequent argument disguised as 'another way' ($\dot{\epsilon}\kappa\epsilon\dot{\iota}\nu\etaς$ $\tau\tilde{\eta}ς$ $\alpha\dot{\iota}\tau\dot{\iota}\alphaς$, 1003^{a}1), and 'this way' ($\dot{\epsilon}\kappa\epsilon\dot{\iota}\nu\omegaς$, 1003^{a}2). The untutored[4] might suppose that these blanks are to be filled by some variant of the word 'actually': after all, Aristotle had announced in B 1. 996^{a}10–11 that he would consider whether the principles existed potentially or actually. And there is no earthly reason to suppose the untutored wrong. But why Aristotle should have been so secretive about it, and what impelled him to flex his vocabulary for 'principles', are beyond my saying.

So the question is: do the principles of things exist potentially, or actually? And the passage then means this:

The principles of things have to be either potential or actual.

But they cannot be actual: if they are actual, they are not principles, because prior to actual things are the potential things that potentially are those actual things (and this is really *priority*, since nothing potential has to be actual).

But neither can they be potential, because if they were, they would constitute too slender a thread by which to hang so great a weight: as we just noted, nothing potential has to be actual,[5] so if the principles of what is were merely potential, the entire brave firmament and all it overhangs could fail to be.

73

S. Knuuttila (ed.), Reforging the Great Chain of Being, 73–115.

There is Aristotle's dilemma. The question for this paper is how he dismantles it. It is an old story,[6] and a true one, that the dismantling is done in Λ 6 and Θ 8; but the story does not relate how the dismantling is carried out, and that is pretty interesting.

Partly, what makes it interesting is its unexpectedness. Others, banking on the obvious fishiness of the second horn of the dilemma, might have opted for the ultimate contingency of things. Not Aristotle: that, he thinks, would put carts before horses, and the page of principles can list no potentialities. So it is the first horn that prods us along the path of error.

Besides, both horns of the dilemma, and the resolution Aristotle gives us (see Λ 6. 1071^{b}13–14, and see below), rest on the claim that potentialities need not be realized. This seems to deny what has sometimes been called the 'Principle of Plenitude' (which I shall occasionally refer to just as 'Plenitude'), that every potentiality must be realized. We may refer to Aristotle's premiss, the apparent denial of Plenitude, as the 'Principle of Scarcity' (or just 'Scarcity'). What is interesting here is that appearances are not everything: it is the second horn of the dilemma that Aristotle will accept, and it requires us to accept the Principle of Plenitude.[7] So, if we are to believe Aristotle, we must accept both Principles.

And, lastly, we have here a main source for Thomas' 'Third Way' of proving the existence of God, which, to some, is still a sharp weapon (sometimes called the 'argument from contingency'). So a look at Aristotle's way of handling the material is not just more dead history.

First consider the above-mentioned fishiness: the trouble with saying that first there are potentialities, and then actualities, is supposed to be that potentialities need not bear fruit. This is Scarcity; it is so far studiedly vague. But it is difficult to see how any clarification of it is likely to help, for the most obvious flaw in the argument is that the conclusion does not even seem to follow from this Principle. It happens that there are things, and, at least so one might think, there might not have been those things, or, indeed, there might not have been any things. And if one thought that, it would not ruffle one's philosophical calm to suppose that first there were potentialities, and then actualities, even though potentialities do not have to become actualities. But supposing this certainly upset Aristotle, especially in Λ 6. Let us turn to that chapter.

2. MET. Λ 6. 1071^{b}3–1072^{a}4: HYPER-ACTUALITIES

Aristotle's overall aim in Λ 6–8 is to establish the existence of at least one "eternal substance that is unmoved" (ἀίδιόν τινα οὐσίαν ἀκίνητον, 1071ᵇ4–5), and possibly a great many of them. We need not follow him all the way; he concludes that there is some eternal being whose eternal activity is not the realization of any potentiality; if it were not for the Hyper-activity of this Hyper-actuality, there would be nothing at all. So actuality would be prior to potentiality; and this is what we are looking for.

He launches his argumentative barge with this (1071ᵇ5–11):

The substances are first among the things that are: if they all are destructible, everything is destructible. But it is impossible for motion either to have come-to-be or to cease-to-be (for it was always), or for time. For there could be no before and after where there was no time. And thus motion is continuous in just the way time is, for [time is] either the same as, or a property of, motion. But no motion is continuous except that in place, and of this [only] that in a circle.

Let us simply grant all this to Aristotle. But we should stop long enough at least to see what we are granting.

The priority of substances among things at large makes everything less dependent for its existence on them. In Δ 11. 1019ᵃ2–4 he says:

Such things are prior in nature and substance as can be without other things, but not those others without them,

and a few lines later (ᵃ11–12) he makes this the focal sense[8] of 'prior'; the author of K uses it (1. 1060ᵃ1) in defining 'principle'. I shall refer to this sort of priority as 'substantial priority'; but there is a labeling problem here (see below, pp. 88–89), and it must not be assumed that whenever Aristotle speaks of 'priority in substance' he means just this.

We must be prepared for a certain relaxing of the rules here. In *Categories* 12–13, he makes allowance for cases in which, although it is not strictly true that x is substantially prior to y, because, in fact, not only does the existence of x entail that of y but also the existence of y entails that of x, he still wants to say that y depends for its existence on x and not conversely. After listing sorts of priority, one of which was substantial priority, where x "does not convert with respect to the entailment of being" with y (12. 14ᵃ30), he says this (14ᵇ10–22):

It might be thought that there is another case of priority apart from the ones mentioned; for where things do convert with respect to the entailment of being, one which is in some way the cause (αἴτιον) of the being of the other might reasonably be called prior by nature. That there are some cases is clear: that there is a man converts with respect to the entailment of being with the true statement about it; for if there is a man, the statement in which we say that there is a man is true, and this converts: if the statement in which we say that there is a man is true, then there is a man; but while the true statement is in no way responsible (αἴτιος) for the thing's being, the thing does seem somehow responsible (αἴτιον) for the statement's being true: it is because the thing is or is not that the statement is called true or false.

Aristotle accepts this, and accordingly adds this priority to his list. But here and in 13. 14^{b}27–33 he is clearly thinking of it as a variant of substantial priority.

It is disappointing that Aristotle gives us no more precision than this. But his example nicely illustrates the point: sometimes we shall want to allow for (what we may call) Existential Dependence even where we have (what we may call) Existential Equivalence.

The substantial priority (in the sense just outlined) of substances over other things is announced at the beginning of Λ (1. 1069^{a}18–21, 24). In establishing the existence of an unmoved eternal substance in Λ 6–8 Aristotle is applying the same notion within the class of substances to show the priority of one or more of them to the others: in 7. 1072^{a}31–32 he tells us that primary among substances is Hyper-actuality, and in 8. 1073^{a}30 he refers to the chief among his forty-seven or fifty-five[9] unmoved movers as 'the primary substance'.[10] To see the relevance of 1071^{b}5–11 to this program, one has to follow out the reminder that immediately precedes it (^{b}3–5):

Since there were three [sorts of] substance, two natural and one unmoved, about this last one must assert: it is necessary that there be some eternal substance that is unmoved.

In Λ 1. 1069^{a}30–^{b}2, Aristotle had partitioned the universe of candidate substances into 'perceptible' and 'unmoved' ones;[11] the perceptible ones are, by definition, subject to motion (see Z 11. 1036^{b}28–30, E 1. 1025^{b}34–1026^{a}3, and Λ 1. 1069^{b}3), and it was this fact that made them subject to natural science (Λ 1. 1069^{a}36–^{b}1). They are the natural sorts of substance above: whether eternal, like the stars and planets, or transient, as we and plants are (1069^{a}30–32).

There are complicated dependences here. In this scheme, if a plant or a planet failed to perform its characteristic motions, it would cease to be. This gives us Existential Equivalence; it is not enough to upset the substantial priority of the plant or the planet over its attributes, including its motions. If my metabolic processes cease, so do I, but it is not as if those processes could go on without bodily support.

On the other hand, plants and planets show an Existential Dependence on whatever it is that enables them to do their things. Plants, and the rest of us organisms, require the sun, moving in its characteristic way (Λ 5. 1071^{a}15–17 with 6. 1072ᵃ9–12 and, more fully, *De gen. et corr.* B 10); for it to do that, it requires certain nested spheres, each moving in its way. Any of these spheres might have done what it does without having the sun glued to the innermost one; and the sun has no need for rutabagas.

So all of the rest of us are dependent on the heavenly bodies and their activities. And what our passage tells us is that there is at least one such activity that is eternal.[12] Aristotle thinks he can prove this by adverting to the impossibility of a time before which there was or after which there will be no time, which gives us the limitlessness of time, and then connecting time with motion (see the fuller version of the argument in *Phys.* Θ 1. 251ᵇ10–28, and cf. *De Gen. et corr.* B 10. 337ᵃ23–24). There will be plenty of trouble: over the limitlessness of time, its connection with motion, and, not least, its continuity: this, Aristotle thinks, means there must be at least one eternal motion, and he is going to have difficulty ruling out the possibility of an eternal relay-race with transient divinities for contestants.

But once he has got this, and puts it together with his picture of the dependencies in the universe, he will have the substantial priority of whatever is responsible for this motion, or these motions, over everything else.

It is all this that we are going to grant him. We can still sustain the anti-Aristotelian intuition that concluded section 1: we must now understand our claim 'first there were actualities, and then potentialities' to mean that there is nothing in the entire, eternal, course of wordly events that is not merely the realization of a prior potentiality – prior in the sense that, without the potentiality, there would have been no realization, although the realization need not have taken place. This is, on the face of it, a perfectly plausible view. And it is this that Aristotle is about to deny.

Since there is at least one eternal motion in the world, he thinks, what keeps it going all the time cannot let up, i.e., must be always acting, or actual (1071ᵇ12–14):

But if there is something capable of moving [things] or of acting, but which is not acting, there won't [therefore][13] be motion: for it is possible for what has a potentiality not to act (ἀλλὰ μὴν εἰ ἔστι κινητικὸν ἢ ποιητικόν, μὴ ἐνεργοῦν δέ τι, οὐκ ἔσται κίνησις· ἐνδέχεται γὰρ τὸ δύναμιν ἔχον μὴ ἐνεργεῖν).

There need be nothing wrong here: if one is going to account for eternal, continuous motion, one cannot do it with a potentiality that merely stands and waits, and the appeal to the Principle of Scarcity merely reminds us that potentialities might just stand and wait.

He goes on to make some points about (Platonic) forms that are similarly

innocuous (there is no question here as to the adequacy of these points as
criticisms of Platonic theory). To begin with, if you don't fit out forms with
potentialities, they won't help you explain motion (1071^b14–16; cf. A 7.
988^b2–4, which protests that the forms are not so fitted out). Further, even
if you do fit out a form or something of the sort with a potentiality, as long
as you fail to provide the push that actualizes that potentiality, you won't
get motion (1071^b16–17). All this is the same old ground, and nothing
daunting: an unactualized potentiality is what it is and not another thing, and
what it is, is unactualized.

But now we read ($^b17$–20):

> But, further, [it will] not [do] even if [the possessor of the potentiality] acts, as long
> as its substance (οὐσία) is potentiality, for there won't [therefore] be *eternal* motion;
> for it is possible for what potentially is, not to be (ἐνδέχεται γὰρ τὸ δυνάμει ὂν μὴ εἶναι).
> So there must be a principle such that its substance is actuality.

Apparently, even an aggressive potentiality will not do: it is still but a potentiality, however it acts, and potentialities are not strong enough to support
eternal motion. And the reason Aristotle gives us for that is the Principle of
Scarcity: after all, they don't *have* to act.

We have been given four candidates for explaining Aristotle's eternal motion. In order of increasing strength, they are (i) something without so much
as a potentiality to get on with (the Platonic forms, he says), (ii) a potentiality, but one that never gets off the ground, (iii) a potentiality that does get
off the ground, but still a potentiality, and (iv) something that necessarily
acts, that acts with no potentiality (of its own) at all. The first two are clear
losers. What is wrong with the third? "The fact that it is still a potentiality"
But we have supposed that it is a potentiality that acts, and so *does* bring
about motion. "Well, but *eternal* motion?" Why not? Suppose it is a potentiality for just that. Or suppose it is just a potentiality for bringing about
motion, and just happens to do that all the time. "But if it's a potentiality,
it might fail; so the motion wouldn't be eternal."

In that last sentence a leap is made that we must look into more closely.
It is this that gets us to an activity that we might call Hyper-activity, on the
part of something that is what it is and does what it does without any potentiality for being or doing it: its essence is its Hyper-activity, and it is a Hyper-
actuality. Since it has no potentiality for that activity, it has so far forth no
matter: this guarantees its eternity (1071^b20–22; cf. N 2. 1088^b14–28). But
why must we have this guarantee? What is wrong with a contingent eternity?

Back in 1071^b6–7, Aristotle had stated his claim about motion by saying that it was 'impossible' for motion to have ever started or ever stop. If he had been sufficiently adamant about this, he might not have needed the leap: if he had read his own claim as saying that his eternal motion was a *necessary* eternal motion, he might have said that potentialities could not account for it because what had to be accounted for was necessary, whereas potentialities could misfire (cf. perhaps *Phys.* Θ 5. 256^{b}7–13). But he does not insist on this in the course of our argument (^{b}17–20), and for all the use he makes of it, what he says in ^{b}6–7 need only mean that it follows from the fact that time doesn't have gaps that motion doesn't. In our argument, he relies only on eternity. Still, it is certainly worth noting that this insistence on necessity would have made the leap easier, for the Principle of Plenitude builds a bridge between eternity and necessity: if every potentiality must sooner or later bear fruit, then where there is never any fruit there was never any potentiality either; and, in particular, where the fruit in question is the cessation of motion in the world, the eternity of that motion rules out the possibility or potentiality for its failure, and it is then necessary that there be motion.[14] But we can hardly appeal to Plenitude without further ado: apart from the fact that Aristotle does not himself explicitly appeal to it, by explaining the highly dubious by the at least as dubious, the argument as we have it rests on Scarcity, which, at least apparently, conflicts with it.

What we have to understand is why Aristotle thinks that potentialities are inadequate for handling eternal affairs just because they can fail. This is one of his pet ideas (cf. *Met.* N 2. 1088^{b}15–25 with 1071^{b}20–22, and see also A 3. 984^{a}19–27, Θ 8. 1050^{b}7–8, 16–17, H 1. 1042^{a}29–30, 4. 1044^{b}6–8, *De int.* 13. 23^{a}23–24, and so on for further expressions of it). One can imagine the following fuzzy argument for this. Suppose you want to account for some state of affairs. What you need (especially if you are Aristotle) is a set of premises from which this state of affairs can be extracted as a conclusion. Suppose one of the premises registers the existence of a potentiality, and the state of affairs to be explained requires, for the explanation to come off, the realization of this potentiality. Potentialities can fail, so there must be something elsewhere in the premises that pushes the potentiality over the edge, something that prevents failure.

Suppose, in addition, that the state of affairs to be explained is an eternal fact of nature. Then the potentiality-pusher must be eternally pushing, eternally forestalling the potential failure. But then why make the explanatorily uneconomical allowance for failure in the first place? Nature, after all, does nothing in vain, and the eternal pusher really is guaranteeing that there is no *genuine* possibility of failure.

I am inclined to think that this rhetoric actually appealed to Aristotle, and that there might, ultimately, be more to it than just rhetoric (although I am not inclined to think that it is, even ultimately, acceptable).[15] It is, at least, charitable to suppose that something, even if only rhetoric, is blinding Aristotle to the badness of such arguments as that of *De caelo* A 12. 281^{b}20–25, where the one offered, as it stands, is this: Suppose something eternal[16] had a potentiality for not being. Now any potentiality can be supposed realized without impossibility resulting. So suppose this one realized. But then an impossibility results: something that is eternally, at some time or other is not. So nothing eternal potentially is not.

This argument involves an extremely simple formal error: when one supposes a presumed possibility actualized, by way of checking on its possibility, and finds a contradiction, that contradiction only rules out the presumed possibility if it is internal to the realization of that possibility (or conflicts with a necessity). If the contradiction is between the realization of the possibility and some other (contingent) fact, nothing very exciting follows at all. Here, when we assume something eternally existent (or eternally the case), and go on to ask as to the possibility of its not existing (or not being the case), we have to be allowing that its eternal existence might turn out to be contingent, or there is no arguing to be done at all. So the conflict between the realization of the presumed possibility of its not existing and the actual fact of its eternally existing shows nothing interesting whatever.

It is of interest that this error runs through Aristotle's modal syllogistic, not so much in the syllogisms themselves as in the arguments offered for them (although it then reflects itself in the oddity of some of those syllogisms); it is of interest that it underlies fatalism and Megarianism, which Aristotle wants to reject, and that it is a variant of what is sometimes called the 'fallacy of compossibility' (which Aristotle can be detected committing in *An. post.* A 15. 34^{a}1–24).[17] But these matters cannot be pursued here; here, what is important is that the argument of the *De caelo*, fallacy and all, is waiting in the wings in the *Metaphysics*, and that it may very well get into the act on prompting by the Principle of Scarcity. That principle tells us that potentialities may fail. Because of that, the argument of the *Metaphysics* tells us, nothing eternally the case can be so by virtue of a potentiality. The argument of the *De caelo* might make the connection: whatever is eternally the case cannot fail to be the case.

But, of course, this would be to commit ourselves to the contrapositive of Plenitude, which seemed not to jibe with Scarcity. Let us return to that.

The fact that potentialities may fail is a versatile sort of fact. We have just seen it used, in Λ 6 and B 6, to establish, however dubiously, that potentialities have no future as 'principles'. It follows, in Λ 6 and B 6, that what principles there are have to be actualities. But in B 6 it was this same fact that showed that the principles couldn't be actualities: where there are actualities, there are potentialities, but not conversely, since potentialities may fail; so potentialities take priority. And in Λ 6, having settled the case in favor of actualities, Aristotle says:

Nevertheless there is a problem [here] ; for it seems that everything that acts is potential, but that not everything potential acts, so the potentiality is prior. But still, if so, none of the things that are will have to be, for it is possible for them to be potential but not yet to be (1071^b22-26).

So what we have, again, is the initial dilemma; this was its first horn, and we are here being told that something is wrong with it. By the time we get to 1072^a3-4, we find that we have seen what:

to put potentiality prior to actuality is in a way well taken and in a way not (it was said how).

Commentators mostly [18] take this to refer to 1071^b22-26, the passage just quoted. If that is what Aristotle intended, he is guilty of blatant question-begging, for all that $^b22-26$ gives us is an argument for the priority of potentiality and the consequence of that thesis, that all things are merely contingent, which, of course, he would have us reject. Presumably it is the fact that this argument has this consequence that creates the difficulty Aristotle has in mind when he says "nevertheless there is a problem here"; the rest of $^b22-26$ merely is explaining what the problem is. Nothing whatever is done about solving it.

Nor is anything done about that in the intervening passage, $1071^b26-1072^a3$. There we learn that we should not generate everything out of night, or anything of that sort, because wood can't move itself, nor can menstrual fluid, nor can earth: one needs a carpenter, sperm, and seed; and that it is no good just saying that there is always motion: it has to be accounted for. There is nothing here for Aristotle's *sotto voce* "(it was said how)" in 1072^a4 to get hold of.

The question of the reference intended is, for us, fairly trivial. [19] The other leading candidate is *Met.* Θ 8; perhaps that is what Aristotle intended, or perhaps in the actual delivery of the lectures for which Θ was a set of notes, Aristotle expanded on the matter. If he did, he presumably said pretty much what Θ 8 says. So next we shall turn to that. Let us first consider exactly what we want from it.

The argument for the priority of potentiality depends on two premisses:

(1)   what is actual is (or has been) potential

and

(2)   what is potential need not be actual.

From (1), which looks (deceptively) like the principle *ab esse ad posse*, it is supposed to follow that there are no actualities without potentialities, and from (2), the Principle of Scarcity, it is supposed to follow that there can be potentialities without actualities.

So it is substantial priority that our argument would establish for potentiality over actuality: potentialities can get along without actualities but not actualities without potentialities. And Aristotle wants to avoid this conclusion. But he must preserve (2), since he needs it for the argument he wants to accept. And since he tells us that it is in a way all right to put potentialities before actualities, his rejection of the argument need not be total: he can allow a properly clarified version of it to establish some sort of priority for potentialities. But they cannot come out substantially prior: actualities must.

3. THE PRIORITIES OF MET. Θ 8

It emerges that actualities win all the priority contests but one, and on that one a draw is declared: they are prior in account or definition, in substance, and half the time, in time; the other half of the time, potentialities are first (1049^b10–12).

(a) *Priority in account* (λόγῳ, 1049^b12–17). This is the simplest of the lot: to give an account of a potentiality you have to say what it is a potentiality *for*, so the account of that must precede the account of the potentiality in the order of understanding; if you want to say what fragility is, you had better be sure everyone knows what breaking is. I shall not stop over this, except to remark that if it is put together with Θ 5 (1047^b35ff.), the result might be that Aristotle had a technique in hand for eliminating references to potentialities altogether, in favor of descriptions, of the conditions under which various things do, or perhaps would, take place. And if so, this might give the foundation for an argument that gives a more substantial sort of priority to actuality. None of this Aristotle does.

(b) *Priority in time* (1049^b17ff.). What comes of this is, in a way, only marginal to the problem of principality, since Aristotle's principles are not temporally first. But the marginalium is very much in order, since it is only here that potentialities come in first at all. So whatever good there is in the first horn of our dilemma is going to have to be found here.

But even here, it turns out, potentialities must split the prize with actualities (Θ 8. 1049^{b}17–32):

And [actuality is] prior in time [to potentiality] in this way: something that is the same in form (τῷ εἴδη, 'in species') is actual beforehand, but not [anything
20 the same] in number. What I mean is this: prior in time to a given man, who at this point is in actuality, and to a given barley-corn, and to a given [case of] seeing, there are the matter, and the seed, and what is capable of seeing, which potentially are [a] man, or a barley-corn, or seeing, but not yet actually; but still, prior in time to these, there are other things that actually are, from which these come-to-be,
25 for what actually is always comes-to-be from what potentially is by the agency of what actually is, e.g., [a] man [comes-to-be] from [a] man, [something comes-to-be] musical by the agency of [something] musical, always from some first thing that moves; and what moves already is actually. In the discussion of substance it was said that everything that comes-to-be something from something and by the agency of something, and that this is the same in species. So it is that it is thought
30 to be impossible that somebody who has done no harping should be a harpist; for one who learns to play the harp learns to play it by playing it, and similarly in the other cases.

That actualities have to come from temporally previous potentialities is not, perhaps, too much to swallow, but it is a pill easily misused, and the restrictions must be made plain. Aristotle believes, and, indeed, in the argument of Λ 6, which we are trying here to amplify, wishes to prove, that there is at least one actuality without a corresponding potentiality. So the appropriate claim here must be only that where actualities have correlative potentialities, the potentialities precede. But further: if there are eternal actualities, these cannot be preceded by anything at all. That makes room for a partisan of Aristotle's cause to argue as follows: you have granted Aristotle the eternity of motion; that cannot have been preceded by any potentiality, and so, according to the current claim, cannot have a correlative potentiality, which is just what Aristotle is trying to prove.

One might be tempted by this to reject the claim that actualities with correlated potentialities must succeed those potentialities. It is, after all, possible to imagine a potentiality and its realization arriving on the scene simultaneously: at the very instant the glass cooled to a point where it could shatter, it did. And, I suppose, it would in the long run be best to find a way of stating the thing that leaves room for such cases: perhaps it would be enough for Aristotle's needs just to say that potentialities never succeed, and in the normal run of events precede, their actualities.

But there is more to it than that: even with the claim unrevised, our partisan cannot prove all he would have to. His argument shows that if we accept the unrevised claim, we cannot suppose that the eternal motion in the universe is the realization of a potentiality *for eternal motion*; such a potentiality would have to precede its actuality, but could not. So one of the suggestions tossed out above (see p. 78), to the effect that there might be such a potentiality, is ruled out if we accept the unrevised claim. But it remains perfectly conceivable that, throughout all the eternity of motion, at any given time, any given motion at that time is the realization of a temporally prior potentiality, just as, as Aristotle himself thinks, throughout all eternity there are human beings, each the product of a pair of temporally antecedent human beings.

So we do not give the game away by accepting Aristotle's claim, even in the form: potentialities come before their realizations.

Or rather, more fully: an *individual* potentiality is prior to its unique realization. This qualification is what the rest of our passage requires, and we must turn to that. But we must also notice that one major difficulty with the fuller formulation is that it may not always be clear how potentialities are to be counted. The main burden of individuation, of course, falls on the individuation of the realizations of potentialities, but that hardly makes it easy. Consider the question we just examined: whether we can allow Aristotle the priority of a potentiality to its realization and still consistently maintain that eternal motion is a matter of realizing potentiality. The answer, we found, turns precisely on what we are to count as the realization here: if the potentiality is one *for eternal motion*, we cannot make the allowance and maintain consistency; if it is a matter of a potentiality or potentialities just *for motion*, whose realization(s) go on continuously and eternally, we can.

In any case, Aristotle will only allow to potentiality a highly qualified temporal priority: it is only where we are speaking of an individual realization that we can say that a particular potentiality must have preceded it; otherwise, actualities are again prior to potentialities. Ultimately, Aristotle wants to infer this from another of his favorite principles, this one a curious vestige of Platonism:[20] the principle that what actualizes a potentiality, the 'efficient cause' of the resulting actuality, is something of the same kind as that actuality. As it is put in Z 7. 1032ᵃ24–25, that "by the agency of which (ὑφ' οὗ)" something comes-to-be is "of the same form", but the form (εἶδος) "is in something else; for it is a human being that begets a human being". As it is put in Z 9. 1034^{a}22–23, "in a way, all things come to be out of [a thing] of the same name (ἐξ ὁμωνύμου)^{21}". Leaning on this formulation, I shall call it the 'Principle of Eponymy' (or just 'Eponymy'; for other formulations and employments, cf. Z 8. 1033^{a}24–28, Λ 3. 1070^{a}4–6, De an. B 5. 417^{a}17–18, ^{b}3–5, Γ 7. 431^{a}3–4, etc.). In our chapter, it is stated elliptically (Θ 8. 1049^b 24–25: see above, p. 83): "what actually is always comes-to-be by the agency of what actually is", but the subsequent examples (^{b}25–26: a man comes from a man, something comes-to-be musical from something musical) show how this is to be read: whatever is actually φ always comes-to-be φ by the agency of something that already is actually φ.^{22}

Unfortunately, there is little to be said in favor of the Principle of Eponymy, and Aristotle has to go to extremes to force the facts to fit it. In Z 7, he first states it for natural, biological coming-to-be (see 1032^{a}15–25: the first of the formulations above comes from this passage); there it is at its best. But he goes on to apply it to the case of 'art' or contrivance as well: in 1032^b 11–14 it is made to cover house-building and health-giving, by making the form of the house or health in the mind of the architect or doctor the eponymous ancestor of the house or the health in the patient. And in 1032^{b}26–28 he makes a feeble stab at extending the principle to the case in which the patient recovers spontaneously (and he apparently has some hope that his attempt can be generalized to cover other cases of spontaneous generation). In Z 8, he faces mules; there he is willing to retreat a step from the demand for identity of species between producer and product to one for identity of the genus next above that (1033^{b}33–1034^{a}2): a mule is no ass, and no horse either, so the identity of type between parent and offspring is achieved only in an anonymous but fortunately mule-ish genus (1034^{a}1–2). Anyway, the mule is something of a flop (1033^{b}33).

It is not clear how much Aristotle would have to give up in order to drop Eponymy. It locks into a number of his tools: the notion of 'nature', the nature of a thing, covers the form of that thing (see Phys. B 1. 193^{a}30–^{b}18, esp. 11–12, Met. Δ 4. 1014^{b}35–36) and also what explains the motion that results in the thing, or keeps it moving after it has arrived (see Phys. B 1. 192^{b}13–34, Met. Δ 4. 1014^{b}18–20); these are, respectively, the 'formal' and 'efficient causes' of the thing (Δ 2. 1013^{a}26–29 = Phys. B 3, 194^{b}26–29; Met. Δ 2. 1013^{a}29–30 = Phys. B 3. 194^{b}29–30), and these two 'causes' coalesce at the species level, just because what produces a member of a species is a member of that species (Phys. B 7. 198^{a}24–27, De gen. an. B 1. 732^{a}4–5, Met. Λ 4. 1070^{b}30–34. Z 8. 1033^{b}29–32, and perhaps De an. B 4. 415^{b}9–12 and ff.). And I suspect that once Aristotle, in Z, has decided that the form of a thing is prior to the compound thing (see Z 3),[23] he hopes to be able to use his version of Eponymy to save himself from Platonism. At any rate, it would not be easy for him to give it up. But it is false.

This is bad enough; there is a further trouble: Eponymy is not enough, by itself, to give Aristotle what he wants, for the fact that an actual φ is needed to realize a potential φ at most will show that any actual φ is preceded by another actual φ (and even here we again have to ignore the possibility of simultaneity), not that any potential φ must be preceded by an actual φ.[24] Here it might be that Aristotle's concentration on barley-corn and sperm led him to miss this point: in these cases, the (bearer of) the potentiality for being φ can only be derived from something actually φ. But I think he would have had more to say: namely, that to talk of a potentiality in the absence of anything that might bring it to life is somehow illegitimate. In Θ 7, his requirements for potentialities are quite stringent:

We must distinguish when each thing is potentially, and when not: for not just at any time [is a thing potentially]. E.g., is earth potentially a human being? Presumably not, but rather at the point at which it has become seed, and even then perhaps not (1048b 37–1049a3).

He then takes up cases in which the coming-to-be is a matter of contrivance, which are not of central concern here; when he gets back to natural genera-tion, he says that here a thing will be potentially

such things as it will be through itself when nothing external prevents it; e.g., the seed is not yet [potentially a human being], for it must be in something, and change (1049a 13–15).[25]

So it sounds as if (again, ignoring the possibility of simultaneity), before you can count yourself as having the potentiality for being φ, you have to be in the presence of whatever else is needed to actualize the potentiality. And then Eponymy tells us that what is needed is an actual φ.

So Aristotle may have a way of handling this last difficulty. I suspect it would lead to difficulties of its own, but I shall forego further consideration here. It is already sufficiently disappointing that we have to accept Eponymy to make out this part of the case.

What bearing does all this have on the dilemma of B 6?

The only sort of priority Aristotle allows potentialities is the temporal priority of an individual potentiality over its particular realization. This, of course, is the most palpable sort of priority: glasses can break but don't, and then they do; people can have children but don't, and then they do.

So the first premiss of the first horn of the dilemma (see p. 82) takes hold here: an individual or a single event that realizes a potentiality is (subject to the qualification about simultaneity) subsequent to that potentiality.

So also the Principle of Scarcity, the second premiss, takes hold: it is perfectly possible that this glass will never break, but (perhaps) be melted down (and cf. Aristotle's own, famous, coat in *De int.* 9. 19ª12–13); it is perfectly possible that this particular couple will never have children; even if the glass does eventually break, or they do have children, the potentialities for these things are there for a long time, at every given moment during which it is perfectly possible that these things should not ensue. There is nothing internal to a potentiality that guarantees its realization in any particular instance, or at any particular time.

And so the argument works here; in fact, it shows more than Aristotle lets on: it shows that, where ϵ (for '$\grave{\epsilon}\nu\acute{\epsilon}\rho\gamma\epsilon\iota\alpha$') is an actual individual or single event, and δ (for '$\delta\acute{\upsilon}\nu\alpha\mu\iota\varsigma$') the potentiality that is realized in ϵ, it is possible to have δ without ϵ but not ϵ without δ, that is, that δ is prior 'in substance' to ϵ.

But if the rest of his case could be made out, no individual (bearer of) a potentiality would exist at all if there had not already been an actual individual (or single event) that realized a potentiality between actually being φ and potentially being φ, where we take that to mean: which come first in the history of the world, actual φ's or potential φ's? Not potential ones, since there can be no potential φ's before there are actual ones. But since Aristotle also wants to claim that, where actualities have correlative potentialities, each actuality must be preceded by a potentiality, actual φ's cannot appear on the scene first, either. So either they arrive simultaneously, a possibility that Aristotle is studiously ignoring, or they do not arrive at all, because they have both been here all along.

This is the most Aristotle can get, but he tries for more: he says that actuality at the species-level is temporally prior to potentiality. This has to be a blunder: he appears to be thinking that since the form precedes each individual case, and since the potentiality (which has to do with the matter of each thing anyway) pertains to the individual case, and form is actuality, actuality is temporally first. But since he does not accept a beginning of things, and, anyway, would not have his forms existing without instantiation, there is no time at which there is a form without there being an individual case of it. All he is entitled to say is that the potentiality for being φ cannot precede all actual cases of φ.

But that is enough to upset the first horn of the dilemma, construed at the species-level. The first premiss stays solid: where there are actual φ's, there have been potential φ's. What goes is the Principle of Scarcity: it is not true that there could be potential φ's without there being actual φ's. What we have now is the Principle of Plenitude instead, and in a fairly strong form: not only is it true that if there are potential φ's there must be actual φ's, but also, if there are potential φ's there have already been actual φ's, indeed, there have always been actual φ's.

If Aristotle had been able to make out the stronger claim that actuality at the species-level is temporally prior to potentiality, it might have seemed that some headway had been made toward substantiating the claims of B 6 and Λ 6. As we shall see, it seemed to somebody that that was so (see pp. 94–95 below). But he cannot make out the stronger claim. And, anyway, the priority he needs is not a temporal one: we learn from Λ 6 that since time has no beginning, neither does motion, and that means we need a pure actuality to keep the motion going. But then this pure actuality has been here no longer than the rest of us. Besides, the present argument cannot be much help in saving the claims of those chapters if it is any part of that task to save the argument of those chapters, for here we are to give up the Principle of Scarcity (at the species-level), and the argument of those chapters uses it as a premiss.

So let us move on.

(c) *Priority in substance.* We have next two rather disparate stretches of argument, both allegedly intended to show that actuality is prior 'in substance' (οὐσίᾳ, 1050ᵃ4). There is a terminological tangle threatening us here; to get on, we must take notice of it and make a decision.

As we noted (p. 75), in *Met.* Δ 11, Aristotle says that one thing is 'prior in nature and substance (κατὰ φύσιν καὶ οὐσίαν)' to another where the latter (roughly) depends for its existence on the former. The phrase 'prior in substance (τῇ οὐσίᾳ)' is used in this way in *Met.* M 2. 1077ᵇ2–3. But Aristotle is not consistent in this usage:[26] he refers to the same sort of priority in *Cat.* 12. 14ᵃ29–35 without any label, and so also in *Phys.* Θ 7. 260ᵇ17–18, where the phrase 'prior in substance (κατ' οὐσίαν)' is used of something else (ᵇ18). A little later (261ᵃ13–14) he states a principle that he is going to use in our first stretch of argument, and which I shall refer to as the 'Principle of the Priority of Ends':

Quite generally, what is coming-to-be is incomplete and proceeding toward a principle, in such a way that what is posterior in coming-to-be is prior in nature (τῇ φύσει),

and within a few lines he has replaced the phrase 'in nature' by 'in substance'

(κατ᾽ οὐσίαν, 261ᵃ19–20). So also in *De gen. an.* B 6. 742ᵃ19–22 and *Rhet.*
B 19. 1392ᵃ19–22 priority 'in substance (τῇ οὐσίᾳ)' is what he takes the
Priority of Ends to establish. And in *Met.* A 8. 989ᵃ15–18 and *Phys.* Θ 9.
265ᵃ22–24 he uses prior 'in nature (φύσει)' in connection with that Principle.

Let us use 'naturally prior' for the priority, whatever it is, that is sup-
posedly established by the Principle of the Priority of Ends, and 'substantially
prior', as before, only where the one thing is something on which the other
depends for its existence. Of course, we do not have Aristotle's permission for
this, and the translations to follow will always reflect what he says, as in the
preceding paragraph, using the phrases 'prior in nature' and 'in substance'.

It is not at all clear that substantial priority and natural priority are the
same priority. It is not even absolutely clear that Aristotle himself thought
they were: in the argument of *Phys.* Θ 7, the substantial priority of spatial
motion is listed (260ᵇ17–18) and argued for (ᵇ19–29) separately from its
natural priority (ᵇ19, 261ᵃ13–23).²⁷ But in *Met.* M 2, less than thirty lines
before using 'prior in substance' for substantial priority (1077ᵇ2–3), he calls
a priority based on the Priority of Ends 'prior in substance' (1077ᵃ18–20).
And so in our chapter, Θ 8, under the heading 'prior in substance' the first
stretch of argument is concerned with natural priority and the second with
substantial priority.

Natural Priority (1050ᵃ4–ᵇ6).

We have here a series of elaborations of one theme; the theme has to do
with Aristotle's views about 'final causes'. Much of it sounds like school metaphysics: an examination answer to the question "How would Aristotle show
the Priority in the Natural Order of Act or Form over Potency?" And, as we
shall see, the examinee at one point gets Aristotle wrong.

We have already seen (1049ᵇ19–23; above, pp. 82ff.) that, at least in the
individual case, a potentiality temporally precedes its realization. This provides the minor, and the Priority of Ends the major, for the desired conclusion
(1050ᵃ4–7):

But then, [actuality is] also [prior to potentiality] in substance; first, because things
that are posterior in coming-to-be are prior in form, i.e., substance (e.g., a man to a child
and human being to seed, for the one already has the form and the other does not).

And then the elaboration sets in: the 'end' (τέλος) of a coming-to-be is
'that for the sake of which' (τὸ οὖ ἕνεκα) the thing comes-to-be (ᵃ8–9); that
for the sake of which the thing comes-to-be is a principle (ἀρχή) of it (ᵃ8);
so an end is a principle (ᵃ7–8); "but the actuality is an end, and it is for its
sake that the potentiality is there" (ᵃ9–10: τέλος δ᾽ ἡ ἐνέργεια, καὶ τούτου

χάρω ἡ δύναμις λαμβάνεται).[28] By way of illustrating this last: animals don't
see so as to have sight: it's the other way around ([a]10–11), as it is with such
deliberately acquired abilities as that of building houses or that of contemplating ([a]11–13).

None of this is very helpful. Conceivably, a thorough review of Aristotle's
teleology would give us more than just words, but this is not the place for
that.[29] For present purposes, let us simply ask: if Aristotle were right here,
would he have shown anything about what we were calling the 'substantial
priority' of actuality: would he have shown that potentialities depend for
their existence on actualities? The rabbit that is conjured up by this word-
magic is that actualities are 'principles' for their potentialities; if we are to
bring this to bear on our initial dilemma, we should like this to mean that
they enjoy this sort of priority. Does it mean that, or can it be made to mean
that?

If the appeal to final causes explains anything, there must be intelligible
and even defensible instances of something like the following schema:[30]

(S)   x has A because that enables it to ψ.

In the present case, A is specified only as the ability to ψ: to see, to build
houses, to contemplate.

Where the ability is a deliberately acquired one, as in the latter two examples ([a]11–13), we get intelligible and defensible instances: the agent in question worked to get the ability to ψ just so that he could ψ. Earlier Aristotle
had reverted to the presumed fact that an ability of this kind cannot be
acquired without the agent actually ψ-ing (1049[b]29–32: see above, p. 83);
there he seemed ready to move from that to saying that the ability depends
for its existence on there having been some actual ψ-ing, which would make
our case here. But he cannot do that here, for here he thinks of this presumed
fact about learning to ψ as speaking *against* the position he adopts, and
accordingly backpedals: people have, he says (1050[a]12–14)

the contemplative [ability] so that they may contemplate; they do not contemplate so
that they may have contemplative [ability], unless they are trainees, and then they
aren't contemplating *except in a way*....[31]

So the contemplation of a student contemplator is not real contemplation,
and to that extent, reversion to the idea that people learn to ψ by ψ-ing in
this chapter is less than cogent. But then, the cases of deliberately acquired
capacities are less than germane.

Consider, then, cases such as sight. A biblical biologist might make sense of an instantiation of (S) for these cases by appeal to God's Providence, but it is not at all clear what this makes prior to what, so it is as well that it is not a route open for Aristotle. An evolutionary biologist might appeal to the genetic pressure favoring x's due to the increased durability they have because they ψ.[32] But this is no more open to Aristotle than appeal to *Genesis*, and for pretty much the same reason: god or gods do no creating, and species are eternal along with the rest of the universe.[33]

But the evolutionist's approach is in certain respects closer to Aristotle's own, so it is worth noting two features of it. First, to the extent that it explains why x's have A (or why there are x's which have A), it does so essentially for the group of x's, not for any particular x. This is reminiscent of Aristotle's maneuver in connection with the temporal priority of actuality at the species-level. Second, it seems to hold some vague hope for the substantial priority of actuality, for, presumably, it requires that there have been x's that have actually lived more fecund lives than (say) the dinosaurs did, and to do that there must have been some actual ψ-ing going on. But this latter hope is a little too vague: in the evolutionist's story the first occurrences of A are (unless he is a Lamarckian) due to genetic occurrences that are not themselves ψ-ings.

But it is precisely this last that is ruled out of Aristotle's 'static' universe: there are no new potentialities turning up that require explanation.[34] So, where ψ-ing is necessary to keep the x's from going extinct, it will always have been going on. And so it is, for example, with touch; an animal that can move about must have this so that it can obtain food and avoid obstacles: "the body of the animal must be tactile, if the animal is going to survive" (*De an.* Γ 12. 434b13–14). If animals had never employed this capacity, there would be no such animals, and so no capacity. So the existence of the capacity turns on its actually being, and having been, employed.

Of course, this is a case of Existential Equivalence: if it weren't for their possession of the capacity, animals wouldn't feel a thing. But one might argue for an Existential Dependence of the capacity on its use anyway, on the ground that the potentiality could not go around without an organism to hold it up, so that any one individual's sense of touch, even if never used (he is, say, unconscious at birth and forever after), is dependent for its existence on other individuals' having actually felt things. This line of thought seems to me promising: it meshes with more than one idea we have already looked at (see on plants and planets, pp. 76ff., and on the species-level priority of actuality, pp. 84ff.). But nailing it down would require the review of Aristotelian teleology we have forsworn.

This much is clear: in order to bring this first elaboration of the natural priority of actuality to bear on its substantial priority, we must go considerably beyond our text. But it might work.

The upshot of our consideration of the second elaboration is going to be quite similar.

There is very little to the second elaboration. His statement of the Principle of the Priority of Ends had been to the effect that proximity to the end meant priority "in form, i.e., substance", and possession of form was taken as an index of that priority (1050ª4–5, 6–7: quoted above, p. 89). Now he says (ª15–16):

Again, matter is potentially, because it may go on to its form, but when it is actually, then it is in its form.

And in b2–4 he sums up:

So it is plain that the substance, i.e., the form, is actuality. And indeed, on this account, it is plain that actuality is prior to potentiality in substance . . . .

There is a clear argument here. Being in a state of actuality is identified with possessing a form: Actuality is Form; but a thing's Substance is its Form, so Actuality if Prior in Substance to Potentiality (that is, it is closer to being a substance – in fact, it *is* a substance). But this is examination-answer stuff, and we surely need more.

The words of b2–3 ("so it is plain . . . ") may suggest that the intervening passage (ª16–b2) contains pertinent argument, but what argument it contains pertains rather to the more general point that actualities stand as ends for their potentialities.

This passage first tells us that some point Aristotle has made holds "in the same way also in the other cases, even where the end is a motion" (ª16–17: ὁμοίως δὲ καὶ ἐπὶ τῶν ἄλλων, καὶ ὧν κίνησις τὸ τέλος). The layout of Θ turns on a distinction (for which see Θ 1. 1045b33–1045ª4, 6. 1048ª25ff., b18–36)[35] between the sort of potentiality that has for its realization or 'completion' (ἐντελέχεια) a *motion* (κίνησις) and the sort that finds its completion in *actuality* (ἐνέργεια). In fact, Aristotle's use of the term 'ἐνέργεια' (which often sounds better translated as 'activity') would, ordinarily (see, e.g., Θ 1. 1046ª1–2, 3. 1047ª30–32), make motion a variety of ἐνέργεια, and in Θ 6. 1048b8–9 the distinction appears as one between potentiality and motion on the one hand and matter and substance on the other. In our passage (in Θ 8), Aristotle has been speaking of 'actuality' (in fact, all the way from the beginning of the chapter); when he gets around to using the priority of form over matter as support for the priority of actuality over potentiality, he is led to recall his distinction, and announces that his current claim is not restricted by it: he means it to cover motion as well as the other sort of actuality.

So nothing specific is there being said in support of the priority of form over matter. And the rest of the passage, down to b2, follows suit. Aristotle tells us that his point (viz., that actualities of either sort take precedence) explains why violin teachers have their pupils give public concerts: the performance, the 'act' (ἔργον) is the goal in acquiring the ability (^{a}17–19, 21),[36] and is the actuality – the word 'actuality' itself is derived from 'act' and has to do with completion (ἐντελέχεια, 'having-its-end-in-it'; ^{a}21–23).[37] Then he tells us that his point also cuts across another distinction: that between cases in which the employment (χρῆσις) of an ability is as far as things go and cases in which there is a further result. A builder puts his ability to work in constructing, but there is something that comes of this constructing, viz., a house, whereas when one exercises one's eyesight, one sees, and that is all (^{a}23–27). But in both cases the actualization of the potentiality is more of an end than the potentiality (^{a}27–28); where it is building, the activity goes on in what is being built, and for just as long as there is something being built (^{a}28–34), and where it is seeing, the activity is in the seer (^{a}34–^{b}2). The sense and relevance of this last are not at all clear; perhaps Aristotle is thinking that these loci for those activities are *in* the things that have form, or even in the forms, as in ^{a}16 the matter (potentiality) when it is actually was said to be *in* its form. But at any rate, we are not getting fresh argument to the priority of form or for its identification with actuality.

So we are left with our examination answer. This, like the argument that simply applies the Priority of Ends, would require for its fleshing out consideration of a great deal of difficult material – here, Aristotle's views on form and matter. So, again, we cannot do it here. But since I have elsewhere said something about this,[38] I shall, with apologies, say what sort of result one might expect from such consideration.

The priority of form over matter for which Aristotle argues in *Met*. Z 3 is, in fact, precisely the priority of actuality over potentiality: a thing's matter is that which might or might not have been that thing, and its form is that by virtue of which the matter is that thing and not whatever it would have been had it been something else. But if it had not been that thing, it *would* have been something else: it would have possessed a different form (the less articulate this alternative form is, the more we should be forced back, in saying what form it had, to the dummy answer that it has the privation of the original form: but this is still a limiting case of possessing a form). To imagine a thing's matter existing just on its own is to imagine a capacity existing just on its own; but capacities for becoming things are capacities *of* things. So they depend for their existence on actual things.[39] This again is a case of Existential Equivalence: since what is potentially the mobile just *is* the heap of cans, the potential mobile and the heap 'convert with respect to the entailment of being', as Aristotle would say. But it still sounds wrong to say that, if it were not for the potentiality of a Calder mobile, there would be no heap of cans. Potentialities need things to have them.

Again we have a case for the priority of actuality over potentiality that might work.

Either of them might even provide us with a way of arguing, as B 6 wanted, that potentialities cannot be the 'principles' of things. But we need not feel too shame-faced about shunning the labors of unpacking Aristotelian teleology or hylomorphism here. For, in fact, neither argument is the sort of thing B 6 and Λ 6 are after. We may accept the idea that the sense of touch must have been used to exist, in the sense explained, and that the capacity or bag of capacities that constitute a thing's matter must have a form to exist. We may, additionally, accept Aristotle's universe, in which there have always been things and motions, dependent for their existence on whatever accounts for the motions of the heavenly spheres. The trouble is that no way of putting together these concessions will yield a Hyper-actuality. Support for the line of thought of B 6 and Λ 6 is yet to come.

Someone, somewhere along the line, made a feeble attempt to connect these considerations with that line of thought. It occurs in the next few lines of text; immediately after Aristotle announces the identity of actuality and substance (i.e., form) and the consequent priority 'in substance' of actuality (see p. 92 above), the text continues (1050^b4-6):

... and, as we said, in time one actuality always precedes another back to the [actuality] of that which always primarily moves.

I cannot bring myself to believe that all of these words are Aristotle's. If the reference is to the earlier discussion of priority in time, as it should be, the fact is that 'we' said nothing of the kind.[40] So the natural, and customary, thing to do is take the reference to refer to any passage one can find in which Aristotle speaks of "that which always primarily moves", of the primary unmoved mover; the usual candidate passage is, of course, Λ 6–7.[41] But, although I have not been able to find any commentator who notices this, it cannot be this passage that is being referred to if the author of the reference understood the passage, nor can it be to *any* passage in Aristotle, for the doctrine is not Aristotle's.

Perhaps the oddity would be clearest if we considered what pseudo-Alexander says (*in Met.* 591.6–9, after quoting b2–5):

> For when Socrates actually is, before him there actually was Sophroniscus, and so, always, "back to the actuality of that which always moves"; for no actuality precedes this actuality, but it is first of all things and the cause of their being.

But, once more, Aristotle's universe is eternal. Its first mover is not temporally first. And there is certainly no temporal chain that leads back through Socrates to his ancestors eventually to arrive at that unmoved mover.[42] The only temporal step Aristotle accredits is that from a given potentiality for something to an eponymous something that brings it to blossom (see above, pp. 84–86), which will itself have an antecedent potentiality (pp. 83–84), which will have an antecedent eponymous something, and so on. Even if we give Aristotle (as we should not) that this implies the temporal priority of actuality, this path of somethings brings us no closer to anything that always moves, for it gets no closer to anything at all: species are just as eternal as the first mover and his entourage.[43] There is, as we have seen (pp. 76ff.), a spiral staircase between these levels, but it is there all the time: the heavens turn while the sun goes around the earth and people imitate this in dependence on it by having children.

So our examinee gets failing marks in 1050b3–6. I think the best thing to do with the lines is erase them. In any event, the best thing for us to do is move on.

Substantial Priority (1050b6–24)[44]

> But then, [actuality is prior to potentiality] even more strictly (κυριωτέρως); for the eternal [things] are prior in substance to the destructible [ones], and nothing eternal is potentially (ἔστι δ' οὐθὲν δυνάμει ἀίδιον; b6–8).

Aristotle's saying that this argument makes actuality prior κυριωτέρως[45] — 'more strictly', 'more authoritatively', or 'more importantly' — occasions widely varying responses.

Pseudo-Alexander thinks we have a fourth sort of priority here (*in Met.* 591.12–14):

> Having shown that actuality is prior to potentiality in account, in time, and in substance, he now shows how it is prior not just in those ways, but also 'more importantly', or more worthily (ἀλλὰ καὶ κυριωτέρως ἤτοι τιμιωτέρως).

That is, it is prior because it is better. This strange construction leads him to invoke (591.14–16) a principle from the *Topics* (Γ 1. 116ᵇ12–13),[46] to the effect that the characteristics of better things are themselves better, in order to complete the argument. But there is no hint of such evaluative considerations in the argument that follows (these matters are taken up in Θ 9); they seem to me entirely irrelevant.[47]

In the program announced back in 1049ᵇ10–12 there were only three priorities to be established. So it is natural (and, it turns out, correct) to take the present argument as an additional one for priority in substance. Thomas Aquinas (*in Met.* n. 1867) takes it this way; but he thinks it is supposed to prove its point more strictly, rather than that it proves a stricter point. The proof, he thinks, is stricter in that the actualities and potentialities with which it deals are situated in different things: the actualities are eternal things, but the potentialities are those of destructible ones. One hesitates to compound doubt by doubting Thomas, but it is hard to see how this does the job 'more strictly' (*magis proprie*) or 'makes a more evident proof' (*facit probationem magis evidentem*), or how to read ᵇ6–8 (whether in Aristotle's Greek or William's Latin [48]) as heralding a stricter proof.

Still, Thomas' point of contrast between this argument and those that precede is there, and important: we are here talking about actualities that are not realizations of the potentialities to which they are supposed to be prior, for the actualities here are not realizations of *any* potentialities.

Consider the following passage, which is frequently cited in this connection (*De int.* 13. 23ª21–25):[49]

It is plain from what has been said[50] that what is of necessity, is in actuality, so that if the eternal [things are] prior, actuality is also prior to potentiality. And some things are actualities without potentialities, e.g., the primary substances, others with potentiality, which are prior in nature but posterior in time.

Bonitz, in the course of a quasi-pseudo-Alexandrian interpretation of our lines (*AM* 404: see note 47) cites from this the reference to 'the primary substances' in favor of his view that eternal things have a better claim to the title 'substance' than transient ones. This, I think, is on the right lines, and will explain 'κυριωτέρως'.

What is it that entitles a substance to the label 'primary'?[51] In the *Categories*, "a substance most strictly, primarily, and chiefly so-called" (οὐσία ... ἡ κυριώτατα τε καὶ πρώτως καὶ μάλιστα λεγομένη; 5. 2ª11–12) was an individual, and the primacy of these was, apparently, due to the fact that if they did not exist, nothing else would (2ᵇ5–6 [5–6c Minio-Paluello]). In *Met. Z*, the argument for the primacy of form, which results in Aristotle's calling form 'primary substance' (see 7. 1032^{b}1–2, 11. 1037^{a}5, 28–29, ^{b}1–4) is one to the effect that the matter in a composite of form and matter is not capable of independent existence, and consequently neither is the composite, which leaves the form as that on which it depends for its existence (Z 3: cf. p. 93f above). The argument of Λ 6–7 was an argument to the effect that there were certain beings that could not fail to exist, by contrast with the rest of us, who can; in 7. 1072^{b}13–14 he says that the realm of contingent beings 'depends' (ἤρτηται) on such a non-contingent one.

In short what makes a substance primary, a substance 'most strictly and primarily', is its substantial priority: what, in Δ 11, was nominated as the central notion of priority (see above, p. 75 and note 8).[52] The previous argument(s) for priority 'in substance', that took off from the Principle of the Priority of Ends, made no explicit mention of substantial priority; we had to fill that in if we wanted to see it there, and it was a tenuous business. This one is different: in 1050^{b}19 we shall be told outright that necessary beings are "primary, for if they were not, nothing would be" (καίτοι ταῦτα πρῶτα· εἰ γάρ ταῦτα μὴ ἦν, οὐθὲν ἂν ἦν). It is in that sense that we are here proving that actuality is prior 'more strictly'.

So the desired conclusion ('C') is

(C)   Certain things that are in actuality are substantially prior to any of the things that are in potentiality.

Here, as Thomas noted, the things that are in actuality are different from the things that are in potentiality; if they were not, they would be prior to themselves.

This simple point is unavoidable. It would not do, for example, to appeal to the lenience with which form was allowed priority over matter in spite of the 'entailment of being' running both ways (see pp. 93–94 above). For if one of these actualities is what it is or does what it does by way of realizing a potentiality, it cannot be or do that without the potentiality; but, as the Principle of Scarcity is about to remind us, the potentiality could at any time fail; so the potentiality is substantially prior to the actuality.

Nor would it help at this point to invoke the Principle of Eponymy and insist that there would have to have been a prior actual φ to support or actualize the potential φ whose realization is one of our actualities. Granted, that Principle was used to allow a misty sort of priority to actuality even in cases in which every single one of the actualities was the realization of a potentiality; and granted, this priority was supposed to operate even where the chain of potentialities went back to eternity right along with the chain of actualities, so that although Aristotle spoke of it as temporal priority, it had to involve something more, such as a sort of dependence of the individual on the archetype. The argument of the preceding paragraph is untouched by any of this. These actualities, whether there is only one, or forty-seven, or fifty-five, or six million of them,[53] if they are the realizations of potentialities, are substantially posterior to their potentialities.

So we must here be dealing with something on the order of what Λ 6. 1071[b]20 called (see p. 78 above) a "principle such that its substance is actuality (ἀρχὴ τοιαύτη ἧς ἡ οὐσία ἐνέργεια)": something that is what it is without realizing any potentiality. Let us speak of the rest of things as 'Potential Beings'; some of these are, because the potentiality involved has been realized, and some are not, because it has not.

The argument Aristotle offers in [b]6–8 (above, p. 95) employs two premisses.

In the first of those premisses, he uses the phrase 'prior in substance'; looking forward to our desired conclusion (C), we can write this as

(P1)   The things that are eternal are substantially prior to the destructible ones.

We found that (C) presupposed that its actualities were not the realizations of potentialities; in the same way, (P1) presupposes that eternal things are not destructible: if they were, they would be prior to themselves. And it is worth noting that this presupposition is a cardinal instance of the Principle of Plenitude. But we need not meet this Principle face-to-face yet; we shall have a good deal to do with it shortly, and, in the interest of economy, let us note that Aristotle could have made do with the weaker

(P1*)   The things that are eternal are substantially prior to the ones that are not.

We shall soon see how this would have been enough.

He gives no argument for this premiss in either form, at least not here.[54] But the concessions we have been making to Aristotle, particularly those made in Section 2, amount to giving him the weaker (P1*) but not the stronger (P1). So let us proceed with (P1*).

The second premiss invoked in [b]6–8 is one for which the sequel provides a great deal of elaboration. The overall argumentative structure that emerges is assembled in the appendix to this paper. There, rock-bottom premisses are flagged 'P', as with (P1) and (P1*) above, while consequences are simply numbered, from (1) on. The second premiss (of ᵇ6–8) there appears as line (12); it is

(12)   Nothing eternal is potentially.

To get from (P1*) to the conclusion (C), we need to identify the eternals of (P1*) with the Hyper-actualities of (C), and the transients of (P1*) with the Potential Beings of (C). (12) is the means to the first of these ends: it tells us that eternal beings are Hyper-actualities.

Aristotle fixes his attention on (12); he says (1050ᵇ8–12):

And here is an argument (λόγος δὲ ὅδε): every potentiality is simultaneously for contradictories; for what does not potentially obtain would not obtain in any case, but it is possible for anything potential not to act (τὸ δυνατὸν δὲ πᾶν ἐνδέχεται μὴ ἐνεργεῖν). Therefore, it is possible for what potentially is to be and not to be; therefore the same thing potentially is and is not.

The overall claim here, that every potentiality is for opposites or that what potentially is is also potentially is not, is common enough in Aristotle.[55] He states it in Θ 3. 1047ᵃ20–24 as an anti-Megarian point, in 9. 1051ᵃ5–11 in the course of showing that actualities are worthier than potentialities, and in Rhet. B 19. 1392ᵃ8–12 just as something to keep in mind about potentiality. It gives him a certain amount of trouble in the Organon (see An. pr. A 13. 32ᵃ29–ᵇ1, De int. 12. 21ᵇ12–16, 36, 13. 22ᵇ20–21, 33–35), in effect because it does not square with two other modal principles whose intuitive appeal is enormous: the principles that from necessity actuality follows and from actuality potentiality follows (ab necesse ad esse, et ab esse ad posse bonae consequentiae); if, then, from potentiality there follows the possibility of the opposite, that conflicts with the necessity that started things off.[56] But here that is only what we expect: the actualities we are dealing with are going to have no potentialities, so that, in a certain sense, the principle ab esse ad posse breaks down for them.

Here Aristotle argues for the claim. The first flag he flies, "for what does not potentially obtain would not obtain in any case", signals some confusion: it is irrelevant, and betrays the fact that he is not firmly keeping in mind the last point in the preceding paragraph, since we are supposed to be arguing for certain things obtaining that do not potentially obtain; perhaps, then, it is as well that it is irrelevant. What is relevant can be written thus:

(P2)   What potentially is can fail actually to be,

so

(1)   What potentially is can either be or not be,

and so

(2)   What potentially is, potentially is not.

This is refreshingly straightforward, but that should not blind us so badly that we are unable to recognize old friends: (P2) is the Principle of Scarcity. We are once again on the train of thought first encountered in the second horn of B 6's dilemma, that goes from this Principle to the priority of actuality.

To continue the journey (1050^b12-14):

But what potentially is not, possibly is not, and what possibly is not, is destructible.

These lines, together with the preceding, make it clear that whatever difference Aristotle felt there was between 'potentially' and 'possibly', it is not germane to the argument. For in $^b11-12$ he has it that what potentially is possibly is (". . . it is *possible* for what *potentially* is *to be* and not to be", τὸ . . . δυνατὸν εἶναι ενδέχεται καὶ εἶναι καὶ μὴ εἶναι), in $^b12$ he goes from 'possibly is not' to 'potentially is not' (from the preceding claim he infers "the same thing potentially is and is not", τὸ αὐτὸ ἄρα δυνατὸν καὶ εἶναι καὶ μὴ εἶναι), and here he outright says that what potentially is not possibly is not (τὸ δὲ δυνατὸν μὴ εἶναι ἐνδέχεται μὴ εἶναι). So, although I shall continue to differentiate the two in translating, I shall not worry over the possibility that a real difference is involved.[57]

Similarly, I shall, with Aristotle, ignore the difficulty that "what possibly is not, is destructible" works cleanly only where we are talking about something already with us; goat-stags and whatnot are things that possibly are not — indeed, they actually are not — but that does not mean that they are destructible, but that they might not exist in the first place. This, I think, is minor.

Lines $^b12-14$ give us two further premises, numbered (P3) and (P4) in the appendix, whose conclusion would be

(3)   What potentially is not, is destructible.

Aristotle does not bother to make this explicit, any more than he does the next step, which would be to infer from (2) and (3)

(4)   What potentially is, is destructible.

At this point the train goes onto a side-track; Aristotle notes that 'destructible' can be understood (^{b}14–16)

either simply or in that respect in which it is said possibly not to be, either with respect to place or with respect to amount or quality; what [is destructible] with respect to [its] substance is [destructible] simply.

Here, as in *De caelo* A 12. 281^{a}30-33, Aristotle is merely telling us that the same moves will work for a thing's possible loss of a characteristic as work for the possible loss of the thing: if something is 'destructible in a certain respect', say, the sun, with respect to its being in Capricorn ([Alexander] *in Met*. 591. 35ff.), that means it can cease to be in Capricorn; if it were destructible 'simply', it could just cease to be. If the argument shows anything about things that are just plain indestructible, a parallel one would show something parallel about things that were indestructibly in Capricorn, two feet long, or lemon yellow.

But here we are concerned with the case of 'simply' indestructible; we conclude (1050^{b}16–24):

So none among simply indestructible things potentially is simply (but nothing prevents [its being potentially] in a certain respect, e.g., its quality or place), so they all are actually; and none among the things that of necessity are, either (and these, after all, are primary, for if they were not, nothing would be), nor, indeed, is motion, if there is any eternal [motion], nor, if there is something eternally moved, is it potentially moved except perhaps from one place to another (for nothing prevents the matter for that being there); so it is that the sun, the stars, and the entire heaven always act, and one need not be afraid, as were those [who talked] about nature, that [the whole works] might grind to a halt.

Let us begin at the beginning. Aristotle says: so,

(5)   Nothing indestructible potentially is.

This is equivalent[58] to (4), which is its obverted contrapositive. And it is not hard to take Aristotle's next conclusion,

(6)   Nothing that is of necessity, potentially is,

as a restatement of (5), and the remainder of the passage as instantiating this for motion and thus allaying all our fears as to entropy and whatnot. And the qualifications are not very difficult: the sun, which is indeed in eternal motion, has no capacity for being (or not being) in Capricorn.

The trouble is that this is all there is to the argument: we were trying to establish (12), and Aristotle thinks he has done it. But neither (5) nor (6) is, in fact, (12). We need a further premiss to get to (12), and that premiss is either

(11)   Everything eternal is indestructible,

or

(10)   Everything eternal is of necessity.

With either (5) as major and (11) as minor, or (6) as major and (10) as minor, we get a Celarent whose conclusion is (12). If there is no material difference between (5) and (6), neither is there any between (11) and (10).

Consider (10). In *Met.* Δ 5. 1015ᵃ33–36 (and see ff.), Aristotle makes the focal sense of 'necessarily' *not possibly not*. Contraposing (10) and substituting for 'of necessity' gives

(9)   Every possible non-being is non-eternal,

that is,

(8)   Every possible non-being at some time is not.

And this, which is thus equivalent to (10), is an instance of the Principle of Plenitude.

In fact, it is more than just an instance of that Principle. For Aristotle has already told us that the occurrences of forms of 'to be' here may either be left as is or filled out uniformly to give predications. So (8) is really

(7)   Everything that can fail to be φ, at some time is not φ,

where 'φ' is replaceable by anything or nothing. And being φ is just failing not to be φ, so (7) is equivalent to

(P5)   Everything that can be φ at some time is φ,

where 'φ' is replaceable by anything or nothing.

(P5) is the Principle of Plenitude; so, on this showing, (10) is simply Plenitude in heavy drag.

The moves that show this equivalence, apart from contraposing (10), may seem perverse. So be it: let us call the operation that follows contraposition 'perversion', so that (P5) is the perverted contrapositive of (10). Still, it is not too kinky for Aristotle.

The contraposition itself is, of course, no more recondite than some of

Aristotle's own implicit moves in this chapter (see, e.g., p. 100 above on steps (3)–(4)).

The latter two stages in the perversion of (10), that yield (7) and then (P5), seem the oddest. But back in Section 2 we left an argument from *De Caelo* A 12 awaiting its cue; we may as well bring it back on stage now. Its role was to show that nothing eternal could have a potentiality for not being (see pp. 78–79). The argument itself is perfectly general in just the way our perversion requires: it would show, if it showed anything, that wherever something is eternally so there is no room left for the possibility that it not be so. In particular, Aristotle is explicit there as well as here that the argument is to be understood with 'to be' standing for 'to be φ' (281^{a}30–33), and he treats potentialities for failure as on a par with potentialities for success (see 281^{b}27–29, 282^{a}4ff.; etc.). Then the conclusion of that argument clearly has "nothing that is never so is still possibly so" as a corollary, and the obverted contrapositive of that is "everything that is possibly so is, at some time, so". Then Aristotle is committed to (P5) and to the moves that show it equivalent to (7), (8) and (9).

That leaves the first stage in the perversion of (10), that shows it equivalent to (9). This also works, but it contains a trap. We have noted (p. 99) that the argument leading to (12) requires, at (P2), a sense of 'possible' that does not obey the principle *ab esse ad posse*; in fact, of course, (12) itself requires such a sense of 'potentially', and Aristotle has already collapsed 'possibly' and 'potentially'. But the sense of 'possibly' in which it interchanges with 'not possibly not' is one that *does* obey that rule, as long as we keep to Double Negation and *ab necesse ad esse*. For an instance of this latter rule is

(i)   If necessarily not p, then not p,

whose contrapositive (applying Double Negation) is

(ii)   If p, then not necessarily not p,

and by substituting 'not possibly not' for 'necessarily' in this (and again canceling the double negatives) we have

(iii)   If p, then possibly p.

Aristotle, especially in the *Prior Analytics*, is particularly sensitive to these matters (see, e.g., A 15. 33^{b}25–31, 34^{b}27–31). So, it might seem, he would not allow the first stage of our perversion, for that requires this substitution.

All this brings out a point, it will emerge, about the Principles of Scarcity and Plenitude. But the fact that the interchange of 'necessarily' and 'not possibly not' requires a weak-kneed sort of possibility (one compatible with necessity) where Scarcity (which is (P2)) and (12) require a robust one (that will allow in beings, but no necessary ones) does no damage whatever to the overall argument. The syllogisms, either of which will establish (12), are (see pp. 101–102):

(6)   Nothing that is of necessity, potentially is;
(10)   Everything eternal is of necessity; therefore
(12)   Nothing eternal potentially is;

and

(5)   Nothing indestructible potentially is;
(11)   Everything eternal is indestructible; therefore
(12)   Nothing eternal potentially is.

If we replace 'potentially' in these with 'possibly' (and there is no reason not to) we shall have to bear in mind that this sort of possibility is the robust one. The suggestion here is that Aristotle would argue for (10), or for (11) as another way of putting (10) just as (6) was another way of putting (5), on the basis of (P5), using the interchange. That means that the possibility spoken of in (P5) is the weak-kneed one. And, indeed, the possibility spoken of in *De caelo* A 12 is the weak-kneed one (see 281ᵇ2–25, where the crucial restriction against necessity, present in *An. pr.* A 13. 32ᵃ18–21, is missing). So if we formulated (P5) using 'possibly', there would be two different senses of 'possibly' at work in the same argument. But that does no harm, for the two never meet: the weak-kneed sense vanishes without a trace between (P5) and (10) or (11), which carry us on to (12) without a trace of regret.

So nothing stands in the way of progressing from (P5) to (10), and thence to (12). The Principles of Scarcity and Plenitude employ different sorts of possibility; that much emerges from the above; but it is not a source of error.

From (12) it follows that the eternal beings whose existence is presupposed by (P1) or (P1*) are Hyper-actualities. Presumably Aristotle is saying just that in 1050ᵇ18 (p. 101): "so they all are actually". We can write:

(13)   Everything eternal is in actuality,

where 'is in actuality' means 'is a Hyper-actuality'.

If we stick by Aristotle's stated first premiss, (P1), we can treat it either as universal ("all things eternal are substantially prior to destructibles") with existential import or as particular ("certain eternal things . . ."), put it together with (13) as minor, and grind out

(16)   Certain things that are in actuality are substantially prior to destructible things,

using the appropriate third-figure syllogism (Darapti or Disamis). Then (4) tells us that anything that is in potentiality is destructible, and that with (16) gives (C). (This last step can be beaten into syllogistic shape, but it is fairly tiresome: see "Note" at bottom of appendix.)

But it should now be clear how it is possible to make do with the weaker premiss (P1*): that was weaker just because it presupposed an instance of Plenitude, and we have now made that part of the argument. Formally, what happens is simple. From (P1*), treated as (P1) was, and (13), by either Darapti or Disamis, we get

(14)   Certain things that are in actuality are substantially prior to non-eternal things.

And from (8) and (2), Barbara tells us, it follows that

(15)   Everything that is in potentiality is non-eternal.

This, with (14), gives us (C) just as (4) did with (16).[59]

And that is all there is to it.

4. SCARCITY AND PLENITUDE

In Aristotle's argument there are three crucial premisses ((P3) and (P4) are innocuous). First, (P1*), which tells us that the universe of transients would not be here unless some eternal beings were. This is not here in question, although I know of no good reason to suppose it true. Second, (P2), which is the Principle of Scarcity. This, provided we bear in mind that it involves the robust sort of possibility or potentiality (that excludes necessity), is hard to challenge. Third, (P5), which is the Principle of Plenitude. We have located a source for this in an argument in the *De caelo* that looks poor, but demands closer looking, and will get it, but not here.

Here there is one remaining sore spot we must treat: the Principles of Scarcity and Plenitude seem to contradict each other.

In fact, they do not. What prevents conflict is not the fact that Scarcity employs robust possibility and Plenitude weak-kneed possibility, for every robust possibility, which, Scarcity tells us, may fail, is also a weak-kneed possibility, and, according to Plenitude, must be realized. What prevents conflict is rather that all Scarcity tells us, and all it need tell us for the argument to work, is that a robust potentiality need not, at any given time, be actualized, where Plenitude tells us that every weak-kneed possibility, and, hence, every robust potentiality, must sooner or later be realized. The point then is just that there is no saying when, if all we know is that the potentiality is there.

That cannot be the end of the story. For one thing, it requires some restrictions on the Principle of Plenitude. There cannot, for example, be possibilities that come under that Principle for dated happenings: the possibility that there be a seabattle tomorrow, July 21, 1979, say. For that possibility could as well fail; it is a robust one, and comes under the Principle of Scarcity. But it has only one chance of realization, so if it has to obey the Principle of Plenitude, we have a contradiction. By the same token, no potentialities covered by this Principle could be specified as for eternal events (see also p. 84 above, which for a different reason rejected such potentialities). And similarly, we cannot force possibilities for unique events which conflict with each other to obey the principles. Aristotle's famous coat (see above, p. 87) provides an example: he says there is a possibility of its being cut up, but it won't be; it will wear out first. Presumably there is a possibility of its wearing out first. Then we cannot have both of these possibilities coming under the Principle; we had better have neither. One suggestion[60] is that the Principle only applies to type-possibilities: the possibility that a coat (some coat or other) be cut up, or that one wear out before it is cut up. My own intuition[61] is that the Principle is restricted to possibilities that are around for all eternity, and have all eternity to get realized in. Aristotle's coat's possibility of being cut up is not like that: when the coat wears out, that possibility wears out with it.

But this requires looking at more text.

Appendix: The Argument of Θ 8. 1050^b6–24

		Derivation	Text	Above p.
(P1)	The things that are eternal are substantially prior to the destructible ones.		$^b6$	98
(P1*)	The things that are eternal are substantially prior to the ones that are not.			98
(P2)	What potentially is can fail actually to be.	Scarcity	$^b10$f.	99
(1)	What potentially is can either be or not be.	(P1)	$^b11$f.	100

		Derivation	Text	Above p.
(2)	What potentially is, potentially is not.	(1)	$^b12$	100
(P3)	What potentially is not, possibly is not.		$^b12f.$	100
(P4)	What possibly is not is destructible.		$^b13f.$	100
(3)	What potentially is not, is destructible.	(P4), (P3) X Barbara		100
(4)	What potentially is, is destructible.	(3), (2) X Barbara		100
(5)	Nothing indestructible potentially is.	(4)	$^b16f.$	101
(6)	Nothing that is of necessity, potentially is.	= (5)	$^b18$	101
(P5)	Everything that can be φ at some time is φ.	Plenitude		102
(7)	Everything that can fail to be φ at some time is not φ.	(P5)		102
(8)	Every possible non-being at some time is not.	(7)		102
(9)	Every possible non-being is non-eternal.	(8)		102
(10)	Everything eternal is of necessity.	(9)		102
(11)	Everything eternal is indestructible.	= (10)		102
(12)	Nothing eternal potentially is.	(6), (10), or (5), (11) X Celarent	$^b7f.$	99, 104
(13)	Everything eternal is in actuality	= (12)	$^b18$	104
(14)	Certain things that are in actuality are substantially prior to non-eternal things.	(P1*), (13) X Disamis		105
(15)	Everything that is in potentiality is non-eternal.	(8), (2) X Barbara		105
(16)	Certain things that are in actuality are substantially prior to destructible things.	(P1), (13) X Disamis		105
(C)	Certain things that are in actuality are substantially prior to any of the things that are in potentiality.	(14), (15), or (16), (4).		97

[*Note*: The rule of inference for the last step, whichever pair of premises is used, can only be made out as a syllogism by rewriting the premises; e.g., (14) might be rewritten as "All non-eternal things are substantially posterior to certain things that are in actuality" to stand as major with (15) as minor for a Barbara yielding "Everything that is in potentiality is substantially posterior to certain things that are in actuality", which then becomes (C). This is relatively pointless.]

Florida State University

NOTES

[1] In this and subsequent translations I have tried to keep 'potential' or 'capable' and their cognates for 'δυνατόν' and its cognates, and 'possible' and its cognates, together with 'can', for 'ἐνδεχόμενον' etc. *Met.* Θ 8. $1050^{b}12-14$ shows that the words had different connotations for Aristotle; the same lines also show that there is no difference in the logical force of the words (see p. 100 below).

[2] The last problem was whether there are (Platonic) forms. The kinship of the present problem with that one is rather tenuous. The received explanation (Bonitz, *AM* 170; Ross, *AM* i 250; Tricot, *A: La M* i. 167), that the form is a sort of potentiality realized in actual individuals, is, perhaps, right (see *Met.* Θ 8. $1050^{b}34-1051^{a}2$, but also notice Λ 6. $1071^{b}15$ and A $7.988^{b}2-4$), but it is hardly very helpful.

[3] See below p. 101; Moreau, 'L'être et l'essence dans la philosophie d'Aristote'; Owen, 'Aristotle on the Snares of Ontology'.

[4] Who here follow the tutored: cf. Alexander *in Met.* 235.10–12; Ross, *AM* i 249, 250; Bonitz, *AM* 169–70; Tricot, *A: La M* i. 167 n. 2.

[5] It is not easy to see what Aristotle thinks is added by saying ($1003^{a}4$) "for even what is not yet is capable of being"; see also Λ 6. $1070^{b}25-26$, which repeats the message in support of the same point. But this saying is replaced in $1071^{b}19$ by "it is possible for what potentially is, not to be" (see p. 78 below, and cf. $1071^{b}13-14$), so I have done that here: cf. Alexander *in Met.* 235.26, 28.

[6] Cf. Tricot, *A: La M* i. 168 (n. 4 continued from p. 167); Ross, *AM* i 250. But no-one notices that the argument of Λ 6 simply *is* the dilemma of B 6 with the half of it that Aristotle does not like deactivated, or how one should sort one's senses of 'prior' so as to reject the one horn and preserve the other.

[7] Lovejoy (*Great Chain*, p. 55 w. p. 338 n. 38) supposed that Aristotle rejected the Principle, and Hintikka (*Time & Nec.* 97–99) showed him wrong. One part of the purpose of the present paper is to strengthen Hintikka's case.

[8] Cf. Owen, 'Logic & Met.' 168–70. In Γ 2. $1003^{b}14-15$ Aristotle says that his πρὸς ἕν λεγόμενα are τρόπον τινὰ λέγεται καθ' ἕν, and in Δ 5 he states a claim to the effect that 'necessary' shows focal meaning by saying that all things necessary are spoken of 'by virtue of' (κατά) one particular (variety of) necessary thing ($1015^{a}35-36$), and he then spells out the analysis. He does not do this last here, but it is easy enough to reconstruct: x is prior in knowledge to y where there can be knowledge of x without knowledge of y but not knowledge of y without knowledge of x; x is prior in time to y where there can be (or is) x at time t without yet y but not without already x; and so on.

[9] Or however many there are: see Ross, *AM* ii 393f. *ad* Λ 8. $1074^{a}12-14$, and especially Hanson, *Constellations* 69ff.

[10] Cf. Owens, *Doctrine of Being*, 456. I do not know why Berti ('Logical and Ontological Priority', p. 60 w. n. 31, p. 67) thinks it possible that this passage refers to the stars.

[11] The text in that passage is a notorious mess, and the approach to it above is reminiscent of Alexander's to the Gordian knot. But it is common enough: see Ross, *AM* ii 348 (paraphrase *ad* $^{a}30$) and 350 (*ad* $^{a}30-32$).

[12] In particular, there is the eternal motion of the 'first heaven': see Oehler, 'Der Beweis in $1071^{b}3-20$', 71–82.

[13] See Ross, *AM* ii 369 *ad* ^{b} 13, referring to Bonitz, *Ind.* $754^{b}5-12$.

[14] More formally: represent 'there is no motion at time t' by '$\sim Mt$'. Then Plenitude tells us:

$$\Diamond\,(\exists t)\,\sim Mt \to (\exists t)\,\sim Mt$$

So, contraposing:

$$\sim(\exists t)\,\sim Mt \to \sim \Diamond\,(\exists t)\,\sim Mt,$$

i.e.,

$$(t)\,\sim Mt \to \Box\,(t)\,\sim Mt.$$

Cf. Hintikka, *Time & Nec.* 95–96.

[15] This was the burden of my doctoral dissertation, *Possibility and Eternity in Aristotle* (Harvard, 1965), in which the argument of *De caelo* A 12 played a central role. See also Hintikka, *Time & Nec.* (esp. Chapter V) and Hintikka *et al., Aristotle on Modality.*

[16] Actually, the argument works with infinite time; but the effect of the end of A 11 and the whole of A 12 is to obliterate the distinction between this and eternity.

[17] Cf. refs. in note 15. In 34a1–24 Aristotle states and tries to prove '$(p \to q) \to (\Diamond\, p \to \Diamond\, q)$', and then takes as an instance of it '$(pq \to r) \to (\Diamond\, p \cdot \Diamond\, q \to \Diamond\, r)$'. That this is the 'fallacy of compossibility' can be seen by substituting 'pq' for 'r'.

[18] Bonitz, *AM* 492; Ross, *AM* ii 371 *ad* a4; both of these give rather full discussion with no awareness of any questions being begged. See also Jaeger, *AM, apparatus ad* a4, and Elders, *Aristotle's Theology* 153. Pseudo-Alexander (*in Met.* 691.16–27) gives an interpretation of the passage that incorporates book Θ and the *De anima*, but is not specific about the reference; Schwegler (*MA* iv 254) and Apostle (*AM* 400 n. 25) simply refer to Θ 8.

[19] It would be less trivial if we were considering the views of Jaeger. He believes that Λ is an early work, Platonistic in its disregard for mundane things (*Aristotle* 219–20 *et seqq.*), as B is but as Θ is not. So the reference (if it is Aristotle's own: Elders, *loc. cit.* n. 17, thinks it probably is not) cannot be to Θ. But Jaeger's view will not do in any case: he also thinks that 1002b33–1003a5, our initial dilemma, is a late addition to B (*Aristotle* 213–14), and then, of course, it is a trifle odd that this passage in Λ should address itself to the resolution of that dilemma. As far as I can tell, Jaeger simply ignores this fact; I imagine if it had occurred to him the entire passage in Λ would, in *AM*, have been bracketed with '[[' and ']]' to indicate that this, too, was part of a later edition (perhaps this is unfair; the dilemma in B is not so bracketed).

[20] See refs. in next note. In Z8, where Aristotle discusses the Principle, he is largely concerned to show that adoption of it will enable one to avoid Platonism: the eponymous something from which you are derived is not a Form but another living human being.

[21] For this use of 'ὁμώνυμος' cf. Bonitz, *Ind.* 514b13–18 and *AM* 330; for a relevantly similar occurrence, see A 6. 987b10 (although there is some difficulty over the text there: cf. Ross, *AM* i 161–62, Bonitz *AM* 89; Bonitz would drop 'ὁμώνυμα'). But this use is non-standard, and it would only invite confusion to call the Principle the 'Principle of Homonymy'. So I have used the label 'Eponymy': 'ἐπωνυμία' and its cognates are not, as far as I know, used by Aristotle in this connection, but they are by Plato: cf. *Phd.* 102b2.

[22] See note 3 above, and p. 101 below.

[23] See 'On Some of Aristotle's Second Thoughts'.

[24] And cf. Ross, *AM* ii 260 *ad* b24–25, and top of p. 261.

²⁵ This fits well with the distinction drawn in *De gen. an.* A 18. 724^b12–22, but, as Balme notes (*A's De Part.* 145), Aristotle does not in the *De gen. an.* stick to that distinction, and so he, Peck (*A: De Gen.* 76 n. a) and Drossaart Lulofs (*ADGA, apparatus* and text *ad loc.*) regard these lines with varying degrees of suspicion: Balme says they are an insertion that "need not be non-Aristotelian", Drossaart Lulofs has them in '[[ ]]', and Peck just brackets them (contrast Louis, *A: DGA* 211, n. 1 to p. 27). No-one refers to our passage in this connection, but it does show that the lines in question are 'not non-Aristotelian'.
²⁶ Indeed, in Z 1. 1028^a33–34 he apparently refers to what I am calling 'substantial priority' as priority in *time*.
²⁷ In the text for this passage, substantial priority has no label at all, natural priority is called priority 'in substance' in 260^b19, 261^a19–20, and priority 'in nature' in 261^a14.
²⁸ The logic of this is nicely laid out by Ross, *AM* ii 262 *ad* ^a7–10.
²⁹ Cf. Balme, *Aristotle's Use*, Nussbaum, 'A. on Teleological Explanation'.
³⁰ Cf. Wright, *Teleological Explanations* 39.
³¹ I pass by the crux in 1050^a14, whose difficulties (see Ross, *AM* ii 262–63 *ad loc.*) are fortunately irrelevant. But I do not think the words can simply be dropped, as Jaeger (*AM ad loc.*) would do.
³² See Ruse, *Philosophy of Biology*, Chapter ix.
³³ See Torrey and Felin, 'Was Aristotle an Evolutionist?'. They conclude from a review of relevant passages "Our conclusion is that Aristotle was not, in fact, either a cosmic or a racial evolutionist" (p. 15), and ". . . Aristotle had adopted early and retained throughout his life the conception of immutable specific types" (16). Sarton's footnote (*History* 535 n. 40) is stupefying: he refers to this article and says "After reviewing all the evidence they cannot answer yes or no". The article was critical of, among others, Sarton's own earlier view that Aristotle "outlined the theory of evolution" (see Torrey and Felin, p. 5). Either Sarton is being dishonest or he did not read the article, at least not with enough care to see what the point of it was.
³⁴ Here, as often elsewhere, I am studiously ignoring such potentialities as derive from human effort (the arts, e.g.).
     If Aristotle had taken a fancy to evolutionary theory, he would no doubt have been happier with Lamarckism: then actual ψ-ing would have given rise to the capacity.
³⁵ On which cf. Ackrill, 'Aristotle's Distinction'; Penner, 'Verbs and the Identity of Actions'; Hintikka *et al., Aristotle on Modality* 65–75 (§ § 24–28).
³⁶ Again, I pass by obscurities I hope are irrelevant: the saying that 'nature does likewise', i.e., acts like these violin teachers, in ^a19, and the problem of 'Pauson's (or Pason's) Hermes' in ^a19–21. In both cases, Ross' n. (*AM* ii 263–64 *ad* ^a19) should be enough to make it clear that matters are not clear.
³⁷ There is a fascinating, and somewhat perverse, discussion of this word by W. C. Ritter, 'Why Aristotle Invented the Word *Entelecheia*'.
³⁸ 'On Some of Aristotle's Second Thoughts'.
³⁹ Here again I pass by an ernormous difficulty, having to do with the relationship between the form of a thing and the thing itself. Cf. the conclusion of 'Second Thoughts'.
⁴⁰ Correctly pointed out by Ross, *AM* ii 264 *ad* ^b4, but he only sees that Aristotle had not there mentioned the prime mover, and misses the point that follows.
⁴¹ So Ross, *ibid.*, Bonitz, *AM* 404 (which says, oddly enough, "^b4 ὥσπερ εἴπομεν, cf. 1049^b17–29. – ^b5 τὸ ἀεὶ κινοῦν πρώτως, cf. Λ 6, 7."), Apostle, *AM* 360 n. 25.

[42] As Thomas Aquinas knew: in *S. T.* Ia q. 46 art. 2 *ad* 7 he says "... it is not impossible for a man to be generated by a man to infinity" (see Brown, 'Infinite Regression' 511–12 [in Kenny 216–17]). So it is that, while Thomas believes it within the competence of reason to prove the existence of God, using regress arguments to do it, he holds that "[the tenet] that the world did not always exist we hold by faith alone .... The reason for this is that the newness of the world cannot be demonstrated from the world itself" (*S. T.* Ia q. 46 art. 2): his regress arguments involve no temporal steps (or not exactly: see this article *ad* 1 for some complications). Yet Thomas' paraphrase of our passage (in his commentary: *in Met.* n. 1866) misses the point just as pseudo-Alexander's does, as do the commentators mentioned in the last note (*locc. cit.*), and as does Stallmach, *Dynamis und Energeia* 201.

[43] On the modern predicament, by contrast, see Lovejoy's *Great Chain*, Chapter ix ('The Temporalizing of the Chain of Being') and Gillispie, *Genesis and Geology*, Chapters i and ix. I have not seen much emphasis placed on Newton's first law in connection with the temporalizing of the regress arguments. This law is the point at which a change in the idea of causality is consolidated (see Koyré, *Newtonian Studies* 66–67; Hanson, 'Newton's First Law', Ellis, 'Newton's Laws', and Hanson's 'Response'): after this, temporal antecedence plays a more central role in causality, and theology will never be the same (if Aristotle's or Thomas' Gods had died, so would the rest of us).

[44] I stop commenting without dealing with: why the heavens do not get tired ([b]24–28), how fire and earth ape the indestructibles but other things do not ([b]28–34), and what effect the argument might have on the Platonic theory of ideas ([b]34–1051[a]2).

[45] Grayeff (*Aristotle and His School*, p. 201) thinks it cannot be Aristotle speaking: the form of the word "is, no doubt, late (mid-Hellenistic)". This is simply false; for a list of comparative adverbs in '-ως' drawn from Herodotus, Plato, Aristophanes, Thucydides, Isaeus, Isocrates and Demosthenes, see Kühner-Blass i 577 Anm. 1. One example there cited (also in Liddell-Scott *s. v.* ἀσφαλής, -ές): ἀσφαλεστέρως, Th. iv 71 (line 26 in Jones' OCT).

[46] Cf. Brunschwig, *Ar.: Top.* 155 n. 6.

[47] But there are vestiges of this idea in strange places. Schwegler (*MA* iv 181 *ad* § 27) is content to quote the above passage from pseudo-Alexander without further comment. Bonitz, whose understanding of the overall argument does not require appeal to such considerations, precedes his comments with the lemma "1050[b]6–34 κυριωτέρα ἡ ἐνέργεια τῆς δυνάμεως" (*AM* 404: "actuality is more authoritative than potentiality"?), and at *Ind.* 416[a]42–43 he cites the occurrence of κυριωτέρως in 1050[b]6 along with occurrences of κύριος and its cognates that have to do with importance, pre-eminence, and so on (occurrences having to do with strictness of sense are listed later, 416[a]56ff.). And Ross, whose understanding of κυριωτέρως is the one I adopt (but see note 52 below) still thinks, quite unfathomably, that the *Topics* principle is needed to complete the argument (see *AM* ii 264 *ad fin.*).

[48] William, at the very least, punctuated the text differently (and there must have been more to it than that): See Thomas *in Met* p. 449, William's text at 792.

[49] I ignore the last line. [Alexander] also refers to this passage, but Hayduck (*apparatus ad* 591.21) mistakenly takes the reference to be to *De int.* 9.

[50] In fact, it is not at all plain from what has been said; Ackrill, indeed, thinks it a later addition (*A's Cat. & De Int.* 153), perhaps Aristotle's own. That could be right.

[51] The answer to this that follows differs considerably from that given by Berti, 'Logical

112   R. M. DANCY

and Ontological Priority' 44–45; see 'Aristotle's First Thoughts' 338–39 for reasons against accepting his. The trouble is that 'οὐσία' is a word he shares with Plato, and the question is, 'which things are the οὐσίαι?'; if, then, Aristotle simply *meant* by 'οὐσία' subject, ὑποκείμενον, he would be begging the question against Plato.

[52] Ross bases the same understanding of substantial primacy entirely on this passage (*AM* ii 265 top); I think that is too little to do on.

[53] See above, note 9.

[54] Ross (*AM* ii 264 *ad* 1050^{b}6) says about (P1): "assumed here, but cf. B. 999^{b}5, Z. 1032^{b}30, Λ. 6, 7". But, in fact: for present purposes, adverting to Λ would be traveling in circles; Z 7. 1032^{b}30–31 tells us that there can be no coming-to-be without something pre-existent, but has to do with the Principle of Eponymy and so does not lead us toward eternity (see above, pp. 94–95); and while B 4. 999^{b}5–6 does state that if there were nothing eternal, coming-to-be would not be possible, the first obscure argument for that (^{b}6–8) would prove, if anything, the eternity of matter (see Ross himself, *AM* i 241 *ad* ^{a}6 and ^{a}8), which is not in question in our passage in Θ (indeed, given the association between matter and potentiality, it would be disastrous to introduce this consideration), and the second, even more obscure, argument (^{b}8–12) would prove, if anything, the eternity of the 'termination' (πέρας) or 'end' (τέλος) of something that comes-to-be (see Ross himself, *AM* i 241 *ad loc.*), where the eternal actualities of Θ 8 are not such terminations or ends – anyway, B is the problem-book, and this passage in it is surrounded by claims Aristotle would not have accepted without qualifications (see ^{b}4–5, 12–16), so there is no reason to believe he would have accepted either obscure argument.

[55] He points out below (a bit confusedly) that in making this overall claim he is not withdrawing from the position explained at length in Θ 2. 1046^{b}4–24 and in Θ 5 (cf. *De int.* 13. 22^{b}38–23^{a}6) to the effect that the only potentialities *properly* for contraries are the 'rational' ones (the ones κατὰ λόγον), such as the doctor's capacity to kill or cure.

[56] On the resulting two sorts of possibility, see below, pp. 103 ff., where they are called 'robust' and 'weak-kneed' (the latter obeys *ab esse ad posse*, and so is compatible with necessity), and Hintikka, *Time & Nec*, Chapter ii.

[57] Cf. note 1 above. I am, then, on the side of Ross (*AM* ii 245 *ad* 1047^{a}26) and Ackrill (*A's Cat. & De Int.* 149) against Waitz (*Ar. Org.* i 376 *ad* 25^{a}37), Bonitz (*AM* 386–87), and possibly Kneale ('Modality' 622).

[58] In a universe that contains indestructible things. Similar problems over existential import can, throughout this treatment, be similarly brushed aside.

[59] If we contraposed (11), we would get (suppressing double negations)

Everything destructible is not eternal.

We could then use this to get from (P1*) to (P1) in the way we above got to (C) from (16) *via* (4), or from (14) *via* (15), and then we could get from (P1) to (C) as above. It is faintly conceivable that Aristotle would then say: "that is just what I meant to do all along; when I said, at 1050^{b}8, 'And here is an argument' (p. 99 above), I meant the argument to be in support of *both* (12) *and* the residue in (P1) over and above (P1*). I think he would be having us on if he said that.

[60] Hintikka's, emphasized more strongly in the earlier 'Necessity' (see pp. 74–75) than in the later *Time & Nec.*: see next note.

61 Also Hintikka's: see *Time & Nec.* 100–101 (pp. 62–63 of this volume); he apparently wants to make the former suggestion a consequence of the latter, and I am a bit suspicious about this.

BIBLIOGRAPHY

Ackrill, J. L., 'Aristotle's Distinction Between *Energeia* and *Kinesis*', in R. Bambrough (ed.), *New Essays on Plato and Aristotle*, Routledge & Kegan Paul, London 1965, pp. 121–141.

Alexandri Aphrodisiensis In Aristotelis Metaphysica commentaria, M. Hayduck (ed.), (*Commentaria in Aristotelem graeca*, Vol. I, Part 1), G. Reimer, Berlin 1891.

Apostle, H. G., *Aristotle's Metaphysics. Translated with Commentaries and a Glossary*, Indiana University Press, Bloomington & London 1966.

Balme, D. M., *Aristotle's De Partibus Animalium I and De Generatione Animalium I*, Clarendon Press, Oxford 1972.

Balme, D. M., *Aristotle's Use of the Teleological Explanation*, Inaugural Lecture, Queen Mary College, University of London 1965.

Berti, E., 'Logical and Ontological Priority Among the Genera of Substance in Aristotle', in J. Mansfield and L. M. de Rijk (eds.), *Kephalaion: Studies in Greek Philosophy and Its Continuation Offered to Professor C. J. de Vogel*, Van Gorcum, Assen 1975, pp. 55–69.

Bonitz, H., *Aristotelis Metaphysica*, Vol. 2., Marcus, Bonn 1849; photoreprint G. Olms, Hildesheim 1960.

Bonitz, H., *Index aristotelicus. Aristotelis Opera*, Vol. 5, G. Reimer, Berlin 1870; photoreprints Akademische Druck- und Verlagsanstalt, Graz 1955; W. de Gruyter, Berlin 1961.

Brunschwig, J., *Aristote: Topiques*, tome 1, Société d'édition 'Les belles lettres', (Budé), Paris 1967.

Brown, Patterson, 'Infinite Causal Regression', *Philosophical Review* 75 (1966), 510–25; reprinted in A. Kenny (ed.), *Aquinas: A Collection of Critical Essays* (Modern Studies in Philosophy), Doubleday, Garden City, N.Y. 1969, pp. 214–236.

Dancy, R. M., 'On Some of Aristotle's First Thoughts About Substances', *Philosophical Review* 84 (1975), 338–73.

Dancy, R. M., 'On Some of Aristotle's Second Thoughts About Substances: Matter', *Philosophical Review* 87 (1978), 372–413.

Drossaart Lulofs, H. J., *Aristotelis De generatione animalium*, Clarendon Press, Oxford 1965.

Elders, L., *Aristotle's Theology: A Commentary on Book Λ of the Metaphysics*, Van Gorcum, Assen 1972.

Ellis, B., 'The Origin and Nature of Newton's Laws of Motion', in Colodny (see under Hanson, 'Newton's First Law'), pp. 29–68.

Gillispie, C. C., *Genesis and Geology: The Impact of Scientific Discoveries Upon Religious Beliefs in the Decades Before Darwin*, Harvard University Press, Cambridge, Mass. 1951; Harper & Row, New York 1959.

Grayeff, F., *Aristotle and His School: An Inquiry into the History of the Peripatos with a Commentary on Metaphysics Z, H, Λ, and Θ*, Barnes & Noble, New York 1974.

114   R. M. DANCY

Hanson, N. R., 'A Response to Ellis's Conception of Newton's First Law', in Colodny (see under 'Newton's First Law'), pp. 69–74.

Hanson, N. R., *Constellations and Conjectures*, W. C. Humphries, Jr. (ed.), D. Reidel Publ. Co., Dordrecht 1973.

Hanson, N. R., 'Newton's First Law: A Philosopher's Door into Natural Philosophy', in R. G. Colodny (ed.), *Beyond the Edge of Certainty: Essays in Contemporary Science and Philosophy* (University of Pittsburgh Series in the Philosophy of Science 2), Prentice-Hall, Englewood Cliffs, N.J. 1965, pp. 6–28.

Hintikka, J., 'Necessity, Universality and Time in Aristotle', *Ajatus* 20 (1957), 65–90.

Hintikka, J., *Time and Necessity: Studies in Aristotle's Theory of Modality*, Clarendon Press, Oxford 1973.

Hintikka, J., w. U. Remes, and S. Knuuttila, *Aristotle on Modality and Determinism* (Acta Philosophica Fennica 29, 7), North-Holland Publ. Co., Amsterdam 1977.

Jaeger, W., *Aristotle: Fundamentals of the History of His Development*, transl. by R. Robinson, Clarendon Press, Oxford 1934 (second edition 1938).

Jaeger, W., *Aristotelis Metaphysica*, Clarendon Press, Oxford 1957.

Kneale, W. C., 'Modality *De Dicto* and *De Re*', in E. Nagel, P. Suppes, and A. Tarski (eds.), *Logic, Methodology and Philosophy of Science*, Stanford University Press, Stanford, Cal. 1962, pp. 622–33.

Koyré, Alexandre, *Newtonian Studies*, Harvard University Press, Cambridge, Mass. 1965; reprint, University of Chicago Press 1968.

Kühner R. and F. Blass, *Ausführliche Grammatik der griechischen Sprache*. Erster Teil: Elementar- und Formenlehre, 2 Vols., Hahn, Hanover 1966 (1890).

Louis, P., *Aristote: De la génération des animaux*, Société d'édition 'Les belles lettres', (Budé), Paris 1961.

Lovejoy, A. O., *The Great Chain of Being: A Study of the History of an Idea*, Harvard University Press, Cambridge, Mass. 1936.

Moreau, J., 'L'être et l'essence dans la philosophie d'Aristote', in *Autour d'Aristote: Recueil d'études de philosophie ancienne et médiévale offert à Monseigneur A. Mansion*, Publications Universitaires, Louvain 1955, pp. 181–204. German translation: 'Sein und Wesen in der Philosophie des Aristoteles', in F.-P. Hager (ed.), *Metaphysik und Theologie des Aristoteles*, Wissenschaftliche Buchgesellschaft, Darmstadt 1969, pp. 222–50.

Nussbaum, M. C. 'Aristotle on Teleological Explanation', Essay 1 in Nussbaum's *Aristotle's De Motu Animalium*, Princeton University Press 1978, pp. 59–106.

Oehler, K., 'Der Beweis für den unbewegten Beweger bei Aristoteles (Metaph. Λ 6. 1071^{b}3–20)', *Philologus* 99 (1955), 70–92.

Owen, G. E. L., 'Aristotle on the Snares of Ontology', in R. Bambrough (ed.), *New Essays on Plato and Aristotle*, Routledge & Kegan Paul, London 1965, pp. 69–95.

Owen, G. E. L., 'Logic and Metaphysics in Some Earlier Works of Aristotle', in I. Düring and G. E. L. Owen (eds.), *Aristotle and Plato in the Mid-Fourth Century* (Studia Graeca et Latina Gothoburgensia XI), Almqvist & Wiksell, Göteborg 1960, pp. 163–190.

Owens, Joseph, *The Doctrine of Being in the Aristotelian Metaphysics: A Study in the Greek Background of Mediaeval Thought*, Pontifical Institute of Mediaeval Studies, Toronto 1963 (second edition).

Peck, A. L., *Aristotle: Generation of Animals* (The Loeb Classical Library), Heinemann,

London; Harvard University Press, Cambridge, Mass. 1943.

Penner, T., 'Verbs and the Identity of Actions: A Philosophical Exercise in the Interpretation of Aristotle', in O. P. Wood and G. Pitcher (eds.), *Ryle: A Collection of Critical Essays* (Modern Studies in Philosophy), Doubleday, Garden City, N.Y. 1970, pp. 393–460.

Ritter, W. C., 'Why Aristotle Invented the Word *Entelecheia*', *Quarterly Review of Biology* 7 (1932/33), 377–404, 9 (1934/35), 1–35.

Ross, W. D., *Aristotle's Metaphysics*, 2 Vols., Clarendon Press, Oxford 1924; corrected reprint 1958.

Ruse, M., *The Philosophy of Biology*, Hutchinson University Library, London 1973.

Sarton, G., *A History of Science: Ancient Science Through the Golden Age of Greece*, Harvard University Press, Cambridge, Mass. 1959.

Schwegler, A., *Die Metaphysik des Aristoteles*, 4 Vols., L. F. Fues, Tübingen 1847/48; photoreprint Minerva, Frankfurt am Main 1960.

Stallmach, J., *Dynamis und Energeia: Untersuchungen am Werk des Aristoteles zur Problemgeschichte von Möglichkeit und Wirklichkeit* (Monographien zur philosophischen Forschung 21), Anton Hain, Meisenheim am Glan 1959.

Thomas Aquinas, *In duodecim libros Metaphysicorum Aristotelis expositio*, M.-R. Cathala and R. M. Spiazzi (eds.), Marietti, Torino 1950.

Torrey, H. B. and F. Felin, 'Was Aristotle an Evolutionist?', *Quarterly Review of Biology* 12 (1937/38), 1–18.

Tricot, J., *Aristote: La Métaphysique*, 2 Vols., J. Vrin, Paris 1953.

Waitz, T., *Aristotelis Organon graece*, 2 Vols., Hahn, Leipzig 1844–1846; reprint W. C. Brown, Dubuque, Iowa n. d.

Wright, L., *Teleological Explanations: An Etiological Analysis of Goals and Functions*, University of California Press, Berkeley 1976.

EILEEN F. SERENE

ANSELM'S MODAL CONCEPTIONS

Modal concepts play a central role in the works of Anselm of Canterbury (1033–1109).[1] The notions of necessity and possibility are particularly important in the arguments which dominate his earlier writings: the ontological proof of the existence of God and the defense of freedom of the will. Later, Anselm's conception of necessity is a crucial component of the extensive and innovative project in rational theology in which he proposes 'necessary reasons' for the redemption of mankind through the Incarnation. Although many of his writings had involved modal concepts, near the end of his career Anselm acknowledged the need to provide a thorough account of his ideas about possibility and necessity, in conjunction with the concepts of capacity and freedom.[2] Of course he accepted the equivalences articulated by Aristotle between 'necessarily' and 'not possibly not' and between 'possibly' and 'not necessarily not'; but he was interested in investigating what further considerations determine the meaning of modal predicates.[3] A late incomplete treatise, the *Lambeth Fragments*, represents at least a partial fulfilment of Anselm's intention to elaborate and defend his understanding of modality.[4] Scholarly studies based primarily on his other writings tend to portray Anselm's treatment of modal concepts as unclear or inconsistent, since the evidence in these writings, though substantial, is so scattered and sketchy that a plausible guiding rationale is difficult to discern.[5] This difficulty hampers attempts to understand and assess a variety of Anselm's best-known contentions: Did he intend to argue in the *Proslogion* and the *Reply* for the necessary existence of God?[6] Or did he indeed deny that God has any properties necessarily, since he asserts in the *Proslogion* and in *Cur Deus Homo* that necessity involves constraint, and thus is incompatible with divine omnipotence?[7] Yet if he held that we should not impute necessity to God, what could he mean by proposing 'necessary reasons' for the Incarnation?

In the *Fragments*, Anselm begins to present a general account of ascriptions of modal predicates, in an effort both to refine and extend the semantic theory developed in his earlier writings, and to explain and defend his characteristic treatment of possibility and necessity. My interpretation of the *Fragments'* account, which rests on a reconstruction of pertinent segments of its analysis, invites new consideration of some basic questions: Does

117

S. Knuuttila (ed.), Reforging the Great Chain of Being, 117–162.
Copyright © 1980 by D. Reidel Publishing Company.

Anselm present and defend a coherent conception of necessity and possibility? How consistent is the treatment of modal notions throughout Anselm's writings? Does this study of Anselm's modal conceptions yield insights for the inexhaustible project of interpreting his arguments for God's existence? The three sections of my study take up these questions in turn; while one essay could hardly suffice to settle these issues, it may succeed in opening new avenues for appreciating the ingenuity and persistence of this Benedictine logician.

I

In his final effort to formulate a plausible account of modality suited to the rational exposition and defense of Christian doctrines, Anselm anchors his analysis of modal predicates in a general semantic theory. He introduces this theory in *De Veritate,* and in *De Grammatico* presents an account of the signification of nouns and intimates his theory's utility for analyzing predicates.[8] Since the material in the *Fragments* appears to be part of this broader theory, we will survey its foundation before considering the later account of predication, and the question of its applicability to the modal assertions which specially interest Anselm.

In *De Veritate,* Anselm and his interlocutor seek a definition of truth which will undergird the Augustinian identification of truth with God, a view Anselm had endorsed in the *Monologion.* In their discussion of the truth of propositions, Anselm propounds a distinction between two sorts of truth which incorporates an influential semantic assumption.[9] A proposition has 'first' truth, Anselm holds, when what it signifies to be the case is so; thus a proposition's having 'first' truth depends on whether the state of affairs happens to correspond to what is asserted. Since 'first' truth is equivalent to the standard conception found in correspondence theories of truth, what other sort of truth could Anselm envision? 'Second' truth is a natural, non-accidental property a proposition always has in virtue of signifying in its literal way; in effect, a proposition's 'second' truth is its literal meaning. (Positing the presence of 'second' truth in all propositions helps Anselm maintain that truth, like God, can be in all things, even in propositions which lack 'first' truth.) Whatever the plausibility of this view may be, it involves an assumption which not only has been influential in the history of semantics, but also is central in Anselm's treatment of modality. Following Aristotle and Augustine, Anselm holds that a word acquires its primary signification by the initial imposition of meaning on a sound; thus he must identify a word or proposition's constant 'second' truth with its original or 'proper' meaning.[10] While he explicitly attributes 'second' truth to propositions, I believe he intends a similar point to apply to words as well.

If words or propositions have a constant natural signification, how can Anselm's theory account for broader meanings words might evolve, and how can it explain metaphorical uses of language? Although Anselm does not really answer these questions here, he recognizes that extended or 'improper' as well as paradigmatic 'proper' uses of language occur. But his explication of examples of 'improper' ascriptions of predicates remains inconclusive here and throughout his early writings.[11] He insists that 'proper' formulations are more perspicuous than 'improper' ones; thus, if 'ought' 'properly' ascribes an obligation, the statement "You ought to love me" is clearer than "I ought to be loved by you". Similarly, if 'can' 'properly' ascribes a power, "Achilles can overcome Hector" is clearer than "Hector can be overcome by Achilles". Whether rhetorical or straightforward, the advice to avoid 'improper' uses of language in the interest of precision and clarity does not repair the theory's lack of an adequate treatment of 'improper' ascriptions. Anselm neither pronounces 'improper' assertions false, nor provides an account of their truth-conditions. Applying a strict version of his theory to the first example, he writes, "Certainly if I truly ought to be loved by you, then I am indebted to render what I owe, and am culpable if I am not loved by you."[12] But he immediately denies that this is what the 'improper' assertion means. Throughout his earlier writings, Anselm appears to have recognized this liability in his semantic theory as a potential theological asset. If a predicate's usual force is blunted in an 'improper' ascription, we can, for example, begin to reconcile the statements (1) "'Necessity' 'properly' denotes constraint", (2) "God is necessarily just", and (3) "God is omnipotent" by deeming (2) an 'improper' ascription of necessity. While this move might strike a skeptical reader as arbitrary, Anselm never abandoned the hope of enhancing its plausibility by providing an independent account of 'improper' predication.

In the *Fragments*, Anselm presents a general analysis of predication and of the bases for 'proper' and 'improper' ascriptions; he also proposes a single criterion for distinguishing these two sorts of ascription. Especially since a long section of the text broaches two modal paradoxes, it seems clear that at least part of his aim is to elucidate the status of 'improper' ascriptions of modal predicates. Raised here by an anonymous student, the two paradoxes are familiar from Anselm's earlier writings; the first concerns the ascription of a capacity to a subject which does not yet exist, and the second concerns ascriptions of incapacities to God. First the student presents the following *reductio ad absurdum*:[13]

(1)   Something which can F can do so only in virtue of its capacity
        to F.
(2)   Something which does not exist has no capacities.
(3)   Therefore, something which does not exist has no capacity for
        being, and no capacity for not being. (2)
(4)   Therefore, something which does not exist cannot be and cannot
        not be. (1, 3)
(5)   From "something which does not exist cannot be" it follows that:
        (a) it is not possible for it to be, and
        (b) it is impossible for it to be, and
        (c) it is necessary for it not to be.
(6)   From "something which does not exist cannot not be" it follows
        that:
        (a) it is not possible for it not to be, and
        (b) it is impossible for it not to be, and
        (c) it is necessary for it to be.
(7)   Therefore, it is both impossible and necessary for something
        which does not exist to be. (5b, 6c)
(8)   Therefore, it is both necessary and impossible for something
        which does not exist not to be. (5c, 6b)

Since each premise looks unexceptionable to him, yet the conclusions are contradictory and even self-contradictory, he asks Anselm to unravel the paradox.

It is easy to appreciate the student's concern over what exactly is asserted in the proposition he uses to exemplify this paradox, 'A nonexistent house can exist'. In a 'proper' ascription, the assertion that it is possible for something to exist designates a capacity inherent in that thing, according to Anselm's views which will be presented in detail in the next section. But if the thing which possibly exists is only a future entity, the location of the corresponding capacity is problematic. Although Anselm could, and in his early writings did, try to analyze such an assertion in terms of the unproblematic capacities of existing agents or entities, e.g. a carpenter and his tools and materials, this strategy is not satisfactory.[14] It may provide truth-conditions for the problematic assertion, but it does not directly elucidate the sense of the original statement. To do so, Anselm needs to explain the relationship between 'proper' ascriptions of possibility, in which the grammatical subject names the relevant capacity-bearer, and 'improper' ones, in which the subject does not or cannot do so.

The paradoxical status of the future house is symptomatic of two gaps in the Aristotelian-Boethian view of modalities: the lack of a systematic explanation of the relationship between capacity and possibility, and the lack of an adequate treatment of antecedent ascription of capacity or possibility to particular subjects. Apparently Anselm takes the student's paradox as an indication of general difficulties in the theory of predication and modality, since he says that a response to the paradox will call him to 'greater things', then introduces a far-reaching array of what he calls 'preliminary considerations'.[15] Since the treatise breaks off before Anselm shows how this broad foundation applies to the paradox, our interpretation must show how, and how successfully, this material helps to resolve the problem at hand and the general difficulties to which Anselm alludes.

Before the reply begins, the student raises a second paradox.[16] We sometimes ascribe impossibility and necessity to God, e.g. when we say that he cannot lie or must be just; but if impossibility entails incapacity, and necessity entails constraint, these plausible assertions conflict with the doctrine of divine omnipotence. What is novel in this passage is that the student preempts Anselm's usual response by saying, "If you reply that this impossibility and necessity signify an insuperable strength in God, then I want to know why this strength is designated by names signifying weakness."[17] Thus the second paradox too calls for a direct explanation of the meaning of a statement whose 'proper' sense is problematic, rather than an indirect analysis in terms of the inability of other agents to tempt God to act unjustly.

In response to these problems, Anselm presents a general theory of predication which consists mainly in what he claims is an exhaustive account of the possible bases for ascription of '*facere*', a verb of broad scope which means 'to do', 'to make', or 'to bring about'.[18] Anselm believes that this analysis will apply to predication in general, since he holds that any predicate whatsoever can be paraphrased by means of '*facere*' plus the specification of some outcome.[19] He provides two lines of reasoning in support of this extension of his analysis to predication in general; while a full discussion of these arguments is beyond our present purview, a brief indication of their character is in order. Surprisingly, the first is an 'ordinary language' argument which rests on the claim that for each predicate there is at least one context in which it serves as an acceptable reply to the question "What is he doing?".[20] Naturally this claim makes sense for action-verbs used in the active voice, but it is hard to see how Anselm could have considered it applicable to predicates with verbs in the passive voice, or to existential verbs such as 'to be' or 'to become'. There is little reason to suppose that this argument for the

substitutivity of *'facere'* for any predicate is more plausible in medieval Latin
than it is in English.[21] Perhaps because he recognizes the dubious character of
this argument, Anselm provides a second and more theoretical justification
for considering the analysis of *'facere'* a general account of predication.

This argument alleges that *'facere'* can be substituted *salva veritate* for any
instance of any predicate because there is always at least one sense in
which a subject can be considered a cause of its predicate.[22] Again, Anselm's
point appears most sensible with respect to action-sentences, in which the
subject-term names the efficient cause of the action predicated. But Anselm
must think that the subject, or subject-term, is always a cause of the predicate
in the sense that it is a necessary condition of that particular instance of
predication, if his argument is to apply to assertions such as "The snow is
white" or "The chair is carried". The depiction of subjects as necessary
conditions and of necessary conditions as causes may strike modern readers
as Pickwickian at best; but this strategy would not have appeared so con-
trived in the twelfth century.[23] Since the applicability of the analysis of
'facere' to modal predicates depends on the claim that it yields a general
theory of predication, one might expect this essay to scrutinize the thin
thread of plausibility in these two arguments. Although I have done so elsewhere, a detailed critical discussion is unnecessary here since we can appreciate the ingenuity and coherence of Anselm's position without reaching a
settled judgment regarding its plausibility.[24]

An initial assumption of Anselm's analysis of *'facere'* and, by extension, of
his analysis of predication, is that not all instances of agency are cases in
which the agent (or subject-term) directly and literally does what he, she, or
it is said to do.[25] For example, one basis for asserting that Jones brought
about Smith's death is that Jones directly murdered Smith, and another
possible basis is that Jones hired the murderer, thereby indirectly bringing
about the death. A major point of Anselm's analysis is to clarify the variety
of bases for such indirect ascriptions of agency; to this end, he articulates
what he thinks are all the possible bases for ascriptions of agency. There are
two possible bases for, or modes of, direct ascription; an agent is said to bring
about a state of affairs in virtue of his action which directly produces it, or
in virtue of his direct failure to prevent the state of affairs from occurring.
In the four indirect modes of ascription, an agent is said to bring about a state
of affairs in virtue of some other action or omission which is a partial cause of
the outcome ascribed. Anselm's analysis of these modes may be summarized
in the following scheme.[26] If *A* is a subject, *s* is a state of affairs which
occurs, and *m, n, o,* and *r* are other states of affairs causally related to *s, A*

may be said to bring about s only if at least one of these six conditions is satisfied:

(1)   A directly brings about s;

(2)   A directly fails to prevent s from occurring;

(3)   A brings about m, and m causally contributes to s's occurring;

(4)   A fails to bring about n, and n's not occurring causally contributes to s's occurring;

(5)   A prevents o from occurring, and o's not occurring causally contributes to s's occurring;

(6)   A fails to prevent r from occurring, and r's occurring causally contributes to s's occurring.

According to Anselm, these modes constitute a disjunctive necessary condition for ascriptions of agency with respect to a specified outcome.

Ascriptions in mode one are straightforward; they include but are not limited to bodily movements. The reason for including mode two as a direct mode may not be so clear, unless we recognize that under some circumstances we do ascribe causal responsibility to a person who fails to prevent an outcome. Since Anselm's plan is to enumerate an exhaustive list of the possible bases for ascriptions of agency, he must then include mode two. Because it is possible for such an ascription to be based only on the person's omitting to act, rather than on any particular alternative act he performs, mode two seems to count as a direct mode. The reason for having four distinct indirect modes is that Anselm distinguishes (a) cases in which the agent acts from (b) cases in which he fails to act, and he further distinguishes (c) cases in which the agent brings about the relevant intermediate outcome from (d) cases in which he prevents the relevant intermediate outcome from occurring.

Among the many interesting issues raised by this analysis of predication and agency, what matters most for understanding Anselm's modal conceptions is his explication of the relationship between the modes of predication and the distinction between 'proper' and 'improper' uses of predicates. Symmetry would prevail if this distinction corresponded to the division between direct and indirect modes of predication, but the situation is not so simple.[27] According to Anselm, only ascriptions made in mode one are 'proper', since this is the only mode in which the agent's action directly causes the outcome ascribed to him. Ascriptions in mode two are 'improper' because the directly relevant factor is the agent's failure to act rather than his directly doing what is ascribed to him. Anselm specifies that, " . . . every verb is said in accordance with the first mode if it is said of something 'properly', so that the thing does just what is said."[28] The indirect modes also represent 'improper' uses, since in these modes again the agent does not directly and literally do what is ascribed to him. Anselm emphasizes that 'propriety' pertains only to ascriptions in mode one: "But if it is not the case that a thing does just what is said, then it is said in accordance with a mode other than the first."[29]

To appreciate the significance of these points for Anselm's modal conceptions, we must delve further into his account of 'improper' predication in general, and 'improper' modal predication in particular. Anselm produces a clearer explanation of the distinction between 'proper' and 'improper' ascriptions of predicates than of the meaning of 'improperly' ascribed predicates. As the passages just quoted indicate, Anselm holds that an ascription of a predicate is 'proper' if and only if its basis is that the subject directly and literally does what is ascribed to him. This criterion involves several assumptions, the most fundamental of which is the view that every predicate has exactly one clear-cut direct signification. But since Anselm embraces this assumption in the doctrine of 'second' truth, it is not surprising that it should recur here.[30] Anselm further assumes, safely enough, that we can generally tell whether the basis for an ascription is in the first mode or one of the others. Thus Anselm's criterion enables us to see that his invocation of the distinction between 'proper' and 'improper' predication is not merely arbitrary. But his use of this distinction in connection with modalities rests on two more controversial and substantive suppositions: that the meaning of a predicate changes when its ascription is 'improper', and that these general semantic theories apply to modal predicates and thereby justify Anselm's treatment of modalities.

Although Anselm's use of the distinction between 'proper' and 'improper' predication clearly assumes that in 'improper' ascriptions part of the 'proper' meaning of the predicate is not ascribed to the subject, he says very little about what is ascribed to the subject. He suggests that we find a complex web of connections between 'improper' ascriptions of nouns or predicates and their 'proper' uses:

It seems to me that whenever a name or a verb is attributed to a thing 'improperly', the thing to which it is attributed bears some relation to the thing of which it is said 'properly' – either like it, or a cause, or an effect, or the genus, or the species, or the whole, or a part, or having the same effect, or shape . . . .[31]

But this comment leaves the necessary conditions for 'improper' ascriptions, and their exact meaning, virtually indeterminate; Anselm commits himself only to the claim that in some sense the referent of an 'improper' ascription resembles the referent of the corresponding 'proper' ascription. Since resemblances can vary widely in degree and kind, this claim as it stands is nearly vacuous. Doubtless it is easier to specify the exact resemblance in particular cases, and thereby to pin down the import of a particular 'improper' ascription.

Does this semantic theory provide a framework for a coherent account of modal predicates? If we accept Anselm's assumptions that the predicate 'is necessarily F' 'properly' ascribes a constraint to its subject, and the predicate 'is possibly F' ascribes a capacity to its subject, we can identify cases for which his account of predication yields a straightforward analysis. Consider, for example, ascriptions of two capacities to Smith: "Smith can run a mile in five minutes" and "Smith can cross the Atlantic Ocean in five hours". In Anselm's scheme, the first is 'proper', because its basis is only Smith's direct act of running, while the second is 'improper', since its basis is Smith's action of boarding a plane for the flight. His ability to board a transatlantic flight can be called a capacity to cross the Atlantic in five hours because it has the same effect as his direct capacity to run the mile in five minutes: he reaches the destination in the time specified.

But even if this analysis is useful for some ascriptions of capacity or constraint, it may not apply equally well to all Anselm's uses of modal predicates. His scheme assumes that the modal assertions to be analyzed can be stated in subject-predicate form, with either a capacity or a constraint attributed to the subject; but frequently modal assertions are couched in the impersonal constructions "It is possible that . . ." or "It is necessary that . . .". While many such statements could be rephrased to locate a plausible subject, at least two kinds of cases seem to resist the form of Anselm's analysis. The first involves attribution of a possibility-predicate to a nonexistent, future subject and the second involves the use of "*necesse est* . . ." to express entailment. It seems slightly odd to think of a conclusion as an object of a literal constraint, particularly when no agent of constraint is specified.

Anselm's distinctions among various senses of the general subject-term 'something' provide a response to the problem of identifying appropriate subjects for modal predicates in difficult cases such as these.[32] A subject or subject-term can count as 'something' in four modes, but is only 'properly' considered 'something' when it satisfies all the requirements of the first mode, when it "is mentioned by name, and is conceived of by the mind, and exists in reality".[33] The second mode lacks the requirement that the subject exist in reality; a chimera, for example, would be called 'something' in mode two. The third mode omits the requirements of existence in reality and of the mental conception of the thing, and includes privative terms such as 'injustice' and indefinite nouns such as 'non-man'. Since these terms acquire their meanings by negating the signification of the corresponding positive or definite terms, they are associated with no full-fledged mental concepts of their own. Anselm adds a final, even weaker mode which lacks all three of the above requirements, on the rationale that the absence or 'not being' of some thing or state of affairs may cause an outcome, as the absence of the sun causes darkness.[34] If these modes are intended as a general analysis of subjects, just as the modes of '*facere*' are an analysis of predication, a suggestion emerges for identifying appropriate subjects for problematic modal assertions.[35] If its subject-term does not directly designate something which satisfies the requirements for 'proper', mode one status, a proposition is 'improper' regardless of the status of its predicate. Thus we could ascribe possible existence to a chimera, for example, explaining that the assertion was 'improper' in virtue of the subject-term's status. Anselm could use the same approach to explain the 'impropriety' of attributing necessity to a conclusion, while maintaining his view (to be discussed in the next section) that propositions cannot constrain the truth of other propositions; if a proposition is 'something' only in an 'improper' sense, it can be necessitated only 'improperly'.[36] The textual evidence is insufficient to argue for a definite interpretation of the generality of the analysis of 'something'. Since the *Fragments* elaborates Anselm's earlier remark about the signification of predicates, found in *De Grammatico*, we might surmise that it similarly elaborates his account of subjects.[37] The strongest reason for assuming that Anselm intends his account of the modes of 'something' to apply to subjects in general is that this supposition allows us to reconstruct a reasonable Anselmian response to the paradox of the possible existence of the future house.

In Chapter XII of his treatise on the fall of the devil, *De Casu Diaboli*, Anselm had confronted the question of how it was possible for the world to exist, prior to its creation. His response that the world both could and could not exist then – it could because of God's ability to create it and it could not in virtue of its own powers – violated the common sense belief of his interlocutor that it is true *simpliciter* to say that the world could exist prior to creation. The *Fragments'* analysis enables Anselm to endorse this belief without immediately capitulating to the student's paradox. An attribution of the capacity to come into existence to something which does not yet exist represents an 'improper' use of language, since the subject-term is only 'improperly' something. Just as the capacity to exist cannot be ascribed to it 'properly', neither can the capacity for nonexistence. Hence Anselm could resolve the student's paradox by blocking its third premise, which initiates the contradiction by maintaining that the future house has no capacity for being and no capacity for not being. Insisting that the future house is 'something' only 'improperly' weakens the force of the paradox by showing that it does not generate contradictory 'proper' assertions; but Anselm still needs to reconcile the apparent contradiction in these 'improper' assertions.

Anselm could evade this demand by denying that the law of non-contradiction applies to 'improper' assertions, but the evidence in the text suggests a more subtle response. We have already noted that in hard cases Anselm supports the view that a subject is always a cause of the predicate ascribed to it by counting necessary conditions as causes, and that he illustrates the fourth mode of 'something' by saying that something's absence can cause an outcome. With the help of these points, we can supply an Anselmian account of one sense in which a nonexistent house might cause its possible existence. If we can paraphrase the problematic statement "A house which does not yet exist can exist" as "A house which does not yet exist can come into existence" or " . . . can begin to be", then we can interpret the nonexistence of the house as a necessary condition for its beginning to be. Thus the nonexistence of the house counts as a cause, and is in Anselm's terms an instance of the fourth mode of 'something'. This explanation rests on a dubious identification of the nonexistence of the house with the nonexistent house; but, for better or worse, Anselm appears to accept such identifications. For example, in discussing the fourth mode of 'something', he equates the statement "that the absence of the sun causes darkness" with "that the sun through its absence causes the effect".[38] According to this line of interpretation, there is one Anselmian sense, albeit an 'improper' one, in which the nonexistent house can exist. Presumably someone who found this explanation plausible would simply drop the apparently conflicting claim that a nonexistent house cannot exist.[39] The attraction of this claim rests on the belief that one can 'properly' ascribe an incapacity to the future house; so it is difficult to see what would motivate adherence to this general negative claim once it was recognized as 'improper', and the countervailing 'improper' sense in which the future house can exist was proposed. This resolution of the problem of nonexistent possibles will not convince a skeptical reader, and I do not insist on its robust plausibility. But this material bears witness to Anselm's determination to devise a model for modalities consistent with his view that possibility 'properly' means capacity.

The material in the *Fragments* does not similarly supersede Anselm's earlier response to the paradox of attributing necessity, and thereby constraint, to an omnipotent God, nor does it answer the question why we sometimes depict God's rectitude in terms which ordinarily designate weakness. But several features of his later analysis enhance the coherence and plausibility of his treatment of allegations such as 'God cannot lie' as alternate 'improper' designations of divine strengths or perfections. Anselm consistently assumes that the predicate 'is necessarily *F*' has one 'proper' signification which denotes that its subject is constrained to be *F* (or is prevented from being not-*F*). He also assumes, however, that there are 'improper' uses in which such a constraint is not directly ascribed to its subject. If in the paradoxical assertion "God is necessarily just" the predicate is ascribed 'improperly', the statement need not imply that an omnipotent entity is under constraint. If God's putative inability to lie or otherwise abandon justice is a consequence of his direct action of always willing righteousness, the ascription of his inability to err has its basis not in the first but in the third mode of predication. Anselm can affirm that God's necessary justice is a result of his upright will, and not vice-versa, only because he holds that an agent directly causes his own acts of willing. It makes sense to say that God is necessarily just because the effects of his unfettered ability to will righteously in some way resemble constraints; but since this is not a 'proper' ascription, it does not compromise God's omnipotence.

This response to the paradox of divine incapacities rests heavily on Anselm's assumptions about the inalienable autonomy of the will. Although a critical scrutiny of his doctrine of capacity and the will is a project in itself, we can consider other ways in which the *Fragments*' analysis supports Anselm's solution.[40] Most importantly, it diminishes the apparent arbitrariness of Anselm's use of the distinction between 'proper' and 'improper' ascriptions of necessity to God. As we have seen, Anselm provides a detailed semantic setting for this distinction which includes a version of a causal theory of predication, the assumption that each word has exactly one 'proper' meaning, and a general criterion for distinguishing 'proper' from 'improper' predication.

But a skeptical reader might still object to Anselm's resolution of the problem of putative divine incapacities on the grounds that it involves special pleading on God's behalf. Perhaps Anselm assumes too hastily that God's liabilities or constraints are always a function of his strength and perfection. Anselm has two forceful rejoinders to such an objection. The first has its source in *Proslogion* V, where Anselm propounds as a generalized version of a crucial principle in his ontological argument that God is whatever it is better

to be than not to be.[41] By means of a premise to the effect that it is better
for an agent to will righteousness than not to do so, Anselm can conclude
that God always wills righteousness. A second rejoinder rests on the generality
of Anselm's depiction of willing; he holds that 'doing well' consists in willing
to maintain righteousness, and 'doing badly' consists in failing to do so,
whether the agent is divine or human. Likewise, he holds that there can be
no external constraints on either a divine or a human agent's will; hence
'properly' speaking no agent can ever be constrained to do badly. Thus
Anselm's solution is general and not *ad hoc* with respect to the concept of
volition involved.

To summarize, the *Fragments* shows that Anselm's modal conceptions are
consistent with his general semantic theory, and so need not be viewed as
obscure singularities in his philosophy. In Anselm's account of meaning, each
word has a 'proper' signification which is its constant value; but words and
propositions also acquire various extended senses associated with their
'improper' uses. In these cases, we can recognize some resemblance between
the 'improper' ascription and the corresponding 'proper' one; but there is also
some difference which accounts for the 'impropriety' and for the fact that
the 'proper' signification of a term or proposition is not fully deployed. For
reasons discussed in more detail in the next section, Anselm takes the 'proper'
signification of necessity to be 'external constraint', and the 'proper' signification of possibility to be 'inherent capacity'. Since these significations
assign narrowly delimited and literal senses to modal terms which occur in
a broad range of philosophical and theological contexts, it is not surprising
that many uses of modalities standard in theoretical discourse fall into the
'improper' category. Since their meanings cluster loosely around their 'proper'
significations, related by various forms of resemblance and chains of causa-
tion, Anselm's theory has considerable leeway in which to construct explanations of 'improper' uses of modal terms as well as having many such uses to
explain.

While Anselm makes progress towards explaining the status and signification of 'improper' ascriptions of modal and non-modal predicates in his
Fragments, the account remains far from satisfying. One striking gap is the
lack of an adequate discussion of truth-conditions for 'improper' ascriptions.
Apparently Anselm assumes that 'improper' assertions can be analyzed in
terms of a set of 'proper' assertions, whose truth is directly determinable.[42]
But this assumption is most plausible for the analysis of 'improper' ascriptions
of action-verbs whose subjects efficiently cause the outcomes ascribed; it is
relatively easy to evaluate 'improper' ascriptions of agency when the subject

was indirectly an efficient cause of the outcome. But the analysis of 'improper' ascriptions is less lucid in cases where the subject is not an efficient cause or where the relevant predicates are not action-verbs, but are existential or modal. The problems we noted in connection with the initial claim that all predicates can be paraphrased in terms of '*facere*' plus an outcome recur to compound the problem of providing truth-conditions for 'improper' ascriptions. Indeed, Anselm's open-ended account of the possible connections between the referents of 'proper' and 'improper' ascriptions makes it hard to see how an 'improper' ascription could be fully false. Even if Anselm has succeeded in showing how they can be meaningful or true, his semantic theory needs refinement if the bases for 'improper' ascription are so broadly described that any 'improper' assertion has a claim to truth. But these objections do not undermine the coherence of the semantic framework developed in the *Fragments* to support Anselm's modal conceptions and to provide solutions to the modal paradoxes which specially interested him. A theory can be coherent without being correct.[43]

II

How consistent is the treatment of modalities in Anselm's writings? The variety of uses of necessity in works prior to the *Fragments* appears to call into question the received view that Anselm's fundamental ideas remained constant throughout his career.[44] But if the *Fragments'* semantics for modal predication explains or supersedes the problematic features of his earlier use of modal notions, the eventual consistency of Anselm's treatment of modalities can be defended. One could present such a case for consistency by examining the patterns in his uses of modalities apart from their particular contexts rather than by reviewing the unfolding of his conceptions from one treatise to the next. But since the latter approach also illuminates their role in the exposition of Anselm's characteristic theological positions, this section will survey significant instances of modal reflection and reasoning in his major treatises as a step toward assessing the consistency of his conceptions. Because interpretation of the proofs for God's existence in the *Proslogion* and the *Reply* is singularly controversial, discussion of the modal features of these arguments is relegated to Section III.

In his first work, the *Monologion*, Anselm presents a proof for the existence of God which closely resembles Augustine's argument in *De Libero Arbitrio*, Book II. Like Augustine's, Anselm's arguments rest on the tenet of Platonic metaphysics that human mental operations such as judgments of goodness and truth require the existence of an independent ultimate cause or criterion, the Good or the True. While Augustine's reasoning emphasizes Truth, and Anselm's stresses Goodness, they both assert that the ultimate cause in question is to be identified with God. (This difference is only one of focus, since by the doctrine of transcendentals Truth and Goodness are 'convertible'.) Although the conception of necessity does not play a central, explicit role in this treatise, Anselm uses *'necesse est'* or a related expression of necessity nearly once per chapter in drawing conclusions. If he used expressions of necessity only to indicate straightforward entailment, this treatise would yield no special insight into the conception of necessity Anselm subsequently develops, except that it includes the idea of conditional necessity or entailment. But there are hints of what is to come.

In the preface, he remarks that he has undertaken the present project in accordance with his brothers' wishes, not in accordance with his capacity to succeed; surprisingly, the word he uses for 'capacity' is *'possibilitas'* rather than *'potentia'*.[45] In itself, this disclaimer would not bear much interpretive weight, partly because the abbreviations for the interchanged terms are so similar that the manuscript tradition could have been contaminated. But its phrasing makes sense in the light of his later definition of possibility as capacity and lack of external constraint. Two other aspects of Anselm's use of necessity here deserve comment, since we are likely to discount them as rhetorical flourishes. He writes as if necessity were a force which requires something to be the case, saying for example, "inevitable necessity requires that ... " and "necessity coerces ... ".[46] Several times he suggests that the force of necessity can admit of degree, asking for example, "What could be more necessary than ... ", or, in his next work, describing his arguments as 'necessary enough'.[47] While these phrases might strike us as metaphorical, in Anselm's view the situation is the reverse: the 'proper' literal sense of 'necessity' signifies an unavoidable force or constraint, and so its 'improper' use in connection with entailment or logical necessity will be metaphorical.

Since Anselm uses phrases indicative of necessity frequently in the *Monologion,* it seems surprising that he relies on them so sparingly in his next treatise, the *Proslogion.* Indeed, there are no uses of these phrases in the famous ontological argumentation in Chapters II and III; and even though modal reconstructions of these arguments often strike modern critics as more plausible than nonmodal ones, I remain unconvinced that they represent Anselm's views. Although I defer discussion of these doubts to Section III, two other chapters containing material regarding attributions of necessity to God merit immediate attention. In Chapter VII, Anselm considers how to harmonize the notion of divine omnipotence with the idea that God has certain incapacities, e.g. he cannot lie.[48] His initial reply to the problem is to interpret God's inability to be unjust or his necessary justice by saying that nothing else has the power to make God fail to be just. According to this strategy, all God's putative incapacities can be analyzed into incapacities of other agents; for example, "God cannot lie" is based on the assertion that "Nothing else has the power to make God fail to be truthful". Thus the ascription of the incapacity to lie is 'improper' or metaphorical, since it does not directly and literally represent the basis for the ascription. Unless Anselm has a convincing and general reason for counting God's insuperable strength of veracity as more fundamental an attribute than his inability to lie, this strategy seems arbitrary. At this point, Anselm does not argue for the adequacy of his strategy to account for putative divine incapacities, but only shows that there is a way to do so. The only reason he offers for considering an inability a strength is that an inability to do "what is not to one's advantage or what one ought not to do" is actually a strength, the direct result of correctness (*rectitudo*) of the will.[49]

Although Anselm does not explicitly apply this strategy to the task of showing that necessary existence need not conflict with divine omnipotence, it is easy to see that he could do so by reasoning along the following lines. If God necessarily exists, he cannot cease to exist. But such an inability to cease to exist is actually a strength, since existence is an advantage. Thus, the ascription of this inability to God is compatible with his omnipotence because its basis is his insuperable strength with respect to existing. Some scholars must suppose that Anselm embraces such an argument, since the reading of *Proslogion* XXIII followed by standard English translations characterizes God as a necessary being. Where Anselm writes, "*et hoc sit unum necessarium, quod est omne et totum et solum bonum*", Charlesworth translates, "and that this is the one necessary being which is altogether and wholly and solely good".[50] But this passage may not require an interpretation which explicitly espouses the view that God is a necessary being, if what Anselm considers necessary is not God himself, but the description of God as "that which is altogether and wholly and solely good". This alternative reading is possible, since Anselm's Latin has no quotation marks to signal that words are mentioned rather than used.

Several features of the context suggest that the alternative reading may be Anselm's meaning. In the preceding chapters, he has argued that God possesses a variety of attributes; Chapter XXIII effects a transition from these points to the pastoral remarks in Chapters XXIV and XXV which bring the treatise to its close. By means of the phrase under discussion, Anselm in effect terminates the exercise of articulating various descriptions of God's perfections, emphasizing the priority of divine goodness as he had in the *Monologion*. The subsequent and final two chapters maintain that a recognition of and response to this goodness is obligatory and sufficient for his readers' salvation, commanding them to: "Lift up your whole understanding and think as much as you can on how and how great that good is" and to "Desire the simple good which contains all goodness, and that is enough".[51]

A different reason for doubting that this phrase commits Anselm to the view that God is a necessary being arises from recognizing that it is a quotation from Luke 10:42.[52] The phrase "Moreover, one thing is necessary" is part of Jesus' rebuke of Martha for being concerned about many things, while her sister Mary is concerned about only one thing, his teaching. The assertion that only his teaching is necessary (ἑνὸς δὲ ἐστι χρεία) means that it is obligatory for salvation.[53] Since the subsequent chapters contain no fewer than twelve additional Biblical quotations, it is likely that Anselm intended this phrase as a quotation also. Thus it is possible to hold that throughout the *Proslogion* Anselm consistently refrains from characterizing God as a necessary being, even though he introduces a strategy in Chapter VII which, if properly developed, might explain and justify doing so. Section III will discuss the grounds for Anselm's reluctance to endorse necessary existence as a divine perfection.

Anselm unsuccessfully confronts the issue of nonexistent possibles in his dialogue *De Casu Diaboli*, in which a student asks how it was possible for the world to exist, prior to its creation.[54] The student is puzzled because he believes that it was possible, but he cannot locate the relevant capacity in the then future world. Anselm's contradictory answer that before creation the world both could and could not exist receives an appropriately cool response from the student. Section I has suggested that in the *Fragments* Anselm explains the student's intuition by showing that a capacity to exist can be ascribed in an 'improper' sense to a nonexistent possible since its nonexistence is a necessary condition for its beginning to be. This explanation supersedes the earlier flatly contradictory response, and should exonerate Anselm's thought from charges of inconsistency or confusion based on his earlier inadequate reply.

Anselm's dialogue on the freedom of the will, *De Libertate Arbitrii*, defends the Christian doctrine of free will be contrasting necessity and free choice. Anselm thinks it is possible for an agent *A* to perform an action *d* just in case *A* has the freedom to choose to *d*.[55] *A* has the freedom to *d* if and only if (1) there are no external constraints against A's doing d, and (2) A has a capacity to d.[56] Thus, for an agent to have a given possibility requires that he have a corresponding capacity and not be externally constrained, but does not require that the capacity in fact be actualized. So a man with the strength to subdue a bull has the strength to subdue a ram, even when he tries but fails to do so, and a normal person has the capacity to see a mountain even when no mountain is present.[57]

But the application of this definition of freedom to the problem of free will rests on an example of a different complexion. By analogy with his ram-holding man, Anselm could say that a person who resisted a stronger temptation could resist a weaker one, even if he in fact fails to do so. But for his defense of free will, Anselm needs to make the broader claim that generally any person has the capacity to resist temptation, even someone who has never resisted a stronger temptation, or perhaps any temptation at all. Anselm justifies this broader claim by means of an analysis of the nature of the will and willing. He defines resisting temptation as maintaining *rectitudo*, the correct state of the will.[58] Since states of the will are purely internal, they are subject to no external constraints, and we always have the innate capacity to will what we want to will.[59] So the will is free, and it is always possible for agents to maintain *rectitudo*. Thus Anselm's defense of free will rests on his assumption of the inalienable autonomy of the will and his definition of freedom, and not on the ram-and-bull analogy.

Although a full discussion of the subtleties and liabilities of this defense of free will is beyond our present purview, we can consider what this argument shows about Anselm's modal conceptions. To anyone accustomed to alethic interpretations of possibility and necessity, the associations of possibility and capacity, and of necessity and constraint, may seem odd.[60] But if the 'proper' significations derived from the modal terms' roots imply capacity and constraint, Anselm's semantic theory requires these associations. This semantic doctrine may not be as straightforward in practice as it is in theory, though, since medieval opinions about etymologies can be elusive or fanciful. The roots of '*possibilitas*' clearly support Anselm's assumptions; it is the abstract noun corresponding to the verb '*posse*' or 'can' whose root is most obvious in the participate '*potens*', which yields the nouns '*potentia*' and '*potestas*' which signify power or capacity. The etymology of '*necessitas*' provides less explicit but still substantial support for Anselm's assumption that it 'properly' signifies constraint or prevention. It is curious to note that the evolution of 'ἀνάγκη', which first meant force or constraint, later fate, and finally mental compulsion, supports Anselm's story perfectly.[61] Although '*necessitas*' translates '*ἀνάγκη*', its development is more complicated. The root '*ne*' plus some lost substantive form of '*cedo*' may suggest, but fails to specify, a literal force or source of constraint.[62] Ancient and early medieval meanings cluster around the idea of inevitability and of something, sometimes a force of nature, which cannot be avoided or turned back. Although the etymological evidence available today suggests a more complex development, Anselm shows no hesitation in associating 'necessity' in its 'proper' sense with an irresistable force; for example, in arguing in *De Libertate Arbitrii* that Satan sinned freely, he asserts: "And therefore he is justly blamed, because since he had freedom of his own will, he sinned not by some compelling force — by some necessity — but of his own accord".[63]

Anselm's conception of necessity occupies a central position in his most extensive work in rational theology, *Cur Deus Homo*, which proposes 'necessary reasons' for the redemption of mankind through the Incarnation. Understanding his conception of necessity is important not only for interpreting the work's aim, but also for appreciating his reservations about its success, since Anselm admits that the argument depends on assumptions about possibility, necessity, capacity, and the will which require a justification he has yet to provide.[64] It is not hard to find what might worry Anselm in the two main discussions of necessity in this treatise, the explanation of the nature and force of 'necessary reasons' in Book I, Chapter X, and the account in Book II, Chapter XVII of ascription of necessity to an omnipotent God.

In Chapter X of Book I, Anselm takes up an objection which his student and interlocutor Boso had raised in Chapter IV:

Therefore when we lay these appropriate reasons which you mention before the infidels, they suppose we are so to speak painting on a cloud, since they consider what we believe not a thing accomplished, but a picture. Therefore first the rational solidity of the truth must be shown, i.e. the necessity which proves that God ought to have or could have been abased to this truth which we proclaim.[65]

Anselm responds to this challenge only in Chapter X after Boso reiterates his hope for a proof that the means he believes God chose for the redemption might be shown 'reasonable and necessary'. Surprisingly, Boso accepts without demur the reply that:

Since in this inquiry you take on the role of those who are willing to believe nothing except what has been shown by reason, I want to make an agreement with you: inasmuch as in relation to God not even the smallest inappropriate thing should be accepted by us, also not even the smallest reason should be rejected, if a more important one does not oppose it. For just as in God however small the inappropriate thing, an impossibility follows, so however small a reason, if it is not overridden by a greater, a necessity should follow.[66]

This is the principle on which Anselm's argumentation will turn: that we must attribute only appropriate properties and actions to God, and we must attribute to him every appropriate property, unless an overriding reason opposes it. Why does Boso concur in this sweeping principle when Anselm has just reminded him of his special role as representative of the infidels? The principle and Boso's response must be understood in the light of the principle of divine perfection — that God is anything it is better to be than not to be — posited in *Proslogion* V as a general upshot of Anselm's ontological arguments.[67] If Boso assumes that this principle has been established by reason in the ontological arguments, it makes sense for him to accept its more elaborate restatement in *Cur Deus Homo*, even though he represents those who do not accept items of Christian doctrine on faith.

But what does Anselm mean by saying that whatever is appropriate to attribute to God has the force of necessity? In the excellent introduction of his translation of *Cur Deus Homo* into French, Roques characterizes Anselm's idea as the logical necessity of the inferences to be drawn from the small number of presuppositions which Anselm shares with his imaginary interlocutors, including Jews and Muslims as well as inquisitive Christians. In accordance with this line of explanation, Roques draws a parallel between what he calls 'Anselm's axiomatic method' and axiomatic methods in modern logic.[68] While his points are well-taken, two related points deserve emphasis in conjunction with this suggestion. Roques supposes that Anselm's argument begins from a small number of axioms; but in my judgment, the primary importance of the principle of divine perfection, which establishes the continuity between the *Proslogion* and *Cur Deus Homo*, ought to be recognized. Secondly, as Roques realizes, his point about 'Anselm's axiomatic method' does not fully explain or exhaust the senses in which Anselm considers the Incarnation and its reasons to be necessary, since as a Christian Anselm believes the Incarnation to have the same necessity which all past events have.

Even if we add these qualifications, it is still not satisfactory to identify Anselm's 'necessary reasons' with the modern notion of logical provability without considering an ambiguity in Boso's original challenge, and an echoing ambiguity in Anselm's response. The original request, to show the necessity by which God ought to have *or* could have submitted to the particular means of redemption which Christians accept as fact, has two components.[69] Anselm should either show that the Incarnation was necessary for salvation or show that at any rate it was not an unreasonable and inappropriate strategy. Anselm's principle that whatever is appropriate ought to be ascribed to God with the force of necessity (unless there are overriding considerations) now comes into play. In effect, it enables Anselm to count a response to the second component of Boso's request as a response to the first, presumably more onerous part. Thus any reason which shows the appropriateness of the Incarnation will be deemed to have the force of necessity, so long as there are no stronger countervailing considerations.[70]

But the exercise of this approach is not entirely free from ambiguity. Although Anselm makes numerous arguments for the appropriateness of the Incarnation, he says it will suffice if only one of them is "invigorated by ineluctable truth".[71] Even if this concession is rhetorical, he would be right to admit that the proposed 'necessary reasons' might be rebuttable. By his own agreement with Boso, he can only count arguments as 'necessary reasons' provided there are no overriding considerations; but he fails to make an exhaustive or even serious search for such considerations. So long as this task is left undone, Anselm's 'necessary reasons' can be asserted only conditionally. Thus if the necessity Anselm imputes to them is intended to indicate logical provability, then consistency requires him to add the 'no overriding considerations' proviso to his conclusions, or else to trivialize his argument by arbitrarily assuming as a premise that there are no such considerations. Since Anselm describes this argument as providing 'necessary reasons',[72] perhaps he invokes an 'improper' sense of 'necessary' which can fall short of ineluctable cogency, as he sometimes does in his first two works.[73] For Anselm's argument to be successful, his premises must be 'necessary' in this sense, i.e. be regarded as plausible by his readers, and the conclusion must be 'necessary' in the sense of being validly entailed by the premises. Thus one need not conclude from the ambiguity suggested by the double function of 'necessary reasons' that Anselm was seriously confused. It makes sense for Anselm to respond to the two components of Boso's request on two levels; he hopes to provide the framework for an unequivocal deduction of the necessity of the Incarnation, and he tries to provide persuasive reasons which might in any case serve a useful apologetic purpose. But we can see nevertheless why Anselm might have been dissatisfied with this aspect of his treatment of necessity; in my interpretation, his argument thus far involves two senses of 'necessity' − characterizing the entailment of a conclusion and the persuasiveness of a premise − which are 'improper' according to his own semantics. Only in the *Fragments* does Anselm begin to provide a general account of 'improper' uses of language.

A second major discussion of necessity occurs in response to Boso's objection that Anselm's arguments impute necessity, and thereby constraint, to God. His response appears paradoxical, since he concedes that all necessity involves constraint (i.e. compulsion or prevention), but then introduces a distinction between necessity which is constraining and that which is not.[74] But a close reading of the text can mitigate this initial impression. Chapters XVII and XVIII of Book II reply to the concern that Anselm's arguments imply that Christ, the God-man, died of necessity rather than freely, contrary to the idea of divine omnipotence and to the belief that Christ's death freely merited human redemption. First Boso objects that since redemption through Christ's death was willed as part of God's plan, it must have been necessitated by God's will.[75] In reply, Anselm invokes his doctrine of the will: no agent's will is subject to external constraints, so Christ's willingness to die cannot have been necessitated.[76] Next Anselm invokes the doctrine of the Trinity to show that in any case Christ's immutable will and God's are identical, so Christ's willingness to die could not have been externally constrained by the divine will.[77] Rather than questioning these points, Boso revises his objection to argue that Christ's death was necessitated not by God's will but by the prior truth of the proposition that he was to die.[78] Anselm's response contains a theological argument explaining why necessity cannot be 'properly' attributed to God, and a more general argument maintaining that the prior truth-values of propositions about events and choices do not constrain what happens.

The theological argument follows a by now familiar strategy, with rather inconclusive results. First Anselm argues that necessity cannot be ascribed to God 'properly' since 'necessity' signifies constraint, which cannot be ascribed 'properly' to God.[79] What is interesting here is that Anselm recognizes the insufficiency of the argument to dispel Boso's doubt, and tries to explain what 'improper' ascriptions of necessity pertinent to his concern might mean. He illustrates some possible bases for 'improper' ascriptions, but I cannot see that his examples resolve the issue. He takes up the question whether God can change the past, for example, and says that he cannot. But this is only an 'improper' ascription of constraint to God, he says, since the basis of this divine incapacity is God's free and immutable choice that the truth-value of propositions about the past remain constant.[80] While this example could show a contemporary reader that he need not accept Peter Damian's suggestion that the past is subject to revision, its assumption about what God has immutably chosen needs further support.[81]

The next argument, designed to convince Boso that the prior truth-value of a proposition does not constrain an agent, is more general and more carefully drawn. At its heart is a distinction between what Anselm calls 'preceding' and 'subsequent' necessity. Preceding necessity is not just a sufficient condition, but also a genuine efficient cause of what is necessitated, while subsequent necessity is not in itself an operative constraining cause of what is necessitated. Subsequent necessity applies to everything: "Whatever has been necessarily has been. Whatever is, necessarily is . . . . Whatever is to be, necessarily will be."[82] But in no case is it genuinely constraining, as Anselm insists in several texts. Anselm begins his response by subsuming Boso's objection under the rubric of subsequent necessity: "If it is said that it was necessary for him to die . . . because faith or the prophecy which preceded it was true, this is not different from your saying that it necessarily was as it would be, because it will have been so."[83] Immediately Anselm denies that this is genuine necessity by calling it inoperative.[84] In the ensuing discussion he uses 'necessity' in its subsequent sense without always reiterating that it is inoperative necessity he has in mind. But the end of his argument again indicates that he intends to exclude subsequent necessity from counting as genuine necessity: " . . . if you wish to know the real necessity of all the things which he [Christ] did and suffered, know that they all were of necessity because he himself willed them."[85] Acceding to this conclusion, Boso says, "You have satisfied me that it cannot be proven that he was subjected to death by any necessity."[86] Thus they agree that the death was genuinely necessitated by Christ's free choice; but because the will is autonomous, he subjected himself to death, and was not subjected to it by any external constraint.[87] In addition, because it was true that Christ would die, his death was subsequently necessary. This passage does not provide a full explanation or defense of Anselm's conception of subsequent necessity; perhaps he thinks he has already established that it cannot count as a constraint by maintaining in De Veritate that the truth of thoughts or propositions cannot be the cause of any truth.[88] Regardless of the plausibility of this claim, Anselm's strategy is clear; he wants to hold that 'necessity' in its 'proper' sense signifies constraint, but that 'improper' ascriptions of necessity, including subsequent necessity, do not impute constraint to their subjects. Anselm might well be dissatisfied with this strategy's progress thus far, since it stands in need of a clearer account of subsequent necessity and a fuller account of the nature of 'improper' ascription. We have seen in Section I how the Fragments elucidates Anselm's general notion of 'improper' ascription, but we should consider in particular the problem of 'improper' ascription of subsequent necessity.

What does Anselm mean by subsequent necessity? A promising conjecture suggested by D. P. Henry equates the distinction between preceding and subsequent necessity with the Boethian distinction between simple and conditional necessity, and with the modern distinction between physical and logical necessity.[89] In mooting these analogies, Henry introduces enough qualifications to render his position inconvenient to criticize; so it will be simpler to consider the following relatively bald version instead:

(1)   Anselm's distinction between preceding and subsequent necessity is equivalent to Boethius' distinction between simple and conditional necessity; and

(2)   subsequent necessity is equivalent to the modern notion of logical necessity, since it amounts to the logical thesis "for all p, if p then p".

While each of these claims is provocative and helpful, each requires more explicit qualification than Henry provides. I agree with him that Anselm's modal conceptions profit from acquaintance with Boethius' commentaries on *De Interpretatione* and that the distinctions under discussion are similar in their purpose, to block determinism. But the authors' characterization of their distinctions differ significantly.

In the first version of his commentary, Boethius contrasts simple necessity with temporal necessity.[90] Whatever else he might hold, Boethius believes that a proposition has simple necessity just in case it is true universally, i.e. at all moments of time, and a proposition has temporal necessity just in case it is true when its specified temporal index is satisfied. Thus for Boethius, the proposition "What is, necessarily is, when it is" imputes only temporal necessity to a true temporally definite proposition at the exact time specified in its temporal index.[91] In his second commentary, Boethius draws a slightly more general and complex distinction between simple and conditional necessity.[92] Here he addresses not only the problem that prior truth-values of propositions about future contingencies appear to imply determinism, but also the compounded problem that an omniscient God will know these truths. It seems that events must occur not only because it is true that they will occur, but also because it is infallibly known that they will occur. According to Boethius, true propositions about future contingencies have conditional necessity, either in virtue of God's knowledge of their truth or in virtue of their temporal necessity. But neither temporal nor conditional necessity imposes constraint on human choices, unlike simple necessity. God's knowledge does not impinge on human freedom because, since he is atemporal, it is atemporal, and so is not strictly speaking foreknowledge.[93]

While Anselm's distinction between preceding and subsequent necessity is also part of a strategy to deny determinism, it differs from Boethius' distinctions in several respects. Unlike Boethius and Aristotle, Anselm has no trouble in maintaining, for example, that Socrates' sitting at t_1 is compatible with his possibility of standing at that moment. Since Anselm defines possibility in terms of capacity and lack of external constraint and recognizes that not all genuine capacities are actualized at a given moment, for him the subsequent necessity of Socrates' sitting at t_1 is clearly compatible with the genuine possibility at t_1 of his standing then.[94] (The proviso that subsequent necessity is not genuine enables Anselm to square his acceptance of unactualized possibilities with his assumption that 'necessarily' is equivalent to 'not possibly not'.) But philosophers such as Aristotle and Boethius who conceive of necessity primarily in terms of the truth of a proposition (or the existence of an entity) at all times encounter more difficulty in explaining the status at a given time of unactualized possibilities, since if the temporally definite proposition "Socrates is sitting at t_1" is true at t_1, his putative possibility of standing can be analyzed only by reference to his actualized possibility of standing at other times.[95] *Ceteris paribus*, this difference should weigh in favor of Anselm's account.

Secondly, Anselm thinks that the Boethian solution to the problem of determinism apparently implied by divine omniscience is inadequate; if God's knowledge is a problem, its objects seem to be necessitated despite its atemporal character.[96] In his late treatise on foreknowledge and predestination, grace and free will, *De Concordia Praescientiae et Praedestinationis et Gratiae Dei cum Libero Arbitrio,* he considers an addendum to Boethius' view. Even if God is atemporal, truths are not; so if God knows all truths, his knowledge must be temporally affected in ways Boethius' account does not appreciate. If it is true that Socrates is sitting at t_1, what God knows prior to t_1 is that Socrates will sit then, and what he knows afterwards is that he did sit then. Since the only moment when God knows the truth that Socrates is sitting at t_1 is t_1 itself, his knowledge is simultaneous with the act of sitting, and this knowledge cannot be a prior cause of it.[97]

Finally, insofar as the material in the *Fragments* clarifies the 'impropriety' of ascriptions of subsequent necessity, Anselm's claim that this sort of necessity does not imply constraint has a more persuasive theoretical basis than Boethius' counterpart claims for temporal and conditional necessity have. Unfortunately, it is not clear how to reconstruct a detailed characterization of their 'impropriety'. Of course Anselms thinks that if 'Socrates is sitting at t_1" is true, then Socrates is sitting at t_1; but he thinks that the protasis' truth subsequently, not genuinely necessitates Socrates' sitting. Perhaps he thinks that since the truth of a proposition is not an entity existing outside the mind, it cannot be an external efficient cause of anything.

Hence an ascription of subsequent necessity cannot belong to the first mode of predication, but must belong to one of the 'improper' modes. Presumably Anselm thinks that the constant conjunction of truth-values we find in cases of subsequent necessity is directly or indirectly a result of God's will or nature; since the constancy of these conjunctions resembles natural constraint, we use 'necessity' in an 'improper' extended sense to describe them. Because of the speculative nature of this reconstruction, I conclude only that once again Anselm's systematic intentions and strategy are clearer than their development.

The conjecture's second thesis, which assimilates Anselm's distinction between preceding and subsequent necessity to a modern distinction between physical and logical necessity, also requires qualification. Since Anselm connects necessity and constraint, it sounds plausible to link genuine, preceding necessity with physical necessity and to link subsequent necessity with logical necessity. But we cannot evaluate this thesis until its advocate specifies which version of 'the' modern distinction between physical and logical possibility it assumes.[98] Henry's version of the conjecture assumes that in the notion of subsequent necessity Anselm asserts the logical thesis "for all p, if p then p", a thesis Henry describes as an empty tautology which tells us nothing about how things are.[99] There are, however, two overt discrepancies between Anselm's distinctions and most modern distinctions. Although Anselm accepts the thesis "if p, then p", he does not consider the occurrence of subsequent necessity empty or trivial; God is responsible for the stability and consistency of a proposition's truth-values in Anselm's view, not the truth of any propositions or ideas. So even the assertion of subsequent necessity involves a metaphysical as well as a logical point. Another difference is that Anselm maintains that subsequent necessity is not genuine, but only an imitation of the real thing. Modern distinctions between physical and logical necessity typically do not relativize the latter by saying that it is only a metaphorical echo of the former. As we have seen, Anselm's distinction between preceding and subsequent necessity can to some extent be explicated by reference to the semantic and metaphysical views which provide its setting; but these broader Anselmian views are so idiosyncratic that analogies to similar distinctions in other philosophers have only limited applicability.

How consistent is Anselm's treatment of modalities in the passages we have considered? Although the variety of his uses of modalities can create an impression of inconsistency, Anselm consistently maintains his central intuitions that:

(1)   'necessity' 'properly' signifies a causally efficient external
        constraint;
(2)   'possibility' 'properly' signifies a capacity and the lack of external
        constraint;
(3)   all other uses of 'necessity' and 'possibility' are 'improper';
(4)   in 'improper' propositions the literal signification of a modal term
        is not fully deployed.

But Anselm's consistent respect for these central intuitions may not add up
to what we would recognize as a consistent treatment of modalities, since (4)
allows so much latitude in the 'improper' signification of modal terms.
Because the narrowly prescribed 'proper' uses of necessity and possibility
are literal, many theoretical uses of modal terms are 'improper'. So to assess
the degree of consistency in Anselm's use of modalities, we must ask whether
his 'improper' uses of necessity and possibility exhibit any consistent pattern.

How many types of 'improper' ascription of modal terms does Anselm
actually introduce in the passages we have surveyed? Admitting that an
exhaustive study of Anselm's writings might yield further senses, and that
finer distinctions can always be drawn, I find one main basis for 'improper'
ascription of possibility, and two main bases for 'improper' ascription of
necessity in the passages we have discussed. Ascriptions of possible existence
to future entities, and of possibilities which are better described as liabilities,
as in "Hector can be overcome", rest on the same basis. In each case the
subject is, in Anselm's view, a cause of what the predicate ascribes only by
serving as a 'nonefficient' cause or logically necessary condition for that
ascription; the future house's nonexistence is necessary for its coming to be,
and Hector is a necessary condition for *his* being vanquished. The 'improper'
uses of 'necessity' in our texts fall into two general groups.[100] Frequently a
proposition ascribes necessity without designating the appropriate efficient
cause. Where moral necessities are ascribed, as in ascriptions of the predicates
'is necessarily just' or 'cannot lie' to God, they simply identify consequences
of the unspecified appropriate cause, in this case, God's correctness of will.
Similarly, in cases of entailment and subsequent necessity, we 'improperly'
say that propositions which in modern terms constitute or jointly constitute
logically sufficient conditions necessitate their consequents. In Anselmian
metaphysics, however, God or the Supreme Truth, not the truth of the premises, is the consequents' genuinely necessitating cause. We can distinguish
another basis for Anselm's 'improper' use of 'necessity' and 'necessary' in his
characterization of reasoning which is forceful but not absolutely ineluctable

as 'necessary' or 'necessary enough'. Thus, at least rhetorically, he describes some of his arguments as 'necessary' which he hopes are sufficient for persuasion of at least some readers; unlike genuine necessity, necessity in this sense admits of degree. Doubtless there are finer strands in the fabric of Anselm's 'improper' uses of modalities, but these uses comprise the main parts of a rather consistent and simple pattern.

Can we judge with any certainty how intentionally or systematically Anselm maintained this degree of consistency in his use of modal notions? Perhaps not; but surely he must have appreciated both the utility and fragility of his account of modality. On the one hand, his defense of free will rests on the narrow 'proper' sense of possibility; on the other, the project of finding 'necessary reasons' for the Incarnation exploits the latitude and ambiguity in the 'improper' uses of necessity. Anselm's efforts in the *Fragments* to provide a systematic account of 'improper' ascription in part represent an attempt to merit this utility and to overcome the fragility of his earlier use of an inadequately justified distinction between 'proper' and 'improper' assertions. Without exaggerating the success of Anselm's constructive analysis of 'improper' ascription of modal predicates, we can see that dismissing his treatment of modalities as inconsistent, or assimilating it to Boethian or modern accounts, involves overlooking much Anselmian ingenuity.

III

Does our study of his modal conceptions yield insights for the inexhaustible project of interpreting Anselm's arguments for the existence of God? Although a detailed treatment of the arguments in the *Proslogion* and the rejoinders to Gaunilo's *Reply on Behalf of the Fool* far exceeds the scope of this section, it is possible to identify and moot a few salient and perhaps provocative implications of our interpretation. In commenting on his ontological argument, many philosophers have explicitly or implicitly accused Anselm of 'modal oversights'. Various authors present and assess modal versions of the ontological argument moving from Anselm's initial premise which defines God as "something than which nothing greater can be conceived of" *via* some supplied modal premises to the conclusion that God necessarily exists.[101] While these arguments are typically proposed as plausible reconstructions of the best line of Anselmian reasoning, they raise the question whether Anselm intended, or should have intended, to argue for God's necessary existence. As early as the thirteenth century, Duns Scotus made the point, later pressed by Leibniz, that Anselm's argument requires a premise asserting the possibility of God's existing.[102] Recently, Robert M. Adams has observed that Anselm's reply to Gaunilo contains an argument for God's necessary existence which is more cogent than the *Proslogion*'s arguments, provided we supply a version of the missing possibility-premise.[103] Assuming that these complaints of 'modal oversights' have some plausibility, how can we explain Anselm's alleged failure to exploit the unrealized potential in his arguments?

The difference between Anselm's semantics for modalities and modern conceptions undermines the supposition that any of our modal reconstructions directly represents his intentions. For example, in *Proslogion* III Anselm argues that it is impossible to conceive of God as not existing.[104] If one makes the Humean assumption that inconceivability and impossibility are equivalent, this conclusion entails that God's existence is necessary.[105] This gloss has enabled some readers to think that Anselm proves God's necessary existence, although he fails to mention 'necessity' explicitly in Chapter II or III.[106] Despite its independent interest, this reading cannot serve as an interpretation of Anselm's thinking without evidence that he too equates inconceivability and impossibility. To my knowledge, such evidence cannot be found.

The thesis that necessary existence should count as one of God's perfections is clearly problematic within Anselm's early semantic theory, and remains so, though to a lesser degree, in the *Fragments'* account. In its 'proper' sense the predicate 'exists necessarily' would attribute constraint to God, contrary to the doctrine of divine omnipotence. Although Anselm could maintain that God exists necessarily using one of the 'improper' senses of the predicate, this would require a careful explication. In fact, Anselm never tries to explain in detail which 'improper' sense this would involve, how it would relate to necessity in its 'proper' sense, or why anyone would want to use an expression which describes God's existence in the 'highest degree' so inappropriately. Even the more fully articulated account of 'improper' predication in the *Fragments* fails to take up these questions. Even if they could be resolved, the use of a predicate whose 'proper' ascription to God is heterodox would invite misunderstanding. Hence Anselm's semantic theory dictates avoiding 'proper' ascription of necessary existence to God, and prudence would direct avoiding its 'improper' ascription, absent a satisfactory account of its meaning.

Fortunately, Anselm has no need to ascribe to God the 'improper' predicate 'exists necessarily', since all divine perfections can be derived from the general principle in *Proslogion* V that God is whatever it is better to be than not to be. If it is better for God to exist at all moments of time, eternally, or in all possible worlds, or to be self-caused and self-sustaining, or a suitable object of worship, by the principle of divine perfection these properties are his. If an ascription of necessary existence reduces to one or more perfections such as these, then the problematic predicate 'exists necessarily' is dispensable for Anselm. This interpretation allows us to discount a paradoxical claim recently suggested by Jonathan Barnes that there can be no Anselmian version of a modal ontological argument because Anselm cannot derive "God exists" from "God necessarily exists".[107] Barnes thinks that by analogy to the treatment of God's necessary justice in *Proslogion* VII, Anselm must hold that (1) "God necessarily exists" means (2) "Nothing has the power to bring it about that God fails to exist". But since (2) does not entail (3) "God exists", then (1) must not either. Surely Barnes is right in insisting that (2) does not entail (3); but it is mistaken to take (2) as Anselm's definitive interpretation of (1). In my view, Chapter VII suggests that the explanation Anselm would give for accepting either (1) or (2) is that God has the advantage of existence in the highest degree. If God has this advantage, then *a fortiori* he exists; so (1) is an 'improper' ascription of necessity, since God's unavoidable existence is an effect of his perfection in existing. The inability of other agents posited in (2) is likewise an effect of this same perfection, and not a full explication of (1). By comparison with his later accounts, we can see that Anselm does not provide a full account of the meaning of any 'improper' ascription in *Proslogion* VII, so it is premature to base a paradoxical claim on this text. Furthermore, Anselm could infer that God exists from the reason he would most likely give for the truth of (1) and (2). Surely Anselm realized that many of his predecessors and contemporaries considered God a necessary being. Occasionally, e.g. in *Proslogion* XXIII and in the first argument in his reply to Gaunilo, he fails to insist unequivocally on his semantic scruples against characterizing God's existence as necessary. But both these passages are comparatively rhetorical interludes in Anselm's writings; the first passage is based on a Scriptural quotation, and the second is frankly described as an *ad hominem* rejoinder. So although Anselm has a way to explain the compatibility of divine perfection and necessary existence, and has precedent for counting necessary existence as a perfection, he has good reasons to prefer alternate descriptions of God's perfection in existing, and respects these reasons.

Does Anselm have an equally reasonable response to the allegation that his arguments ought to include an explicit assertion of the possibility that God exists? Traditionally, readers have recognized that the logic of the ontological argument in *Proslogion* II requires the missing possibility-premise; perhaps some felt that Anselm's own faith or his theistic environment partially explained the omission. Adams' realization that a certain version of this missing premise together with material from the first chapter of the reply constitutes a cogent argument focuses fresh attention on Anselm's omission. In view of an interesting twist in the version of the possibility-premise Adams' reconstruction supplies, and of its compact clarity, I have chosen to use this version of a modal reconstruction as a backdrop for explaining the semantic constraints on Anselm's ability or willingness to provide this missing link.

Adams begins his examination of this argument by extracting these three theses from chapter one of the reply:[108]

(1)   "No one ... doubts that if it [that than which a greater cannot be thought] did exist, its nonexistence, either in actuality or in the understanding, would be impossible. For otherwise it would not be that than which a greater cannot be thought."

(2)   "But as to whatever can be thought and does not exist – if it did exist, its nonexistence, either in actuality or in the understanding, would be possible."

(3)   "Therefore, if that than which a greater cannot be thought can even be thought, it cannot be nonexistent."

According to Adams' reconstruction of this argument in modern terms, the first premise claims that necessarily, if God exists, he exists necessarily, i.e. he is a logically necessary being.[109] The proof then turns on the principle introduced in premise (2), whose generalization is a statement of Brouwer's Axiom, which holds that for every existential proposition p

(1) $p \supset NMp$.

What Anselm asserts is that where p is an affirmative existential pro-position,

(b) $-p \supset NM\text{-}p$, or equivalently,

(c) $-p \supset N\text{-}Np$.

In conjunction with a version of the premise that it is possible for God to exist, Brouwer's Axiom, even in Anselm's less general version, yields the conclusion that he does exist. If Anselm explicitly assumes what he appears to take for granted, that God's existence is possible, then he could endorse Adams' Anselmian argument for g, "God exists", and for Ng, "God exists necessarily":

(1)	$g \supset Ng$	premise (1) above.
(2)	$-N\text{-}Ng$	strong version of a possibility premise.
(3)	$-g \supset N\text{-}Ng$	premise (2) above and substitution in (c).
(4)	Therefore $-\text{-}g$	(2), (3), *modus tollens*.
(5)	Therefore g	(3), double negation.
(6)	Therefore Ng	(1), (5), *modus ponens*.

The insight that Anselm could make this simple and forceful argument if he assumes premise (2) raises a number of interesting issues. Adams points out that the cogency of this reconstruction depends not only on accepting a system of modal logic which includes Brouwer's Axiom, but also on accepting certain semantic rules to define necessity.[110] Thus the argument is not sound if one takes 'Np' to mean only that p is logically provable, but does hold if one takes it to mean that p is true in all possible worlds, or by virtue of our rules of language. But our investigation of Anselm's modal semantics indicates that these modern conceptions simply do not correspond to his intuitions. Were he alive today, Anselm might insist that "God exists" is true in all possible worlds, but I find no evidence that he considered this as a possible interpretation of "God exists necessarily". He recognizes existence without spatio-temporal limitation as a divine perfection, saying, "You [God] are nevertheless not in place or time, but all things are in you".[111] But the view he espouses is not that God exists in all things, but that they exist in him! Nor does Anselm define necessity simply as what is true in virtue of the rules of language. At the heart of his ontological argument rests the belief that, upon reflection, the definition of God as "that than which nothing greater can be conceived of" yields a substantive existential claim. In part because of this unique argument, and in part because he rejects the view that the truth of ideas or propositions can cause truths, Anselm makes no firm distinction between what is true *simpliciter* and what is true by virtue of the rules of language.

Is there any way Anselm could embrace the elegant argument Adams reconstructs, despite the discrepancies between his modal conceptions and ours? His conception of possibility creates two stumbling-blocks to positing Adams' crucial second premise, one which affects only the special formulation required for Adams' argument, and one which affects any version of a possibility-premise. Both difficulties stem from the view that in its 'proper' sense 'possibility' signifies a capacity and lack of external constraint, together with the assumption that a philosophical theologian should either use predicates 'properly' or be prepared to provide specific explanations of the bases for their 'improper' ascription. The first difficulty is that Anselm's semantic theory offers no natural mechanism or strategy for analyzing the iterated modal operators required in premises (2) and (3). If possibilities must 'properly' be literal capacities residing in agents, and necessities must 'properly' be literal constraints on agents, Anselm's theory cannot accommodate such iterated modalities without risk of infinite regress. Anselm needs to take this risk seriously, since his defense of free will depends on there not being a regress from a given capacity to the capacity to exercise it; he asserts only that we can maintain correctness of will, not that we can in fact always exercise this capacity.[112] Perhaps one could extend his theory to provide an interpretation of 'improper' ascriptions of iterated modal predicates, and not incur the risk of infinite regress, but I see no solid evidence for supposing that Anselm saw a way to do so.[113] So even if he had recognized the power of the argument Adams discovered, the dubious status of iterated modalities within his semantic theory should have given Anselm pause.

But his semantic theory also creates a more general problem for propounding the possibility of God's existing. As we have seen, a fully 'proper' attribution of possibility signifies that an actual subject has an inherent capacity. Since this presupposes that the subject already exists, Anselm could not assert the premise "God possibly exists' in its 'proper' sense without assuming his conclusion that God actually exists. His persistent efforts in subsequent writings to explain 'improper' ascriptions of the predicate 'can exist' testify to his interest in finding an interpretation that could, *inter alia*, clarify the status of nonexistent possibles and repair the missing link in his ontological argument. Although he makes considerable progress in understanding 'improper' predication, his last and best account of 'improper' ascription of 'can exist' in the *Fragments'* solution to the paradox of the possibility of the future house does not elucidate the 'improper' premise "God possibly exists". According to the interpretation developed in Section I, Anselm's solution first converts the problematic proposition "A house which does not yet exist can exist" into the more tractable assertion "A house which does not yet exist can come into existence". Then, with the help of assumptions discussed and criticized in Section I, Anselm can explain that the future house causally contributes to its coming into existence because its present nonexistence is a necessary condition for its beginning to be. But if Anselm's God exists, he exists without a beginning, and so we cannot use this solution to analyze the assertion 'God possibly exists'.

Alternatively, Anselm could stress that this premise uses its subject-term 'improperly', thereby protecting the argument from the charge of circularity.

Thus, in asserting the possibility-premise one would assume only that 'God' acts as 'something' in the second mode, referring to our concept of God. But I doubt that this purely conceptual version of the premise would be strong enough to satisfy Anselm's critics. More probably, Anselm would assume that the possibility-premise applied to God either 'properly' or 'improperly', in the way he uses 'God' and 'something' in the initial premise that God is "something (*aliquid*) than which nothing greater can be conceived of." Strictly speaking, both this premise and the missing possibility-premise involve the well-recognized ontological assumption that properties can be cross-predicated of something *in intellectu* and *in re*. [114] But in rhetorical terms the possibility-premise poses more danger, first by implicitly raising the question of the possibility of God's existing, and secondly by overtly confronting the reader with the argument's dubious assumption of ontological cross-predication.

Was Anselm aware of these semantic snares involved in asserting "God possibly exists" or "God necessarily exists"? The wide berth he gives modal premises in his *Proslogion* and his subsequent efforts to develop a systematic account of 'improper' modal assertions suggest that to some extent he was aware of their problematic nature. The characteristic ingenuity of his final account of predication in the *Lambeth Fragments* supports the surmise that we would do well to accord the benefit of the doubt to Anselm's philosophical acumen.

Yale University, New Haven

NOTES

[1] I would like to thank Professors Marilyn Adams, K. J. J. Hintikka, and Norman Kretzmann, and Doctors D. P. Henry and Simo Knuuttila for stimulating comments. I am grateful to the Academy of Finland and the American Council of Learned Societies for their support.

[2] Anselm writes in *Cur Deus Homo* I, 1: "Est et aliud propter quod video aut vix aut nullatenus posse ad plenum inter nos de hac re nunc tractari, quoniam ad hoc est necessaria notitia potestatis et necessitatis et voluntatis et quarundam aliarum rerum, quae sic se habent, ut earum nulla possit plene sine aliis considerari. Et ideo tractatus earum opus suum postulat, non multum, ut puto, facile, nec omnino inutile; nam earum ignorantia quaedam facit difficilia, quae per earum notitiam fiunt facilia." "Another reason makes me think that it is either very difficult or impossible to examine this subject fully here; to do so it is necessary to understand the concepts of capacity, necessity, will – and several others as well – which are so closely related that none can be analyzed fully apart from the others. And so the treatment of these topics requires a separate work, one which in my opinion will not be very easy, or entirely useless, because ignorance of these matters creates difficulties which can be resolved through

understanding them." (Schmitt II, 49. 7–13) Citations of Anselm's writings refer to the volume, page, and line numbers in F. S. Schmitt (ed.), *Anselm of Canterbury, Opera Omnia,* Edinburgh 1938–51. For a discussion of the chronology of Anselm's treatises, see Schmitt's, 'Zur Chronologie der Werke des hl. Anselm von Canterbury', *Révue Bénédictine* **44** (1932), 322–350; these findings are summarized in Jasper Hopkins, *A Companion to the Study of St. Anselm,* Minneapolis 1972, pp. 9–16.

³ Aristotle discusses these equivalences in *De Interpretatione,* Chapters 12 and 13. For a brief survey of some of their intervening history, see W. and M. Kneale, *The Development of Logic,* Oxford 1962, pp. 117–128. *Cur Deus Homo* II, 17 illustrates Anselm's use of these equivalences and also his interest in squaring modal semantics with divine omnipotence: "Quidquid namque cogitur esse prohibetur non esse, et quod cogitur non esse prohibetur esse; quemadmodum quod necesse est esse impossibile est non esse, et quod necesse est non esse impossibile est esse, et conversim. Cum autem dicimus aliquid necesse esse aut non esse in deo, non intelligitur quod sit in illo necessitas aut cogens aut prohibens sed significatur quia in omnibus aliis rebus est necessitas prohibens eas facere et cogens non facere contra hoc quod de deo dicitur." "For whatever is constrained to be the case is prevented from not being so, and what is constrained not to be is prevented from being, just as if it is necessary for something to be the case, it is impossible for it not to be so, and if it is necessary for it not to be the case, it is impossible for it to be so, and conversely. However, when we say that something necessarily is or is not in God, we do not understand there to be a constraining or preventing necessity in him, but we signify that there is a necessity in all other things which prevents them from doing – and constrains them not to do – anything incompatible with what is said of God." (Schmitt II, 123. 24–30; I have corrected a typographical error in line 29.)

⁴ The treatise was originally edited by F. S. Schmitt in *Ein neues unvollendetes Werk des hl. Anselm von Canterbury* (Beiträge zur Geschichte der Philosophie und Theologie des Mittelalters, Band XXXIII, Heft 3, 1936). Schmitt first published the fragments in an order of his own devising; subsequently he and R. W. Southern published the text as it appears in Lambeth MS 59 in *The Memorials of St. Anselm,* London 1969. The text is partially translated in D. P. Henry, *The Logic of St. Anselm,* Oxford 1967, and is fully translated in Hopkins; it is translated more literally in my *Anselm's Philosophical Fragments: A Critical Examination* (Ph.D. Diss., Cornell University, 1974). There has been some debate over the authenticity and dating of the fragments. Although I assume that the work is Anselm's, it would not affect my interpretation of the texts if they were composed by one of Anselm's students. I also assume that this is a late work. The main external evidence for a late dating is the remark from *Cur Deus Homo* quoted in note 2, together with the location of the text in a codex containing Anselm's late correspondence.

⁵ For examples of such criticisms, see Jonathan Barnes, *The Ontological Argument,* London 1972, pp. 23–25; M. J. Charlesworth, *St. Anselm's Proslogion,* Oxford 1965, pp. 32–40; Henry, pp. 172–180, and also his *Medieval Logic and Metaphysics,* London 1972, p. 109; Hopkins, pp. 50–51; and René Roques, *Pourquoi Dieu S'est Fait Homme,* Paris 1963, pp. 75–91.

⁶ Extensive bibliographies of this literature may be found in Barnes and in Richard A. La Croix, *Proslogion II and III: A Third Interpretation of Anselm's Argument,* Leiden 1972. For the view that Anselm argues for God's necessary existence, see Norman Malcolm, 'Anselm's Ontological Arguments', *Philosophical Review* **LXIX** (1960), 41–62,

reprinted in Alvin Plantinga (ed.), *The Ontological Argument,* Garden City, N.Y. 1965.
[7] "Omnis quippe necessitas est aut coactio aut prohibitio." "Naturally every necessity is either constraint or prevention." (Schmitt II, 123. 23) But Anselm holds that ascriptions of necessity to God are 'improper': "Iam dicimus quia deus improprie dicitur aliquid non posse aut necessitate facere." "We have already said that God is 'improperly' said to be unable to do something, or to do something by necessity." (Schmitt II, 122. 25) Anselm's distinction between 'proper' and 'improper' ascription, and his related remarks in *Proslogion* VII will be discussed in detail below.
[8] "Cum enim in definitione nominis vel verbi dicitur quia est 'vox significativa', intelligendum est non alia significatione quam ea quae per se est." "For when one says in the definition of a noun or a verb that it is a significant utterance, this should be understood only by means of its direct signification." (Schmitt I, 161. 16–18)
[9] Anselm contrasts these two kinds of truth in *De Veritate* Chapter II: "Alia igitur est rectitudo et veritas enuntiationis, quia significat ad quod significandum facta est; alia vero, quia significat quod accepit significare. Quippe ista immutabilis est ipsi orationi, illa vero mutabilis. Hanc namque semper habet, illam vero non semper. Istam enim naturaliter habet, illam vero accidentaliter et secundum usum." "Thus, on the one hand an utterance is true and correct because it signifies that what it is signifying is the case; but on the other hand, it is true because it signifies the meaning imposed on it. Of course this truth is unchanging in its expression, but the other is variable. For an utterance always has the one, but does not always have the other. For it has this one naturally, but has the other accidentally and according to the occasion." (Schmitt I, 179. 10–15)
[10] Anselm's treatment of the distinction between 'proper' and 'improper' use of terms provides some support for several approximate paraphrases; it contrasts a term's direct and indirect signification, its narrow and broad use, its original and extended sense, or its literal and metaphorical meaning. More precisely, *'proprius'* and *'improprius'* mark the Greek grammatical distinction between ἴδιος and ἄκυρος. Thus a word's 'proper' meaning is its particular or peculiar signification; when it is used 'improperly' its peculiar signification is to some extent changed, blocked, or not fully deployed. Because *'proprie'* and *'improprie'* are technical terms which to my knowledge have no satisfactory simple English translation, I use the transliterated terms in scare-quotes. But I stress that it is a mistake to suppose Anselm regards 'improper' use of language as seriously wrong; he recognizes its pervasiveness and devotes considerable effort in the *Fragments* to explaining its foundation. For the early history of this distinction, see Priscian's *Institutiones Grammaticae* II, 18 in H. Keil, *Grammatici Latini,* Lipsiae 1855, p. 55, and see G. E. Owen, 'Proof in the PERI IDEON', *Journal of Hellenic Studies* 77 (1957), 103–111. For the medieval reception of this distinction, see R. W. Hunt, 'Studies on Priscian in the Eleventh and Twelfth Centuries', *Mediaeval and Renaissance Studies* 1 (1941–43), 211–214, especially his remark on the association between 'propriety' and etymology: " . . . the nature of its invention, that is the purpose for which it was principally or properly (*proprie*) invented is the criterion by which we ought to judge a word . . . ." (p. 212)
[11] The text containing these examples is: "Cum ergo dico quia debeo amari a te, non ita dicitur quasi ego aliquid debeam, sed quia tu debes amare me. Similiter cum dico quia non debeo amari a te, non aliud intelligitur quam quia tu non debes amare me. Qui modus loquendi est etiam in potentia et in impotentia. Ut cum dicitur: Hector potuit vinci ab Achille, et Achilles non potuit vinci ab Hectore. Non enim fuit potentia in illo qui vinci potuit, sed in illo qui vincere potuit; nec impotentia in illo qui vinci non potuit,

sed in illo qui vincere non potuit." "Therefore when I say that I ought to be loved by
you, I do not assert that I have some quasi-obligation, but that you ought to love me.
Likewise, when I say that I ought not to be loved by you, what is understood is that you
ought not love me. This way of speaking also occurs in connection with capacity and
incapacity, for example, when we say that 'Hector can be overcome by Achilles', and
'Achilles cannot be overcome by Hector'. For there may be no capacity in the one who
can be overcome, and there may be no incapacity in the one who cannot be overcome,
but in the one who cannot overcome." (Schmitt I, 188. 15–22)

12 "Si enim vere debeo, debitor sum reddere quod debeo, et in culpa sum si non amor a
te." (Schmitt I, 188, 10–11)

13 Southern and Schmitt, p. 341.7–39; Hopkins, pp. 215–216.

14 Anselm uses this strategy in *De Casu Diaboli*; see Schmitt I, 253.4–254.9.

15 "Siquidem iam a longe prospicio quod ad maiora me vocas, si respondere incepero.
... Ad haec autem quae quaeris investiganda, necessarium intelligo aliquid praeponere
de verbo quod est facere, et quid sit proprie 'suum alicuius', ne, cum iis opus erit, digres-
sionem pro eis cogamur interserere." "Indeed I foresee now from far off that you are
calling me to greater things should I begin to reply.... For the topics you want to have
investigated, I think that it is necessary first to introduce something about the verb
'*facere*' (to do, to bring about) and about what is 'properly' ascribable to something. In
that way we shall not be forced to insert a digression on these topics when our work
concerns them." (Southern and Schmitt, p. 342.17–23)

16 Southern and Schmitt, p. 342.1–9; Hopkins, p. 217.

17 "Quod si respondes impossibilitatem hanc et istam necessitatem fortitudinem in deo
significare insuperabilem, quaero cur designetur ista fortitudo nominibus significantibus
infirmitatem." (Southern and Schmitt, p. 342. 6–9)

18 "Sex ergo modis 'facere' pronuntiamus ...." "We therefore use '*facere*' in six ways
...." (Southern and Schmitt, p. 344.11)

19 "Verbum hoc quod est 'facere' solet poni pro omni verbo cuiuslibet significationis,
finito vel infinito, etiam pro 'non facere'." "The verb '*facere*' is customarily put for any
verb of any signification, finite or infinite, even for 'not to do'." (Southern and Schmitt,
p. 342. 26–27) After making this observation, Anselm explains why what he describes
is linguistically acceptable.

20 Southern and Schmitt, p. 342.26–343.8; Hopkins, pp. 218–219.

21 It is interesting to note that '*Quid agis?*' has a colloquial classical usage nearly as
broad as the one Anselm imputes to '*Quid facit?*'; examples from Cicero and Horace
were probably available to Anselm at Bec. This parallel is pertinent because Anselm comments that he considers '*facere*' and '*agere*' equivalent; see Southern and Schmitt,
p. 338.22–25 and Serene, pp. 94–97.

22 "Denique omne de quo aliquod verbum dicitur, aliqua causa est ut sic hoc quod
verbo illo significatur; et omnis causa usu loquendi 'facere' dicitur illud cuius causa est.
Quare omne de quo verbum pronuntiatur aliquod, facit quod eodem significatur verbo."
"Finally, everything of which a verb is said is some cause of the occurrence of what is
signified by the verb; and in ordinary usage every cause is said to bring about that of
which it is the cause. Therefore, everything of which any verb is said brings about what
is signified by that verb." (Southern and Schmitt, p. 343.9–12)

23 Anselm follows Cicero and Beothius in dividing causes into two classes, efficient and
nonefficient. The latter class includes material causes and what we would call logically

necessary conditions; see Southern and Schmitt p. 338.35–339.3.

[24] Serene, pp. 103–113 and 120–137.

[25] More often than not, Anselm presents his analysis as an account *de dicto*, not *de re*. But he regularly ignores this distinction here, as well as elsewhere.

[26] Southern and Schmitt, p. 334.8–335.4; Hopkins, pp. 221–223.

[27] For an alternative to the interpretation I present, see Henry, *Logic*, p. 20.

[28] "Nam omne verbum, si proprie dicitur de aliqua re ut hoc ipsum faciat quod profertur . . . secundum primum modum dicitur." (Southern and Schmitt, p. 347.15–21)

[29] "Si vero non ita est ut hoc ipsum faciat quod pronuntiatur . . . secundum alium modum dicitur quam per primum." (Southern and Schmitt, p. 347.22–25)

[30] See notes 9 and 10.

[31] "Videtur mihi, quotiens attribuitur alicui rei aut nomen aut verbum improprie, quia illa res, cui attribuitur, est illi, de qua proprie dicitur, aut similis aut causa aut effectum aut genus aut species aut totum aut pars aut idem valens aut figura . . . ." (Southern and Schmitt, p. 347.5–8) Similar accounts of possible relationships between literal and metaphorical uses of words are found in the pseudo-Ciceronian *Rhetorica ad Herrenium* and in Augustine's *De Dialectica*.

[32] Southern and Schmitt, p. 336.11–337.7; Hopkins, pp. 239–240.

[33] "Dicimus enim 'aliquid' proprie, quod suo nomine profertur et mente concipitur et est in re . . . ." (Southern and Schmitt, p. 336.12–13)

[34] The distinguishing characteristic of a fourth mode 'something' is its lack of an associated concept and of a uniquely specifiable name. Because this mode is both difficult to grasp and important for the resolution of the paradox of the future house, I quote at length: "Ut si dicitur, 'dies est et nox non est propter praesentiam solis', sive 'nox est et dies non est propter absentiam solis', idem est ac si dicatur 'praesentia solis facit esse diem, et non esse noctem'; et 'absentia solis facit esse noctem et non esse diem'. . . . Dicitur enim saepe causa aliqua facere esse et non esse per praesentiam et absentiam, quamvis non addatur praesentia vel absentia. Ut si dicitur, 'sol facit diem esse et non esse, et facit noctem esse et non esse'. Sed alia facit per praesentiam, alia per absentiam." "If it is said, 'It is day and not night because of the sun's presence' and 'It is night and not day because of its absence', it is the same as if one were to say, 'The sun's presence makes it day and not night', and 'The sun's absence makes it night and not day' . . . . For often some cause is said to bring something about or to prevent something through its presence and absence, even though 'presence' or 'absence' is not mentioned. Thus one says, 'The sun causes day and night to be or not to be'. But the one cause operates through its presence, the other through its absence." (Southern and Schmitt, p. 340.29–40)

[35] This is a reasonable supposition in light of Anselm's remark that his reply to the paradoxes requires two preliminary analyses: one of '*facere*' and the other of 'proper' ascriptions of predicates to subjects; see note 15.

[36] Since Anselm says only that his modes of 'something' constitute an exhaustive analysis, and does not claim that the 'improper' modes are mutually exclusive, the distinctions among the second through fourth modes are not so crucial.

[37] Henry, *Logic*, pp. 17–21; for a discussion of this treatise, see Henry's *The De Grammatico of St. Anselm: The Theory of Paronymy*, Notre Dame 1964, and *Commentary on De Grammatico: Historical-Logical Dimensions of a Dialogue of St. Anselm's*, Dordrecht 1974.

38 This text appears in note 34. One point of disanalogy is that the absent sun exists while the future house does not; but since the fourth mode of 'something' does not require even a well-defined concept of the subject, Anselm does not consider this difference crucial for his analysis.

39 Such a reader must also assume that the identification of a cause satisfies the need to locate the relevant capacity-bearer.

40 For a discussion of Anselm's treatment of the will, see Hopkins, pp. 139–167; I discuss Anselm's views of capacity and agency in relation to the analysis of *facere* in a paper forthcoming in *Anselm Studies*.

41 "Tu es itaque ... quidquid melius est esse quam non esse." (Schmitt I, 104.15–16)

42 For examples, see note 11.

43 This remark need not assume that we have in hand a 'correct' semantics for modality. A definitive evaluation of Anselm's modal accomplishments must also take into account the serious difficulties in the theories which serve as Anselm's sources. Since a full treatment of these sources exceeds the scope of this paper and a partial treatment is a dubious bargain, I defer discussion of the sources as much as possible. For evidence concerning Anselm's acquaintance with the relevant works of Augustine, Boethius, and Peter Damian, see R. M. Rhodes, *The Ancient Libraries of Canterbury and Dover*, Cambridge 1903, p. 7, and see J.-P. Migne (ed.), *Patrologiae Cursus Completus*, Paris 1847, 150, cols. 770–779 for the pertinent Bec catalogue.

44 One reason given for this consistency is that he published nothing before the age of 43! See Hopkins, p. 4.

45 "Cuius scilicet scribendae meditationis magis secundum suam voluntatem quam secundum rei facilitatem aut meam possibilitatem hanc mihi formam praestituerunt." "It is more in accordance with their wish than with my capacity (*possibilitatem*) or facility for it that they have chosen for me this form for the writing of my mediation." (Schmitt I, 7.7)

46 " ... inevitabilis necessitas exigit ... " and "necessitas cogat ... ". (Schmitt I, 40.15 and 16.16)

47 For example, in the *Monologion* he uses the phrase "quid magis necessarium quam ... " in Chapters XII and LIII (Schmitt I, 26.29 and I, 66.10). In Chapter X of his reply to Gaunilo, Anselm uses the phrase "satis necessaria argumentatione ... ". (Schmitt I, 138.28–29)

48 Schmitt I, 105.8–106.2

49 Anselm's reasoning is this: "Sic itaque cum quis dicitur habere potentiam faciendi aut patiendi quod sibi non expedit aut quod non debet, impotentia intelligitur per potentiam; quia quo plus habet hanc potentiam, eo adversitas et perversitas in illum sunt potentiores, et ille contra eas impotentior." "Thus in the same way, when someone is said to have a power to do or undergo something which is not to his advantage or which he ought not to do, then what is understood by 'power' is impotence, because the more he has this 'power', the more adversity and perversity have power over him, and the more impotent he is against them." (Schmitt I, 105.23–27)

50 Schmitt I, 117.4–5; Charlesworth, p. 145.

51 Anselm urges, " ... erige totum intellectus tuum, et cogita quantum potes, quale et quantum sit illud bonum." (Schmitt I, 117.25–26) and also, "Desidera simplex bonum, quod est omne bonum, et satis est." (Schmitt I, 118.17)

52 Schmitt I, 117.20

156   EILEEN F. SERENE

53 This reading is given in notes in the *Oxford Annotated Bible* and the *Jerusalem Bible.*
54 Schmitt I, 253.4–254.9
55 Anselm contrasts necessity with freedom in asserting that Satan and Adam sinned not by necessity, but by free choice: "... per potestatem peccandi ... et per liberum arbitrium et non ex necessitate ... ". (Schmitt I, 209.27–28)
56 This definition emerges from several passages. In Chapter V Anselm asserts that an agent's consent is derived not from nature or necessity, but from himself: "quem consensum non naturaliter nec ex necessitate ... sed ex se aperte videtur habere." (Schmitt I, 216.10–11) Although an external force can attack a resisting will, it cannot overcome it without the agent's consent: "Impugnare namque potest invitam voluntatem, expugnare nequit invitam." (Schmitt I, 218.7) In Chapter III he says that every freedom is a capacity: "Ergo quoniam omnis libertas est potestas ...." (Schmitt I, 212.19) In the second edition of his commentary on *De Interpretatione,* Boethius reports that the Stoics defined necessity in terms of external constraints which prevent what is the case from being otherwise. See Kneale, pp. 123–126.
57 The ram example appears in Chapter VII (Schmitt I, 219. 24–31); the mountain example is in Chapter III (Schmitt I, 213. 5–25). Apparently Anselm does not regard the absence of a mountain as a constraint.
58 "... quoniam voluntas non nisi sua potestate vincitur. Quare nullatenus potest tentatio vincere rectam voluntatem; et cum dicitur, improprie, dicitur. Non enim aliud intelligitur, quam quia voluntas potest se subicere tentationi ...." " ... since the will is not overcome except by its own power. Therefore, no temptation can overcome a correct will; and if it is said to do so, this is asserted 'improperly', for nothing is understood except that the will can subject itself to temptation ...." (Schmitt I, 216.31–217.3)
59 Correctly, Anselm does not consider it plausible to say that the sinner lacks an additional capacity to exercise his capacity to maintain righteousness in a particular case, since this would risk an infinite regress.
60 A central intuition in an alethic interpretation is that something is possible if it is so in some possible world, and necessary if it is so in all possible worlds. For seminal accounts of 'possible worlds' semantics for modalities, see K. J. J. Hintikka, 'The Modes of Modality' and S. A. Kripke, 'Semantical Considerations on Modal Logic', in *Acta Philosophica Fennica* **XVI** (1963), 65–81 and 83–92.
61 For this history, see Liddell and Scott, *Greek-English Lexicon*, Oxford 1963 and F. E. Peters, *Greek Philosophical Terms*, New York 1967.
62 For slightly varying accounts of this subject, see A. Ernout and A. Meillet, *Dictionnaire Etymologique de la Langue Latine: Histoire des Mots*, Paris 1967, p. 434, A. Walde and J. B. Hofmann, *Lateinisches Etymologisches Wörterbuch*, Heidelberg 1938, Vol. II, pp. 152–153, and DuCange, *Glossarium Mediae et Infimae Latinitatis*, Graz 1954, Vol. IV, p. 583.
63 "Et ideo iuste reprehenditur, quia cum hanc haberet arbitrii sui libertatem, non aliqua re cogente, non aliqua necessitate, sed sponte peccavit." (Schmitt I, 210.4–6)
64 See note 2.
65 "Quapropter cum has convenientias quas dicis infidelibus quasi quasdam picturas rei gestae obtendimus, quoniam non rem gestam, sed figmentum arbitrantur esse quod credimus, quasi super nubem pingere nos existimant. Monstranda ergo prius est veritatis soliditas rationabilis, id est necessitas quae probet deum ad ea quae praedicamus debuisse

aut potuisse humiliari . . . ." (Schmitt II, 51.21–52.5)

[66] "Quoniam accipis in hac quaestione personam eorum, qui credere nihil volunt nisi praemonstrata ratione, volo tecum pacisci, ut nullum vel minimum inconveniens in deo a nobis accipiatur, et nulla vel minima ratio, si maior non repugnat, reiciatur. Sicut enim in deo quamlibet parvum inconveniens sequitur impossibilitas, ita quamlibet parvam rationem, si maiori non vincitur, comitatur necessitas." (Schmitt II, 67.1–6)

[67] See note 41. For a discussion of this principle from a theological point of view, see W. Courtenay, 'Necessity and Freedom in Anselm's Conception of God', in *Analecta Anselmiana: Untersuchungen über Person und Werk Anselms von Canterbury*, Helmut Kohlenberger (ed.), Frankfurt 1975, IV: 2, 39–64.

[68] Roques, pp. 81–85.

[69] See note 65.

[70] But it *would* be at least equally difficult to give a logical proof in response to the second part of Boso's request. It will not do simply to enumerate and then rule out possible overriding considerations; Anselm would need to show that there can be no such considerations.

[71] "Verumtamen, si vel una de omnibus quas posui inexpugnabili veritate roboratur, sufficere debet." (Schmitt II, 94.19–20)

[72] In Book II, Chapter VI, Anselm concludes that if it is necessary for the heavenly kingdom to include men, then it is necessary for a God-man to make satisfaction: "Si ergo, sicut constat, necesse est ut de hominibus perficiatur illa superna civitas, . . . necesse est ut eam faciat deus-homo." (Schmitt II, 101.16–19) Later Anselm asserts that he has sufficiently answered Boso's questions: see, for example, Schmitt II, 131.13.

[73] See notes 46 and 47.

[74] See note 7; I use 'constraint' to include both '*coactio*' and '*prohibitio*'.

[75] " . . . si non mori vellet, non magis hoc posset, quam posset non esse quod erat. Nam ad hoc erat homo ut moreretur . . . ." " . . . if he wished to avoid death, he could no more do so than he could not be what he was. For he became man in order to die . . . ." (Schmitt II, 120.29–30)

[76] "Si se sponte voluit hominem facere, ut eadem immutabili voluntate moreretur . . .?" "Who freely willed to become man, so that by the same immutable will he should die . . .?" (Schmitt II, 121.9–10)

[77] "An non similiter apparuit ex iis quae dicta sunt, filium dei et assumptum hominem, unam esse personam, ut idem sit deus et homo, filius dei et filius virginis?" "Likewise, has it not appeared from the things which have been said that the son of God and the man he became are one person, such that God and the man who was the son of God and of a virgin, are the same?" (Schmitt II, 121.22–24)

[78] "Sed quaecumque fuerit causa, verum est tamen quia non potuit non mori et necesse fuit illum mori." "But whatever the cause was, it was still true that he could not avoid death, and that it was necessary for him to die." (Schmitt II, 122. 14–15)

[79] Schmitt II, 122.25–123.3; for a discussion of some theological implications, see Courtenay, especially pp. 54–55 and 60–64.

[80] "Et sicut cum deus facit aliquid, postquam factum est, iam non potest non esse factum, sed semper verum est factum esse; nec tamen recte dicitur impossibile deo esse, ut faciat quod praeteritum est non esse praeteritum nihil enim ibi operatur necessitas non faciendi aut impossibilitas faciendi, sed dei sola voluntas, qui veritatem semper, quoniam ipse veritas est, immutabilem, sicuti est, vult esse." "And just as when God

brings something about, after it is done, from this time it cannot be undone, but always it is true that it was done; still it is not correct to say that it is impossible for God to change the past. For no necessity of not doing something, or impossibility of doing something, is operative here, but only the will of God who, since he himself is the Truth, wills that truth always remain immutable." (Schmitt II, 123.3–8)

[81] Damian's dramatic assertion is found in Chapter IV of the titlepiece in *De Divina Omnipotenita E Altri Opuscoli*, P. Brezzi (ed.), Firenze 1943: "Fateor, plane fateor, nullumque timens cavillatoriae contentionis obloquium constanter affirmo quia valet omnipotens Deus multinubam quamlibet virginem reddere, incorruptionisque signaculum in ipsa eius carne, sicut ex materno egressa est utero, reparare." "Fearful of no reproach of jeering contention, I acknowledge – flatly acknowledge – and resolutely affirm that omnipotent God is capable of making a woman a virgin, however many times she was married, and of repairing the mark of virginity in her flesh, just as when she came from her mother's womb." (Brezzi, p. 70) In a less dramatic explanation, Damian holds only that God could change the truth-value of any proposition which is coeternal with himself. (Brezzi, pp. 146–152) To my knowledge, Anselm did not have this book.

[82] "Quidquid fuit, necesse est fuisse. Quidquid est, necesse est esse .... Quidquid futurum est, necesse est futurum esse." (Schmitt II, 125.18) See *De Interpretatione* 19ª23 ff.

[83] " ... si dicitur: necesse erat ut ... moreretur, quia vera fuit fides sive prophetia quae de hoc praecesserant: non est aliud quam si dicas necesse fuisse ita futurum esse, quoniam sic futurum erat." (Schmitt II, 125.4–6)

[84] According to Anselm, preceding necessity differs from subsequent necessity by being an efficient cause which necessitates its effect: "Huiusmodi autem necessitas non cogit rem esse, sed esse rei facit necessitatem esse. Est namque necessitas praecedens, quae causa est ut sit res; et est necessitas sequens, quam res facit. Praecedens et efficiens necessitas est ...; sequens vero et quae nihil efficit ...." "Necessity of this sort, however, does not force a thing to be, but the being of the thing brings about the necessity. For preceding necessity is that which is a cause of a thing's being, and subsequent necessity is that which the thing brings about. Preceding necessity is efficient ...; but subsequent necessity effects nothing." (Schmitt II, 125.6–11)

[85] "Et si vis omnium quae fecit et quae passus est veram scire necessitatem, scito omnia ex necessitate fuisse, quia ipse voluit." (Schmitt II, 125.28–29)

[86] "Satisfecisti mihi illum non posse probari ulla necessitate mortem subisse ...." (Schmitt II, 126.3–4) Anselm consistently assumes that one cannot be constrained or subjected by his own will; see note 58.

[87] Since this necessity is chosen by God, Anselm holds that it is compatible with divine freedom and omnipotence; see Courtenay, pp. 54–60.

[88] "Ut cum veritas quae est in rerum existentia sit effectum summae veritatis, ipsa quoque causa est veritatis quae cognitionis est, et eius quae est in propositione; et istae duae veritates nullius sunt causa veritatis." "Indeed as the truth which is in states of affairs is an effect of the highest truth, it itself is also the cause of the truth of a thought, and of that which is in a proposition; and those two truths are the cause of no truth." (Schmitt I, 190.9–12) Anselm's Platonic point is that Truth is the cause of the truths of thoughts and propositions.

[89] Henry, *Logic*, pp. 177–180.

[90] Explaining Aristotle's solution in *De Interpretatione* to the problem of future

contingents, Boethius distinguishes simple from temporal necessity: " . . . ergo quod est, quando est, ex necessitate est . . . . Non tamen omnia quaecumque sunt aut non sunt, aut ex necessitate sunt, praeter temporis praesentis nuncupationem, aut ex necessitate non sunt, nulla mentione praesentis temporis facta. Quare non est, inquit, idem temporaliter necessarium esse, ut est mihi cum sedeo et simpliciter ex necessitate esse, ut homini mortalitas." " . . . therefore whatever is the case, necessarily is so, when it occurs . . . . Nevertheless not all events either are or are not the case, or are so by necessity, except by the proclamation of the present moment; in other words, they are not necessitated without reference to the present moment. Why, he asks, is it not the same for something to be temporally necessary – e.g. just as I must sit when I am sitting – and to be necessary *simpliciter* – e.g. just as a man must be mortal . . . ." (Migne, Vol. 64, col. 339B)

91 For example, Boethius writes: " . . . necesse est mihi tunc sedere cum sedeo, sed ipsum sedere mihi non ex necessitate inest, possum enim surgere." " . . . it is necessary for me to sit at the moment when I am sitting, but my sitting is not necessitated, for I can get up." (Migne, Vol. 64, 339A)

92 In the second edition of his commentary, Boethius characterizes the distinction more broadly: "Duplex modus necessitatis ostenditur, unus qui cum alicujus accidentis necessitate proponitur, alter qui simplici praedicatione profertur, ut cum dicimus solem moveri necesse est, non enim solem quia nunc movetur, sed quia nunquam non movebitur, idcirco in solis motu necessitas venit. Aliter vero qui cum conditione dicitur talis est, ut cum dicimus Socratem sedere necesse est, cum sedet . . . ." "Two modes of necessity are presented, one which is proposed in connection with the necessity of some accident, the other which is asserted by a simple predication, as when as say that it is necessary for the sun to be moved; for it is not because the sun is moved now, but because it will always be moved, that there is necessity in its motion. But in fact conditional necessity is asserted otherwise, when for example we say that it is necessary for Socrates to sit, when he sits." (Migne, Vol. 64, 514A)

93 Anicii Manlii Severini Boethii *Opera* I, *Philosophia consolatio,* ed. L. Bieler, Turnholti 1957, Bk. V, 6.7–30; for a more detailed discussion of Boethius' modal conceptions, see Simo Knuuttila's article in this volume, 'Time and Modality in Scholasticism', pp. 163–257.

94 For example, he thinks that the man strong enough to subdue the bull has a genuine, albeit unactualized, capacity to subdue a ram, even when the ram is escaping his grasp; see note 57.

95 For discussions of the deterministic tendencies in the 'statistical' or temporal model for modalities, see Knuuttila and K. J. J. Hintikka, *Time and Necessity: Studies in Aristotle's Theory of Modality,* Oxford 1973.

96 In other words, Anselm thinks a defense of free will must more directly address people's pervasive impression that it makes sense to say that divine knowledge imposes some sort of necessity on us. In chapter II of *De Concordia,* Anselm wants to acknowledge this intuition, but show that it involves an 'improper' ascription of necessity. Once we understand the basis for this 'improper' ascription, we are supposed to see that God's knowledge does not impose genuine necessity or constraint on us.

97 "Denique si quis intellectum verbi proprie considerat: hoc ipso quod praesciri aliquid dicitur, futurum esse pronuntiatur. Non enim nisi quod futurum est praescitur, quia scientia non est nisi veritatis. Quare cum dico quia si praescit deus aliquid, necesse est illud esse futurum: idem ac si dicam: Si erit, ex necessitate erit. Sed haec necessitas nec

cogit nec prohibet aliquid esse aut non esse. Ideo enim quia ponitur res esse, dicitur ex
necessitate esse; . . . non quia necessitas cogat aut prohibet rem esse aut non esse. Nam
cum dico: Si erit, ex necessitate erit: hic sequitur necessitas rei positionem, non prae-
cedit. . . . Non enim aliud significat haec necessitas, nisi quia quod erit non poterit simul
non esse." "Finally, if one considers the 'proper' meaning of the verb, one realizes that
when something is said to be foreknown, it is asserted that it will occur, since there is no
knowledge except of the truth. Thus when I say that if God foreknows something, it
is necessary for it to be in the future. It is the same as if I should say 'If it will be, of
necessity it will be'. But this necessity neither constrains nor prevents something from
being or not being the case. For when I say: 'If it will be, of necessity it will be', the
necessity follows from the positing of the thing, it does not precede it . . . . For this
necessity signifies nothing except that what will be the case cannot at the same time not
be the case." (Schmitt II, 248.5–249.9)

[98] Of course not all modern philosophers accept a sharp distinction between physical
and logical necessity; Quine, for example, rejects standard formulations of this distinction.

[99] Henry, *Logic*, p. 179.

[100] Anselm also uses 'necessary' in the sense of 'obligatory', though not in the texts
central to our discussion; for examples, see the texts in notes 2, 15, and 50.

[101] See note 6.

[102] Scotus makes this point in part two of article two of his question in the *Opus
oxoniense* on the existence of God. His point that the defining formula for 'God'
should specify that he is the greatest entity conceivable without contradiction may be
found in A. Wolter, trans., *Duns Scotus: Philosophical Writings*, Indianapolis 1962, p. 77.
Leibniz's point from the *New Essays Concerning Human Understanding* may be found in
Plantinga, pp. 55–56.

[103] Robert Merrihew Adams, 'The Logical Structure of Anselm's Arguments', *Philosophical Review* **LXXX** (1971), 28–54.

[104] "Sic ergo vere est aliquid quo maius cogitari non potest, ut nec cogitari possit non
esse. Et hoc est tu, domine deus noster." "Therefore, something than which a greater
cannot be thought exists so truly that it cannot be thought not to exist." (Schmitt I,
103.1–3)

[105] For a more detailed discussion of this point, see G. B. Matthews, 'On Conceivability
in Anselm and Malcolm', *Philosophical Review* **LXX** (1961), 110–111, and Barnes, p. 23.

[106] For example, see note 8.

[107] Barnes, pp. 24–25.

[108] The argument may be found in Schmitt I, 131.6–11: (1) "Nullus . . . dubitat quia
si esset, nec actu nec intellectu posset non esse. Aliter namque non esset quo maius
cogitari non posset." (2) "Sed quidquid cogitari potest et non est: si esset, posset vel
actu vel intellectu non esse." (3) "Quare si vel cogitari potest, non potest non esse 'quo
maius cogitari nequit'."

[109] Here I am summarizing the arguments in Adams, pp. 41–48.

[110] Adams, pp. 45–46.

[111] ". . . non es tamen in loco aut tempore, sed omnia sunt in te." (Schmitt I, 115.14–15)

[112] See notes 58 and 59.

[113] For Anselm's analysis of the modes of '*facere*' to be exhaustive, as he claims, it must
apply to compound predicates of various sorts; but I see no way to generalize his strategy
for iterated possibility- and necessity-operators.

[114] See, for example, Adams pp. 32–34 and Barnes, pp. 67–81.

BIBLIOGRAPHY

Adams, R. M., 'The Logical Structure of Anselm's Arguments', *Philosophical Review* 80 (1971), 28–54.
Anselm of Canterbury, *Opera omnia I–V*, ed. by F. S. Schmitt, T. Nelson, Edinburgh 1946–1951.
Barnes, J., *The Ontological Argument* (New Studies in the Philosophy of Religion), Macmillan, London 1972.
Boethius, *Commentarii in librum Aristotelis Perihermeneias I–II*, ed. by C. Meiser, Teubner, Lipsiae 1877–1880.
Boethius, *Philosophiae consolatio*, ed. by L. Bieler (Corpus Christianorum, Series Latina 94), Brebols, Turnholti 1957.
Charlesworth, M. J., *St. Anselm's Proslogion*, Oxford University Press, Oxford 1965.
Courtenay, W., 'Necessity and Freedom in Anselm's Conception of God', in *Analecta Anselmiana* IV, 2, ed. by H. Kohlenberger, Minerva, Frankfurt am Main 1975, pp. 36–64.
Du Cange, C. D., *Glossarium Mediae et Infimae Latinitatis*, Graz 1954.
Duns Scotus, *Philosophical Writings*, a selection edited and translated by A. Wolter, T. Nelson, Edinburgh 1962.
Ernout, A. and Meillet, A., *Dictionnaire Étymologique de la Langue Latine: Histoire des Mots*, Librairie C. Klincksieck, Paris 1967.
Henry, D. P., *Commentary on* De grammatico: *The Historical-Logical Dimensions of a Dialogue of St. Anselm's* (Synthese Historical Library), D. Reidel, Dordrecht 1974.
Henry, D. P., *The* De grammatico *of St. Anselm: The Theory of Paronymy*, University of Notre Dame Press, Notre Dame, Indiana 1964.
Henry, D. P., *The Logic of St. Anselm*, Oxford University Press, Oxford 1967.
Henry, D. P., *Medieval Logic and Metaphysics*, Hutchinson & Co, London 1972.
Hintikka, J., 'The Modes of Modality', in *Proceedings of a Colloquium on Modal and Many-Valued Logics, Helsinki 23–26 August 1962* (Acta Philosophica Fennica 16), Societas Philosophica Fennica, Helsinki 1963, pp. 65–81.
Hintikka, J., *Time and Necessity: Studies in Aristotle's Theory of Modality*, Oxford University Press, Oxford 1973.
Hopkins, J., *A Companion to the Study of St. Anselm*, University of Minnesota Press, Minneapolis 1972.
Hunt, R. W., 'Studies on Priscian in the Eleventh and Twelfth Centuries', *Mediaeval and Renaissance Studies* 1 (1941–1943), 194–231.
Kneale, W. and M., *The Development of Logic*, Oxford University Press, Oxford 1962.
Knuuttila, S., 'Time and Modality in Scholasticism', this volume, pp. 163–257.
Kripke, S., 'Semantical Considerations on Modal Logic', in *Proceedings of a Colloquium on Modal and Many-Valued Logics, Helsinki 23–26 August 1962* (Acta Philosophica Fennica 16), Societas Philosophica Fennica, Helsinki 1963, pp. 83–94.
La Croix, R. A., *Proslogion II and III: A Third Interpretation of Anselm's Argument*, E. J. Brill, Leiden 1972.
Liddell, H. G. and Scott, R., *A Greek-English Lexicon*, revised and augmented by M. S. Jones with R. McKenzie, Oxford University Press, Oxford 1976.
Malcolm, N., 'Anselm's Ontological Arguments', *Philosophical Review* 69 (1960), pp. 41–62, reprinted in A. Plantinga (ed.), *The Ontological Argument*, Doubleday, Garden City, N.Y. 1965, pp. 136–159.

Matthews, G. B., 'On Conceivability in Anselm and Malcolm', *Philosophical Review* 70 (1961), 110–111.

Owen, G. E. L., 'A Proof in the PERI IDEON', *Journal of Hellenic Studies* 77 (1957), 103–111.

Peter Damian, *De divina omnipotentia e altri opusculi,* ed. by P. Brezzi and B. Nardi (Edizioni nazionale dei classici del pensiero italiano 5), Firenze 1943.

Peters, F. E., *Greek Philosophical Terms,* New York University Press, New York, University of London Press, London 1967.

Plantinga, A. (ed.), *The Ontological Argument,* Doubleday, Garden City, N.Y. 1965.

Priscian, *Prisciani Grammatici Caesariensis Institutionum grammaticarum libri XVIII* ex recensione Martini Hertzii (*Grammatici latini* ex recensione H. Keilii, II, III), Teubner, Lipsiae 1855–1859.

Rhodes, R. M., *The Ancient Libraries of Canterbury and Dover,* Cambridge 1903.

Roques, R., *Pourquoi Dieu S'est Fait Homme,* texte, introd., trad. et notes (Sources Chrétiennes 91), Les Éditions du Cerf, Paris 1963.

Schmitt, F. S. (ed.), *Ein neues unvollendetes Werk des hl. Anselm von Canterbury* (Beiträge zur Geschichte der Philosophie und Theologie des Mittelalters 33, 3), Verlag der aschendorffschen Verlagsbuchhandlung, Münster 1936.

Schmitt, F. S., 'Zur Chronologie der Werke des hl. Anselm von Canterbury', *Révue Bénédictine* 44 (1932), 322–350.

Serene, E., *Anselm's Philosophical Fragments: A Critical Examination* (Ph. D. Diss., Cornell University 1974).

Southern, R. W. and Schmitt, F. S. (eds.), *The Memorials of St. Anselm* (Auctores Britannici Medii Aevi 1), Oxford University Press, London 1969.

Walde, A. and Hofmann, J. B., *Lateinisches etymologisches Wörterbuch I–II,* 3. Aufl., Carl Winter, Heidelberg 1938–1954.

SIMO KNUUTTILA

TIME AND MODALITY IN SCHOLASTICISM

1. INTRODUCTION

In this paper I shall study the fate of the Aristotelian theory of modality in the hands of scholastic philosophers and theologians — how they used this theory, how they modified it, and how they criticized it. By and large, I shall consider the problem from the vantage point of the so-called Principle of Plenitude:

(P)   no genuine possibility can remain forever unrealized.

Its role in Western thought was studied by Arthur O. Lovejoy in his book *The Great Chain of Being*.[1] Lovejoy thought that this principle originated in the ancient Platonic tradition, and he claimed that Aristotle did not adopt the principle. In his works on Aristotle's theory of modality Jaakko Hintikka has disproved Lovejoy's view, and he has also spelled out the part the principle plays in Aristotle's works.[2]

Modal theory had a prominent status in scholastic thought, since many central theological doctrines turned on the notions of possibility and necessity. The techniques of conceptual analysis used by the scholastics were to a large extent derived from Aristotelian logic. From this logic Aristotelian Scholasticism borrowed a theory of modal notions which may be called a 'statistical' model of modality. When Ernest A. Moody writes about the distinction between 'simple' material consequences and 'as of now' material consequences in his article 'Medieval logic' in *The Encyclopedia of Philosophy*,[3] he in effect gives a short description of one kind of statistical interpretation of modal notions. Moody says that in certain authors "this distinction corresponds strikingly to that between the Philonian and the Diodorean definitions of implication, and like those, it involves the notion of contingent propositions' being true at one time and false at another, with necessary propositions being of the kind that are 'always true'."[4] Moody's description features a version of the 'statistical' interpretation of modality, according to which a temporally indefinite sentence is necessarily true if it is true whenever uttered, possibly true if it is true sometimes, and impossible if it is always false. In this paper I shall try to explain, how and why this model

163

S. Knuuttila (ed.), Reforging the Great Chain of Being, 163–257.
Copyright © 1980 *by D. Reidel Publishing Company.*

was introduced into scholastic thought as well as to spell out its actual use, significance, and eventual rejection in Scholasticism. It will be seen that the problem of determinism is intricately interwoven with discussions about modalities in the Aristotelian tradition.

One of the most zealously pursued lines of research in the logic of the Middle Ages was the study of different kinds of fallacies.[5] This practice had a solid foundation in the scholastic method. One of the tasks of this method was to discover general sentences from which other true sentences could be derived and which would thus help to master the vast tradition:

Sunt ergo memoriter tenenda uerba auctorum, sed ea maxime que plenas sententias explent, et que commode possunt ad multa transferri, nam et hec integritatem scientie seruant, et preter hoc a seipsis tam latentis quam patentis energie habent plurimum. (*Ioannis Saresberiensis Metalogicon*, III, 4)[6]

In so far as scholastic method can be characterized as an attempt to organize the tradition into the form of deductive systems, it was necessary to explain in what way apparently contradictory sentences in the authoritative tradition could be understood and analyzed so as to exclude contradiction from these systems. Right from the beginning this practical end lent to scholastic method the character of conceptual analysis. In his commentary on Boethius' tract *De sancta trinitate*, Gilbert of la Porreé sets forth how a *quaestio* arises and how it must be solved by means of an analysis of the ambiguity, if one wants to combine seemingly contradictory sentences within the same authoritative tradition:

Hic commemorandum est quod ex affirmatione et ejus contradictoria negatione quaestio constat. Non tamen omnis contradictio quaestio est. Cum enim altera contradictionis pars esse vera, altera vero nulla prorsus habere argumenta veritatis videtur, ut, omnis homo est corporeus, non omnis homo est corporeus; itemque, nullus homo est lapis, quidam homo est lapis; aut cum neutra pars veritatis et falsitatis argumenta potest habere, ut, astra paria sunt, astra paria non sunt: tunc contradictio non est quaestio; cujus vero utraque pars argumenta veritatis habere videtur, quaestio est.[7]

In the process of inquiry conducted by means of *quaestiones* and *disputationes*, certain sentences stood out the analysis of which caused exceptionally great problems. They were later called *sophismata*. The sophismata and their solutions had a central status in medieval scientific thinking: they were used as means of solving other problems which structurally resembled those presented in the sophismata and analysed in their resolutions.[8]

One frequently discussed sophism was the sentence "A sitting man can walk" (or its parallel form "A black thing can be white"). In one form or

another the solution of this sophism is found within the context of almost
any analysis of problems where modal notions play an important part (as for
example in the question of the relationship between Divine Providence and
determinism). In his work *Sophistici elenchi* (166a22–30) Aristotle had
demonstrated how this sentence could be analysed so as to be true in one
sense and false in another sense. In Section 2 below I will show how this
Aristotelian solution goes together with the statistical interpretation of modal
notions. In the Aristotelian scholasticism the same solution (often called a
distinction between the composite and the divided senses) is explicitly understood in terms of the statistical interpretation of modal notions containing
(P).

I shall then show how this model is accepted in medieval theories of
modality. Because the Aristotelian solution to the sophism mentioned above
was often used in the Middle Ages so that it clearly implied the statistical
interpretation of modality, I will discuss in considerable detail its applications
to different kinds of problems. Section 5 below is devoted to this topic, but
it is also discussed in Section 3 ('Aristotelian Ideas in Boethius'), in Section 4
('Abaelard's Modal Theory'), and in Section 8 ('The Statistical Interpretation
of Modality in Thomas Aquinas'). In these sections I also present other
evidence for my claim that the Aristotelian statistical interpretation of
modality was (together with certain Neoplatonic ideas explicitly connected
with the Principle of Plenitude as Lovejoy has shown) a prominent modal
theory until the late thirteenth century. This evidence consists, for the most
part, of well-known medieval doctrines, and I believe that my treatment
of them in this context increases possibilities of understanding those
doctrines in a more adequate way.

The principle (P) was usually not accepted in the Middle Ages without
qualification because it was thought to restrict God's power and freedom. In
Section 7 God's possibilities are discussed, and it will be found that the
adherents of the statistical interpretation of modal notions understood supranatural possibilities as constituting an exception to (P). However, this did
not belie their acceptance of (P) for natural possibilities.

In Section 6 I treat the ideas of a group of twelfth century writers known
as *nominales* by their later critics. They rejected (P) more or less consciously.
It is difficult to evaluate the historical significance of this deviation from the
acceptance of (P). But at the end of the thirteenth century and at the beginning of the fourteenth century we meet a new theory of modality in which
(P) is consciously rejected and in which the apparent difficulties of the
statistical model are discussed. It seems that Duns Scotus had a dominant

status in creating principles of modal thought which are no longer bound to the limitations of the statistical interpretation of modality. In Section 9 below Duns Scotus' modal theory is presented as the predecessor of the modern understanding of modality.

If the reader is not familiar with the previous chapters of this book, it may be easier for him to follow the argumentation of this paper having first read Section 10 ('Concluding Remarks').

2. ARISTOTLE AND THE STATISTICAL INTERPRETATION OF MODALITY

In book Θ of his *Metaphysics*, Aristotle criticizes the Megarians according to whom only that what is actual is possible (*Met.* 1046b29–32). This doctrine Aristotle claims to do away with both motion and becoming, because "what does not happen, cannot happen" (1047a11–12). And so it seems that nothing can be otherwise than it is (now). In fact this conclusion follows from what Aristotle takes to be the Megarian doctrine only if the actuality 'now' is thought to determine what at all times is possible or impossible.[9] This is what Aristotle thinks the Megarians do, for according to him it follows from their doctrine that "he who stands will always stand, and he who sits will always sit, since if he is sitting he will not stand up, because it is impossible that anything which cannot stand up should stand up" (*Met.* 1047a15–17). In Aristotle's opinion this is absurd, and therefore it must be accepted that something can be and yet not be (*Met.* 1047a21–22). But in order to differentiate between possible and impossible Aristotle adds that "it cannot be true to say that 'this is possible but will not be'", which would imply the disappearance of impossible things" (*Met.* 1047b4–6). In the same way Aristotle says earlier: "he who says that something which cannot happen is or will be, will be in error, for this is what impossible meant." (1047a12–14).

This passage clearly shows how the assumption that each genuine possibility is realized at some moment of time was one of the presuppositions of Aristotle's thinking. But if this principle, according to which every genuine possibility is actualized in time, is applied to possibilities whose actualization refers to a definite moment of time, it seems to follow that, for every moment of time, what at that time can be actual must then be actual. Thus we have the result stated in so many words in the famous Chapter 9 of *De interpretatione*: "What is, necessarily is, when it is; and what is not, necessarily is not, when it is not" (19a23–24). So the circle seems to be closed: we are right back at the Megarian doctrine of possibility if presented in the form that what is actual at a given moment, is exactly what can be in that moment. In *De interpretatione* 19a7–23 it becomes apparent that Aristotle believes he can give this doctrine an indeterministic interpretation. This is achieved by transferring attention from a temporally definite event or from a sentence concerning one to similar events and sentences without temporal qualification (19a23–27).[10]

This way of thinking was natural for Aristotle, because it was based on his inclination to regard the typical form of a declarative statement as temporally unqualified. So the truth-value of a statement concerning changeable things is changeable[11], and it is easy to identify necessary statements with those which are true whenever uttered, contingent propositions with those which are sometimes true, and impossible ones with those which are never true. According to this view every temporally definite proposition is necessarily true if it is true, because its truth-value cannot change. If on the other hand the temporal specification is removed, the proposition often becomes one the truth-value of which changes. This in short is Aristotle's way out of the Megarian type of determinism.

What I have said up to now is essentially based on Professor Hintikka's studies in Aristotle's theory of modality. He has shown how the Aristotelian solution functions in terms of the conceptual presuppositions of Aristotle's thinking, although shifting the focus of attention from temporally qualified cases to temporally unqualified ones naturally says nothing about the possible alternatives of a state of affairs at a given moment. The generalization with respect to time leaves fully untouched the deterministic implications of Aristotle's assumptions concerning temporally determined events and sentences.

Additional light may be shed on this complexity when we realize that Aristotle obviously thought that the Megarian doctrine derived from some sort of conceptual confusion, or more exactly from a fallacious analysis of structurally ambiguous, temporally unqualified modal sentences.

In *Soph. el.* 166a22–30 Aristotle shows how the meaning of a statement changes according to whether its elements are understood συνϑείς or διελών (in the composite sense or in the divided sense):

Such statements as "a man can walk while sitting", and "he can write while not writing" depend on the composition. The meaning is namely not the same if one divides the words and if one combines them in saying that "it is possible to walk-while-sitting". And the same holds for the latter, if one combines the words "to-write-while-not writing", for then it means that it is possible for him to write and not to write at once. But if one does not combine them, it means that when he is not writing, he has the power to write. (*Soph. el.* 166a23–30)

According to Aristotle the sentences "a man who is not writing can write" and "a sitting man can walk" are false, when the possibility is understood to qualify a composition of two mutually exclusive predicates with the same subject at the same time. And Aristotle thought that the Megarian doctrine which maintained that only what is actual is possible was based on the falsity of precisely this sort of sentence *in sensu composito.* Thus we read in *Met.* 1047a16–17 that according to the Megarians he who is sitting will always sit "since if he is sitting he will not stand up, because it is impossible that anything which cannot stand up should stand up".

But although it might be true that a man who is not writing cannot write while not writing, and while not writing he is necessarily not writing, the same can be analysed *in sensu diviso* and it is then true that someone not writing can write. Here we have a counter-example which shows to Aristotle's satisfaction that the Megarian conceptual determinism is fallacious (cf. *Met.* 1047a23–24).

In Aristotle's opinion, a modal sentence concerning the possibility of mutually exclusive predicates is structurally ambiguous, because the possibility can refer to a supposed actuality of predicates at the same time (*in sensu composito*) or at different times (*in sensu diviso*). The distinction is, in the last analysis, reduced to a temporal distinction between the simultaneity and non-simultaneity of actualization of predicates. In fact Aristotle explicitly says that, in the divided sense, the possibility must be actualized at some other time because otherwise the distinction cannot be made:

A man has at the same time the capacity of sitting and standing, because when he has the one he also has the other; but this does not mean that he can sit and stand simultaneously, but only at different times. But if a thing has for an infinite time more than one capacity, there is no other time and it must realize the other power simultaneously. Thus if anything which exists for an infinite time is destructible, it will have the capacity of not being. If it exists for an infinite time, let this power of not being be realized. Then it will both be and not be in actuality at once. (*De caelo* 281b16–23).

We can now clarify our description of Aristotle's strategy in his discussion of the Megarian doctrine in book Θ of the *Metaphysics.* The criticism is based on the idea that the sentence "he who is sitting can stand" is, according to Aristotle, understood by the Megarians only *in sensu composito* without considering the possibility of understanding it as a temporally unqualified sentence *in sensu diviso*. On the latter reading, it is, in Aristotle's opinion, true if it is sometimes true to say of the sitting man in question that he is standing. Aristotle did not realize, however, that although he can thus claim that there is the possibility of standing while someone is sitting, this possibility is not an alternative to this very act of sitting, because it refers to an actualization at another time. Since, according to this treatment, every possibility must be actualized at some time in order to be a genuine possibility, the structural ambiguity of the sentence above is reduced to a distinction between the simultaneous and non-simultaneous actuality of predicates. By thinking of possibilities from the point of view of their actualization in one temporal reality (world history), Aristotle implicitly countenances those deterministic assumptions which he elsewhere wanted to exorcise.

Aristotle's discussions of modality are related to several different ideas. I have stressed the link with the concept of time because it seems to be relevant to the subsequently influential distinction between the composite and divided meanings of modal sentences in which the possibility of mutually exclusive predicates is maintained. Although Aristotle never defined modal concepts in terms of purely temporal notions, I think that there is sufficient textual evidence for the claim that the statistical interpretation of modal notions as applied to temporally indefinite sentences was one of the conceptual presuppositions of his thought. The reason for calling this model of modality statistical is that on it modal notions are, in the last analysis, reduced to extensional terms which are merely means of classifying what happens in the one and only world of ours at different moments of time.

It may be in order to mention briefly other Aristotelian modal paradigms, although I will later discuss mainly the history of the statistical model. Aristotle makes much use of the idea of potentiality as a power which strives to realize itself. (P) is clearly connected with this model, too. According to Aristotle, the absence of external hindrances must be built into the definition of such a possibility (see *Met.* 1048a23–24). But then it follows that a potentiality which is prevented from being actualized by an external hindrance is not a genuine possibility. It is true (although only a trivial point) that there are all sorts of unrealized partial possibilities in Aristotle. They do not, however, save him from the difficulties of the Megarian type of determinism described above, for only total possibilities are relevant to this problem, and when such a possibility is present, it seems to be realized immediately (see, e.g., *Met.* 1048a5–21, 1049a5–14, *Phys.* VIII, 4, 255b3–12).[12]

The idea of partial potentialities is not a happy solution to the problem of how to find room for unactualized potentialities *qua* potentialities. There is, however, a more promising way of meeting this difficulty in Aristotle. He made a distinction based on the concepts *kinesis* and *energeia* according to which potentialities of *energeiai* aim at *energeiai* and are instantaneously realized through *energeiai* (see *De an.* 425b26–426a1, *Phys.* 202a18ff, *Top.*

138b30ff.). The potential outcome of a *kinesis* is realized step by step through *kinesis*, which, according to Aristotle, is the actuality of what exists potentially in so far it exists potentially (see *Phys.* 201a10–11).[13] In terms of this distinction potentiality and actuality can be kept separate. It fails, nevertheless to provide room for potentialities which are not actualized, for as far as a potentiality which is actualized through a *kinesis* is a total potency of the final result, it must not be impeded by any external hindrance.[14]

The fourth Aristotelian paradigm might be called the logical definition of possibility. According to this paradigm, what is possible can be assumed to be actual without any impossibility resulting from this assumption (*An. pr.* I, 13, 32a18–21). It has sometimes been thought that this model contains an idea of purely logical possibility, which would be a counterexample to his acceptance of (P). However, this does not appear to be the case. Aristotle did not make any sharp distinction between logic and ontology, and in many places he uses his 'logical' definition of possibility outside logical contexts.[15] And in *De caelo* 281b15–21 he uses the definition in order to show that a possibility cannot remain forever unactualized. For if it is never realized, something impossible will follow from supposing it to be realized.

3. ARISTOTELIAN IDEAS IN BOETHIUS

In Aristotelian Scholasticism the question of Divine Providence and Foreknowledge was mainly understood as being analogous to the problems involved in Aristotle's discussions of the Megarian doctrine. The apparatus developed by Aristotle was used in order to show that Providence does not imply determinism. The most common way out was an analysis similar to that presented in *Sophistici elenchi* 166a22–30. Abaelard seems to be the first Latin author to refer explicitly to this text.[16] However, in his commentaries on *De interpretatione*[17], Boethius introduces the example of a sitting and possibly standing man in order to clarify why everything does not happen necessarily, although it is true that what is, necessarily is when it is:

sed si, quando est, eam esse necesse est, non idcirco simpliciter et sine temporis praesentis descriptione ex necessitate. quando enim sedeo, non potest fieri ut non sedeam et necesse est mihi tunc sedere cum sedeo, sed ipsum sedere mihi non ex necessitate inest, possum enim surgere (*In Arist. Periherm* I, 121.25–122.4).

This comment on the crucial sentence of Aristotle's sea-fight discussion shows that, in Boethius' opinion, a possibility must refer to those moments of time at which the opposite state of affairs is not actual. Therefore, at each moment of time, only what is actual is possible at that moment. This temporal necessity, as it is called by Boethius, is exactly the deterministic corollary implicit in the Aristotelian statistical modal theory. Temporal necessity is made relative by considering what can happen at other times. This erroneous strategy is based on the Aristotelian habit of treating states of affairs first in a temporally indefinite way. Even if my sitting now is necessary, my sitting is not always actual, and therefore it is true to say that I can stand.

For Boethius, the basic form of a singular declarative statement is temporally indefinite. The truth-value of a sentence changes if the sentence is not necessary or impossible, *i.e.*, always true or untrue. The connection between the change of the truth-value and the statistical model of modality is explicitly stated by Boethius as follows:

sola enim sunt quae et esse et non esse contingit, quae non semper sunt et non semper non sunt. Si enim semper essent, status eorum mutari non posset atque ideo ex necessitate essent; si autem semper non essent, ea non esse necesse esset. etenim sicut ipsa natura rerum evenientium est varia, ita quoque altera pars contradictionis habet variabilem veritatem. (*In Arist. Periherm.* I, 124.30–125.7)

In the second edition of his commentary on *De interpretatione* Boethius applies the distinction *necessarium temporale-necessarium simplex* to the truth of propositions. He takes it to be a solution to the problem of the apparent necessity of true sentences at the time of their utterance or temporally definite sentences. The necessity depends on the reference to the moment of time, and it often disappears when the temporal qualification is taken away:

at vero illa quae cum condicione dicitur, ut cum dicimus Socratem sedere necesse est, tunc cum sedet, id quod proponimus tunc cum sedet et hanc condicionem temporis si a propositione dividamus, de tota propositione veritas perit. non enim possumus dicere quoniam Socrates ex necessitate sedet. potest enim et non sedere. (*In Arist. Periherm.* II, 241.29–242.5)

While presenting this solution, Boethius states in so many words that if something happens to be the case, the opposite state of affairs is not possible with respect to the same time. So you cannot accept the formula

(1) $\quad p_{t_1} \,\&\, M\text{-}p_{t_1}$

for, if the possibility is assumed to be actualized, it would lead to the impossibility

(2) $\quad (p_{t_1} \,\&\, \text{-}p_{t_1})$.

Although the impossibility of (2) is a valid modal thesis, (2) does not follow from (1) assumed to be actualized, except when possibilities are understood as descriptions of the state of affairs at some moment of time in the one and only historical reality.

When Boethius here concludes that the possibility of standing must refer to another time, he is bound by the presuppositions of the Aristotelian 'statistical' theory of modality. I have pointed out earlier that Aristotle's distinction between *sensus compositus-sensus divisus* is in certain cases reduced to the distinction between simultaneous and non-simultaneous actuality of elements of a modal sentence. Boethius' distinction *necessarium temporale-necessarium simplex* is an instance of this semantical analysis, which is built on the prevalence of temporally indefinite sentences and on the presupposition that genuine possibilities refer to a realization in the real history of the actual world.

Boethius does not, however, explicitly discuss the example of structurally ambiguous sentences in *Soph. el.* 166a22—30. Commenting on Aristotle's reference to tricks of sophists (*De int.* 17a34—37) he presents a group of six fallacies which he also lists in other contexts. It had taken shape in the Aristotle-commentaries of late Antiquity and is based on Aristotle's definition of the concept ἔλεγχος in *Soph. el.* 167a23—27. According to this characterization, apparent contradictions can occur in the following cases:

(a)   fallacia secundum aequivocationem: Cato se Uticae occidit — Cato se Uticae non occidit,

(b)   fallacia secundum univocationem: homo ambulat — homo non ambulat,

(c)   fallacia secundum diversam partem: oculus albus est — oculus albus non est,

(d)   fallacia secundum diversum relatum: decem dupli sunt — decem dupli non sunt,

(e)   fallacia secundum diversum tempus: Socrates sedet — Socrates non sedet,

(f)   fallacia secundum diversum modum: catulus videt — catulus non videt.[18]

Like Aristotle, Boethius resolves the implicit determinism of the statistical (temporal) theory of modality by referring to the temporal ambiguity of temporally unqualified sentences; the *tempus* and *modus* fallacies are interesting from this point of view. In *In Arist. Periherm.* II, p. 133, 9—29 Boethius writes:

at vero nec si ad aliam et aliam partem adfirmatio negatioque ponatur, fit in ipsis ulla veri
falsique divisio, sed utrasque veras esse contingit: . . . nec si diversum tempus in adfirmatione ac negatione sumatur, ut cum dico Socrates sedet, Socrates non sedet. alio enim
tempore sumpto sedere veram facit adfirmationem, alio tempore non sedere veram
negationem. amplius quoque si diverso modo quis dicat in negatione quod aliter in
adfirmatione proposuit, vim contradictionis intercipit. si quis enim dicat adfirmationem
potestate, negationem vero actu, possunt et adfirmatio et negatio uno tempore con-
gruente veritate constitui: ut si quis dicat catulus videt, catulus non videt. potestate enim
videt, actu non videt.

The corresponding passage in *Introductio ad syllogismos categoricos* runs as
follows:

Item si quis de Socrate proponat dicens, Socrates sedet, atque alius neget, Socrates non
sedet, utraeque verae esse queunt, si ad diversa tempora referantur. Potest enim nunc
quidem Socrates sedere, alio vero tempore non sedere. . . . Item, si quis ovum animal esse
constituat, aliusque ovum animal esse neget, utraeque a veritate non dissonant: namque
ovum potestate animal est, actu animal non est. (PL 64, 778–779).

Fallacia secundum diversum tempus is caused by the fact that a temporally
indefinite sentence can be true or untrue when uttered at different moments
of time. This does not concern sentences which are necessarily true or false,
because then the condition for the existence of the fallacy – that the
sentence could be uttered at different moments with different truth-values –
is not fulfilled. When Boethius maintains about mutually exclusive sentences:
utraeque verae esse queunt, si ad diversa tempora referantur, he puts into
words precisely the principle by which Aristotle tries to overcome the difficulties of statistical modalities in connection with temporally definite sentences.
While the tempus-fallacy (fallacy (e)) is brought about by a change of
truth-value of temporally unqualified sentences, the modus-fallacy (fallacy
(f)) is based on the fact that sentences referring to the same moment of utterance can both be true if one refers to a potential state of affairs and the other
to an actual state of affairs. The sentences can then be true *uno tempore*. It
is strongly presupposed here that the potency will be actualized, because
otherwise the contradiction would not only be an apparent one. And correspondingly it is thought that if x can be A, it is true to say that x is such a
being to which the property A belongs – even if it does not always possess it.
In the treatments of both fallacies, the possibility is understood within
the framework of the statistical interpretation of modality. In both cases,
Boethius tries to show a mistake in claiming that only what is actual is
possible, if things at another time are otherwise.[19] The problems of the
Megarian type of determinism can be solved on the basis of this analysis by

demonstrating that they are caused by a semantical confusion: only one of the meanings of certain ambiguous sentences is heeded.

An early example of the use of this strategy for the problems of Divine Foreknowledge and determinism is the last speech of Lady Philosophy in the fifth book of Boethius' *Philosophiae consolatio*.[20] In the first part, *Philosophia* shows that Divine Foreknowledge does not import necessity on events. Boethius explains that God as an eternal and atemporal being is simultaneous with every instant of time and so all of history is immediately before the divine vision. To be seen by somebody does not make the actual state of the seen object necessary.[21]

While Boethius has thus shown that Divine Foreknowledge does not cause things to happen necessarily, he still has to explain how determinism can be avoided if, however, it is a fact that what God sees to happen cannot not happen:

Hic si dicas quod euenturum Deus uidet id non euenire non posse, quod autem non potest non euenire id ex necessitate contingere, meque ad hoc nomen necessitatis adstringas, fatebor rem quidem solidissimae ueritatis, sed cui uix aliquis nisi diuini speculator accesserit. (*Philos. cons.* V, 6, 25)

The answer is based on a distinction between a simple and a conditional necessity, and on the claim that the necessity with a condition is not incompatible with indeterminism:

Respondebo namque idem futurum cum ad diuinam notionem refertur necessarium, cum uero in sua natura perpenditur liberum prorsus atque absolutum uideri. Duae sunt etenim necessitates, simplex una, ueluti quod necesse est omnes homines esse mortales, altera condicionis, ut si aliquem ambulare scias eum ambulare necesse est .... Hanc enim necessitatem non propria facit natura sed condicionis adiectio .... Eodem iqitur modo, si quid prouidentia praesens uidet, id esse necesse est tametsi nullam naturae habeat necessitatem. (*Philos. cons.* V, 6, 26–30)

Medieval authors interpreted this distinction of Boethius as a distinction between *necessitas consequentiae-necessitas consequentis,* which became a commonplace in later medieval literature.[22] It was applied to show that there is an ambiguity in such sentences as "If God knows that *p,* then necessarily *p.*" The true meaning of the sentence according to scholastics was the *necessitas consequentiae*:

(3) $N(K_G p \supset p)$.

From (3) the untrue and deterministic *necessitas consequentis* does not follow:

(4) $K_G P \supset Np$.

I shall return later to the problems of this distinction in order to show that, contrary to the belief of even many modern commentators, it did not solve the problem of Divine Foreknowledge and determinism, at least in the form in which it was used in Aristotelian scholasticism. Although the distinction contains the sound insight that (4) does not follow from (3), the medieval Aristotelians did not without question deny (4). On the contrary, for reasons already indicated (4) was in a sense accepted. For God's knowledge concerns, of course, all temporally indefinite propositions at those moments when they are true.

Howard R. Patch has tried to show that Boethius' distinction is tantamount to the Aristotelian distinction between simple (ἁπλῶς) necessity and hypothetical (ἐξ ὑποθέσεως) necessity. With a reference to *Physics* 200a Patch writes: "One can recast the examples he [Boethius] gives to fit the logic of Aristotle: 'If you know that a man walks, he must needs walk' can be restated thus: 'If you are to know that a man walks, he must needs walk'. The situation is unchanged, and the example is precisely like the case in Aristotle. The cause 'for the sake of which' is now clearly discernible, but it was implicit before. The same point holds true with the proposition on which the argument of the two types of necessity bears: 'If God foresees that we shall do something, we must do that certain thing' becomes 'If God is to foresee that we shall do something, we must do that certain thing'. By this statement it is clear that we are bound only by hypothetical necessity."[23]

When Patch is thus recasting Boethius' examples "to fit the logic of Aristotle", he, in effect, changes them so that they can be understood as cases similar to (3). However, this kind of interpretation[24] does not have real textual support. In the texts quoted, Boethius is not discussing the presence of an object as a necessary condition for God's knowledge. He is clearly interested in the necessity of the object in the sense of (4) and in the problem of how the necessity belonging to the consequent could be made relative:

Eodem igitur modo, si quis prouidentia praesens uidet, id esse necesse est tametsi nullam naturae habeat necessitatem. Atqui deus ea futura quae ex arbitrii libertate proueniunt praesentia contuetur; haec igitur ad intuitum relata diuinum necessaria fiunt per condicionem diuinae notionis, per se uero considerata ab absoluta naturae suae liberate non desinunt. (*Philos. cons.* V, 6.30–31)

It seems that in (4) God's knowledge of *p* as the antecedent specifies those moments, at which *p* cannot be false. When *p* is true at a given moment, it cannot be false then because of the temporal necessity. But if *p* is considered without any temporal qualifications, then it is sometimes true and sometimes

false, if it is not necessary in a simple way. We see now that the possibility
of regarding the putative inference from Providence to determinism as a
fallacy is, in Boethius, based on the reliance on the statistical interpretation
of modal notions as applied to temporally indefinite sentences. A sentence is
possible, if it is true at some moment of time, and so the temporal or conditional necessity of a sentence does not mean that things cannot be otherwise,
because the contradictory sentence may be possible, too. As in the Aristotelian
distinction between expositions *in sensu composito* and *in sensu diviso* of
possibility sentences containing mutually exclusive predicates, the possibility
of being otherwise refers to periods of time different from that during which
the temporal necessity holds true. It is a sad fact that all attempts to criticize
determinism by using the statistical modal theory necessarily miss the target
in the literal sense of the expression.

Another example of the difficulties caused by temporally definite sentences
is Boethius' discussion of assertoric sentences signifying singular future contingent events. According to Boethius, one should not use such sentences at
all:

si vere dicat futurum esse id quod praedicitur non possibile sit non fieri, hoc autem ex
necessitate sit fieri. ergo qui dicit, quoniam erit aliquid eorum quae contingenter
eveniunt, in eo quod futurum esse dicit id quod contingenter evenit fortasse mentitur;
vel si contigerit res illa quam praedicit, ille tamen mentitus est: non enim eventus falsus
est, sed modus praedictionis. (*In Arist. Periherm.* II, 212.5–13)

According to the statistical theory of modality, a temporally definite true
sentence is necessarily true, because its truth-value cannot change. If someone
has to speak about contingent future events, it is better that he explicitly
mentions that they are happening contingently, in order to avoid the impression that they will happen necessarily. To happen contingently means,
according to Boethius, that what happens could fail to happen:

oportet enim in contingentibus ita aliquid praedicere, si vera erit enuntiatio, ut dicat
quidem futurum esse aliquid, sed ita, ut rursus relinquat esse possibile, ut futurum non
sit. haec autem est contingentis natura contingenter in enuntiatione praedicare. (*In Arist.
Periherm.* II, 213.7–12)

One might now think that Boethius in fact rejects the statistical model of
modality. It seems that, for any contingent future event, there is a real
possible alternative which remains unrealized. The description Boethius offers
for contingent future events is, however, a statistical one, and so it remains
problematic, whether a singular contingent event really actualizes only one of
many alternative possibilities:

et quaecumque sunt possibilia mutabiliter evenient. quae enim secundum aliquam possibilitatem dicuntur, non eveniunt secundum necessitatem. unde fit ut manifestum sit quoniam non omnia ex necessitate vel sunt vel fiunt, sed quaedam sunt quae aequali modo vel fiunt vel non fiunt. et hoc est utrumlibet fieri. alia vero in pluribus quidem fiunt, in paucioribus vero non fiunt. et aequaliter quidem fiunt, ut egredientem domo amicum videre. fit enim hoc et non fit aequaliter. quaedam vero frequentius fiunt quam non fiunt, ut sexagenarium canescere frequentius fit quam non fit, et tamen ita hoc potest fieri, ut et non fieri impossibile non sit. (In Arist. Periherm. I, 120.21–121.3)

In the light of this characterization, a singular future event is contingent, if it is of such a generic type which in certain kinds of situations is sometimes exemplified, sometimes not. This definition takes no account of the real alternatives of a singular event.

Richard Bosley has argued that what Aristotle says in De int. 19a33–39 is that it is necessary for a member of a contradiction to be true or false; not, however, for it to be either only true or only false. According to this interpretation, Aristotle's main thesis in Chapter 9 is that, if it is once true to say something about particular events, it does not follow that it is always true to say so. Correspondingly, if one of a pair of contradictory statements is either true or false it does not follow that it is either only true or only false. "Both aspects are inferred from the single insight that 'once true' does not mean 'always true'."[25] Thus Aristotle neither abolishes the Law of Excluded Middle in the case of future contingents nor modifies it.

In Bosley's opinion, this interpretation is supported by the traditional interpretation of De interpretatione as presented in the commentaries of Ammonius and Boethius. They say that, in a pair of contradictory sentences with respect to contingent events, truth and falsity are divided in an indefinite way. According to Bosley, this means that, even if it is always true to say that one member of a contradictionary pair is true, it is not necessarily the same member.[26]

There are passages in Boethius' commentaries on De interpretatione which agree with this interpretation. I have already partially quoted the text where the changeability of the truth of either member of certain contradictions is stated:

etenim sicut ipsa natura rerum evenientium est varia, ita quoque altera pars contradictionis habet variabilem veritatem. et semper quidem vera vel falsa est, non tamen una definite, ut hoc verum sit determinate aut illud, sed utrumlibet, ut sicut status ipse rerum mutabilis est, ita quoque veritas aut falsitas propositionum dubitabilis sit et eveniat quidem, ut in aliquibus frequentius una sit vera, non tamen semper, et una rarius vera, non tamen eam falsam esse necesse sit. (In Arist. Periherm. I, 125.5–14)

In this text the members of a contradiction are understood in a temporally indefinite way. Although it holds for each moment of time that the affirmation and the corresponding negation divide between themselves the two truth-values truth and falsity, the division is not always made in the same way. This happens only if we are concerned with necessary or impossible states of affairs. If a real change of the truth-value is demanded from members of a contradiction as a sign of an indefinite division of truth and falsity, what happens to temporally definite pairs referring to singular future events? Boethius' examples are usually of this type, but he only states that they are indefinitely true or false.[27] Perhaps what he is doing is systematically applying statistical ideas to individual events and temporally definite sentences without realizing that they are irrelevant as far as their temporal necessity is concerned.[28] So he says that, if you have a pair of contradictory sentences referring to a certain future event, necessarily one of them is true and the other is false. It does not follow, however, that one is necessarily true and the other is necessarily false. While explaining this, Boethius refers to the temporal necessity, which disappears if the temporal qualification is omitted. Then he continues:

ita in contradictione contingenti adfirmationem quidem vel negationem veram esse necesse est, non tamen vel adfirmationem simpliciter ac definite veram vel negationem, sed utramlibet et quam certae veritatis constituerit eventus. (*In Arist. Periherm.* I, 124.2–7)

4. ABAELARD'S MODAL THEORY

Abaelard did not feel much enthusiasm for the group of six fallacies presented by Boethius. He did not consider them philosophically interesting, and he thought that even Aristotle had treated them only because the historical situation demanded that he refute the fallacies of the sophists.[29] Concerning the *diversus modus* case presented by Boethius, Abaelard observes that, if the contradiction *ovum est animal-ovum est non animal* is refuted by maintaining that *est* in the former sentence can be understood *secundum potentiam* and in the latter *secundum actum*, we must remember that the former interpretation is not rational nor is it used.[30]

But there is another model for conceptual analysis which Abaelard considered important for the accurate understanding of sentences containing modal expressions. And it is exactly the συνθείς-διελών distinction presented in *Sophistici elenchi.* Abaelard refers to this when he shows how the structural ambiguity that appears in sentences containing modal expressions can be eliminated by differentiating expositions *per compositionem* and *per divisionem:*

Videntur autem duobus modis exponi posse, veluti si dicam 'possibile est stantem sedere'. Ut enim docet Aristoteles in sophisticis elenchis, alius est sensus per divisionem, alius per compositionem; per compositionem vero si stare et sedere simul in eodem subiecto coniungatur, ac si dicatur possibile est stantem sedere manentem stantem, id est sedere simul et stare, ac si dicamus: *"possibile est ita contingere, ut haec propositio dicit: stans sedet"*, quae omnino falsa est, quia iam duo opposita simul inesse eidem possent, et tunc quidem possibile quasi ad integrum sensum propositionis applicatur, ac si dicatur posse evenire ut haec propositio dicit: *'stans sedet'*. Si vero ita accipiatur, quod is qui stat, possit sedere quandocumque, non iungimus sibi opposita et ad rem ipsam, non ad propositionem *'possibile'* referimus dicentes: rem quae stat, posse quandocumque sedere, sed non posse contingere, ut dicit propositio *'stans sedet'*. (*Log. Ingred.* 489.1–14)[31]

Abaelard also calls this distinction a difference between *expositio de sensu* and *de re*.[32] In the first case, the possibility is a predicate which belongs to the meaning of the corresponding non-modal sentence, and in that case the possibility qualifies the composition of subject term and predicate term in its totality. According to the latter interpretation, the possibility constitutes the meaning of the sentence; it qualifies how the subject is what the predicate says.[33]

It is essential to our subject matter that, in the above example, Abaelard considers the first interpretation false, because, in that case, mutually exclusive predicates would be taken as belonging to the same subject at the same time; according to the *de re* analysis the sentence is true, because a sitting man can at some time stand. He thus preserves in his analysis the possibility of saying, for example, that a man now sitting can stand, if he can stand at some point in time. And so as not to connect opposite qualifications with a subject we must obviously also think that if a sitting man can stand, there must be at least one moment of time at which he in fact does stand, because otherwise the untrue *de sensu* interpretation would hold for all moments of time. By means of the same model, Abaelard analyses the sentence *possibile est hominem mortuum esse* in the second *Tractatus* of the *Dialectica*:

Si enim possibile est quod illa dicit propositio, possibile simul mortuum et hominem cohaerere, quod quidem falsum est, cum ex natura oppositionis alterum non possit pati alterum. Neque enim homine[m] vivente in eodem existere possunt, quippe cum *'mortuum' 'vitam'* non perferat, nec homine[m] mortuo, quippe cum *'hominem' 'mors'* non patiatur. Quia ergo nec homine vivente nec mortuo nec etiam antequam homo crearetur, natura hominem et mortuum patiatur, numquam simul ea patitur. Nullo itaque modo videtur vera haec propositio: *'possibile hominem mortuum esse'*, ut scilicet de sensu simplicis exponatur. Cum vero de rebus exponitur, vera videtur hoc modo: *'possibile est hominem esse mortuum'*, idest id quod est homo, potest mortuum fieri. (*Dial.* 196.32–197.4)

Because the concepts *homo* and *mortuus* cannot ever be simultaneously applied to the same thing, the modal sentence is untrue in *de sensu* meaning, but it is true in *de re* meaning because what now is a man can be dead in the future (i.e., when he is no longer a man). But if man were immortal, then the state of affairs, which makes the *de sensu* case false, would always hold true and the *de re* analysis could not be true.

In both the above-mentioned cases, the application of a modal distinction presupposes the possibility of transfering the focus of attention from a temporally qualified case to a treatment in which time is indifferent. At the same time, modal concepts are given the statistical interpretation which we previously said arose naturally from the conceptual presuppositions of Aristotle's thought. I would now like to consider briefly the influence of these interlocked conceptual presuppositions on Abaelard's thought.

In considering assertoric sentences, Abaelard defines the word *dictio* following Aristotle as *vox significativa ad placitum cuius partium nihil extra designat.*[34] The next step towards the definition of an assertoric sentence is the definition of *oratio: vox significativa ad placitum, cuius partium aliquid significativum est separatum.*[35] An *oratio* containing a finite verb is *oratio perfecta.* When Abaelard has in view *oratio perfecta* as an actual linguistic act of asserting, he calls it *propositio.* What is asserted in a proposition is *dictum.*[36]

Dictum corresponds to some extent to the modern concept of the proposition. The truth-value of Abaelard's *propositio* cannot change, because it is a unique linguistic event. G. Nuchelmans, whose book *Theories of the Proposition* I have followed above, says that a proposition is too short-lived for its truth-value to have time to change.[37] *Propositio* is, according to Abaelard, only secondarily true. Primarily true or untrue is *dictum*, and its truth-value depends on whether things correspond to what is claimed.[38] It must be noticed here that Abaelard is not very consistent in his use of terms. The basic form of *dictum* or its counterparts is temporally unqualified and its truth-value is changeable in case where it concerns a changing state of affairs. Thus Abaelard writes while discussing the status of the Law of Excluded Middle in Aristotle's logic:

Sed prius nobis inspiciendum est qualiter ipsius antecedens Aristoteles intellexerit, a quo argumentatio incipit, hoc videlicet: omnium affirmationum et negationum necesse est alteram esse veram, alteram esse falsam, ut hoc prius discusso ipsum ab inconvenienti facilius absolvamus. Potest autem et vere et falso accipi, sicut et illud quod in tractatu oppositorum de eisdem affirmationibus et negationibus dixit, alteram scilicet semper esse veram et alteram falsam, veluti istarum: *'Socrates est sanus'*, *'Socrates non est sanus'*. Si enim ita intellexeris quod uni et eidem semper verum inhaereat, falsum est, cum potius neutra illarum veritatem custodiat, sed modo vera sit eadem, modo falsa. Si vero ita sumpseris ut *'alteram'* non circa unam tantum teneas, sed indifferenter accipias ac si dicas alterutra(m), verum est. (*Dial.* 219.32–220.7)

From the above text it is clear that the idea of a necessary sentence as an omnitemporally true statement is connected with the doctrine of the change of truth-values. The same conception is also put forward elsewhere:

Quod autem necessarium est, sempiternum est nec principium novit. Unde et id quod ista consequentia vera proponit: "si est homo, est animal", ita est semper ut dicitur, sive solae res ipsae de quibus agitur, permaneant, sive non; et omnes verae consequentiae ab aeterno sunt verae. Categoricarum autem propositionum veritas, quae rerum actum circa earum existentiam proponit, simul cum illis incipit et desinit. (*Dial.* 279.13–20)

According to Abaelard, every statement is necessarily true while it is true and everything necessarily is while it is, but this depends on the temporal qualification in the sentence and it does not make the statement or the thing necessary *simpliciter, i.e.,* true or actual always without temporal indices:

Ex his itaque Aristoteles manifeste demonstrat ipsas affirmationes et negationes in proprietate veri ac falsi sequi illos eventus rerum quos enuntiant, gratia quorum tantum verae esse vel falsae esse dicuntur, in eo scilicet quod quemadmodum quamlibet rem necesse est esse, quando est, vel non esse, quando non est, ita quamlibet propositionem veram necesse est veram esse, dum vera est, vel non veram non esse veram, dum vera non est. Sed non ideo omnem veram necesse est esse simpliciter nec omnem quae non est vera, necesse est non esse veram; alioquin numquam quae vera est, posset esse non vera nec ea quae non est vera, posset fieri vera: quod enim ex necessitate est, aliter esse non potest. (*Dial.* 221.3–13)

Correspondingly Abaelard often uses the example that a man whose leg is cut off, cannot afterwards be a biped or walk although he can be a biped or walk *simpliciter.*[39] In this case the generalisation in respect to time makes the impossible possible because what is said to be possible at some moment in time has been actual. But Abaelard also has examples in which something is claimed to be possible although it is never actual:

'Possibile' quidem et 'contingens' idem prorsus sonant. Nam 'contingens' hoc loco non quod actu contingit accipimus, sed quod contingere potest, si etiam numquam contingat, dummodo natura rei non repugnaret ad hoc ut contingat, sed patiatur contingere; ut cum dicimus: "Socratem possibile est esse episcopum", etsi numquam sit, tamen verum est, cum natura ipsius episcopo non repugnet. (*Dial.* 193.31–36)

More complex is the claim in *Introductio ad theologiam,* that the contingent foreknown by God could forever remain unactualized, with God nevertheless remaining infallible.[40]

Are these counterexamples to my interpretation, according to which Abaelard's theory of modalities can be characterized as a statistical interpretation of modality where every genuine possibility must be realized in a temporal reality? In both examples Abaelard refers to nature (*natura*); in fact, in the above quotation he defines possibility as freedom from contradiction with nature. Now, according to one definition of modal concepts, often repeated by Abaelard necessity is identified with what nature demands, possibility with what nature allows, and impossibility with what nature forbids. The concept 'nature' in this connection means the metaphysically invariant structure of the world.[41]

On the epistemological level, nature refers to the reality made up so that its structure is reflected in universal concepts and their relationships, which the intellect separates by abstraction from the sensual world.[42] Although Abaelard seems to leave the ontological status of universal concepts undefined, in the same way as that of *dictum*,[43] in principle his idea of abstraction strongly resembles Aristotle's doctrine of knowledge. Thus Abaelard's epistemological position, which he leaves largely undeveloped, may be described as moderate realism.[44] According to this view, we obtain our knowledge of the nature of things by inductive abstraction. But then our knowledge about what nature in general allows can be derived only from what in fact has been exemplified in some individuals. Thus Abaelard writes:

Quod enim in uno particularium videmus contingere, id in omnibus eiusdem speciei individuis posse contingere credimus; potentiam enim et impotentiam secundum naturam accipimus, ut id tantum quisque possit suscipere quod eius natura permittit, idque non possit quod natura expellit. Cum autem omnia eiusdem speciei particularia eiusdem sint naturae — unde etiam dicitur ipsa species tota individuorum substantia esse —, idem omnia recipere potentia sunt et impotentia. (*Dial.* 385.1–8)

And the example previously mentioned that Socrates can be a bishop, continues with an argument stating why the modal sentence is true:

... verum est, cum natura ipsius episcopo non repugnet; quod ex aliis eiusdem speciei individuis perpendimus, quae proprietatem episcopi iam actu participare videmus. (*Dial.* 193.36–194.1)

Now we see that examples of unrealized possibilities are not in contradiction with our interpretation. Unrealized possibilities are unrealized only in a relative sense, for the presupposition behind their use is that, in another member of the same species, the possibility in question has already been realized. In the same way as Abaelard considers it possible to make a generalization with respect to time, he also takes it to be possible to generalize with respect to instances of species. In connection with the generalization with respect to time, one might well ask to what extent it says something about the possibilities at the original moment, and analogously the generalization to other members of the species leaves us with the problem of the possibilities open to a particular member of the species. A presupposition needed for the rationality of Abaelard's procedure seems to be that we take our knowledge to be primarily of species and only secondarily of individuals.

Explicit applications of the statistical model are found in Abaelard's discussion about specified modal sentences. He first distinguishes between two kinds of qualifications. In an internal determination, the predicate of the sentence containing a modal notion is repeated in the determination (*possibile est Socratem esse hominem dum est homo*). In an external determination, the added predicate is different from that of the original sentence (*possibile est Socratem esse hominem, dum vivit*).[45]

Abaelard remarks that sentences of this kind can be interpreted as *hypotheticae temporales*. It means that sentences like "Socrates necessarily is running when he is running" or "Socrates can run when he is sitting" are read so that they express a conjunction of two sentences uttered at a specified moment of time. So the latter sentence means that, at the moment of Socrates' sitting, Socrates is sitting and it is possible that he is running.[46] In Abaelard's opinion, this reading is true and the reason seems to be that the point of time to which the possibility refers is indefinite. This interpretation is supported by the fact that Abaelard next discusses the examples above as 'genuine modal sentences', viz. in the sense that the *dum* phrase expresses the time of the state of affairs which is claimed to be possible or necessary. And, in this sense, the sentence "Socrates can run when he is sitting" is not true. What is, necessarily is, when it is and, correspondingly, if something is determinately possible, it must then be actual:

Si vero illud 'dum' modo praedicato tantum apponatur, tunc proprie modales erunt cum determinationibus et vere, quando scilicet modus determinatur sic: Socrates currere est necesse, dum currit vel Socratem currere est possibile, dum sedet. Sic enim expositis vera est prima et falsa secunda. (*Dial.* 206.33–37)

While the temporal determination in Abaelard's conceptual system *de facto* meant an inevitable actualization at the moment in question, *Peripateticus Palatinus* had difficulties with sentences in which something was said to be possible for something as long as it is. If Socrates can sit as long as he lives, can he sit even when he is not sitting?

In the part of the Commentary on Aristotle's *De interpretatione* edited by Minio-Paluello[47], Abaelard treats the problem by stating that the omnitemporal possibility must, in such cases, be understood *indifferenter, i.e.,* it refers to the period of time during which the possibility is sometimes actualized. This is in accordance with the Aristotelian analysis of the sentence: a sitting man can stand. The possibility refers to those periods of time when the man is not sitting.

Si vero sedere indifferenter utamur pro omni tempore et non sedere pro presenti, et de eo loquamur qui aliquando sedet et modo non sedet, satis concedendum videtur a toto, quo videlicet, cum sit possibile eum sedere omni tempore vite sue, possibile sit sedere dum sedet, et rursus possibile sit sedere dum non sedet. Quod si inferatur ergo sedet et non sedet, non est inconveniens, cum sedet indifferenter acceptum sit omnis temporis (ac si diceretur sedet nunc vel sedit olim vel sedebit) et non sedet presentis tantum sit temporis. (*Super Perierm.* 38.17–26)

We have seen that Abaelard was faced with the problem that every temporally determined sentence seems to be necessarily true if it is true. He tried to avoid this type of determinism by means of the Aristotelian method of replacing the sentence by a temporally indefinite one. This 'solution' was needed to show that even if sentences as objects of God's knowledge are temporally definite and thus necessarily true, they are not therefore necessarily true in a simple way, *i.e.,* without the temporal qualification:

Et nota quod cum vera sit haec propositio modalis cum determinatione "impossibile est rem non ita evenire, cum Deus providerit evenire", non tamen vera est simplex, quae ait: impossibile est non ita evenire. Nam et ista vera est: impossibile est hunc hominem habere duos pedes, postquam amiserit, vel impossibile est hunc hominem sedere, dum stat, nec tamen ideo verum est simpliciter, quod impossibile est vel hunc habere duos pedes vel hunc sedere. (*Log. Ingred.* 429.18–25)

This solution is the same as we found in Boethius, and Abaelard says it is a Boethian idea. In the work *Introductio ad theologiam,* Abaelard quotes the main lines of the corresponding passage in Boethius' *Philosophiae consolatio*[48] and then makes the following comment:

Ex his philosophiae verbis, tam videlicet de absoluta quam determinata necessitate, liquidum est quod supra distinximus; singula videlicet quae eveniunt necessario evenire, si ad divinam referantur providentiam, hoc est, necessario evenire, cum Deus ita evenire providerit: sed non ideo simpliciter debere dici quod necessarium sit ea evenire. (*Int. ad theol.,* ed. Cousin, p. 146)

In this connection Abaelard discusses Chapter 9 of Aristotle's *De inter-pretatione* in order to show that this solution is based on the Aristotelian treatment of the problem as to how the definite truth of singular sentences concerning future contingent events fits together with indeterminism. According to Abaelard, Aristotle proves that, from the fact that sentences about the future necessarily are true or false, it does not follow that all happens by necessity. Such a claim is namely based on a sophistical argument. To solve this sophism, one has to make a distinction between two different interpretations of a proposition containing the concept of necessity.

Haec quippe propositio: Necesse est navale bellum cras futurum esse, vel non esse cras futurum, duos habet sensus; unum quidem in quo hypothetica disjuncta est falsa, ac si ita diceremus, necessarii nomen bis ponentes: Necesse est navale bellum cras esse futurum, vel necesse non esse cras futurum: alium vero in quo categorica est vera, habens disjunctum subjectum, et quasi disjunctam in subjecto positam, et necessarii nomen semel positum in praedicato. (*Int. ad. theol.* pp. 142–143)

This distinction shows some similarity to the fact known in modal logic that it is fallacious to conclude from

(1) $N(p \lor q)$

to

(2) $Np \lor Nq$.

The situation is complicated, however, by the fact that in some cases this conclusion, p and q being contradictory sentences, is valid according to Aristotle. For if p and q are temporally definite sentences, they are neces-sarily true if they are true. Therefore (1) and (2) must be qualified so that *praedicatio necessarii* in them is *simplex* and not *determinata*. When Abaelard qualifies the necessity in the distinction so that it becomes a simple neces-sity, at the same time he gives a temporally indefinite interpretation to the sentences in question.[49] Then (1) means that, of any pair of contradictory sentences, one of the two is true whenever the pair is uttered. But if the sentences are about contingent things, it is not always the same part which is true. So (2) does not follow from (1). The distinction between (1) and (2) as applied to temporally indefinite sentences seems to be the Abaelardian interpretation of Aristotle's assertion:

everything necessarily is or is not, and will be or will not be; but one cannot divide and say that one or the other is necessarily. (*De int.* 19a28–29).

Abaelard tries to apply this distinction to Divine Knowledge so that although God knows at every moment of each temporally unqualified pair of contradictory sentences which one of them is true, it does not follow that the same sentence is always true. This argument takes no account of the fact that, at a certain moment, only what actually happens or what God infallibly sees as happening can happen. As for Aristotle, so for Abaelard, it was enough to show a fallacy in the argument which purported to conclude impossibility to be otherwise (at another time) and consequently simple necessity from the necessity at a certain moment:

Cum ergo singula provideat evenire ita ut eveniunt, profecto ita ipse evenire necesse est. ... Et nos quidem, quam diximus Aristotelis sententiam sequentes, concedimus de singulis, quia necesse est ita evenire, cum ipse ita evenire providerit; non tamen ideo simpliciter concedere cogimur, quia necesse est ita evenire, cum videlicet, ut dictum est, simplex necessarii praedicatio nequaquam consequatur determinata. (*Int. ad theol.* p. 143)

Even if Abaelard's modal discussion is dominated in many cases by the 'statistical' interpretation of modality as applied to temporally indefinite sentences, he seems to apply the distinction between possibilities *de dicto* and *de re* as a modal distinction, too, and not only as a distinction between simultaneous and non-simultaneous actuality. The context in question is his analysis of the sentence *"Si possibile est rem aliter evenire quam evenit, possibile est Deum falli"*.[50] This thesis was known to Abaelard from Augustine's *De Civitate Dei*, where it is presented as Cicero's argument against the omniscience of God.[51]

Abaelard considers the argument to be a sophism. In *Logica Ingredientibus* he says that the antecedent is untrue when read *de sensu* and true when it is read *de re*. And when it is untrue, the possibility of God's error does not follow from it. But does it follow if the antecedent is true? Abaelard's negative answer is based on the belief that *de re* analysis of the antecedent as such saves us from this conclusion. Here Abaelard does not say that *de re* concerns the possibility to be otherwise at another time and God therefore cannot err. (See *Log. Ingred.* 430.5–27) This would be consistent with his other treatments according to which everything necessarily is as it is with respect to God's knowledge. Here he seems to think that *de re* possibility is a purely modal alternative. From the possibility of being otherwise the possibility of God's error does not follow, because if things were otherwise, God would possess a different knowledge of them. A similar idea is presented in *Dial.* 218.3–219.24.

I have mentioned earlier that Boethius sometimes applies double-edged possibilities to individual events in a way which does not go well together with his usual way of handling modal notions within the frame of the statistical interpretation. Thus it may be that the idea of contrafactual possibilities was not totally beyond his purview, and, with Abaelard, this seems to be even more clearly the case. On the other hand there are many passages in Abaelard which are not readily comprehensible if one fails to realize that the statistical interpretation of modal notions formed an integral part of the presuppositions of his thought. He does not appear to have been troubled by the fact that (P) is in different ways implied by his arguments.

So it is not surprising that there is another modal paradigm in Abaelard in which (P) is explicitly accepted. One of the group of 19 Abaelardian propositions condemned as heretical by Pope Innocent II runs as follows:

Quod ea solummodo possit Deus facere vel dimittere vel eo modo tantum vel eo tempore quo facit, non alio.[52]

This charge, unlike certain others, was well-founded. Abaelard writes in *Introductio:*

Quantum igitur aestimo, cum id tantum Deus facere possit quod eum facere convenit, nec eum quidquam facere convenit quod facere praetermittat; profecto id solum eum posse facere arbitror quod quandoque facit . . . (*Int. ad theol.* 128)

and

Praedictis itaque rationibus, vel objectorum solutionibus liquere omnibus reor, ea solummodo Deum posse facere vel dimittere, quae quandoque facit vel dimittit, et eo modo tantum vel eo tempore quo facit, non alio. (*Int. ad theol.* p. 131).

Abaelard adopted this doctrine from the well-known argument of neo-platonic theology, according to which the Omnibenevolent is not envious and therefore He must actualize all His possibilities for good — other kinds of possibilities He does not have.[53] This "theological form of the Master Argument of Diodorus" — as Faust calls it — leads to the same result as the statistical model for modality, according to which every possibility must be realized sooner or later.[54]

5. MODALITY, COMPOSITION, AND DIVISION IN THE
TWELFTH AND THIRTEENTH CENTURIES

In early commentaries on Aristotle's *Sophistici elenchi* in the twelfth and thirteenth centuries, as well as in tracts concerning *sophismata*, it is easy to

trace the way in which the statistical model for modality as applied to temporally unqualified sentences was disseminated in medieval thought. In the
oldest known and still extant medieval commentary on *Sophistici elenchi*[55]
the following gloss is made upon the passage 166a22–30:

Secundum conpositionem autem huiusmodi, ut posse sedentem anbulare, idest possibile
est quod sedens simul anbulet, vel possibile est quod sedens alio tempore anbulet. Si
quis didicit litteras, possibile est nunc discere litteras quos scit. Hec oratio significat
aliquem didicisse litteras et eum nunc posse illas litteras discere, que coniunctim sunt
falsa, quia aliquis non potest didicisse litteras et simul discere; sed divisim potest aliquis
didicisse et discere. Sicut si Deus providit Socratem legere, possibile est Socratem ⟨legere⟩.
(*Log. Mod.* I, 210.10–17)

Instead of De Rijk's supplement on line 17, we shall read *non legere*, for
didicisse and *discere*, like *sedere* and *anbulare*, are mutually exclusive predicates. And then we have here another instance of the well-known strategy
for avoiding determinism in connection with Divine Providence.

Summa sophisticorum elencorum[56] is another commentary from the
twelfth century, in which the following *sophisma conpositionis* is presented:

Possibile est sanum esse egrum,
ergo idem potest esse sanus et eger,
ergo '*sanum*' et '*egrum*' possunt predicari de eodem.

Sophisma est conpositionis, quia prima propositio potest intelligi composita et divisa.
Si intelligatur composita, idest quod possibile sit sanum et egrum esse simul, falsum est.
Si vero intelligatur divisa, scilicet quod possibile sit id quod est sanum, esse egrum alias,
verum est (*Log. Mod.* I, 316.1–7)

In both of the above texts, the possibility *in sensu diviso* refers explicitly
to a difference in the time of actualization. This is needed as possibilities are
taken to be actualized in actual history. When discussing *sophismata* caused
by *amphibolia* the sitting of Socrates is used as an example:

Hec enim: '*Socrates sedet*' in eodem tempore potest esse vera cum ista: '*Socrates non
sedet*'. Cum enim in hoc tempore vera sit ista: '*Socrates sedet*', in eodem vera potest esse
ista: '*Socrates non sedet*' ... Igitur possunt simul esse vere. Solutio. Cum dicit Aristotiles:
"due contradictoria non possunt simul esse vere", idest: *non possunt simul habere
potentiam existendi vere*; non dixit quando una contradictoria est vera, quod non contingat alteram quandoque esse veram. (*Log. Mod.* I, 311.8–15)

The most natural application of this analysis for medieval writers was to
the relation between Providence and determinism, but it was used in other
contexts, too:

Iste est peccans mortaliter
istum mereri vitam eternam est possibile
ergo istum peccantem mortaliter mereri vitam eternam est possibile. . . .

Et latet fallatia circa conclusionem. Nam in hac forma vocis '*istum peccantem mereri*' sunt due orationes, quarum altera est composita et falsa. Si scilicet hec oratio: '*istum peccantem mereri*' sit subiectus terminus et hic terminus '*possibile*' predicatur, sic designato quoniam iste potest mereri peccando. Altera est divisa et vera diviso hoc termino '*mereri*' ab hoc termino '*istum peccantem*' et constructo hoc termino '*possibile*' ex parte predicati ut sit subiectus terminus hic terminus '*istum peccantem*', predicatus hic terminus 'mereri possibile', designato quoniam qui quandoque peccat potest in alio tempore mereri. (*Log. Mod.* II, 2, 687.21–688.1)

In a commentary on *De interpretatione* from the mid-twelfth century the question is raised whether a white thing can be black, and the same presuppositions can be found there. The falsity of the exposition *de compositione* is based on the fact that then the possibility of mutually exclusive predicates belonging to the same subject at the same time is asserted. It cannot be the only analysis, however, because then the possibility of actualization of the predicates at different times would be neglected:

Compositio est, ut, si quis dicat: '*possibile est album esse nigrum*' ⟨et alius dicat: '*non est possibile album esse nigrum*'⟩, uterque verus esse poterit. Si enim unus sic intelligat dividendo: '*possibile est rem esse que alba est nigram*', verum est. Alius vero compositionis facit sophisma dicens: '*non est possibile album esse nigrum*', idest aliquid manens album nigrum esse; et ita hic totum *album esse nigrum* subicitur equivoce. (*Log. Mod.* I, 613.23–28)

The same example is discussed in a manuscript from the latter part of the 12th century, which is called by De Rijk *Dialectica Monacensis*[57]:

Secundum igitur compositionem fiunt paralogismi ex eo quod aliqua dictio modalis potest ordinari ad diversa. Ut patet hic: '*possibile est album esse nigrum*', '*possibile est ambulantem sedere*'. Est enim utraque istarum multiplex ex eo quod modus potest ordinari ad id dictum quod actualiter ibi exprimitur et sic oratio debet intelligi de dicto – sive de maiori compositione sive composita, quod idem est. Et tunc falsa est. Vel potest modus ordinari supra quoddam enuntiabile quod potestate ibi est, hoc scilicet: '*aliquid in quo est albedo possibile est esse nigrum*', ita ut hoc attributum '*esse nigrum*' attribuatur ei quod est album gratia substantie solum et non gratia accidentium. Et sic debet oratio intelligi de re – vel de minore compositione vel divisa, quod idem est. Et sic vera. (*Log. Mod.* II, 2, 570.18–29)

When the writer applies the *compositio-divisio* distinction to his examples, he may have in mind the generalization both with respect to time and with respect to species; the possibility in the *de re* case is founded on an actuality at some time or in some instance of the species. This is implied in the locution that the possibility *de re* is said *gratia substantie solum et non gratia accidentium.* By 'possibility' the writer does not imply an alternative state of affairs to a temporally definite case because he believes that every true statement about the present is necessarily true: *omne dictum de praesenti verum et affirmativum est necessarium.* [58] This being the case, an unactualized possibility can only refer to future times. Hence the distinction between possibility *de dicto* and possibility *de re* appears to be a temporal distinction. In another passage the writer states that possibility does not refer to the future in a universal way but indefinitely with respect to some time. Correspondingly, impossibility denies the potency universally:

Sicut enim possibile ponit potentiam indefinite respectu alicuius temporis futuri et non universaliter respectu cuiuslibet, impossibile vero privat potentiam eandem non indefinite sed universaliter pro quocumque tempore futuro, similiter separabile indefinite et non universaliter dicit potentiam separandi respectu temporis et subiecti, inseparabile privat eandem potentiam universaliter respectu temporis et subiecti (*Log. Mod.* II, 2, 512.28– 34)

The writer does not at this point discuss the question as to whether a genuine possibility can remain eternally frustrated. However, I think that while he speaks about future times to which his possibilities refer, they in fact are the times of their actualization. This assumption is supported by the fact that his introductory remarks on modal notions clearly presuppose the statistical interpretation of modal notions as applied to temporally indefinite sentences. He says that a sentence *necessarium per se* is infallible at all times, i.e., in the past, present, and future, and a sentence *necessarium per accidens* cannot be false either now or in the future although it might have been false in the past, as "This man has studied in Paris". When the criterion of the necessity of a sentence is the immutability of its truth-value, it follows that every true sentence is necessarily true when it is uttered, although not necessarily *per se*. A possible sentence must be true sometimes, because otherwise its negation would be immutably true and the sentence itself impossible *per se.* [59] These ideas are repeated in many logical tracts from the twelfth and thirteenth century in virtually identical terms. [60]

In his textbook of logic, William of Sherwood also discusses the sample question of whether something white can be black. He formulates the sophism as follows:

> What is possible will be true
> A white thing can be black
> Therefore, it is true that a white thing is black.

According to William the first premiss, which entails (P), is not problematic.

In the second premiss, the composite and the divided senses are to be distinguished, and the distinction is typically interpreted as a temporal distinction between the simultaneous actuality and actuality at different times. The problematic conclusion is said to rely only on the composite meaning. The text runs as follows:

Quicquid est possibile, erit verum.
Album esse nigrum est possibile.
Ergo album esse nigrum est verum.

Et dico, quod minor propositio est multiplex scilicet ex eo, quod ista duo album et esse nigrum possunt componi respectu eius, quod est possibile. Et sic significatur, quod hoc dictum compositum est possibile et sic est oratio composita, vel possunt dividi ab invicem et tunc significatur, quod compositio huius predicati esse nigrum ad aliud, quod tunc est album, est possibile, quia ly album eo quod dividatur ab hoc predicato: esse, quod habet tempus amplissimum. Per hoc, quod dico possibile non trahit suam suppositionem ab illo, ut supponat pro albis illius temporis, sed supponit pro hiis, que nunc sunt alba. Est ergo minor vera propositio divisa et quia ipsa composita est, eadem illi secundum substantiam.[61]

William of Sherwood was one of the most influential teachers of logic in the 13th century. He apparently taught in Paris in the 1240's. Without taking any stand here *vis-à-vis* the open question of William's chronology and relations of influence involving him[62] it is interesting to note that in their discussions about the *compositio-divisio* distinction in connection with modal sentences, many 13th century writers more or less openly repeat the same kind of statistic-temporal interpretation of modality as I have been discussing.

Albert the Great specifies the possibility that a non-writing agent can write in his commentary on *Soph. el.* 166a22–32 by adding to the context the temporal word '*nunc*':

Si quis autem non componat accusativum cum verbo, tunc significat quod qui nunc non scribit, habet possibilitatem ut scribat: et haec est vera.[63]

As an additional condition, Albert presupposes that the possibility will at some time be actualized. In his commentary on Aristotle's *Metaphysics* he writes:

Unde haec duo non sunt simul vera: aliquid possibile est esse et quod illud idem omnino non erit. (*Metaph. lib.* 9, *tract.* 2, *cap.* 2)[64]

In the *Summulae Logicales*[65] of Peter of Spain we read the following analysis of the question:

"Quemcumque ambulare est possibile, contingit quod ipse ambulet
sed sedentem ambulare est possibile
ergo contingit, quod sedens ambulet".

Minor est duplex, quia si hoc dictum 'sedentem ambulare' per se subiciatur huic predicato 'est possibile', sic est sensus unus. Et est oratio falsa in illo sensu, quia tunc actus oppositi sibi invicem coniunguntur, . . . Si autem illud dictum supponat predicto predicato pro parte sui, scilicet pro subiecto ipsius dicti, tunc est sensus talis: "sedens habet in se potentiam ad ambulandum"; et hoc sensu est vera minor. (*Tract.* VII, 68).

Peter of Spain then states that the distinction can also be interpreted so that in one case the participle *sedens* determines the temporal area of *ambulare* and in the other case that of *posse*. But it is characteristic that, according to Peter of Spain, this latter interpretation can be reduced to the former, *i.e.*, the temporal and modal versions of the *compositio-divisio* analyses coincide:

Dicunt ergo quod predicte orationes sunt duplices, quia concomitantia importata per hoc participium 'sedentem' potest significari respectu huius verbi 'ambulare'; – et tunc est sensus istius "sedentem possibile est ambulare" idest: "dum sedeo, me ambulare est possibile"; quod falsum est –; vel potest concomitantia denotari respectu predicati; et tunc est sensus istius "sedentem possibile est ambulare" idest: "dum sedet, potentiam habet ad ambulandum postea"; et hoc est verum. Sed ista distinctio in idem redit cum priori, quia quando denotatur concomitantia respectu huius verbi 'ambulare', tunc ponitur possibilitas supra totum dictum, et sic est falsa; quando autem denotatur concomitantia respectu predicati, tunc possibilitas ponitur supra subiectum dicti, et sic est vera. (*Tract.* VII, 70–71)

The last-mentioned version is presented by Lambert of Auxerre in his logical *Summa*. As Peter of Spain could hardly quote this work, the writers may have had common sources.[66] Lambert's text is a beautiful example of the *compositio-divisio* distinction as a distinction between simultaneous and non-simultaneous actuality of mutually exclusive predicates in temporally indefinite sentences:

Ad hoc dicendum quod minor (sc. sedentem ambulare est possibile) est duplex: nam iste accusativus 'sedentem' potest componi cum isto infinito 'ambulare', vel potest dividi ab eo: primo modo est composita et falsa et est sensus hoc: "dictum sedentem ambulare est possibile" et hoc falsum est. Nam sic dicendo significatur quod iste actus ambulare insit sedenti pro tempore in quo sedet, et sic sequitur quod sedens ambulet. Secundo modo est divisa et vera et est sensus: "ille qui nunc sedet habet potestatem ut postea ambulet", et hoc est verum, quia sic dicendo significatur quod ille actus qui est ambulare possit inesse sedenti non pro tempore in quo sedet, sed pro alio. (*Summa Lamberti,* ed. F. Alessio, p. 158)[67]

The temporal interpretation of *compositio-divisio* distinction is not always stated as explicitly as in the above examples. The shift to another time is not mentioned, *e.g.,* by Thomas Aquinas or Roger Bacon in their discussion of the sentences "black can be white" or "a sitting man can walk".[68] However, both of these writers state explicitly that a true affirmation about the present time is necessarily true and, therefore, deny the possibility of Socrates' standing now if he is now sitting.[69]

The following much discussed sophism is relevant in this context: *Anima Antichristi necessario erit.* In *Dialectica Monacensis,* the sophism and its solution are presented in the following way:

Iuxta fallaciam compositionis solvitur hoc sophisma: anima Antichristi erit necessario. Distinguendum est ex eo quod modus potest determinare compositionem, que est actualis, vel compositionem huius participii ens, quod potentiale est ibi, scilicet per subintellectum. Si primo modo, composita est et falsa; si secundo modo, divisa est et vera. (De Rijk, *Log. Mod.* II, 2, 571.9–13).

William of Sherwood discusses the same sophism in his works *Introductiones in logicam* and *Syncategoremata.* In the latter work the sophism is treated as follows:

sciendum quod haec dictio necessario potest esse categorema vel syncategorema. Si categorema, sic est determinatio praedicati, si syncategorema, tunc compositionis. . . . Sic solvitur hoc sophisma: anima antichristi erit necessario. Probatio: anima antichristi habebit esse necessarium quia aliquando habebit esse non cessans incorruptibile. Contra: contingenter erit quia possibile est ipsum non fore. Et patet quod probatur secundum quod est categorema; improbatur secundum quod est syncategorema et determinatio praedicati ratione compositionis, quia sic est haec vera: anima antichristi contingenter erit, alio modo falsa.[70]

The solution presented is that the sentence is false *in sensu composito* and true *in sensu diviso.* Modern interpreters have not found this solution immediately clear. In particular, the falsity of the *compositio* case has caused difficulties. In his translation of William of Sherwood's *Syncategoremata,* Norman Kretzmann quotes as by way of explanation a remark made by Peter Geach. According to him, "the most usual reason for the choice of Antichrist as an example is that here we have a future individual who can be identified, and whose existence is epistemically certain (being quaranteed by revelation), but yet, like any unborn man's, is future contingent ontologically speaking."[71] If this were the reason why William of Sherwood did not accept the necessary truth of the sentence *Anima Antichristi erit,* he would here accept ideas different from the modal principle *quicquid est possibile, erit verum* mentioned earlier. This however is not the only possible interpretation. If we consider the statistical interpretation of modal concepts as applied to temporally indefinite sentences, another and perhaps more plausible solution suggests itself. The sophism is said to be true in the categorematic sense because the soul is eternal. When necessity is, thus, identified with omnitemporality, the sophism may be false in the syncategorematic sense, because it would then always be true to say that Antichrist will be but never that he is. When William of Sherwood writes: *contingenter erit quia possibile est ipsum non fore,* the sentence can be understood so that Antichrist ceases to be a non-actual future being when he is actual.

This view goes well together with the definition of *necessarium per se* and *necessarium per accidens* given by William of Sherwood and the author of *Dialectica Monacensis.*

Et similiter dicitur necessarium per se, quod non potest nec potuit nec poterit esse falsum ut deus est. Necessarium autem per accidens est, quod non potest nec poterit esse falsum, potuit tamen ut: ego ambulavi. Item possibile et contingens dupliciter dicuntur.[72]

Correspondingly the sentence "Antichrist is coming in the future" is not necessary *per se* although it is true and has always been true. For it will not always be true, because Antichrist is not always something belonging only to the future. The accidental necessity of the sentence "William has studied in Paris" is based on the past tense of the expression. Correspondingly a future tense sentence concerning a being "whose existence is epistemically certain" can be interpreted as being necessary *per accidens* but not *per se.* And in fact this example was explicitly put forward in a twelfth century treatise edited by L. M. De Rijk under the title *Logica 'Ut Dicit'.* There the necessity is first divided into absolute and relative necessity. The absolute necessity is said to be either *per se* or *per accidens.* An example of the last-mentioned necessity is the sentence "Antichrist will be":

Per se, quod non potest nec poterit esse nec potuit esse falsum, ut Deus est. Per accidens, quod non potest nec potuit esse falsum, poterit tamen; et tale est verum de futuro, ut Antichristum fore; ... (*Log. Mod.* II, 2, 390.20–22)

There is an analogy with this solution in Stoic logic. According to Alexander of Aphrodisias, some stoic philosophers maintained that the statement "There will be a sea battle tomorrow" is only possible and not necessary, because, even if the statement is true, it does not necessarily remain true after the battle has taken place.[73] It is supposed here that a necessary statement is true whenever uttered.

The interpretation offered by Kretzmann and Geach is perhaps applicable to Robert Grosseteste. In *De veritate propositionis*, he considers the sentences *Antichristus erit* and *Antichristus est futurus* and states that they are true but not necessary because it is possible that Antichrist will never be.[74] This claim needs further specification, however, for as well shall see later, Grosseteste had a special theory about the contingency of the world.

We have seen that it was natural for early medieval authors to have a double treatment of sentences. It was possible to discuss their truth or falsity at the same time when something else holds or without such temporal restrictions, *i.e.*, with respect to any time. In the statistical interpretation of modality, a sentence is necessarily true without qualification, if its truth-value never changes. It is temporally or conditionally necessary, if its truth-value remains unchanged under certain conditions. In fact it is supposed that the truth-value of a merely temporally necessary sentence will change, because otherwise the contradictory sentence would be impossible without qualification and the sentence in question would be necessary without qualification, too. In addition to the *compositio-divisio* -distinction as applied to possibility sentences containing mutually exclusive predicates, the interrelated ideas of statistically interpreted modal concepts and changing truth-values were used by some authors in connection with the doctrine of *consequentia ut nunc.* Some scholars have noted this fact.[75]

In the work *Tractatus logicae minor,* which perhaps mistakenly has been attributed to Ockham, the writer characterizes the distinction between inference 'simple' and inference 'as of now' by stating that the 'as of now' inference is one which does not always hold. It holds true only at a determinate time. What is known as inference 'simple' always holds true.[76] This is not what Ockham seems to think in his other works and may, therefore, speak for the unauthenticity of the tract.[77] But, when the validity of the simple consequence is said to be based on the impossibility of the conjunction of the antecedent and the denial of the consequent, it seems, as Marilyn M. Adams has stated, that the modalities are to be interpreted in terms of time, so that a proposition is necessary if and only if it is always true, impossible if and only if it is never true, and possible if and only if it is true at some time.[78] The necessity of an 'as of now' inference is then a kind of temporal necessity — the truth-value cannot change at the time when a contingent condition is actual.

6. NOMINALES AND TEMPORALLY DEFINITE SENTENCES

The statistical interpretation of modalities discussed above is connected with the habit of treating sentences in a way which makes them indefinite in respect to time (or individuals). E. A. Moody makes the following criticism of this way of thinking in another medieval context: "The controversy rests, in part, on the false assumption that a sentence of present time, stated at two different times, is the same sentence; only on this assumption is it possible to speak of a sentence being true and becoming false. If the relativity of time range in the sentence, to the time of its utterrance, were eliminated by introducing explicit dates into the sentences composing the conditional, it would be unequivocally true, or false, regardless of when it might be stated."[79] Against this background it is interesting that in the twelfth century attempts were made to base philosophical and theological thinking on temporally definite sentences. Although many influential thinkers of the thirteenth century strongly condemned these attempts, it is possible that they were one source of the modal theories of the fourteenth century which displaced the Aristotelian doctrine.[80]

The interest in temporal definiteness can be seen from twelfth century texts in which Abaelard is accused of maintaining that *'Socrates legit' aliud significat cum profertur in hoc tempore et aliud cum profertur in alio tempore*. This was taken to be in contradiction to Aristotle's doctrines:

Hic confunditur error Magistri Petri dicentis quod Socrates sedet est alia oratio prolata a Socrate et alia prolata ab eodem in alio instanti. Sed Aristotiles vult quod hec oratio possit esse vera et falsa. Sed hoc non potest secundum Petrum, quia alia oratio est cum profertur in hoc instanti et alia cum profertur in alio instanti.[81]

Now we have seen that although the truth-value of the Abaelardian *propositio* cannot change, he treated *dictum* in a good Aristotelian fashion. The criticism is, therefore, partly unjustified. But there were, nevertheless, people who seriously believed that the *dictum* (in the Abaelardian sense) must be taken as temporally definite.

The birth of the theory of temporally definite propositions was at least partly connected with the problem which Augustine, among others, presents in his commentary on the Gospel according to St. John (*PL* 35, 1722). According to Augustine, those people who lived before Christ had exhibited the same belief, by believing in the articles concerning Christ contained in the Apostolic Creed, as those, who lived at the time of Christ or after.[82] In the Middle Ages there was a wide consensus that what *antiqui* and *moderni* believed was the same. But since for the former the propositional object of their faith must have been in the future and for others in the present or past, the problem arose as to how to explain the identity of the articles despite the differences in such expressions as *Christum nasciturum esse, Christum esse natum.*[83]

When the problem of the identity of the articles of faith is considered in the thirteenth century, a solution presented by *nominales* is often mentioned:

Alii dixerunt contrarium, quia posuerunt quod enuntiabile, quod semel est verum, semper est verum, et ita semper scitur. Et ut melius pateat, videnda est eorum positio et ratio positionis. Fuerunt qui dixerunt, quod albus, alba, album, cum sint tres voces et tres habeant modos significandi, tamen, quia eandem significationem important, sunt unum nomen .... Et ista fuit opinio Nominalium, qui dicti sunt Nominales, quia fundabant positionem suam super nominis unitatem (Bonaventura, *Sent. d.*41, *a.*2, *q.*2).[84]

Nominales maintained that, in the same manner as the same *nomen* can occur in different grammatical forms, the same *dictum* or *enuntiabile* can be uttered in different tense. When the original proposition is temporally definite, uttering it at different times demands the use of different tenses. But the truth-value of the proposition cannot change. Peter of Poitiers writes (*c.* 1170):

Sed quia quidam insurgunt contra nos dicentes: Vos creditis passionem Domini, et navitatem etc., sed falsum est illos articulos esse. Ergo vos creditis ea quae falsum est esse, falsitas subest fidei vestrae: ideo possumus assignare articulos per dicta propositionum, ut Christum esse natum, Christum esse passum etc. Hoc idem credidit Abraham, sed sub aliis verbis Christum esse nasciturum, Christum esse passurum.[85]

If a *dictum* is once true, it is always true. Its truth-value does not change.[86]

An anonymous *Quaestiones* written *circa* 1220 presents the following summary of the subject matter:

Sicut plures voces sunt unum nomen, ita plura enuntiabilia sunt articulus unus, et sicut mutatur vox, non tamen mutatur nomen, nam si dicam albus, alba, album, idem est nomen et tamen vox mutatur, ita cum diceretur olim: Christum esse passurum, et modo dicatur: Christum esse passum, idem est articulus at tamen sunt enuntiabilia diversa. Et hoc provenit ex hoc quod tempus aliter est de esse articuli, aliter de esse enuntiabilis; tempus enim secundum suam substantiam est de esse articuli: secundum differentias suas de esse enuntiabilis.[87]

Nominales treated in the same way the question whether God's knowledge can change if once he knew, e.g., that Christ will be born but cannot any more know that he is going to be born. The proposition which is the object of knowledge is temporally definite, and one's knowledge of it at different times must be formulated in different tenses.[88]

It is significant that the more or less orthodox Aristotelians of the thirteenth century unanimously rejected this doctrine. In his theological *Summa* Thomas Aquinas denies what *antiqui nominales* had claimed, viz. *idem enuntibile esse Christum nasci et esse nasciturum et esse natum*, because

198   SIMO KNUUTTILA

diversitas partium orationis diversitatem enuntiabilium causat: tum etiam quia sequeretur
quod propositio quae semel est vera, semper esset vera: quod est contra Philosophum qui
dicit quod haec oratio Socrates sedet vera est eo sedente, et eadem falsa est, eo surgente.
(*S. Th.* I, *q.*14, *a.*15 *ad*3).

According to Thomas Aquinas, *tempus consignificatum* belongs to the
meaning of the proposition and therefore it is not true, e.g., that God knows
everything he has known. But although many of the propositions known by
God are not always true, that fact does not necessitate a change in God's
knowledge, because His knowledge as a whole is an atemporal corpus.[89]

Like Thomas, other critics were sceptical of the theory that there is no
change of truth value, which, according to the Aristotelian theory of
modality, would mean that propositions are only necessary or impossible.[90]
But it seems that at least some of the criticized writers thought that it was
not possible to apply the statistical model to temporally definite sentences at
all. And rather than abandoning their theory of temporally definite sentences,
they questioned the statistical model of modality. Thus Peter of Poitiers says
that although a true proposition can be false, it cannot begin to be false.
(*Sent.* 1, 12.212–215.) It follows that at every point in time, there are
unrealized possibilities which describe states of affairs alternative to those
which are actual (cf. I, 12, 172–173). It is now clear that if Socrates is sitting
at the moment t_1, it may be possible that he is not sitting at the moment t_1
(see I, 13, 138–145). No reference to another time is needed, because the
true sentence "Socrates is sitting at t_1" can be false – even if it were an
object of God's knowledge. According to the Aristotelian doctrine, a temporally definite true sentence cannot be false as such, because there is no time
at which it could be false. Peter of Poitiers seems to consider it fallacious to
consider possibilities from the point of view of their actualization in the one
historical reality:

Fallacia: aliquis potest esse predestinatus qui non est predestinatus; ergo potest incipere
esse predestinatus, vel: aliquis potest non esse predestinatus qui est predestinatus, ergo
potest desinere esse predestinatus; vel aliqua anima potest esse salvanda que non est
salvanda; ergo potest incipere esse salvanda (*Sent.* I, 12, 202–207).

In the thirteenth century traditional philosophical doctrines eclipsed
thoughts presented by *nominales;* only at the end of the century did the
critics of Aristotle return to similar themes.

7. GOD'S POSSIBILITIES IN EARLY SCHOLASTICISM

The idea of unactualized possibilities as such was not a new invention in the twelfth century. In the Christian tradition it was realized very early that, in order to avoid many difficulties, the possibilities of God must be assumed to be greater in number than what happens in the actual world. The source for this idea was the Bible, where the actual world is in many places not taken as an exhaustive manifestation of God's omnipotence (see, e.g., *Gen.* 18:14, *Mark* 10:27, *Matt.* 19:26, *Matt.* 26:53, *Luke* 1:37, *Luke* 18:27).

One of the applications of this idea was Tertullian's emphasis on the imitation of nature. Because God has selected the actual form of the world from a set of possibilities, nature possesses normative significance for men:

Quis enim est vestium honor iustus de adulterio colorum iniustorum? Non placet deo quod non ipse produxit. Nisi si non potuit purpureas et aerinas oves nasci iubere. Si potuit, ergo iam noluit; quod deus noluit, utique non licet fingi. Non ergo natura optima sunt ista, quae a doe non sunt, auctore naturae. Sic a diabolo esse intelleguntur, ab inter-polatore naturae.[91]

Although the Christian doctrine virtually contained a denial of the Principle of Plenitude (P), at least in so far as God's possibilities are concerned, (P) was introduced into Cristian thought owing to its important role in ancient philosophy, as Lovejoy has shown. A good example of the tension thus created is Augustine's answer to the Tribuse Marcellinus in *De Spiritu et littera*. Marcellinus had asked along the lines of (P) how Augustine could say that something is possible although there is no example of it in the world. In his answer Augustine denies (P) of God's possibilities on the basis of the Bible. The reason for this restriction of (P) is a theological one. God can make a man sinless although man has lost his *posse non peccare*.[92]

However the role of unrealized possibilities remains obscure. In other passages Augustine is inclined to think that God has realized in the world all possible kinds of creatures. He also seems to guide events so that his un-realized possibilities cannot be alternative states of affairs with respect to the actual course of events.[93]

Augustine thought that his deterministic view of the world, which included a doctrine of double predestination, did not exclude the freedom of will, because he defined the latter as an absence of external constraints. Although man cannot himself determine the theologically relevant direction of his will, *liberum arbitrium* is, nevertheless, in operation when one man chosen to be saved loves God and another one determined to the fires of hell hates Him:

Scimus eos qui corde proprio credunt in Dominum, sua id facere voluntate ac libero arbitrio. (*Ep.* 217 *ad Vit., PL* 33, 985)

Nam liberum arbitrium usque adeo in peccatore non periit, ut per illud peccent, maxime omnes qui cum delectatione peccant et amore peccati. (*Contra duas epistolas pelagianorum* I, 2, 5, *PL* 44, 552)[94]

Discussions about God's possibilities were dominated in the twelfth century by two radical theses. Peter Damian had claimed that Divine Omnipotence cannot be restricted in any way. On the other side there was the Abaelardian doctrine that the actual world is an exhaustive manifestation of God's omnipotence and that God, therefore, cannot do anything he does not in fact do. In his work *De divina omnipotentia*[95] Peter Damian takes as a starting point the claim of Hieronymus according to which God cannot restore lost virginity.[96] The writer refers to a discussion with his friend, abbot Desiderius of Monte Cassino, who had accepted Hieronymus' view and developed it to such a theory that God cannot do things which he does not want to do.[97] Peter Damian finds this solution problematic. If God cannot do anything he does not will to do and if he does what he wills, God cannot do anything else than what at every moment is actualized.[98] Peter Damian takes this to be a restriction of Divine Omnipotence, and, in order to avoid it, one should realize that God does not will everything he can do. If this is the case, then you cannot see from the actual course of events everything God can do. However, it is strange that after having stated this Peter Damian tries to allow for God's unrealized possibilities by referring to such extraordinary cases as for example restoring lost virginity.[99] Even if a simultaneous prevalence of contradictory states is impossible according to principles generally accepted, this impossibility must, according to Peter Damian, not be extended to Divine Omnipotence.[100]

Before I attempt to elucidate the reasons which led Peter Damian into the position mentioned, it is in order to mention briefly that one general line in Peter Damian's argumentation is the doctrine that God is outside time. He says that, for this reason, the use of tenses in connection with Omnipotence may be misleading:

non inepte possumus dicere quia potest Deus facere, in illa inuariabili et constantissima semper aeternitate sua, ut quod factum fuerat apud hoc transire nostrum, factum non sit, scilicet ut dicamus: Roma quae antiquitus condita est, potest Deus agere ut condita non fuerit. Hoc quod dicimus: potest, praesentis uidelicet temporis, congrue dicitur quantum pertinet ad inmobilem Dei omnipotentis aeternitatem; sed quantum ad nos, ubi continuata mobilitas et perpes est transitus, ut mos est, potuit conuenientius diceremus . . . (*De div. omnip.*, *PL* 145, 619A)

The text quoted may make the impression that Peter Damian explains how certain paradoxical formulations of the Divine power can be avoided by using, e.g., tenses so that the Law of Contradiction is not violated. This is not, however, the point intended in the work. A stronger polemical thesis is defended, and the main object of Peter's attack are thinkers who thoughtlessly apply dialectical and rhetorical arguments to the mysteries of Divine Omnipotence.[101] While so doing they limit God's freedom, because Peter believes that the following state of affairs holds in logic:

Sed quantum ad consequentiam disserendi, si futurum est ut pluat, necesse est omnino ut pluat, ac per hoc prorsus inpossibile est ut non pluat. Quod ergo dicitur de praeteritis, hoc consequitur nichilominus de rebus praesentibus et futuris, nimirum ut, sicut omne quod fuit, fuisse necesse est, ita et omne quod est, quamdiu est, necesse sit esse, et omne quod futurum est, necesse sit futurum esse. Atque ideo, quantum ad ordinem disserendi, quicquid fuit, inpossibile sit non fuisse, et quicquid est, inpossibile sit non esse, et quicquid futurum est, inpossibile sit futurum non esse. (*PL* 145, 603A–B)

It is worth noticing that Peter understands philosophical modal notions along the lines of the Diodorean modal theory, according to which only what is actual at a given moment is then possible. We have seen how a generalization with respect to time or species was proposed as a solution to deterministic consequences of this modal theory. Peter Damian mentions this proposal by referring to certain 'wise men of this era' who introduced the '*ad utrumlibet*'- contingency in order to show that something can be otherwise than it is. Peter remarks, however, that this solution is based on the variable nature of things, and therefore does not seem to solve the problem contained in the claim that what is, necessarily is when it is.[102] Neither is a reference to states of affairs at other times a proper way of discussing God's possibilities, because then the familiar course of natural events would be the criterion of God's possibilities.[103]

We can see now that Peter Damian was in fact concerned with the same temporal necessity which caused trouble in the statistical interpretation of modality. If it is true that what is, necessarily is, when it is, then at whatever moment of time the actual state of affairs excludes all alternative states of affairs with respect to that time as impossibilities. Now Peter Damian is not contented to say that these 'impossibilities' are Divine possibilities. Instead he maintains that God can make things with mutually exclusive properties, which is tantamount to denial of the Law of Contradiction:

Factum quoque aliquid fuisse et factum non fuisse unum idemque inueniri non potest. Contraria quippe inuicem sunt adeo ut si unum est, alterum esse non possit. Nam quod fuit non potest uere dici quia non fuit et e diuerso quod non fuit non recte dicitur quia

202 SIMO KNUUTTILA

fuit. Quae enim contraria sunt in uno eodemque subiecto congruere nequent. Haec porro
inpossibilitas recte quidem dicitur si ad naturae referatur inopiam; absit autem ut ad
maiestatem sit applicanda diuinam. (PL 145, 612 A–B).

It is possible that the denial of the Law of Contradiction in Peter Damian's
thought is based on a confusion. It seems that, in the text quoted above, he
takes

$$(1) \qquad -M\,(p_{t_1}\,\&\,-p_{t_1})$$
and
$$(2) \qquad -(Mp_{t_1}\,\&\,M\text{-}p_{t_1})$$

to be equivalent. We have seen that a purely modal distinction between (1)
and (2) was not used in early medieval thought. Hence a confusion between
them was perhaps natural. When Peter Damian wanted to deny (2), which
was accepted by philosophers as a temporal impossibility, he thought that the
denial of (1) follows, too.

One could ask, of course, if there is real confusion in Peter Damian's argument. His denial of the Law of Contradiction seems to be a natural sequence
of his acceptance of the statistical interpretation of modality as the starting
point of the discussion. Within the framework of this model, God's unrealized
possibilities seem to break the laws of logic. At the beginning of his work,
Peter briefly states that not all natural possibilities are realized (PL 145,
597A–B). If he had taken this idea at face value and if he had followed the
idea of several alternative states of affairs, he could have avoided the irrational
conclusions which now exist in his theory of supranatural modalities.

In his work De sacramentis christianae fidei, Hugh of St. Victor rejects
both the opinion of Peter Abaelard and that of Peter Damian. If the doctrine
of Peter Damian is characterized by the claim that nothing is impossible for
God, Hugh withdraws from this view by saying that God cannot do impossible things; such an ability would not be a proof of potency but rather of
impotency:

Ergo summe potens est qui potest omne quod possibile est; nec ideo minus potest, quia
impossibilia non potest, impossibilia posse non esset posse sed non posse (De Sacramentis, PL 176, 216).

This solution was often repeated in later medieval literature.

In Hugh's opinion, Divine Providence is unchangeable but it does not
follow from this that God cannot direct the world otherwise than he does:

Sed nos ad hoc respondemus, quod si mutaretur eventus quod fieri potest, nec mutaretur nec cassaretur providentia; quia hoc omnino fieri non potest. Sed potius nunquam fuisset praevisum quod nunquam fuerat futurum; et constaret providentia in eo ut non fieret. (*ibid.* 215)

According to this view, Divine Omnipotence contains more possibilities than what will happen according to Providence. Thus it is natural that Hugh should next pose the question of whether God can make a better world. Hugh first gives two tentative arguments against a positive answer:

Sive ideo non potest melior esse quia summe bona est ita ut nulla omnino boni perfectio ei desit, sive ideo non potest esse melior quia majus bonum quod ei deest capere ipsa non potest. (*ibid.* 216).

Hugh considers the first argument to be incorrect, because the world would then be as good as God. In the second case, it seems that in order to be the actual world the world cannot be better. God can increase the capacity of the world to receive goodness, however, and in this sense the world could be better:

Ergo in se non potest, in Deo potest, quia ipsa non potest, sed Deus potest et quantum ipse potest dici non potest. (*ibid.* 216)

The same ideas are to be found in the work *Summa sententiarum* (*PL* 176, 41–174); they are supported there by many quotations from Augustine. (*PL* 176, 63.70).[104]

In the last quotation, a distinction is made between God's possibilities and natural possibilities. This distinction was a commonplace in the twelfth and thirteenth centuries. It is interesting that the distinction is frequently made so that the kinds of natural possibilities are in fact defined by means of (P), whereas (P) is refuted vis-à-vis supranatural possibilities. Peter Damian writes:

Ventilent quaestiones suas qui uolunt, iuxta modum et ordinem disserendi, dum modo per ambages suas et scolaris infantiae nenias contumeliam non inferant Creatori; sciantque inpossilitatem istam in ipsa rerum esse natura et uerborum ex arte procedentium consequentia, non ad uirtutem pertinere diuinam, nichilque supernae maiestatis euadere posse potentiam, ut dicatur iuxta solius naturae ordine uerborumque conditionem ... (*PL* 145, 615 A–B)

When an instantiation in nature is the criterion for possibilities, miraculous events are impossibilities from the natural point of view:

Utrumque nimirum, et uirginem parere et aedificium ruere, homini Deum ignoranti inpossibilia uidebatur. (*PL* 145, 614 D)

Similarly William of Auxerre writes in his *Summa aurea:*

Stultam fecit deus sapientam huius mundi. Sapientia mundi impossibile iudicat quod in naturis rerum non videt. Hanc autem stultam fecit deus possibile fore declarando atque faciendo quod ipsa impossibile iudicat. Ergo non solum illud est possibile quod est possibile secundum causas inferiores.[105]

Alain of Lille writes that *possibile secundum inferiorem causam* is said *secundum cursum naturae.* It can also be characterized as *consuetudo,* which is *altera natura.* Kinds of natural possibilities are thus possibilities which are already examplified in the course of time. *Cursus naturae* and *consuetudo* show which are the kinds of possibilities *secundum inferiorem causam.*[106] Correspondingly, God's possibilities can be impossibilities according to nature, which fixes the simple use of the concept possibility:

Possibile vero secundum superiorem causam dicimus id quod superior causa, id est Deus, facere potest, quamvis in natura non sit, ut fieri possit, ut asinam Balaam loqui, virginem parere, et hujusmodi. Illud autem quod possibile est secundum naturam, simpliciter dicitur possibile: quod vero dicitur impossibile secundum inferiorem causam, non simpliciter dicitur possibile, sed possibile Deo.[107]

The role of (P) as the criterion of natural possibility figures clearly in the discussions about the value of pictures presenting *chimairas* and other fantastic objects. The proponents of the philosophical theory of art (*ars imitatur naturam*) found such pictures problematic and so did Bernard of Clairvaux, who condemned them because they disturbed religious meditation.[108] Alain of Lille writes:

O nova picturae miracula. Transit ad esse quod nihil esse potest. Picturaque simia veri arte nova ludens, in res umbracula rerum vertit, et in verum mendacia singula mutat. (*PL* 210, 491)

In Alain's opinion, such pictures present impossibilities. If the definition of possibility requires an instantiation in the actual world, there is no problem in making pictures of impossibilities. In fact as far back as the first century B. C. Vitruvius had condemned such pictures which present things which cannot be.[109] Lovejoy has omitted these examples from his extensive catalogue of obvious applications of the Principle of Plenitude.

The above examples show that, in the twelfth and early thirteenth centuries, in certain contexts it was usual to refer to supranatural possibilities when something is impossible according to the natural modalities. Insofar as supranatural possibilities were defined so that (P) did not hold of them, this pattern of thought could actually reinforce the belief that (P) is applicable to all kinds of natural possibilities. On this line of thought Divine possibilities offer metaphysical alternatives to the actual course of events. As such they could have served as a basis for a logical theory of modality, and such attempts can perhaps be found in Peter of Poitiers. When (P) was usually accepted for natural possibilities, Divine possibilities remained, however, more or less only *ad hoc* tools for explaining certain theological problems.

In its most sophisticated form the early scholastic speculation about God's possibilities is found in the works of Robert Grosseteste. In his work *De libero arbitrio*[110], Grosseteste maintains that things do not happen necessarily although God as an infallible being knows them and is unchangeably willing them. Grosseteste's strategy is based on a distinction between two kinds of necessity:

Dico igitur, quod est necessarium duplex: uno modo, quod non habet posse aliquo modo ad eius oppositum vel cum initio vel fine, cuiusmodi est hoc: duo et tria esse quinque. Istud enim posse non habuit neque ante tempus, neque in tempore ad non esse verum. Et tale est necessarium simpliciter. Est et aliud necessarium, quod neque secundum praeteritum, neque secundum praesens, neque secundum futurum habet posse ad eius oppositum, sine tam initio fuit posse ad hoc et fuit posse ad eius oppositum, et tale est antichristum fore futurum et omnium eorum, quae sunt de futuro, quod eorum veritas, cum est, non potest habere non-esse post esse, ut supra ostensum est. Est tamen posse ad hoc, ut ab aeterno et sine initio fuerint falsa. Et ad talem possibilitatem ab aeterno ad esse et non-esse sequitur, quod res est in se contingens, et non quia potest habere non-esse post esse. Plura enim sunt contingentia, quae non habebunt non-esse post esse, sicut anima antichristi. (*De libero arbitrio,* ed. Baur, 168.26–169.15)

It is interesting to see in this connection that, according to Grosseteste, true statements concerning contingent future events are necessarily true because their truth-value cannot change. This seems to be an explication of one particular consequence of the Aristotelian statistical interpretation of modality. Grosseteste's opinion that such statements can be false *sine initio* refers to another providential program. Grosseteste also seems to be aware of the problematic character of this solution as regards the real alternatives of the actual world. So he gives a tentative counter-argument to the doctrine that God can know things different from those He in fact knows. According to the argument, if x is A and x can be $-A$, then $-A$ can be actualized. The actuality of A at a moment is taken to frustrate the possibility of the actualization of $-A$ then. Because a frustrated possibility is not a genuine possibility, x is necessarily A when it is A:

esse aliquid dum est, est necessarium, et maxime si loquamur de esse instanti, ut: si

Scorates est albus in hoc instanti, non est posse ad hoc, ut non sit albus in hoc instanti; quia si potest illud posse vel, potest reduci in actum, vel non. Si potest, reducatur. Tunc sequitur, quod sit albus et non sit albus simul et in eodem indivisibili, quod est impossibile. Si non potest reduci in actum, tunc est posse frustra. Sed nulla est possibilitas frustra. (*Idem* 173.15–174.2)

Unfortunately, Grosseteste does not offer separate comment on this argument. But he clearly believes that the distinction made between different necessities can also be applied to it. Even if it were true in the actual world that God cannot know anything other than what he in fact knows, the stronger necessity (*ab aeterno et sine initio*) would not follow from this claim:

Similiter, cum Deus sciat aliquid, non est posse ad hoc ut, postquam scierit illud, non sciat illud. Est tamen aeternum posse ut sine initio non scierit illud, quod scit. (*Ibid.* 169.38–39, 170.33)[111]

It seems that there is a domain of Divine possibilities part of which is actualized in the history. It is historically important that in this approach possibilities are understood as alternative states of affairs. In the discussions of the twelfth and early thirteenth century unrealized Divine possibilities presented the theological problem of reconciling Divine power (*potentia Dei absoluta*) with Divine goddness and justness rather than a basis for a new modal theory.[112] But even if the epistemic status of God's unrealized possibilities remained unclear and their relevance to the question of the real alternatives of the actual course of events doubtful, this doctrine had some influence on the late medieval modal theory in which logical and real possibilities are distinguished and (P) is no more accepted for either one.

As Eileen Serene has shown in her paper included in this volume, Anselm of Canterbury developed a modal theory without (P) based on the concept of potency. I have already mentioned that there were even in the Aristotelian tradition all kinds of unfulfilled potencies understood as partial possibilities. It remains problematic whether Anselm really had insights principally different from the idea of unrealized partial possibilities.

There was a corresponding discussion among Jewish and Muslim writers. In *The Guide of the Perplexed*[113] (I, 73, the tenth premiss) Moses Maimonides reports that the Mutakallimun maintained that "everything that may be imagined is an admissible notion for the intellect". And, Maimonides continues, "they say of the existent things – provided with known forms and determinate sizes and necessarily accompanying modes that are inchangeable and immutable — that their being as they are is merely in virtue of the continuance of a habit."

These thoughts were a part of the argument for the creation of the world. Because there is an immense group of different imaginable possibilities concerning the world, there must be an agent who is the cause of its being as it is. H. A. Wolfson has shown that one source of Maimonides was the *Nizāmiyyah* of Juwaynī.[114]

Maimonides' criticism of this idea is based on the claim that the Mutakallimun discuss possibilities on the basis of the imagination and not according to the intellect. And in fact there was a tendency in the Kalam to make the class of absolute impossibilities very small. While Christian writers usually considered the Law of Contradiction as a limit to the Divine Omnipotence, many Muslim writers took it as a restriction of God's power only with respect to the actual world. They did not accept any absolute limits to the omnipotency other than certain doctrines concerning the unity of God.[115]

Maimonides in his criticism appears uncertain about the criterion by which one can distinguish whether something is said to be possible only by imagination or by intellect, especially as far as God's possibilities are concerned. In his third philosophical argument for God's existence Maimonides uses the principle that if something is possible, it is sometimes actualized.[116] And it seems that he takes this as a philosophical criterion of possibility. But as such it is not directly applicable to Divine possibilities. Maimonides writes: "For if the philosopher says, as he does: That which exists is my witness and by means of it we discern the necessary, the possible and the impossible; the adherent of the law says to him: The dispute between us is with regard this point. For we claim that that which exists was made in virtue of will and was not a necessary consequence. Now if it was made in this fashion, it is admissible that it should be made in a different way, unless intellectual representation decides, as you think it decides, that something different from what exists at present is not admissible" (I, 73, *loc. cit.*). Even if the Principle of Plenitude can serve as an epistemic criterion of natural possibilities, we cannot know all Divine possibilities. Then we should not speculate about unrealized divine possibilities, because we cannot decide if they are dedicated to Him truly or only by false imagination (III, 15).

8. THE STATISTICAL INTERPRETATION OF MODALITY
IN THOMAS AQUINAS

I have discussed elsewhere the modal notions of Averroes, who defines them
explicitly by means of temporal concepts.[117] His statistical and temporal
interpretation of modality was accepted by such Latin authors as Siger of
Brabant and John of Jandun; the latter presented in 1318 an answer to the
question *"Utrum omne generabile de necessitate generabitur"*, which is
perhaps the biggest defence of the Principle of Plenitude in medieval literature. There John first disproves fifteen different counterexamples to the
principle.[118]

An Averroistic theory of causes had a prominent part in the thought of
Latin Averroists. It was also used by Thomas Aquinas who believed that it
provides at least a partial solution to the problem as to why everything does
not happen necessarily in the world although God guides everything according to the immutable providence.

In the natural philosophy of the thirteenth century Aristotelians two
central terms were *causa efficiens* and *effectus*.[119] A general background to
the causal theory was Avicenna's definition of the relationship between *causa*
and *effectus*. It maintains that every effect is necessary in relation to its
cause:

Omnis effectus est necessarius respectu suae causae.[120]

It was usual to think that everything in the world has a *causa proxima* or
(as with accidental events) a *causa remota*. Hence it seems that, whatever
happens in the world, can be characterized as necessary in the sense of having
a necessitating cause. Thus Thomas Aquinas wrote:

. . . in natura nihil est causale secundum relationem ad causam primam, quia omnia sunt
a Deo provisa; sed sunt aliqua casualia per comparationem ad causas proximas. (*De malo*,
q. 2, a. 5. ad 6).

As this text shows, there were theological reasons for accepting the view
that everything is necessary with respect to its cause. By using this idea
writers aimed to avoid the improper thought that anything in the world could
happen by mere accident and outside Divine Providence. From this point of
view it also seems that, at every moment of time, what happens then happens
necessarily. The adherents of this theory claimed, however, that in another

sense everything does not happen by necessity. This denial could be maintained on the basis of the Aristotelian or at least Boethian distinction *necessitas simplex* vs. *necessitas temporalis*. In physics, a somewhat more complicated devise was used.

According to Averroes, Avicenna's causal principle must be understood so that the effect is necessary when the cause is not impeded from producing the effect. And the central interest of the thirteenth century theory of causality concerned the classification of causes with regard to their possible hindrance.[121] Aquinas presents this idea in his commentary on Aristotle's *Metaphysics* as follows:

> Sed sciendum, quod dictum Avicennae intelligi debet, supposito quod nullum impedimentum causae adveniat. necesse est enim causa posita sequi effectum, nisi sit impedimentum, quod quandoque contingit esse per accidens. (*Metaph.* 1193)[122]

A necessary cause is one which is never impeded from producing the effect when it is in the state of a cause. It is called *causa ut semper*. We see that the modal character of the cause is here explicitly defined statistically and the same holds for contingent causes, too. They are divided into three groups. *Causa ut in pluribus* produces the effect in most cases, *causa ut in paucioribus* or *ut in raro* only in a few cases and *causa ad utrumlibet* presents the special case of fifty percent incidence rate.[123]

If a cause can be impeded from producing the effect, it is sometimes actually impeded, because a necessary cause (*ut semper*) is different from a contingent one precisely in that it never is impeded. And when the modal status of an effect was defined by referring to the nature of the corresponding cause, it could be claimed that an effect is contingent even if it necessarily is when it is. Its cause is such that it can be impeded at other times.

The idea appears clearly from Siger of Brabant's discussion of the question *Utrum omnia futura necessarium sit fore antequam sint.* At a certain moment, the causes of the next effect are not impeded, and therefore it follows necessarily from the causes. For effects of contingent causes this necessity is, according to Siger, of the same type as the necessity employed in the Aristotelian principle: what is, necessarily is when it is. But, because the cause can be impeded at some other time, its effect is contingent even in the case just mentioned.[124] We see that the contingency here is a result of a generalization in respect to time, and Siger's defence of indeterministic physics is, therefore, an application of the statistical modal theory.

Thomas' commentary on Chapter 9 of *De interpretatione* is based on a similar idea of indeterministic causality. He first presents a picture of the world based on causality and modality in the manner of Averroes' Aristotle-interpretation:

Sunt autem differentiae entis possibile et necessarium; et ideo ex ipsa voluntate divina originantur necessitas et contingentia in rebus et distinctio utriusque secundum rationem proximarum causarum: ad effectus enim, quos voluit necessarios esse, disposuit causas necessarias; ad effectus autem, quos voluit esse contingentes, ordinavit causas contingenter agentes, id est potentes deficere. Et secundum harum conditionem causarum, effectus dicuntur vel necessarii vel contingentes. (*In Periherm.* I, *lect.* 14.22).

This is the general background of Thomas' discussion of the problems of future contingent events and the truth of sentences which refer to them. He believes that Aristotle wanted to show that singular future sentences are not in the same way *determinate vera* as other true sentences. If they were determinately true, everything would happen by necessity. As it is not so, there must be a *dissimilitudo* in such sentences in comparison with the others (*op. cit. lect.* 13.6).

One reason for denying the claim that all happens necessarily is, according to Thomas, that the acceptance of this claim would annihilate the apparent threefold contingency (*triplex genus contingentium*):

Quaedam enim contingunt ut in paucioribus, quae accidunt a casu vel fortuna. Quaedam vero se habent ad utrumlibet, quia scilicet non magis se habent ad unam partem quam ad aliam, et ista procedunt ex electione. Quaedam vero eveniunt ut in pluribus; sicut hominem canescere in senectute, quod causatur ex natura. Si autem omnia ex necessitate evenirent, nihil horum contingentium esset. (*In Periherm.* I, *lect.* 13.9)

For this argument to make sense Thomas must have meant by necessity the necessity *ut semper* concerning a cause which never fails in producing its effect. Thomas does not take this necessity to be universal, because there are causes which do not always produce an effect. For this reason, there are different classes of contingent effects. When the focus of attention is on singular future events, Thomas follows the Aristotelian manner of examining the modality of singular events by treating them as representatives of certain classes of events. While Aristotle had in mind what happens in other similar cases and bases the contingency of a definite singular event on a comparison with them, Thomas considers the type of cause in question. When the modal status of an effect is determined by the quality of the cause in question, the treatment is thereby transferred from the definite event to the behaviour of that type of cause in general.

Thomas now takes it as adequately shown that everything does not happen by necessity, but he immediately remarks that singular statements concerning future effects *ut in pluribus* are, however, *determinate vera:*

De eo enim quod est magis determinatum ad unam partem possumus determinate verum dicere quod hoc erit vel non erit, sicut medicus de convalescente vere dicit, iste sanabitur, licet forte ex aliquo accidente eius sanitas impediatur (*In Periherm.* I, *lect.* 13.9).

But where is the dissimilarity promised earlier with respect to other propositions? The answer is that it does not concern the determinateness of their truth, but the way in which they are determined:

cum verum hoc significet ut dicatur aliquid esse quod est, hoc modo est aliquid verum, quo habet esse. Cum autem aliquid est in praesenti habet esse in seipso, et ideo vere potest dici de eo quod est: sed quamdiu aliquid est futurum, nondum est in seipo, est tamen aliqualiter in sua causa: quod quidem contingit tripliciter. Uno modo, ut sic sit in sua causa ut ex necessitate ex ea proveniat; et tunc determinate habet esse in sua causa; unde determinate potest dici de eo quod erit. Alio modo, aliquid est in sua causa, ut quae habet inclinationem ad suum effectum, quae tamen impediri potest; unde et hoc determinatum est in sua causa, sed mutabiliter; et sic de hoc vere dici potest, hoc erit, sed non per omnimodam certitudinem. (*In Perherm.* I, *lect.* 13.11)

According to this view, a contingent effect of the type *ut in pluribus* is in its cause before its occurence in a determined way, albeit changeably. Therefore a true assertoric statement about the occurrence of the effect is determinately true, although its truth-value may change. There are two ways of understanding this claim. We have seen that, in the Aristotelian statistical interpretation of modality, it was common practice to consider the truth-value of a definite sentence changeable by treating the sentence as a member of such a group of temporally indefinite sentences which, when uttered, are sometimes true and sometimes false. Statements about effects the causes of which are impeded *ut in raro* would then allow the characterization that they are true changeably. The other possible interpretation is as follows. Suppose that a future effect is now present in its cause, which is of the type *ut in pluribus*. It is now true to say that this effect is present in its cause without a hindrance. This utterance-token of the sentence concerning the state of the cause may prove to be false, if a hindrance later arises. Both of these alternatives suffer from the same weakness. They explain the changeable truth of a temporally definite singular sentence by referring to properties which the sentence could have were it not a temporally definite sentence. Anyway, the change into temporally indefinite treatment was an Aristotelian method to avoid difficulties caused by temporally definite sentences. And it is in Thomas' opinion an acceptable device for showing that from the determinate truth of singular sentences concerning future contingent events of the type *ut in pluribus* it does not follow that they are happening by necessity.

All future events are not, however, already present in their causes. Therefore Thomas also needs contingency *ad utrumlibet*:

Tertio, aliquid est in sua causa pure in potentia, quae etiam non magis est determinata ad unum quam ad aliud; unde relinguitur quod nullo modo potest de aliquo eorum determinate dici quod sit futurum, sed quod sit vel non sit. (*In Periherm.* I, *lect.* 13.11)

Thomas says that the truth of sentences concerning these kinds of events is not denied by Aristotle. But because the event is not present in the causes, such sentences are not determinately true or untrue. Their truth-value cannot be known, either, because

futura autem non cognoscit in seipsis, quia nondum sunt, sed cognoscere ea potest in causis suis: ... nullo autem modo, si in suis causis sunt omnino in potentia non magis determinata ad unum quam ad aliud, sicut quae sunt ad utrumlibet. (*In Periherm.* I, *lect.* 14.19)

Thomas thinks that this kind of contingent event may as well occur as fail to occur. It is, however, difficult to see what the undetermined truth of sentences concerning such events could mean other than the fifty-fifty statistical division of the two truth-values in the class of corresponding temporally indefinite sentences.

Thomas' belief that a determined truth-value of singular contingent future sentences would lead to determinism is based on the Aristotelian assumption according to which actuality excludes the possibility for something to be otherwise in respect to the same time. And correspondingly the unchanging truth-value of a singular sentence referring to a certain moment of time makes it necessarily true.

We have seen how Thomas tries to qualify singular future sentences so that their truth-value would be changing or indefinite. According to my interpretation he is, in both cases, trying to introduce statistical ideas which do not affect the truth of the singular sentence under discussion. However, by so doing he follows the Aristotelian habit of transferring the discussion from temporally definite cases to temporally indefinite ones. This strategy is stated by Thomas as follows:

Et ideo manifeste verum est quod omne quod est necesse est quando est; et omne quod non est, necesse est non esse *pro illo tempore* quando non est: et haec est necessitas non absoluta sed ex suppositione. Unde non potest simpliciter et absolute dici quod omne quod est, necesse est esse, et omne quod non est, necesse est non esse; quia non idem

significant quod omne ens, quando est, sit ex necessitate, et quod omne ens simpliciter
sit ex necessitate; nam primum significat necessitatem ex suppositione, secundum autem
necessitatem absolutam. (*In Periherm.* I, *lect.* 15.2)

It is clear from the text that *necessitas ex suppositione* means the temporally definite case. Then the temporal word in the sentence *omne quod est,
necesse est esse, quando est* also expresses the condition on which the necessity is in force. Hence the distinction is the same as the Boethian distinction
necessarium temporale vs. *necessarium simplex.* [125]

From this discussion it is already clear how Thomas can maintain that
Divine Omniscience goes hand in hand with indeterminism. From the statistical interpretation of modality, it follows that a temporally definite singular
sentence is necessarily true when it is true. The same holds true for a sentence
as far as it is qualified as being an object of God's knowledge. The traditional
Aristotelian way out of the former dilemma was to see how the truth-value of
the corresponding indefinite sentence behaves at other times. Likewise, if a
sentence or a state of affair necessarily is as it is, insofar as it is an object of
God's definite knowledge, it is not in all cases necessary in the statistical
sense:

Actus divinae cognitionis transit supra contingens, etiam si futurum sit nunc, sicut
transit visus noster supra ipsum dum est; et quia esse, quod est, quando est, necesse est;
quod tamen absolute non est necessarium, ideo dicitur, quod in se consideratum est
contingens, sed relatum ad Dei cognitionem est necessarium, quia ad ipsum non refertur
nisi secundum quod est in esse actuali. (*Sent.* I, *d.* 38, *q.* 1, *a.* 5, *ad.* 3.)

On the basis of the statistical interpretation of causes, an analogous
method could be applied. When the modal status of an effect is primarily
determined by the general nature of the corresponding cause, an effect can
be contingent even if it necessarily is when it is:

Unde manifestum est, quod contingentia et infallibiliter a Deo cognoscitur, inquantum
subduntur divino conspectui secundum suam praesentialitatem, et tamen sunt futura
contingentia suis causis comparata. (*S. Th.* 1 *q.* 14. *art.* 13)

In the light of these distinctions, it was possible to characterize two
different variants of necessity. Although it is necessary that, if God knows
that *p,* then *p* (*necessitas consequentiae*), it does not follow that if God
knows that *p,* then *p* is necessary (*necessitas consequentis*).[126] The latter
necessity does not follow because at a time different from that under discussion things can be otherwise. That this is the interpretation that was given
to the *consequentiae-consequentis* distinction can be seen from the fact that,

according to Thomas, the consequent as a temporally determined sentence is, after all, necessarily true:

Et similiter, si dicam, si Deus scivit aliquid, illud erit, consequens intelligendum est prout subest divinae scientiae, scilicet prout est in sua praesentialitate. Et sic necessarium est, sicut et antecedens: quia omne quod est dum est, necesse est esse, ut dicitur in I Periherm. (*S. th.* I, *q.* 14, *a.* 13 *ad* 2)

Thus understood the logical distinction between *necessitas consequentiae* and *necessitas consequentis* also includes the Aristotelian shift of focus of attention to temporally indefinite sentences. Hence it is analogous to the Aristotelian *compositio-divisio* analysis of possibility sentences containing mutually exclusive predicates. Its basic nature as a distinction between simultaneous and non-simultaneous actuality of predicates appears clearly when Thomas Aquinas discusses the sentence *Omne scitum a Deo est necessarium.* Suppose that a subject has the predicates "known by God to be black" and 'white'. According to Thomas, those predicates cannot belong to the subject *in censu composito* but they can belong to it *in sensu diviso.* While giving this solution in *De veritate* I, *q.* 2, *a.* 12, *ad* 4 Thomas says that the divided sense is true because the subject can be discussed with respect to the time during which it is said to be an object of God's knowledge or without this qualification. The possibility to be white refers thus to those moments of time at which the subject is not seen by God to be black. Although a thing is necessarily black when God sees it to be black, it can have another colour if God does not always see it as black. In this sense the original sentence is false:

refertur enim res ad Dei cognitionem secundum quod est in sua praesentialitate: praesentialitas autem rei non semper ei convenit; unde res potest accipi cum tali dispositione, vel sine ea; et sic per consequens potest accipi illo modo quo refertur ad Dei cognitionem, vel alio modo.

Perhaps the best known mediaeval example of the statistical interpretation of modality occurs in Thomas' third proof of God's existence (*tertia via*). A decisive step in it is the claim

... quod possibile est non esse quandoque non est.[127]

Thomas' proof is similar to one of the proofs of Maimonides mentioned above. As is well-known, Thomas uses this Aristotelian principle in his theodicy, too. If the perfection of the universe requires that there should be some beings which can fail in goodness, then actual failures must occur.[128]

Like his forerunners, Thomas thought that God's possibilities are not all realized. This idea is, however, seldom used in his discussions of philosophical problems. In most cases, Thomas seems to be satisfied with the solutions achieved by applying the statistical interpretation of modality. And even if God's unrealized possibilities are needed in some connections, e.g., in the definition of Divine Omnipotence,[129] it is enough to know that there are such possibilities. It is not important what they are.

This limitation was natural because, according to Thomas, knowledge about the contents of God's unactualized possibilities is beyond the epistemic possibilities of men *in statu viae*. This idea is often repeated by Thomas. It is based on his Aristotelian epistemology. As we saw in Abaelard, the statistical theory of modality may be interpreted in an epistemic way so that we can know whether something is possible only if there is a real example of it. Although, according to Thomas, we can know that there are unrealized possibilities, we cannot know what they are.[130]

In his article 'Aristotle and Corruptibility' C. J. F. Williams had made certain interesting remarks on Thomas' modal theory which seem to contradict my interpretation.[131] He has analysed Aristotle's modal concepts in *De caelo* 281b and he tries to show that a fallacy occurs in Aristotle's argument there. Williams presents as a central distinction the difference between statements of the form

(1) $-M(-p_{t_1} \& p_{t_1})$

and of the form

(2) $-M(-p_{t_1} \& p_{t_2})$

where the former is a special case of Aristotle's statement in 281b12–24 and true, while the latter is a special case of 281b9–11 and false. Williams thinks that Aristotle's mistake is to assume that because the temporal distinction loses its significance if either term is always true, the corresponding modal distinction would likewise become impossible. In fact a purely modal distinction between

(3) $Mp \& M-p$

and

(4) $M(p \& -p)$

is still available, however, although the temporal *compositio-divisio* distinction

(5) $p_{t_1} \& -p_{t_1}$

and

(6) $p_{t_1} \& -p_{t_2}$

does not function any more if one of the terms is eternal. According to Williams, Aristotle had in mind only the temporal distinction and did not realize the feasibility of the modal distinction. Williams does not, however, realize that, with respect to Aristotle's own conceptual presuppositions, he does not make any mistake.[132] Aristotle thought of possibilities from the point of view of their actuality in the one temporal reality of ours. Then Mp and $M-p$ cannot both be true with respect to the same time. Furthermore, if p or $-p$ is always actually true, the other proposition cannot be true, i.e., it is impossible.

According to Williams, Thomas has, in his commentary on *De Caelo*, called attention to this same logical error in Aristotle's thought.[133] This is supposed to be evident from the following text:

Quamvis enim nullius potentia sit ad hoc quod duo opposita sint in eodem tempore in actu, tamen nihil prohibet quod potentia alicuius sit ad duo opposita respectu eiusdem temporis sub disiunctione, aequaliter et eodem modo: sicut potentia mea est ad hoc quod cras in ortu solis vel sedeam vel stem; non tamen ut utrumque sit simul, sed aequaliter possum vel stare non sedendo vel sedere non stando. Sic igitur posset aliquis obviare rationi Aristotelis. Ponamus enim aliquid semper ens, ita tamen quod istud esse suum sempiternum sit contingens et non necessarium. Poterit ergo non esse respectu cuiuscumque partis temporis infiniti, in quo ponitur semper esse: nec propter hoc sequeretur quod aliquid sit simul ens et non ens. Eadem enim ratio videtur in toto infinito tempore, et in aliquo toto tempore finito. Etsi enim ponamus quod aliquis sit in domo semper per totam diem, tamen non est impossibile eum in domo non esse in quacumque parte diei: quia non ex necessitate est in domo per totam diem sed contingenter. (*In De caelo* I, *cap.* 12, *lect.* 26, 6)

It is questionable, however, to what extent Aquinas' distinction corresponds to the modal distinction intended by Williams. For Thomas, it is clear that if p is actual at t_1, $-p$ cannot be actual with respect to the same time and *vice versa*. Therefore Thomas says: *possum vel sedere non stando vel stare non sedendo*. This is, however, not the same thing as the modal thesis Mp_{t_1} & $M-p_{t_1}$, which Williams has in mind, for the condition of truth of both possibilities is their realizability in one and the same historical world.

It might then be thought that, although something eternal is constantly actual, it is nevertheless always possible for it not to be with respect to the next instant of time. Then it would be possible for it not to be infinitely although it cannot not be while it is. Or one could claim that, because it is uncertain whether someone will sit or stand in the near future, both possibilities should be acceptable. For this Thomas gives a little later the following hypothetical argument:

Nihil enim prohibet aliquid esse simpliciter possibile, quod tamen est impossibile aliquo posito: sicut si ponamus Socratem sedere pro aliquo tempore, possibile est simpliciter illum pro illo tempore non sedere, tamen non est compossibile. Ita etiam potest dici quod illud quod fuit tempore infinito, pro tempore illo poterat non esse: non tamen hoc quod est ipsum non esse, est compossibile posito, ut scilicet simul possit poni cum eo quod est ipsum esse. (*In De caelo* I, *cap.* 12, *lect.* 29, 5)

Thomas does not accept in either passage the hypothetical counterargument as proof of the claim that an eternal being could fail to be. And in both cases he refers, as Williams says, to a metaphysical principle irrelevant to the logical topics under discussion:

potentia autem existendi non est ad utrumque respectu temporis in quo quis potest esse; ommia enim appetunt esse, et unumquodque tantum est quantum potest esse. Et hoc praecipue patet in his quae sunt a natura, quia natura est determinata ad unum. Et sic quidquid semper est, non contingenter semper est, sed ex necessitate. (*In De caelo* I, *cap.* 12, *lect.* 26, 6)

From this metaphysical principle it follows that, for every moment of time, what at that time can be actual is then actualized. This is in contradiction with the principle p_{t_1} & $M\text{-}p_{t_1}$ which according to Williams Thomas first accepted. It seems to me, however, that Thomas does not make this logical mistake. I have supposed that Thomas' understanding of possibilities in this context is, from start to finish, based on the assumption that what is possible must sometimes be actual in the temporal reality. When Thomas says that it is true to say with respect to a certain moment of time that someone can sit if he does not stand or he can stand if he does not sit, the mutually exclusive nature of the conditions shows that only one of the alternatives will turn out to be a genuine possibility. This is exactly what is stated in the metaphysical argument.[134]

9. DUNS SCOTUS' CRITICISM OF THE STATISTICAL INTERPRETATION OF MODALITY

In the preceding chapters I have followed the career of modality in scholasticism. I think that there is sufficient evidence to support the claim that one should always bear in mind the possibility of the statistical interpretation of modality in discussing medieval texts containing modal concepts. In this chapter I will put forth a definite limit after which a scholar also has to consider the possibility that the model in question had been rejected on the basis of an entirely different understanding of modality. I mean John Duns Scotus' criticism of the statistical interpretation and his own theory of modality which is based on a distinction between logical and real possibilities, on an extension of the focus of attention to alternative states of affairs with respect to the same moment of time, and on the essential function of the concept of compossibility. I shall concentrate only on Duns Scotus; his possible predecessors, e.g., Henry of Ghent and certain Franciscan thinkers of the thirteenth century, are beyond the intended purview of this paper.

In his *Tractatus de primo principio*,[135] Duns Scotus gives a short account of his theory of what can be said about God as First Principle on the ground of purely philosophical and rational argumentation. The work can thus be characterized as *prolegomena* to a metaphysics, but the actual motive for its writing was perhaps Scotus' intention only to collect together different ideas about the First Principle dispersed in his Commentaries on the Sentences.[136]

In the first chapter, Duns Scotus defines the concept of essential order (*ordo essentialis*) as a category of being (*passio entis*) and shows into which subclasses it can be divided. In the second chapter he seeks to prove that the distinctions made in the first chapter are exhaustive and that their members are mutually exclusive. The third chapter offers the argument that different kinds of orders presuppose a First Principle which can be shown to be one and the same.

The subject of the fourth chapter is the simplicity, infinity, and intellectuality of the First Being. This chapter is especially interesting with respect to our theme because here Scotus tries to demonstrate that both the Aristotelian as well as the Neoplatonic metaphysics include conceptual presuppositions which inevitably lead into difficulties in discussing the contingency of phenomena or, as Scotus says, in saving the contingency.[137]

The basic ideas of Scotus' criticism appear from his proof that the first efficient cause is intelligent and endowed with will (IV, 4).[138] The third argument for this thesis is based on the concept of contingency and runs as follows. Something is caused contingently. Therefore the first cause operates contingently and hence voluntarily. The conclusion from the occurrence of contingent phenomena to the contingent operation of the First Principle is proved by the principle that every secondary cause causes in the same way as it is moved by the first cause. The proof of the second conclusion, according to which the First Principle is endowed with will, is based on a distinction between natural necessity and contingency. The will is the only source of contingency. Every other cause acts according to natural necessity.

The reasons put forth in these proofs are traditional. They resemble discussions about God's possibilities in the twelfth century. The causality proceeding from secondary causes is not metaphysically necessary and pertains to the voluntary character of the first cause. It will be seen, however, that for Duns Scotus unrealized possibilities are no longer entangled with the mysteries of Divine Omnipotence.

Three objections are then proposed against this argument for the intelligent and voluntary operation of the First Principle. According to the first objection, our will could still cause something contingently when the first cause would move it necessarily. The second objection states that Aristotle concedes that something is caused contingently but denies the contingency of the will of God. For he assumes, according to the argument, that the source of contingency in sublunary things is motion. And although motion is caused necessarily insofar as it is uniform, yet difformity and contingency follow from its parts. According to the third objection some moved things can be impeded, and the opposite can, therefore, occur contingently. Thus it seems that no reference to the will as the source of contingent action is needed. The text of the argument and the objections against it run as follows:

Aliquid causatur contingenter; igitur prima causa contingenter causat; igitur volens causat. Probatio primae consequentiae: Quaelibet causa secunda causat inquantum movetur a prima; ergo si prima necessario movet, quaelibet necessario movetur et quidlibet necessario causatur. Probatio secundae consequentiae: Nullum est principium contingenter operandi nisi voluntas vel concomitans voluntatem, quia quaelibet alia agit ex necessitate naturae et ita non contingenter. Obicitur contra primam consequentiam: quia nostrum velle posset adhuc contingenter aliquid causare. Item: Philosophus concessit antecedens et negavit consequens intelligendo de velle Dei, ponendo contingentiam in inferioribus ex motu, qui necessario causatur inquantum uniformis, sed difformitas sequitur ex partibus eius, et ita contingentia. – Contra secundam: Aliqua mota possunt impediri et ita oppositum contingenter evenire.

As far as the first objection is concerned Scotus points out that if there were a necessary first efficient cause with respect to our will, the same would hold good of the will as of other things under the influence of such a cause. Our will would then be necessarily willing, for something else would cause it to will necessarily. The first efficient cause could activate our will either immediately or indirectly, so that it would first move something else which would then move our will. But if the first cause moves necessarily, our will would be necessarily moved by its *causa proxima*, because a second cause functions in the same way as it is moved by the first cause. And another impossibility would follow in Scotus' opinion. Anything caused by a will would be caused necessarily:

Si est primum efficiens respectu voluntatis nostrae, idem sequitur de ipsa quod et de aliis; quia, sive immediate necessario moveat eam, sive aliud immediate, et illud necessario motum necessario moveat, quia movet ex hoc quod movetur, tandem proximum necessario movebit voluntatem; et ita necessario volet et erit volens necessario. Sequitur ulterius impossibile, quod necessario causat quod volendo causat.

When dealing with the second objection, Scotus states that contingency means that, when something happens, its opposite could have happened at the time when it actually did. He also implies that Aristotle uses the concept of contingency in a different way. Scotus says that, if an effect necessarily follows from its cause at a certain moment (*quando causatur*), it cannot then (*tunc*) follow from it contingently in the Aristotelian sense of contengency. If phenomena are seen in a temporally definite way, then everything appears to happen necessarily. Causal chains can, however, be contingent in the other sense if the First Principle does not produce them in such a way that it could not help producing them:

Non dico hic contingens quodcumque non est necessarium nec sempiternum, sed cuius oppositum posset fieri quando istud fit. Ideo dixi: "Aliquid contingenter causatur", non: "Aliquid est contingens". Modo dico quod Philosophus non potuit consequentiam negare salvando antecedens per motum; quia si ille motus totus necessario est a causa sua, quaelibet pars eius necessario causatur quando causatur, hoc est, inevitabiliter, ita quod oppositum tunc non posset causari. Et ulterius: Quod causatur per quamcumque partem motus, necessario tunc causatur, id est, inevitabiliter. Vel igitur nihil fit contingenter, id est evitabiliter, vel primum sic causat, etiam immediate, quod posset non causare.

According to Duns Scotus, the possible hindrance to the cause mentioned in the third objection demands that attention be paid to a stronger cause — in the last analysis to the first cause. When every cause in a causal chain, ultimately proceeding from the first cause, produces its effect necessarily, the impeded cause is necessarily impeded from producing the effect when it does not produce it:

Si alia causa potest impedire istam, nunc potest virtute superioris causae impedire, et sic usque ad primam; quae si immediatam causam sibi necessario movet, in toto ordine usque ad istam impedientem erit necessitas; igitur necessario impediet; igitur tunc non posset alia causa causare contingenter causatum.

The common basic thought underlying these refutations is expressed in the principle according to which the contingency is not sufficiently defined when it is taken to mean such things or events as are changing and hence not necessary. In reality a contingent state of affairs is such that its opposite could occur at the time when it is actual. Next I shall show how this definition of contingency meant a real break in the modal theories of Scholasticism.

The modal thesis of Duns Scotus is incompatible with the Aristotelian modal paradigm which I have called the statistical interpretation of modality. I have mentioned some examples of its applications to theological problems in the middle Ages as well as examples of the method by means of which Aristotle and his medieval followers tried to explain away its implicit determinism. The often used Aristotelian distinction between modal sentences understood *in sensu composito* and those understood *in sensu diviso* was based on temporally or generically indefinite treatment of sentences. When the notion of possibility applied to a sentence containing mutually exclusive predicates is spelled out by reading the sentence *in sensu composito*, then the sentence is false, because possibility would then refer to the simultaneous actuality of incompatible predicates. It can, however, be true *in sensu diviso* and it then allows one of the predicates to be actual when the other is not. So every temporally definite true sentence is necessarily true, but its necessity can be characterized as a merely temporal necessity. This means that its truth-value can change at another time. The writers were not concerned about the fact that the temporal reference presupposed in this solution is variable. On the contrary, they often used in the same context such expressions as "at the time God sees it" and "at another time" while describing how something is only temporally necessary.

A related idea was used in the thirteenth century theory of causality where causes were classified into different groups according to the possibility of their being impeded. This classification is nothing but an application of the statistical theory of modality to physics. If a certain effect is viewed at the moment of its occurrence, it occurs then necessarily, but it can be called contingent if the corresponding cause is of such generic nature that at other times when it is *in statu causae* it does not always produce te effect.

In the part of the *Tractatus de primo principio* quoted above, Duns Scotus calls attention to the fact that, if the processes of the world are reducible to first cause acting necessarily, then it cannot be claimed, at the same time, that there are contingent phenomena in the world. Scotus also denies that the statistical interpretation of modality could be a sufficient basis for maintaining that everything does not happen necessarily. As we have seen earlier, there were writers (such as Thomas Aquinas) who did not accept metaphysical necessitarianism but who thought that the contingency of a number of natural phenomena can be proved in terms of the statistical view without reference to supranatural possibilities. When the influence from the higher causes proceeds in the chain of causes, according medieval Aristotelians, it arrives at contingent causes which in the state of a cause sometimes produce their effect and sometimes do not. So the contingency could be defended without discussing the nature of the first cause. It remained a fact, however, that when the contingent causes produce their effects, they produce them then necessarily (*quaelibet pars necessario causatur quando causatur*). And the opposite effect cannot then (*tunc*) follow from the cause.

The idea of Scotus' criticism is to hold on to this description which is definite with respect to a certain instant of time. When a certain individual effect is under consideration, it cannot be proved to be contingent by alluding to what happened under similar initial conditions at another time. For instance, if at a certain moment Socrates wants to sit and he therefore cannot at that time will anything incompatible with his sitting, his possibility to will otherwise then is not proved by showing that at another moment he wants to stand. Accordingly, Scotus says that the contingency does not mean what is not always the case (as in the statistical interpretation of modality); a contingent event is one the opposite of which could occur at the time when it is actual. This concept of contingency is erroneous from the point of view of the statistical interpretation of modal concepts. According to Scotus, it must, nevertheless, be accepted if one wants to express that something does not happen necessarily.

The basic idea of Scotus' criticism is also clear from his remark concerning the third objection. According to it some causes can be impeded, although all actual effects occur necessarily. Again Scotus discusses the problem in terms of temporally definite events. If the cause C_1 can be impeded at the moment t_1, this possibility is based on a cause C_2, and so on up to the first cause. If it operated in a necessary manner, then the cause C_2 necessarily would impede C_1 from producing the effect and it would then be impossible for it to produce its effect contingently (*tunc non posset causare contingenter causatum*).

Even here Scotus tries to prove the incompatibility of the contingency with a metaphysical necessitarianism by discussing the case explicitly in a temporally definite way. If there is no alternative to a temporally definite event, it is misleading to call it contingent.

According to Duns Scotus the concept of a statistical contingency as applied to temporally indefinite sentences does not take account of the modal status of individual events. Implicitly it presupposes that they are necessary. Francis of Marchia, an Italian scotist, expresses this idea very well in the 38th distinction of the first book of his Commentary on the Sentences:

Ideo talis contingentia, quae est in ordine ad unam causam impedibilem per aliam causam vel ex parte agentis vel ex parte patientis, et non in ordine ad totum ordinem causarum simul, est contingentia secundum quid et non simpliciter. Ideo talis contingentia est contingentia per accidens et non per se, quia est in ordine ad causas accidentales et non in ordine ad causas essentiales nisi inquantum concurrunt cum causis accidentalibus. Est contingentia secundum quid et non simpliciter. Est contingentia privativa et non positiva, quia non est contingentia in ordine ad causas in ultima dispositione in qua possunt agere effectum, sed est in ordine ad causas in dispositione in qua non possunt pro tunc agere effectum . . . . Contingentia vero per se est, qua effectus est contingens in ordine ad causas essentiales, non in ordine ad causas accidentales, quia remotis omnibus causis accidentalibus vel eis positis potest effectus poni ab eis vel non poni . . . .[139]

This new terminology quickly became part of general usage in the science of the fourteenth century. Natural phenomena are now considered to be necessary with respect to their causes. Because the reasons for a possible hindrance were explicated in the initial conditions to which causal rules were applied, the statistical dimension of modality became irrelevant. So the supposed contingency of natural phenomena was, according to John Buridan, based on the fact that certain things appear to be contingent as long as the causal connection of nature are not perfectly clear to men.[140]

These themes are present in Scotus' criticism of traditional metaphysics. Although problems of natural science were not central to the main interest of Scotus, his philosophical work concerning the nature of knowledge and modality produced some important ideas in this area, too. In terms of his new understanding of modality spelt out by considering alternative states of affairs at the same time Scotus could easily make a distinction between conceptual necessity and constitutional necessity of natural events. Although the phenomena of nature are causally necessary, they belong to a whole which is only one of several conceivable worlds.[141] We do not know a priori which possible world we are living in. This idea could inspire research into the laws of the actual world in a way different from the Aristotelian science, in which conceptual necessity is required of scientific truths. From Scotus' point of view, this demand appears to be a restriction of our epistemic possibilities concerning the actual world. Thus Scotus says that, by means of inductive research, we can find out what the actual world is like even if the results do not have the certainty of analytical or logical truths (principia nota ex terminis).[142] However, it must be stated that this is not a description of the fourteenth century physics. The Aristotelian idea of science was transcended there by creating models for physical phenomena *secundum imaginationem*, *i.e.*, for thinkable worlds. The methods of finding the actual world were not much considered.

All the doctrines implied in the three objections mentioned above can be found, e.g., in Siger of Brabant's works.[143] The main object of Scotus' attack is metaphysical necessitarianism. He especially criticizes the attempts to use the statistical interpretation of modality in bringing together the contingency of phenomena and the first cause acting necessarily. But, as we have seen, the use of the statistical model was not restricted to those Aristotelians who accepted the doctrine of the first cause as a necessarily acting agent. While Scotus' replies to the second and the third objection are thus in a sense also relevant to Thomas Aquinas' works, the first objection and its discussions have a more limited scope. In Thomas' opinion, God moves the will *ut indeterminate se habens ad multa* while *determinatio ad volendum hoc vel illud* is the agent's own act. On this theory, God usually has an influence on the will only as sustaining it, and the will in action is, therefore, not a link in any causal chain.[144] I have shown elsewhere the kinds of difficulties which Thomas gets involved when he tries to defend the freedom of will in conjunction with his statistical theory of modality against rational determinism.[145] In this connection it is enough to state that Duns Scotus' first objection does not refer to Thomas' theory of the freedom of will.

Siger of Brabant writes, however, exactly in the way criticized by Duns Scotus. According to Siger, acts of will are caused, and they do not essentially differ from natural events. The freedom of will implies only that the same act of willing does not always occur when the cause is present, because a stronger cause can impede it.[146] Duns Scotus says that this statistical theory of the freedom of will can be criticized in the same way as the application of the statistical model to natural phenomena (*idem sequitur de ipsa quod et de aliis*).

Scotus' medieval predecessors did not accept the statistical model of modality without qualifications. It was thought to limit God's freedom and omnipotency especially in connection with the doctrine of creation. Therefore the earlier mentioned writers usually accepted the view that God does not fulfill all of his possibilities. Ingetrud Pape has shown that δυνατὰ οὐ κατὰ δύναμιν mentioned by Aristotle in *Met.* 1019b21−33 were understood in the Scholasticism as a class of possibilities which are not said according to a natural potency. Such possibilities were needed in the theology of creation because creation took place *ex nihilo*. And while the concept of a natural potency presupposed an actuality sometimes, Divine Omnipotence was defined by reference to other kinds of potencies in order to save His freedom.[147] According to Thomas Aquinas, *possibilia non secundum potentiam* are absolute possibilities and God is said to be omnipotent with respect to them. Absolute possibilities are conceptual possibilities; their criterion is that the subject is not incompatible with the predicate (*praedicatum non repugnat subjecto*). Thomas says that not all such possibilities will be actualized.[148] However, in other context he accepts the statistical interpretation.[149] This practice is based on the view that it does not belong to the epistemic possibilities of man to know what the absolute possibilities of God are. They do not occur in Thomas' philosophical argumentation as rational alternatives to the actual world.[150] They constitute a class of supranatural possibilities and their main function seems to be to serve as the basis of God's sovereignty. Scotus also believed (erroneously) that Aristotle puts forward in *Met.* 1019b a purely conceptual possibility. He calls it *possibile logicum*.[151] But the function of these possibilities in Scotus' thought is very different from their status in Aquinas' thought.

The main lines of Scotus' theory of modality are easy to understand without any speculative interpretations. This depends on the fact that his starting-point is a criticism of the statistical interpretation of modality. An extensive discussion about the theory of modality is to be found in distinction 39 of the first book in Scotus' Commentaries on the Sentences. In accordance with the tradition, this chapter contains a survey of modal concepts because in it God's knowledge about future contingents is discussed.

According to Scotus a *causatum* can be contingent only if the first cause functions in a contingent way. The contingency of phenomena in a causal chain depends on whether the whole universe (which is ultimately reducible to the first cause) could be different. Scotus takes this to be conceptually possible.[152] Therefore *causa prima* does not act necessarily in the sense that it would be bound to the general outlook of the actual world. But although the world as a whole is thus contingent, the phenomena of nature are, nevertheless, causally necessary.

In Scotus' system, the will has an exceptional position in comparison with the natural phenomena. When natural agents act under given initial conditions in a causally determined way, the will as a non-natural agent determines its action itself (*agens liber*). With respect to it, the contingency is not constitutionally conditional (*secundum quid*) as is the case with respect to the natural agents.[153] Using the definition of the contingency of the human will Scotus formed for himself a conceptual model for describing the free action of the First Principle.

For Scotus, the will is not free in the sense that it could at the same time will a thing and its opposite (*non enim est libertas in voluntate nostra ut simul velit opposita obiecta*). But the will is free with respect to the act of willing at any given time (*habet libertatem ad actus oppositos*). Thus Socrates cannot want to sit and stand at the same time but instead of willing to stand he could be not willing it.[154]

This analysis is analogous to the distinction between *sensus compositus* and *sensus divisus* and Scotus' comments on it, therefore, clarify his understanding of modal concepts as compared with the earlier use of the distinction in modal contexts. According to Duns Scotus, this description of the freedom of will ensues first the notion of possibility or contingency which I have earlier called the statistical interpretation of modality. By this one means that the will can successively intend opposite objects:

Una contingentia et possibilitas, ut voluntas successive feratur in obiecta opposita: et haec possibilitas et contingentia consequitur eius mutabilitatem. Et secundum hanc possibilitatem distinguuntur propositiones de possibili quae fiunt de extremis contrariis et oppositis, ut "album potest esse nigrum": et secundum sensum divisionis est propositio vera, prout intelliguntur extrema habere possibilitatem pro diversis temporibus, ut "album in *a* potest esse nigrum in *b*"; unde ista possibilitas consequitur successionem. Et sic etiam haec vera in sensu divisionis "voluntas amans illum, potest odire illum". (*Lect.* I, d. 39, q. 1–5, n. 48)

This kind of contingency is, nevertheless, not a sufficient basis for the freedom of the will. It would only mean that the will can will different things at different times. But this property, which follows from the mere changeability of the will, does not take into account the question of whether the will while willing something could be not willing it then. And if this is not the case, then the will is always willing necessarily when it is willing. That is why the description of the freedom of the will presupposes a different concept of possibility:

Sed adhuc illam libertatem voluntatis consequitur alia potentia, quae est logica (cui etiam correspondet potentia realis). Potentia logica non est aliqua nisi quando extrema sic sunt possibilia quod non sibi invicem repugnant sed uniri possunt, licet non sit possibilitas aliqua in re: ... Haec autem possibilitas logica non est secundum quod voluntas habet actus successive, sed in eodem instanti: nam in eodem instanti in quo voluntas habet unum actum volendi, in eodem et pro eodem potest habere oppositum actum volendi, ... (*Ibid. n.* 49–50)

Scotus gives the following example of this logical possibility. Let us consider the will at some instant of time at which it is willing something. Its actual turning towards the willed object is not, however, its essential property. And because the opposite of an accidental property can be attributed to the subject without a conceptual contradiction, it can be said that, when the will is willing a certain thing at a certain time, it can at that time be not willing it (*voluntas volens a in hoc instanti et pro hoc instanti potest nolle a in eodem et pro eodem*).[155]

The logical possibility as such is not a sufficient framework for the treatment of the freedom of the will. Its meaning for Scotus in this connection is to show that contradictory sentences can be logically possible in the divided sense with respect to the same instant of time. Thus it helps him to get rid of the conceptual difficulties present in the attempts to reconcile the freedom of the will and the statistical interpretation of modality.

The nature of those difficulties can be characterized in the following way. When every genuine possibility is assumed to be realized sooner or later, every possible sentence entails the presupposition that there is, in actual history, at least one instant of time at which the possibility is actualized and the sentence declared to be possible is true.[156] If we have a sentence "It is possible that p", we interpret the possibility as concerning the instants of time at which p can be true or $M(Et)p(t)$. According to the statistical model of modality, this sentence is true only if there is at least one instant of time, say t_1 such that p is true at t_1. But if $-p$ is always true, there is no such instant. It is, therefore, contradictory to think that something could be at a certain moment of time if it is not then, in other words $(t)\,(-p(t) \supset -Mp(t))$.[157] This is also the interpretation often given in the Scholasticism to the Aristotelian principle: "What is necessarily is when it is".

According to Duns Scotus $-p$ & Mp is not a real contradiction. In his opinion, this conjunction is consistent because, for p to be possible, it need not be required that p be sometimes true in the actual world. It is sufficient that it would be true if an alternative to the actual world were actual. The new idea in Scotus' modal theory is to consider several alternative states of affairs at the same time and with respect to the same moment of time. When Scotus introduces in the text quoted above a class of logical possibilities, which are also real possibilities, it seems that all logical possibilities are not real alternatives to the actual world. We have seen earlier that the structure and the laws of the nature set certain limits on real possibilities. But the possibility of willing otherwise is a real alternative because it does not demand that the structure of the actual world be different.

The real possibility needed in the explication of the freedom of the will is connected with the idea of alternatives which is taken to be implicit in the notion of logical possibility. So the temporal distinction between simultaneous and non-simultaneous actualization is no longer of importance to

Scotus' thought. Real possibility is needed because it is a feature of the freedom of the will that the agent could have willed otherwise not only in a
logical sense but in a real sense, too. This real possibility is described by Duns
Scotus in the following way. Every cause is prior with respect to its effect.
Even when the cause and the effect are temporally simultaneous, a real state
of affairs is reflected in this distinction. Therefore the will, at the moment
at which it chooses a certain act of willing, precedes that act of willing. Thus
the will, at the moment of its willing, stands in a contingent relationship to
that act of willing as well as to the corresponding not-willing. And this contingency is not based on a claim that the will had earlier a contingent relationship to the act of willing because the will was then not the cause of the
actual act of willing. It is the cause of the actual act of willing so that *volens
in a potest nolle in a.*[158]

In a traditional manner Scotus then states that the sentence: *volens in a
potest nolle in a* can be understood *secundum compositionem* or *secundum
divisionem*. In the first case, it is false and in the second case it is true. But it
is historically important that Scotus explicitly denies that the reason for the
truth of the latter case is the fact that the mutually exclusive predicates refer
to different points of time (*non quia extrema intelliguntur pro diversis temporibus*). Instead of this analysis, the sentence must be understood as a
conjunction of two sentences. In one of them, an act of willing is stated and
in the other an opposite act of willing is claimed to be possible.[159] The sentence is then explained as follows:

> "voluntas est volens in *a*" et "voluntas potest esse nolens in *a*", – et hoc verum est, quia
> voluntas volens in *a*, libere elicit actum volendi nec est eius passio.
>   Unde si ponitur voluntatem esse tantum in uno instanti, libere vult, et non libere vult
> nisi quia potest nolle. Et ideo vera est in sensu divisionis "voluntas volens in *a*, potest
> esse nolens in *a*" . . . (*Lect.* I, *d*. 39, *q*. 1–5, *n*. 51–52)

After this conceptual analysis Duns Scotus believed he had tools for an
adequate analysis of the question of whether the divine will can be free if it
is never changing. Scotus' answer runs as follows:

> ut sicut est possibilitas in voluntate nostra respectu actus volendi – et logica et realis –
> in eodem instanti et pro eodem respectu eiusdem, ita etiam voluntas divina, quae in
> quantum operativa praecedit se ut productiva, potest in eodem instanti aeternitatis et
> pro eodem instanti aeternitatis velle et nolle aliquid, et sic producere aliquid et non
> producere. (*Ibid. n.* 54)

Next Scotus puts forward three objections to this solution:

(1) When the will at a certain moment is willing a certain thing, it is not

possible that it could be not willing it then because Aristotle says that every-thing necessarily is, when it is.

(2) *Ars obligatoria* embodies the following principle: if a contingent sen-tence now false is supposed to be true, it must be denied that now is the present moment at which it is true. If for example the sentence: "You are in Rome" is now (at the present moment, say *a*) false but if it is assumed to be true, it must be denied that *a* is the present 'now' of discussion. A sentence false at the moment *a* cannot be true then, because it should be possible for it to become true then, whereas there is no motion at an instant.

(3) If the will is willing something at moment *a* and if it can be not willing it, this possibility is a potency with an actuality or before an actuality. It cannot be a *potentia cum actu* and therefore it is a *potentia ante actum* and thus refers to another time.[160]

In his answer to the first objection, Duns Scotus states that the sentence *omne quod est quando est, est necessarium* can be understood *secundum compositionem* and *secundum divisionem*. According to the first reading, the sentence is categorical and true. The meaning is that necessarily everything is when it is. In the divided sense the sentence is conditional and false. Then it means that whenever something is, it then necessarily is. The true reading is based on the fact that it is not possible that something belongs to the sub-ject and does not belong to it at the same time.[161]

The solution which Scotus offers here does not parallel the Aristotelian distinction in *De int.* 19a23–27 according to which the necessity of a tem-porally definite sentence disappears with the removal of the temporal qualifi-cation. For Scotus, both cases are temporally definite. And although every temporally definite sentence expresses a necessary identity in the composite sense, this does not mean that every temporally definite sentence would be necessarily true as Aristotle and his followers before Scotus were inclined to believe.

The second objection seems to be derived from William of Sherwood's work *De obligationibus*.[162] *Ars obligatoria* was a method of logical training frequently used in medieval universities. In the game of obligation, the opponent first proposes a statement which the respondent accepts by binding himself to its truth (*se obligat*). The opponent then proposes other claims and the respondent must accept or deny them in such a way that he will neither accept anything contradictory to the original sentence nor deny anything not contradictory.[163]

In a tract concerning *Ars obligatoria* that dates from the beginning of the 13th century[164] the following rule is to be found: *Quolibet falso possibili posito de instanti quod est, negandum est illud esse.* The rule is then discussed in the light of the following example. Socrates is now black and it is now the moment *a*. The respondent accepts the sentence: "Socrates is white" but then he has to deny the statement: "It is now the moment *a*". This is a clear example of the habit of understanding possibilities as states of affairs actualized successively instead of considering them as alternative states of affairs with respect to a certain moment in time. In an additional remark the writer states that if the black Socrates is said to be white with respect to the instant at which he is black, this is something impossible as such. If the sentence is understood in a temporally indefinite way, it is possible if there is an instant at which he is white.[165]

William of Sherwood discusses the same rule in an analogous way. In addition, he gives the reason mentioned by Scotus that *x* which is *A* at the moment *a* cannot be −*A* at that moment because it cannot become −*A*. The possibility is here considered from the point of view of actualization in the real history as is usual in the statistical modal theory. Thus it seems that *x* can be −*A* only if *x* is not always *A*, i.e., if it at some time is −*A*.[166] Scotus has already presented his idea that the meaning of modal concepts is connected with treating several alternative states of affairs at the same time, and so he is contented with stating that the rule in question is erroneous:

Etsi te esse Romae sit falsum in *a*, potest tamen esse verum in *a*, -sicut licet voluntas velit aliquid in *a*, potest non velle illud in *a*. (*Lect.* I, d. 39, q. 1–5, n. 56)[167]

As to the third objection, Scotus remarks that the question is not about *potentia ante actum tempore* but about *potentia ante actum natura*. The will and the act of willing can be separated within an instant of time and, on the basis of this non-temporal distinction, it can be claimed that even when the will at that instant is willing something it could be not willing.[168]

According to Duns Scotus, it is true of logical and of real possibilities that possibility can be attributed to a contrafactual state of affairs with respect to a certain moment of time. It is therefore easy for him to solve the classical problem about the compatibility of Divine Foreknowledge and indeterminism. We have seen how one popular solution to this problem was to make a temporal distinction between a sentence as an object of Divine Foreknowledge at a certain moment and the sentence without this condition. The possibility to be otherwise at another time is, of course, superfluous to the problem in question. And according to Scotus, this shift in the focus of attention is not needed. Even if God knows that *p* is true at the moment t_1 in the future, p_{t_1} can be false. Even if God knows what Socrates will do at a certain moment in

the future, Socrates could do otherwise. Correspondingly in Scotus' opinion
the possibility of God's error does not follow from the fact that God knows
that *p* in the future while it is possible that —*p*. But such a consequence without modal notions would be valid.[169]

The starting-point of Duns Scotus' modal theory is the concept of logical
possibility (*possibile logicum*).[170] Every sentence which does not contain a
conceptual contradiction is logically possible. Each possibility can be thought
of as being actualized. This is, in fact, the interpretation given to the absence
of conceptual contradiction as a distinguishing mark of conceptual possibilities (*non repugnat sibi esse*).[171] It does not mean, however, that any possibility could be actual in the factual world because all possibilities are not
compossible.[172] In *An pr.* 32a18–20 Aristotle defines possibility by saying
that, when a possibility is assumed to be realized, nothing impossible results.
A statistical exposition of this principle is to be found in *De caelo* 281b3–25
where Aristotle states that if something never actual is assumed to be possible,
something impossible will follow, namely, that something would be and not
be at the same time. In Duns Scotus' theory of modality, nothing impossible
will necessarily follow if something never actual is thought to be actual. It
may be that it cannot be actual in the factual world but, from this incompossibility with the actual world, it does not follow that it would be impossible
as such. Thus the Aristotelian definition must be improved so that, from
supposing a possibility to be actual, nothing impossible follows except in
cases when an incompossibility follows from it:

Et hoc est quod solet dici, quod posito aliquo possibile in esse, non sequitur impossibile
nisi quando resultat aliqua incompossibilitas. (*Lect.* I, *d.* 39, *q.* 1–5, *n.* 72)

According to Scotus, contrafactual states of affairs at a certain moment
are thus not impossible merely because they are not actual. This important
step in the history of modal notions was made possible by Scotus' insight
that possibilities do not presuppose a corresponding actuality in the real
world.

In distinction 43 of the first book of his Commentaries on the Sentences,
Scotus treats the question of whether something is impossible because God
cannot do it or whether God cannot do something because it is impossible.
In this connection, he gives a kind of a metaphysical model for his theory of
modality. In the first instant of being things receive an intelligible being (*esse
intelligibile*) in the intellect of God. Because the intelligible being comprises
the individual nature (*quidditas*) of each thing that can be known, a possible
being (*esse possibile*) follows from the intelligible being in the second instant

of nature. For it holds of everything belonging to the first instant that it is not contradictory for them to be (*formaliter non repugnat sibi esse*).[173]

The possibilities belonging to the second instant of nature are the object of Divine Omnipotence. In this sense possibilities are prior with respect to Omnipotence. Therefore impossible states of affairs are not impossible because God cannot do them. God cannot do something because it is impossible. Impossibility in general then takes the form of a conceptual incompossibility:

Est ergo ibi iste processus, quod sicut Deus suo intellectu producit possibile in esse possibili, ita producit duo entia formaliter (utrumque in esse possibili), et illa 'producta' se ipsis formaliter sunt incompossibilia, ut non possint simul esse unum, neque aliquid tertium ex eis; hanc autem incompossibilitatem, quam habent, formaliter ex se habent, et principiative ab eo – aliquo modo – qui ea produxit. Et istam incompossibilitatem eorum sequitur incompossibilitas totius figmenti, includentis ea, et ex ista impossibilitate figmenti in se et ex incompossibilitate partium suarum est incompossibilitas eius respectu cuiuscumque agentis;... (*Ord.* I, *d.* 43, *q.* u., *n.* 16)

In this model possibilities are classified into equivalence classes on the basis of relations of compossibility. One of the classes into which logical possibilities are partitioned is the actual world. Because these classes contain only mutually consistent propositions, it is impossible according to Scotus that the actual world would contain all possibilities as actual. The relationships between possible states of affairs always exclude part of them from any one joint world. This is the background of Scotus' treatment of claim that if God knows that p and $M-p$, it follows that God is liable to err. Scotus states that nothing impossible follows if it holds that p while it is possible that $-p$ and the possibility is thought to be actual. The contradiction does not follow from the mere assumption that a possibility is actual. In order for it to come about it is crucial that the possibility is incompossible with something else in the same assumed world – for instance with the fact that God knows that p. Then there is an *incompossibilitias quantum ad aliam.*[174]

In the light of this model of modality projected on God's intellectual life, the problem of infallible knowledge about future contingents appears to be as follows. The conceptual combinations produced by the Divine Intellect are classified into groups belonging to the second instant of being (*esse possibile*). From those groups the Divine Will chooses one to be true of the actual world:

Intellectus divinus offert voluntati suae complexionem ut neutram ... et quando ponitur in esse et in effectu per voluntatem determinatam ad unam partem, tunc apprehenditur ut vera, et prius tantum offerebatur voluntati ut neutra .... Intellectus divinus primo non est practicus, nec apprehendit primo aliquid ut operandum, sed ostendit voluntati ut neutram; voluntas autem determinat se ad unam partem, ponendo in esse vel non in esse, et tunc intellectus apprehendit veritatem illius. (*Lect.* I, *d.* 39, *q.* 1–5, *n.* 62–63)

Scotus' followers had some difficulty in trying to understand how the truth of statements concerning contingent future events could be based on God's choice, if the freedom of will was to be defended at the same time.[175] Scotus' own answer would apparently have been that the sentences selected by God to be true of the actual world also include those which specify its real alternatives. Among the true sentences there is, e.g., the sentence which says that Socrates, while sitting at the moment t_1, could have stood at that moment.

Until now I have discussed Scotus' theory of modality insofar as it provided an alternative to the statistical interpretation of modality as used by the thirteenth century Aristotelians. As for the necessary action of the first cause, the target of Scotus' criticism was Neoplatonic metaphysics, especially in the form of Avicenna's theory of emanation.

The Avicennean metaphysics exerted a great influence on scholastic thought. In addition to Avicenna's ideas about causality, especially his doctrine of essence and existence as well as his theory of modality, which was intimately connected with the former doctrine, were subsequently much discussed.[176]

According to Avicenna, most things are such that nothing impossible follows if they are supposed to be unactual. Such things are possible. Because their essence does not imply their existence, they must receive their existence from something else. Another being is the cause of their existence. This chain of the causes of existence cannot continue infinitely without losing its explanatory power, and there must, therefore, be a first cause which does not receive its existence from outside. Its essence implies existence.[177] There is only one such being and according to Avicenna it is a necessary being. All things posterior with respect to the necessary being (*wājib al-wujūd*) are contingent *per se*, because they can not-be on their own ground. But, on the grounds of the causal influence proceeding from the First Being, they are necessarily because everything necessarily is with respect to its cause. Contingent beings (*mumkin al-wujūd*) are thus necessary *per aliud*.[178]

This theory is an application of Plotinus' metaphysics of emanation which Avicenna had adopted. Plotinus was the subsequently most influential neoplatonist. He is also the main witness for the metaphysical form of the Principle of Plenitude which Arthur A. Lovejoy discussed in *The Great Chain of Being*.

The first principle of being according to Plotinus is the One. It is itself
beyond being. It is perfect because it does not seek for anything and as such
"it is as if flowing over and its plenitude gives birth to an Other."[179] According to Plotinus everything which has reached its perfection gives birth to
another. The most perfect being cannot remain shut up in itself, for it is the
unjealous potency of all things (δύναμις πάντων).[180]

Δύναμις πάντων is an expression which Plotinus often uses about the One.
Enn. IV, 8, 5.33—35 gives an indication as to how the concept δύναμις should
be understood in Plotinus' writings. It is said that everywhere only actualization reveals a power, which otherwise would stay hidden and, to be sure,
turn out to be unreal. Thus we can, in a sense, speak about possibilities only
if we at the same time speak about their actualization. So, when it is said that
the One is Δύναμις πάντων, it is in effect also said that all things will be
realized. In *Enn.* IV, 8, 6.12—13 Plotinus says that no such restrictions as,
e.g., jealousy must be made on this power — it proceeds until it has realized
everything that can be (χωρεῖν δὲ ἀεὶ ἕως εἰς ἔσχατον μέχρι τοῦ δυνατοῦ τὰ
πάντα ἥκῃ).[181]

In a way similar to Plotinus Avicenna thinks that the first Being, while
contemplating himself, gives rise to emanation which actualizes all possibilities at different levels of being.[182] Avicenna says that the first being wills
what is produces but since its will is the same as its knowledge of what can
be, the will is not connected with any choice. The will wills everything which
the necessary being knows to follow necessarily from its being.[183] Because it
is better to be than not to be and because the first being is totally benevolent,
its overflowing power calls into existence all that can be. An essence which
does not receive existence in this process is, according to Avicenna, impossible.[184]

Scotus claims that this metaphysics of emanation is self-contradictory. In
order to show this, Scotus first calls attention to the view that things which
are posterior to the first being are contingent *per se* and necessary *per aliud*.
When a contingent thing is such that it can be and not be, it follows that
some alternative possibilities are present in Avicenna's system. The first being
is said to cause necessarily the existence of those beings which can be. But
whatever can be made, can be non-actual *per se*. From this it follows that it is
inconsistent to say that the first being acts in a necessary manner at least in
the sense that it would logically be bound to a realization of only one possible world.[185] Scotus also remarks that there is evil in the actual world. Were
the actual world the only possible one for God, it could not be maintained
that He is omnipotent and benevolent.[186]

10. CONCLUDING REMARKS

The statistical modal theory enjoyed a prominent status among the presuppositions of Western thought from Aristotle until the late 13th century. According to it, modal notions are in the last analysis reducible to extensional terms. They are merely means of classifying what happens in the one and only actual world at different moments of time. This pattern of thought becomes more natural if it is realized that it was connected with the habit of regarding temporally indefinite sentences as typical vehicles of communication. Such sentences contain a reference to the time of utterance as part of their meaning, and it was thought that a necessary sentence is true whenever it is uttered, a possible sentence is at least sometimes true, and an impossible one is never true. An analogous statistical view easily suggested itself in connection with the widely accepted epistemic attitude according to which our knowledge is, in the first place, about the generic properties of a species and only secondarily about individuals as members of a species. One could then think that a necessary property is instantiated in every member of a species, a possible property at least in some of its members, whereas an impossible property never belongs to any member of the species.

We have seen that right from the beginning temporally definite events and sentences presented difficulties to the temporal version of this modal theory. When possibilities are treated in such a way that there must be place for their real actualization in one and the same historical world, it follows that, for every moment of time, what at that time can be actual must then be actual. Furthermore, the truth-value of temporally definite sentences cannot change, and they are therefore necessarily true if they are true. It does not matter whether the temporal qualification refers to the calendar date of the event to which the sentence refers or, as usual, to some specification of the time of utterance of a temporally indefinite sentence.

This problem cannot properly be solved within the statistical interpretation of modal notions. The usual strategy in which the focus of attention is shifted from temporally definite cases or sentences to temporally indefinite ones reintroduces the possibility to be otherwise, but, unfortunately, this possibility does not offer alternatives to the definite event under discussion. It only tells us what can happen at another time.

This mistaken attempt to avoid the deterministic implications of Aristotelian assumptions concerning temporally definite events and sentences was reinforced by the belief that the alleged determinism is based on a conceptual confusion. By distinguishing between the composite and the divided meaning

of sentences like "A sitting man can walk", Aristotle and his medieval followers could claim that the sentence is false in the first sense because it then
means that it is possible that a man sits and stands simultaneously. But it
would be fallacious to believe on this basis that things cannot be otherwise.
For the sentence can be read in the divided sense, and then it means that the
man who is sitting can stand. As I have shown, it was usual to add here the
qualification 'at another time'. Thus there is, in fact, the possibility of standing while the man sits, but this possibility refers to another time. And as this
possibility cannot be eternally frustrated if it is a genuine possibility, the
distinction can be reduced to a temporal distinction between the simultaneous
and non-simultaneous actualization of mutually exclusive predicates.

Analogous difficulties are included in the claim that an individual possesses
unrealized potentialities, viz. those which other members of the same species
have realized. Even if this may be a natural way of motivating assumptions
concerning the capacities of the members of a species, it does not vindicate
the genuine potentialities of a particular member of that species.

It seems that Duns Scotus played an important role in creating principles
of modal thought, which are no longer bound to the limitations of the statistical interpretation of modality. In his modal theory, the meaning of modal
notions is connected with the idea of considering different alternative states
of affairs at the same time. It is historically interesting that this attitude
seems to have been developed as a conscious alternative to the statistical
interpretation of modal notions. Scotus points out especially the difficulties
of treating temporally definite events and sentences in this theory.

Even if the Principle of Plenitude, according to which no genuine possibility remains forever unrealized, was denied for divine possibilities in early
medieval doctrine of Omnipotence, the idea of unrealized possibilities was not
applied to the theory of modality in general. This happens in Duns Scotus'
modal theory where the domain of possibility is accepted as an *a priori* area
of conceptual consistency. It is then divided into different classes of compossible states of affairs of which the actual world is one. Of logical possibilities
(*possibile logicum*) some are real alternatives to the actual world (*possibile
reale*). Such a possibility is characterized by the fact that it could be actual
without any change in the general structure and general laws of the actual
world. Thus it was not Leibniz who invented the idea of possible worlds,
which has similarities with the contemporary understanding of modality as it
is codified in the so called possible worlds semantics. The basic idea is present in Duns Scotus' modal theory, and this new view on modal notions is the
general basis of the fourteenth century modal logic.

The consequences of this new understanding of modal notions can be seen in the fourteenth century theories of supposition. As theories of generality, they contain the idea that the truth of a sentence in which there are general terms is truth-functionally dependent on the truth of those basic sentences into which it can be analysed in different ways. The domain of terms in tense contexts must be ampliated so that, in addition to the appellative present domain, there are domains of past and future *significata*. The domain of possibility is now said to include not only past and future objects but also merely possible ones. The domain of necessity is part of that of possibility.[187]

In this new theory, the distinction between modal statements in the composite and in the divided sense can be understood in a way different from the interpretation which suggests itself within the statistical interpretation of modality. In the latter theory, the composite and the divided sense of sentences like "A sitting man can walk" differ only with respect to the respective moments of actualization of the capacity which the sitting man has. In the new theory, the false composite sense means that it is possible that a man at the same time is sitting and standing. The true divided sense then means that there is a sitting man in the actual world or in a given possible world and this sitting man is standing in another possible state of affairs.

The new modal theory was applied in the fourteenth century to modal syllogistic, which was thus given a turn quite different from the Aristotelian modal syllogistic, which was (at least partially) an application of the statistical modal theory to necessary and possible properties of actual beings. In fact, this is how Aristotle's modal syllogistic seems to have been interpreted, e.g., by Averroes and Albertus Magnus, as I have shown elsewhere.[188] In the fourteenth century, it was usual to present separate treatments of modal sentences in the composite and in the divided sense. The conversion of modal sentences and the relationships between modal statements in the composite and divided sense as well as between modal statements and assertoric statements were regulated by rules which were based on the new understanding of modality. The logical properties of modal sentences in the divided sense were obtained by considering the set of equivalence classes of compossible possibilities. This was taken to be an *a priori* domain of modalized terms and to determine the logical behavior of modal propositions. In this approach, the application of the *dictum de omni et nullo* was used as a natural way of obtaining syllogistic modes in the same way as in the assertoric syllogistic. The rules for modal sentences in the composite sense are obtained by applying to the corresponding assertoric forms general rules of modal inference, especially the following ones:

SIMO KNUUTTILA

$$\frac{p \supset q}{Mp \supset Mq}$$

and

$$\frac{p \supset q}{Np \supset Nq}.$$

In the modal syllogistic of sentences in the composite sense there must be at least one necessary premiss in a valid mode because the compossibility of two possible premisses is not granted.[189]

The break with the Aristotelian theory of modality is a general feature of the fourteenth century modal logic. There is *prima facie* evidence for the claim, too, that the type of modal theory developed by Scotus was intrically linked with the fourteenth century discussions of intensional identity and methods of individuation, the explanatory nature of scientific sentences, and other questions the emergence of which is often allegedly explained by referring only to the general difference between nominalism and realism.

University of Helsinki and
Academy of Finland

NOTES

[1] A. O. Lovejoy, *The Great Chain of Being. A Study of the History of an Idea.* The William James Lectures delivered at Harvard University 1933, Cambridge Mass. 1936.
[2] J. Hintikka, *Time and Necessity: Studies in Aristotle's Theory of Modality*, Oxford 1973, pp. 93–113; partially reprinted on pp. 57–72 of this volume.
[3] E. A. Moody, 'History of Logic, Medieval Logic', P. Edwards (ed.), *The Ensyclopedia of Philosophy* IV, pp. 528–534.
[4] *Ibid.* p. 532.
[5] See L. M. De Rijk, *Logica Modernorum. A Contribution to the History of Early Terminist Logic I. On the Twelfth Century Theories of Fallacy* (Wijsgerige teksten en studies, VI), Assen 1962, pp. 22–23.
[6] *Ioannis Saresberiensis Episcopi Carnotensis Metalogicon*, C. C. I. Webb (ed.), Oxonii 1929, p. 137.7–11 (*PL* 199, 900D). In his work *Die theologische Prinzipienlehre der mittelalterlichen Scholastik*, Freiburg im Breisgau 1964, A. Lang gives many examples of how the methodology of theology and jurisprudence in the twelfth century was guided by the practical need of such general principles (*regulae*) by means of which the tradition could be mastered. The needed theoretical guidance was found in Aristotle's *Topics* and its status can be seen, e.g., in the following quotation from the *Metalogicon* of John of Salisbury: Sine eo (sc. libro Topicorum octavo) non disputatur arte, sed casu" (*Metalogicon* III, 10, Webb (ed.), p. 154.20–21, *PL* 199, 910C). In the early scholasticism, the general principles were usually not given any definite metaphysical or theoretical

justification. It was enough that they were *conceptiones communes animi* and as such useful in the organization of the tradition. See Lang, *op. cit.* pp. 41–105.

[7] *PL* 64, 1258A. A critical text is edited by N. Haring in *Nine Mediaeval Thinkers. A collection of hitherto unedited texts*, J. R. O'Donnell (ed.), (Publications of the Pontifical Institute of Mediaeval Studies, Studies and Texts 1), Toronto 1955. A well-known example of the early medieval conceptual analysis is Abaelard's *Sic et Non*. Its fourth concordance rule runs as follows: "Facilis autem plerumque controversiarum solutio reperietur, si eadem verba in diversis significationibus a diversis auctoribus posito defendere poterimus" (*PL* 178, 1344). Abaelard's interpretation rules were collected from the concordance rules given by scholars before him, as Grabmann and others have noticed; see M. Grabmann, *Die Geschichte der scholastischen Methode* I, Freiburg im Breisgau 1909, pp. 234–239; cf. L. M. De Rijk, *Logica Modernorum. A Contribution to the History of Early Terminist Logie II, 1. The Origin and Early Development of the Theory of Supposition* (Wijsgerige teksten en studies, XVI), Assen 1967, p. 129. For philosophical analysis in the theology of the twelfth century, see also M. D. Chenu, Un essai de méthode théologique au XIIe siècle, *Revue des sciences philosophiques et théologiques* 24 (1935), 258–267, M. D. Chenu, Grammaire et Théologie aux XIIe et XIIIe siècles, *Archives d'histoire doctrinale et littéraire du moyen âge* 10 (1935–1936), 5–28, De Rijk, *Logica Modernorum* I, pp. 153–178.

Abaelard's *Sic et non* is an example of the collections to which the search for general propositions gave rise. They presented theological or canonistic sentences *pro et contra* with respect to supposed rules and served in this way for their critical examination. In canonistics such books were called from the end of the twelfth century *Brocardi* or *Brocarda* collections and their arguments *brocardica* (see Lang, *op. cit.* pp. 71–74, A. Lang, Zur Entstehungsgeschichte der Brocardasammlungen, *Zeitschrift für Rechtsgeschichte* LXII (1942), *Kan. Abt.* XXXI, 119–122, P. Weimar, 'Argumenta Brocardica', *Studia Gratiana* XIV (1967), 107. There has been much discussion about the meaning of these words among the historians of law. (For different suggestions, see Weimar, *op. cit.* pp. 105–109). Somewhat surprisingly, recent scholars have paid no attention to the obvious fact that the counterexamples to *generalia* supported by *pro*-sentences deny the proposed rule in accordance with the syllogistic mood *Bocardo*. Its first premiss expresses a counterexample to the proposed rule. The second premiss states the subject of the first as a case to which the rule should apply. And then the denial of the rule is concluded. (Cf. C. S. Peirce, *Collected Papers*, Vol. II, C. Hartshorne and P. Weiss (eds.), Cambridge Mass. 1932, p. 294.)

In his paper (pp. 115–117) Weimar discusses an example from Pilius where the claim that every pact is valid is criticized by presenting statutes which allow, e.g., a change of mind (*posterioris voluntatis legitima prepositio*). Thus the rule must be modified, because validity is not a feature of a certain agreement which, however, is a pact.

When we know that the forerunners of mnemonic words with letters signifying syllogistic moods were created at the end of the twelfth century (see L. M. De Rijk, *Log. Mod.* II, 1, pp. 400–403), it seems reasonable that *disputatae brocardi* were so called according to mnemonic letters referring to the fifth mood of the third figure of the Aristotelian syllogistic.

[8] The word *sophisma* is used in the Middle Ages in many different ways. In early texts it usually means a faulty argument (see, e.g., Abaelard's *Introductio ad theologiam* in *Opera Petri Abaelardi* II, V. Cousin (ed.), Parisiis 1859, p. 142). Later it is often a

sentence which can be interpreted in different ways, of which one is usually the proper one. See G. Wallerand, *Les Oeuvres de Siger de Courtrai* (Les Philosophes Belges, 8), Louvain 1913, pp. 20–33, M. Grabmann, *Die Sophismatalitteratur des 12. und 13. Jahrhunderts* (Beiträge zur Geschichte der Philosophie und Theologie des Mittelalters, 36, 1), Münster 1940.

[9] Cf. also J. Hintikka, *Time and Necessity*, pp. 197–198.

[10] J. Hintikka has presented this interpretation in 'The Once and Future Sea Fight', *The Philosophical Review* 73 (1964), 461–492. Chapter VIII of his *Time and Necessity* is an expanded version of this article.

[11] *Ibid.* pp. 63–70, 84–86, 149–151. The clearest example is *Cat*. 4a23–b2 where Aristotle says that if the statement '*a* sits' is true, it will be false after *a* has got up. The same claim is repeated, e.g., in *Met*. 1051b13–18.

[12] Cf. J. Hintikka with U. Remes and S. Knuuttila, *Aristotle on Modality and Determinism* (Acta Philosophica Fennica, Vol. 29, No. 1), Amsterdam 1977, pp. 25–28, 35–39, 50–56.

[13] For the distinction between potentialities involving or not involving a reference to motion see *Met*. 1019a15–32, 1019b30–1020a6, 1045b35ff., *De int*. 23a3–16, and for further evidence Hintikka with Remes and Knuuttila, *op. cit*. pp. 59–76.

[14] See *ibid*. pp. 60–64.

[15] *Ibid.* pp. 22–25, 32–33, and I. Pape, *Tradition und Transformation der Modalität I. Möglichkeit – Unmöglichkeit*, Hamburg 1966, pp. 39–43.

[16] *Peter Abaelards Philosophische Schriften*, hrsg. von B. Geyer (Beiträge zur Geschichte der Philosophie und Theologie des Mittelalters, Band 21, 1–3), Münster 1919–1927. *Logica 'Ingredientibus'*, p. 489, 1–14.

[17] *Anicii Manlii Severini Boetii Commentarii in librum Aristotelis Perihermeneias* I–II, C. Meiser (ed.), Lipsiae 1877–1880.

[18] See *In Arist. Periherm* II, 132.21–134.7, *Introductio ad syllogismos categoricos*, *PL* 64, 778–780, *De syllogismo categorico*, *PL* 64, 803. For the titles of the works and Boethius' sources, see De Rijk, *Log. Mod*. I, pp. 24–43.

[19] It is typical that in two Byzantine commentaries on *Soph. el*. the fallacies *secundum diversum modum* and *secundum diversum tempus* coincide; see De Rijk, *op. cit*. pp. 37–38.

[20] *Anicii Manlii Severini Boethii Opera I, Philosophiae consolatio*, L. Bieler (ed.), (Corpus Christianorum, Series Latina 94), Turnholti 1957.

[21] *Philos. cons*. V, 6.1–17.

[22] See, e.g., *S. Thomae Aquinatis Summa contra gentiles*, Marietti ed., Torino 1961, I, c. 67, *La querelle des futurs contingents* (Louvain 1465–1475), textes inédits par L. Baudry (Etudes de Philosophie Médiévale, XXXVIII), Paris 1950, p. 193.

[23] H. R. Patch, 'Necessity in Boethius and the Neoplatonists', *Speculum* X (1935), 402.

[24] Another modern adherent of this interpretation is D. P. Henry. See his book *The Logic of Saint Anselm*, Oxford 1957, p. 178.

[25] R. Bosley, 'In Support of an Interpretation of *On Int*. 9', *Ajatus* 36 (1977), 29.

[26] *Ibid.* pp. 34–40.

[27] See, e.g., *In Arist. Periherm*. I, 120.7–22, 123.18–24, II, 240.8–14, 245.12–18.

[28] In the same way as Bosley, *op. cit*., I cannot agree with Dorothea Frede in her opinion that the traditional interpretation of *De int*. 9 as represented by Boethius would support her view according to which Aristotle restricts the principle of bivalence in regard to

statements concerning future contingent events. See D. Frede, *Aristoteles und die "Seeschlacht"*. *Das Problem der Contingentia Futura in De Interpretatione* 9 (Hypomnemata, 27), Göttingen 1970, pp. 24–27, 70–73.

[29] Petrus Abaelardus, *Dialectica*, L. M. De Rijk (ed.), (Wijsgerige teksten en studies, 1), Assen 1956, p. 183, 8–13; see also De Rijk, *Log. Mod.* I, p. 60.

[30] *Dial.* 182.30–183.2.

[31] See note 16 above.

[32] *Log. Ingred.* 489.16, 21.

[33] *Ibid.* 489.25–27, *Dial.* 198.5–11.

[34] *Dial.* 147.21–22.

[35] *Ibid.* 146.35–36.

[36] See G. Nuchelmans, *Theories of the Proposition. Ancient and Medieval Conceptions of the Bearers of Truth and Falsity* (North-Holland Linguistic Series, 8), Amsterdam 1973, pp. 150–156, M. Tweedale, 'Abailard and Non-things', *Journal of the History of Philosophy* 5 (1976), 329–342, M. T. Beonio-Brocchieri Fumagalli, *The Logic of Abelard* (Synthese Historical Library), D. Reidel, Dordrecht 1969, pp. 71–77. In *Dialectica* Abaelard does not use the term *dictum*. Among others, the expression 'quod propositio dicit' corresponds to it (157.18).

[37] Nuchelmans, *op. cit.* p. 162.

[38] See, e.g., *Log. Ingred.* 367.13–26, and Nuchelmans, *op. cit.* p. 158.

[39] *Log. ingred.* 229.34–36, 274.10–12, 429.21–25 *et passim*.

[40] *Opera Petri Abaelardi*, V. Cousin (ed.), Vol. 2, Parisiis 1859, p. 146: "Nam etsi ad notitiam divinam respiciamus, sic illud evenire videbimus secundum eam, ut posset etiam non evenire. Ita quippe ipse illud providit et scivit eventurum esse, et sciret etiam secundum mutabilitatem naturae rerum, posse numquam evenire . . .".

[41] See also *Dial.* 98.16–18, 196.29–197.31, 204.11–12, 205.30, *Log. Ingred.* 492.34, and J. Jolivet, 'Elements du concept de nature chez Abaelard' in *La filosofia della natura nel medioevo*. Atti del terzo congresso internazionale di filosofia medioevale, Milano 1966, pp. 297–304. Abaelardian views are summarized in the unauthentic part of *Log. Ingred.* edited by Geyer as follows: "Modi isti diversos habent sensus, possibile tantum valet quantum "natura patitur", impossibile "natura repugnat", necesse "natura exigit". Natura autem dicitur prima rerum creatio. (*Log. Ingred.* 496.33–35).

[42] *Log. Ingred.* 27.18–34, *Dial.* 154.25–29; see also De Rijk's introduction to *Dialectica*, pp. XCIII–XCIV.

[43] See Nuchelmans, *op. cit.* pp. 160–161.

[44] So, e.g., F. Copleston in *Mediaeval Philosophy: Augustine to Scotus*, (A History of Philosophy, Vol. 2). Third printing, Westminster, Maryland 1955, p. 151. J. H. Randall, Jr., characterizes Aristotle's doctrine of the essential knowledge in the book *Aristotle*, New York, 1960, p. 119, as follows: "Essence is thus defined as what is knowable and statable about an *ousia*, what the definition of a kind will formulate. It is not the formula (*logos*) or the definition (*horismos*) that is identical with the concrete thing, or can properly be said to be an *ousia*, it is what the logos formulates, the intelligible structure or make-up of the thing, what we know and state when we know the thing." Abaelard presents his opinion about the abstracting knowledge almost in the same words: "Cum enim hunc hominem tantum attendo in natura substantiae vel corporis, non etiam animalis vel hominis vel grammatici, profecto nihil nisi quod in ea est, intelligo, sed non omnia quae habet, attendo. Et cum dico me attendere tantum eam in eo quod hoc habet,

illud tantum ad attentionem refertur, non ad modum subsistendi . . . Separatim namque
haec res ab alia, non separata intelligitur, cum tamen separatim non existat et pure
materia et simpliciter forma percipitur, cum neque haec pure sit nec illa simpliciter, ut
videlicet puritas ista vel simplicitas ad intelligentiam, non ad subsistentiam rei reducantur,
ut sint scilicet modus intelligendi, non subsistendi. . . . Sic et intellectus per abstrac-
tionem divisim attendit, non divisa, alioquin cassus esset." (Log. Ingred. 25.23–26.3)

45 Dial. 206.16–23.

46 Dial. 206.23–33.

47 L. Minio-Paluello, Twelfth Century Logic. Texts and Studies II. Abaelardiana Inedita:
1. Super Periermeneias XII–XIV, Roma 1958.

48 Int. ad theol., Cousin (ed.), pp. 145–146.

49 "Ac si videlicet ita dicimus: Navale bellum cras esse futurum, vel non esse futurum,
hoc videlicet totum necesse est, hoc est, necesse est ut ipsum cras fiat vel non fiat. Et
hoc quidem modo necessarii nomen semel positum et absolute praedicatum veram reddit
enuntiationem: et generaliter ad quaslibet affirmationes et negationes earum praedicatio
ipsius veraciter applicatur: ut videlicet de singulis dicamus, quia hanc vel illam esse veram
est necesse, quod Aristoteles intellexit cum proprietatem assignaret contradictionis.
Non tamen ideo alteri earum necessarii praedicationem absolute possumus applicare, ut
veraciter dicamus quia vel hanc necesse est esse veram, vel illam necesse est esse falsam.
Ideo autem absolute addimus, quia determinatam necessarii praedicationem omnibus
hujusmodi veri propositionibus applicari ipse ibidem edocet, dicens: Igitur esse quod est,
quando est, necesse est: et non esse quod non est, quando non est, necesse est. Sed non
ideo simpliciter dicit quia necesse sit. Non enim sic determinata necessarii praedicatio
simpliciter infert, . . . ". Ibid. p. 143.

50 Log. Ingred. 430.2–3, Dial. 217.27–28.

51 M. Tulli Ciceronis De divinatione I–II, A. S. Pease (ed.), (University of Illinois
Studies in Language and Literature, Vol. VI, 2–3 (1920), Vol. VIII, 2–3 (1923)), II, 18:
"Nihil enim est tam contrarium rationi et constantiae quam fortuna, ut mihi ne in deum
quidem cadere videatur ut sciat quid casu et fortuito futurum est. Si enim scit, certe illud
eveniet; sin certe eveniet, nulla fortuna est; est autem fortuna; rerum igitur fortuitarum
nulla praesensio est." Cf. also M. Tulli Ciceronis De Fato, hrsg. von K. Bayer, Tusculum-
Bücherei, München 1963, 10, 20ff., S. Aurelii Augustini De Civitate Dei V, 9, PL 41, col.
149–150, Log. Ingred. 429.26–34.

52 See D. E. Luscombe, The School of Peter Abelard, Cambridge 1970, p. 134.

53 Int. ad theol. p. 123. This doctrine originates in Plato's Timaeus 29–30; Platon,
Timée, A. Rivaud (ed.), Oeuvres complètes 10, Paris 1925. Plotinus repeats it many
times in the Enneads, see, e.g., Enn. IV, 8, 6.12–14, and V, 4, 1.26–32, 34–36; Plotini
Opera I–II, P. Henry et H.-R. Schwyzer (eds.), (Museum Lessianum, Series Philosophica,
33–34), Paris 1951–1959. See also A. O. Lovejoy, op. cit. pp. 61–63 and J. M. Rist,
Plotinus: The Road to Reality, Cambridge 1967, p. 75.

54 A. Faust, Der Möglichkeitsgedanke. Systemgeschichtliche Untersuchungen I–II,
Heidelberg 1931–1932, Vol. II, p. 193.

55 De Rijk, Log. Mod. I, pp. 82–88.

56 Ibid. pp. 88–89.

57 For an introduction to the work, see De Rijk, Log. Mod. II, 1, pp. 408–415, and the
text II, 2, pp. 435–638.

58 Log. Mod. II, 2, p. 481.32–33.

[59] *Log. Mod.* II, 2, pp. 481.22–482.9.
[60] See *Log. Mod.* II, 2, 390.18–31, 429.1–10, *Die Introductiones in Logicam des Wilhelm von Sherwood*, M. Grabmann (ed.), (Sitzungsberichte der Bayerischen Akademie der Wissenschaften, Phil. hist. Abteilung 1937, 10), p. 41.13–16.
[61] *Introductiones*, p. 90.11–24.
[62] See *William of Sherwood's Introduction to Logic*, translated with an introduction and notes by N. Kretzmann, Minneapolis 1966, pp. 4–8.
[63] *B. Alberti Magni Opera omnia* II, A. Borgnet (ed.), Parisiis 1890, p. 545.
[64] *Alberti Magni Opera omnia* XVI, 2, B. Geyer (ed.), Aschendorff 1964, *lib.* 9, *tract.* 2, *cap.* 2.
[65] Peter of Spain, *Tractatus called afterwards Summule logicales*, L. M. De Rijk (ed.), (Wijsgerige teksten en studies, 22), Assen 1972.
[66] See *ibid.* pp. LXXX–LXXXIV.
[67] Lamberto d'Auxerre, *Logica* (Summa Lamberti), F. Alessio (ed.), Firenze 1971.
[68] See Thomas Aquinas' *De fallaciis* VI, *S. Thomae Aquinatis Opera omnia XVI*, Parma (ed.), photolithographice reimpressa, New York 1950, and *Sumule dialectices magistri Rogeri Bacon*, R. Steele (ed.), *Opera hactenus inedita Rogeri Baconi*, Fasc. XV, Oxonii 1940, pp. 334–335.
[69] See Roger Bacon, *Sum. dial.* pp. 624–625, and *S. Thomae Aquinatis in Aristotelis libros Peri Hermeneias et Posteriorum analyticorum expositio*, Marietti ed., Torino 1964, *In Periherm.* I, *lect.* 15, 2.
A very explicit example of the *compositio-divisio* analysis of modal sentences as a temporal distinction between the simultaneity and non-simultaneity of actualization of predicates is to be found in John of St. Thomas' *Ars Logica* (first published in 1631–1632). In the introductory text (translated by F. C. Wade) John of St. Thomas says that, in the composite sense, the simultaneous presence of two forms in one subject is signified; in the divided sense their union is not meant at the same time, but successively. See John of St. Thomas, *Outlines of Formal Logic*, translated by F. C. Wade (Mediaeval Philosophical Texts in Translation, 8), Milwaukee, Wisconsin 1955, p. 88.
[70] *The Syncategoremata of William of Sherwood*, J. R. O'Donnell (ed.), *Mediaeval Studies* III (1941), pp. 73–74; cf. also *Introductiones in logicam*, Grabmann (ed.), p. 41.32–38.
[71] *William of Sherwood's Treatise on Syncategorematic Words*, translated with an introduction and notes by N. Kretzmann, Minneapolis 1968, pp. 101–102.
[72] *William of Sherwood's Introductiones in logicam*, Grabmann (ed.), p. 41.13–16; see also *Dialectica Monacensis, Log. Mod.* II, 1, p. 481.25–30.
[73] Alexander of Aphrodisias, *De Fato*, I. Bruns (ed.), (Commentaria in Aristotelem Graeca, Suppl. II, 2), Berlin 1892, 177, 7ff. The example is mentioned among other similar stoic opinions by Michael Frede in his book *Die stoische Logik* (Abhandlungen der Akademie der Wissenschaften in Göttingen, phil. hist. Klasse, dritte Folge, 88), Göttingen 1974, p. 47.
I think that the idea of the statistical interpretation of modality as applied to temporally indefinite sentences is the light needed for understanding of certain other sophisms in William's work, too. The sophism following that of Antichrist in the *Syncategoremata* is, e.g., the following: "Contingents necessarily are true". The sentence is said to be true if 'necessarily' belongs to the claim that two forms at one and the same time cohere in the same subject. This is, of course, the traditional temporal necessity.

It is untrue if it signifies that "the form belonging to the predicate necessarily inheres in some suppositum of the subject" (Kretzmann's translation, p. 102). In the meaning of this simple necessity contingents are not necessarily true. See *Syncategoremata*, O'Donnell (ed.), p. 74.

[74] *Die philosophischen Werke des Robert Grosseteste*, L. Baur (ed.), (Beiträge zur Geschichte der Philosophie des Mittelalters, 9), Münster 1912, p. 144.30–31. See also *De scientia Dei, op. cit.* p. 145.22.

[75] See E. A. Moody, *op. cit.* p. 352; E. A. Moody, *Truth and Consequence in Mediaeval Logic* (Studies in Logic and the Foundations of Mathematics), Amsterdam 1953, pp. 73–74; and M. Adams, 'Did Ockham know of Material and Strict Implication?', *Franciscan Studies* 33 (1973), 9–15.

[76] *The Tractatus logicae minor of Ockham*, E. Buytaert (ed.), *Franciscan Studies* 24 (1964), 77.

[77] M. Adams, *op. cit.* pp. 13–14.

[78] *Ibid.* p. 15.

[79] E. A. Moody, *Truth and Consequence in Mediaeval Logic*, p. 75.

[80] See Section 9 of this paper.

[81] L. M. De Rijk, 'Some New Evidence on Twelfth Century Logic', *Vivarium* 4 (1966), 45.

[82] *S. Aurelii Augustini In Joannis euangelium tractatus, PL* 35, 1722; see also *S. Aurelii Augustini De nuptiis et concupiscentia, PL* 44, 450, and *Petri Lombardi Sententiarum libri quatuor* I, d. 44, 2, *PL* 192, 635.

[83] For the whole question, see M. D. Chenu, 'Grammaire et théologie aux XIIe et XIIIe siècles', *Archives d'Histoire Doctrinale et Littéraire du Moyen Age* 10 (1935–1936), 5–28; and Nuchelmans, *op. cit.* pp. 177–189.

[84] *Doctoris Seraphici S. Bonaventurae Opera omnia* I, distr. II, Quaracchi 1883.

[85] *Petri Pictaviensis Sententiarum libri quinque* III, *PL* 211, 1090.

[86] *Sententiae Petri Pictaviensis* I, P. S. Moore and M. Dulong (eds.), (Publications in Mediaeval Studies, VII), Notre Dame, Indiana 1961 (first printing 1943), I, 12, 208–223.

[87] Cited from Chenu, *op. cit.* p. 13.

[88] *Petri Lombardi Sent.* I, d. 41.7, d. 44.4, *PL* 192, 635, 641; see also *Sent. Petri Pictaviensis* I, 13, 211–222, and Nuchelmans, *op. cit.* p. 185–186.

[89] *Sancti Thomae Aquinatis commentum in quatuor libros sententiarum, Opera omnia* IV, Parma (ed.), photolithographice reimpressa, New York 1948, *Sent.* I, d. 41, q. 1, art. 5.

[90] See Chenu, *op. cit.* pp. 18–22; Nuchelmans, *op. cit.* p. 183.

[91] Tertullian, *De cultu feminarum*, A. Kroymann (ed.), (Corpus Scriptorum Ecclesiasticorum Latinorum, 70), Vindobonae 1942, I, 8, p. 68.

[92] "Absurdum enim tibi uidetur dici aliquid fieri posse, cuius desit exemplum, cum, sicut credo, non dubites numquam esse factum, ut per foramen acus camelus transiret, et tamen ille hoc quoque dixit deo esse possibile." *De spiritu et littera*, C. F. Vrba and I. Zycha (eds.), (Corpus Scriptorum Ecclesiasticorum Latinorum, 60), Lipsiae 1913, 1.1; see also 35.63.

[93] See, e.g., *De civitate dei* XI, 22; XXII, 2, *PL* 41; and Lovejoy, *op. cit.* p. 67. H. Blumenberg, 'Nachahmung der Natur. Zur Vorgeschichte der Idee des schöpferischen Menschen', *Studium generale* 10 (1957), 276–277; J. Hick, *Evil and the God of Love* (The Fontana Library), London 1968, pp. 50–51, 76–88.

[94] For the freedom of will in Augustine see also H. A. Wolfson, *Religious Philosophy*, Cambridge, Mass. 1961, pp. 158–176.

[95] Pierre Damien, *Lettre sur la toute-puissance divine*, A. Cantin (ed.), (Sources Chrétiennes, 191), Paris 1972. In the edition, the reference system is that of the text in *PL* 145.

[96] *De div. omnip.* 596C. See *Sancti Eusebii Hieronymi Epistulae* I, I. Hilberg (ed.), (Corpus Scriptorum Ecclesiasticorum Latinorum, 54), Vindobonae 1910, XXII, 5, p. 150: "Audenter loquor: cum omnia deus possit, suscitare uirginem non potest post ruinam."

[97] *De div. omnip.* 596C–597A.

[98] *Ibid.* 597A: "... ergo nichil omnino potest facere eorum quae non facit."

[99] *Ibid.* 600B–601B. The reasons for Peter Damian's defence of Divine Omnipotence were not only theological ones. The voice of a church politician can be heard in the following words: "si hoc diffundatur in uulgus ut Deus in aliquo, quod dici nefas est, inpotens adseratur, ilico plebs indocta confunditur, et christiana fides non sine magno animarum discrimine perturbatur." *Ibid.* 597C.

[100] *Ibid.* 612A–B.

[101] *Ibid.* 603B–C.

[102] *Ibid.* 602D–603A.

[103] *Ibid.* 612B.

[104] For the work see Luscombe, *op. cit.* pp. 198–213.

[105] *Summa aurea in quatuor libros sententiarum a Guillelmo Altissidorensi*, Parisiis 1500, *f.* 25, *col.* 2.

[106] *Alanii de Insulis Regulae de sacra theologia* 57–58, *PL* 210, 648.

[107] *Ibid.* 57. Precisely the same ideas are presented by Simon of Tournai; see *Expositio magistri Symonis Tornacensis super Simbolum*, N. Haring (ed.), *Archives d'Histoire Doctrinale et Littéraire du Moyen Age* XLI (1974), *editio prima* 36–43, *editio secunda* 48–54.

[108] Bernard of Clairvaux, *Apologia ad Guillelmum*, *PL* 182, *c.* 915.

[109] *De architectura* VII, 5; cited in E. De Bruyne, *The Esthetics of the Middle Ages*, transl. by E. Hennessy, New York 1969, p. 41.

[110] Robert Grosseteste, *De libero arbitrio. Die philosophischen Werke des Robert Grosseteste*, L. Baur (ed.), (Beiträge zur Geschichte der Philosophie des Mittelalters, Band 9), Münster 1912.

[111] The text quoted above continues as follows: "Unde Magister in Sententiis: Deus potuit nulla creasse et ita nulla creata praescivisse vel scivisse. Ergo habet potentiam, ut numquam creasset et numquam scivisset multa, quae scit." *Op. cit.* 169.19–170.3. For Grosseteste's theory of modality, see also J. G. Dawson, 'The "De libero arbitrio" of Grosseteste', *La filosofia della natura nel medioevo*. Atti del terzo congresso internationale di filosofia medioevale, Milano 1966, pp. 355–362.

[112] See also D. Siedler, *Intellektualismus und Voluntarismus bei Albertus Magnus* (Beiträge zur Geschichte der Philosophie und Theologie des Mittelalters XXXVI, 2), Münster 1941.

[113] Moses Maimonides, *The Guide of the Perplexed I–II*, translated with an introduction and Notes by S. Pines. Introductory Essay by L. Strauss, third impression, Chicago 1974.

[114] H. A. Wolfson, *The Philosophy of the Kalam. Structure and Growth of Philosophic*

Systems from Plato to Spinoza IV, Cambridge, Mass., and London 1976, pp. 434–444.
[115] *Op. cit.* pp. 578–589.
[116] Moses Maimonides, *op. cit.* II, p. 247; see also p. 249.
[117] S. Knuuttila, 'The "Statistical" Interpretation of Modality in Averroes and Thomas Aquinas', *Ajatus* 37 (1977), 7998; see also G. Jalbert, *Nécessité et Contingence chez Saint Thomas et chez ses prédécesseurs*, Ottawa 1961, pp. 37–40. In the tract on the modality of propositions edited by D. M. Dunlop in *Islamic Studies* (Journal of the Central Institute of Islamic Research, Karachi) 1 (1962), 23–34, and discussed by N. Rescher in *Studies in the History of Arabic Logic*, Pittsburgh 1963, pp. 91–105, Averroes makes a division between the non-temporal and the temporal construction of modal sentences. Both of them are based on the statistical interpretation of modality. In the first case the possible predicate is found in the subject mostly, leastly, or equally; in the temporal construction the possibility is interpreted in terms of the majority of times, as many times as not, and the minority of times. See Rescher, *op. cit.* pp. 93, 99. The Latin version of the text is in *Aristotelis Opera cum Averrois Commentariis*, Venetiis 1562–1574, Vol. I, part 2b & 3, pp. 78–80. On page 94 Rescher estimates the role of temporal modalities in the Middle Ages as follows: "This chronological approach to the logic of modality – derived by the Arabic logicians from the Hellenistic Aristotelians, and probably owing its origin to the early peripatetics and perhaps also Stoic influences – seems to have been lost to the Latin Aristotelianism of the middle ages." I think that the texts presented in this paper totally disprove Rescher's view. For Arabic modal logic, see also N. Rescher, *Temporal Modalities in Arabic Logic* (Foundations of Language, Supplementary Series, Vol. 2), D. Reidel, Dordrecht 1966.
[118] Ms. Firenze BN, Conv. Soppr. I III 6, ff. 109ra–110vb.
[119] See A. Maier, *Die Vorläufer Galileis im 14. Jahrhundert. Studien zur Naturphilosophie der Spätscholastik* (Storia e letteratura, 22), Roma 1949, p. 53.
[120] *Ibid.* p. 226.
[121] *Ibid.* pp. 232–234.
[122] S. *Thomae Aquinatis In duodecim libros Metaphysicorum expositio*, Marietti ed., Torino 1950.
[123] See, e.g., Siger of Brabant's *De necessitate et contingentia causarum* in J. J. Duin, *La doctrine de la providence dans les écrits de Siger de Brabant*. Textes et étude (Philosophes médiévaux III), Louvain 1954, pp. 22–23. Statistical ideas in Thomas' philosophy of nature are also discussed in E. F. Byrne, *Probability and opinion. A Study in the medieval presuppositions of the post-medieval theories of probability*, The Hague 1968, pp. 188–205.
[124] Siger of Brabant, *op. cit.* pp. 28–29, 32–35, 104–108.
[125] See also *The Tractatus de praedestinatione et de praescientia dei et de futuris contingentibus of William Ockham*. Edited with a Study on the Mediaeval Problem of a Three-valued Logic by Ph. Boehner (Franciscan Institute Publications, 2), St. Bonaventure, N.Y. 1945, p. 73.
[126] See also *Summa contra gentiles* I, 67; *De veritate* I, q. 2, a. 12, ad 4, *Quaestiones disputatae* I, Marietti ed., Torino 1953; *De malo* q. 16, a. 7, *Quaestiones disputatae* II, Marietti ed., Torino 1949; and H. Schwamm, *Das göttliche Vorherwissen bei Duns Scotus und seinen ersten Anhängern* (Philosophie und Grenzwissenschaften V, 1–4), Innsbruck 1934, pp. 91–99.
[127] S. *th.* I, q. 2, a. 3c. See also, e.g., *In Aristotelis duodecim libros Metaphysicorum*

expositio, Marietti ed., Torino 1950, *Lib.* IX, *lect.* 9, *n.* 1870: Id quod potest non esse, contingit non esse. Haec enim duo aequipollent. For Thomas' third proof see E. Gilson, *The Christian Philosophy of St. Thomas Aquinas*, London 1957, pp. 68–70; G. Jalbert, *op. cit.* pp. 219–229; D. Bonnette, *Aquinas's Proofs for God's Existence. S. Thomas Aquinas on The Per Accidens necessarily implies the Per Se*, The Hague 1972, pp. 127–139; A. Finili, 'Recent Work on the Tertia via', *Dominican Studies* VII (1954); A. Kenny, *The Five Ways* (Studies in the Ethics and the Philosophy of Religion), New York 1969, pp. 49–69.

[128] See, e.g., *S. th.* I, *q.* 48, *a.* 2c, where Thomas writes: "Ita perfectio universi requirit ut sint quaedam quae a bonitate deficere possint, ad quod sequitur ea interdum deficere." See also C. Connellan, *Why Does Evil Exist*, Hickswille, N.Y. p. 129; and J. Hick, *Evil and the God of Love* (The Fontana Library), London 1968, pp. 99–104.

[129] *S. th.* I, *q.* 25, *a.* 3.

[130] *S. th.* I, *q.* 12, *a.* 8, *ad* 4, *Summa contra gentiles* III, p. 56; *De unione verbi incarnati, q. un., a.* 1 c in *S. Thomae Aquinatis Quaestiones Disputatae II*, Marietti ed., Torino 1949. The idea is perhaps connected with the Aristotelian doctrine that it is necessary for anyone who knows what a thing is to know too that it is. *An. post.* II, 7, 92b4–6. In his commentary on the text Thomas says: "impossibile est scire quod quid est hirco-cervi, quia nihil est tale in rerum natura". *In libros Post. an. expositio*, Marietti ed., Torino 1964, II, 6, 461.

[131] C. J. F. Williams, 'Aristotle and Corruptibility. A Discussion of Aristotle, De caelo I, xii', *Religious Studies* I (1965), 98–99.

[132] See Hintikka, *op. cit.* pp. 210–212.

[133] *In libros Aristotelis De caelo et mundo expositio. Opera omnia*, Leonina ed., Vol. III, Romae 1886, Williams, *op. cit.* p. 99.

[134] For Thomas' modal theory see also the careful analysis in K. Jacobi, 'Kontingente Naturgeschehnisse', *Studia Mediewistyczne* 19 (1977), 7–70. Jacobi does not, however, deal with the problems of the statistical interpretation of modality in Thomas Aquinas.

[135] The text used here is W. Kluxen, *Johannes Duns Scotus: Abhandlung über das erste Prinzip* (Texte zur Forschung), Darmstadt 1974. Other modern editions are, a.o., *John Duns Scotus, A Treatise on God as First Principle*, translated and edited by A. B. Wolter (Forum Books), Chicago 1966; *Joannis Duns Scoti Tractatus de Primo Principio*, F. Müller (ed.), Freiburg 1941; and *The De Primo Principio of John Duns Scotus*, a revised text and a translation by E. Roche, St. Bonaventure – Louvain 1949. All references to the Commentaries on the Sentences in this paper are to the *Ioannis Duns Scoti Opera omnia* (*editio Vaticana* 1950–).

[136] See Kluxen, *op. cit.* pp. XV–XVI.

[137] *Ord.* I, *d.* 2, *pars* 1, *q.* 1–2, *n.* 149; cf. also *Lect.* I, *d.* 39, *q.* 1–5, *n.* 41.

[138] The following arguments are almost word-for-word the same as those in *Ord.* I, *d.* 2, *pars* 1, *q.* 1–2, *n.* 79–88. For the connection of the texts, see C. Balić, Disquisitio historico-critica, *Ioannis Duns Scoti Opera omnia I* (*editio Vaticana*), pp. 161*–164*.

[139] Maier, *op. cit.* pp. 242–243 (Cod. Vat. Chis. B VII 113 f. 94–94).

[140] *Ibid.* pp. 240–244.

[141] For examples, see D. E. Sharp, *Franciscan Philosophy at Oxford in the Thirteenth Century*, New York 1964 (1930), pp. 362–363.

[142] See, e.g., *Ord* I, *d.* 3, *pars* 1, *q.* 4, *n.* 235–237; an English translation in *Duns Scotus, Philosophical Writings*. A selection edited and translated by A. Wolter, Edinburg 1962,

pp. 111–112. See also J. R. Weinberg, *Abstraction, Relation, and Induction. Three Essays in the History of Thought*, Milwaukee 1965, pp. 139–141.

[143] See *De necessitate et contingentia causarum* in J. J. Duin, *op. cit.* pp. 20, 28–29, 32–35; and *Sigeri de Brabantia quaestiones in Metaphysicam*, J. J. Duin, *op. cit.* pp. 103–108.

[144] See, e.g., *S. th.* II–1, *q.* 9, *a.* 4, *q.* 10, *a.* 4, *q.* 17, *a.* 5, *ad* 3.

[145] S. Knuuttila, De libero arbitrio in *Iustificatio impii*. Juhlakirja professori Lauri Haikolan täyttäessä 60 vuotta, Helsinki 1977, pp. 135–149. Relevant texts are, a.o., *S. th.* I, *q.* 83, *a.* 1c, II–1, *q.* 10, *a.* 2c, *q.* 13, *a.* 6c, and *ad* 3, *De malo q.* 6, *a. un. c, q.* 16, *a.* 5c, and *In Periherm.* I, 14, 24.

[146] *Quaestiones magistri Sigeri super librum de causis*, A. Marlasca (ed.), (Philosophes Médiévaux, XII), Louvain 1972, pp. 101.13–20, 102.50–55. See also A. Zimmermann, Thomas von Aquin und Siger von Brabant im Licht neuer Quellentexte in *Literatur und Sprache im europäischen Mittelalter. Festschrift für Karl Langosch zum 70. Geburtstag*, Darmstadt 1973, pp. 440–441.

[147] I. Pape, *Tradition und Transformation der Modalität I, Möglichkeit-Unmöglichkeit*, Hamburg 1966, pp. 45–50. See also J. Stallmach, *Dynamis und Energeia. Untersuchungen am Werke des Aristoteles zur Problemgeschichte von Möglichkeit und Wirklichkeit* (Monographien zur philosophischen Forschung, XXI), Meisenheim am Glan 1959, pp. 18–20.

[148] See *S. th.* I, *q.* 25, *a.* 3, *q.* 46, *a.* 1, *ad* 1.

[149] See Section 8 above.

[150] See note 130 above.

[151] E.g., *Ord.* I, *d.* 7, *q.* 1, *n.* 27.

[152] "Nulla est naturalis conexio et causae et causati simpliciter necessaria in creaturis, nec aliqua causa secunda causat naturaliter vel necessario simpliciter, sed tantum secundum quid." *Ord.* I, *d.* 8, *pars* 2, *q.u., n.* 306.

[153] See C. Balić, 'Une question inédite de J. Duns Scotus sur la volenté', *Recherches de théologie ancienne et médiévale* 3 (1931), 193–199. See also L. R. Roberts, 'Indeterminism in Duns Scotus' Doctrine of Human Freedom', *The Modern Schoolman* 51 (1973), 1–8. According to Roberts, Duns Scotus cannot prove that the will while willing could have been willing otherwise. I do not think that Scotus wanted to prove this in any empirical way; it is what it means for the will to be free. Cf. also P. Scapin, Il significato fondamentale della libertà divina secondo Giovanni Duns Scoto. *De doctrina Ioannis Duns Scoti. Acta Congressus Scotistici Internationalis Oxonii et Edimburgi 11–17 sept. 1966 celebrati, Vol. II, Problemata philosophica* (Studia Scholastico-scotistica, 2), Romae 1968, pp. 530–537.

[154] *Lect.* I, *d.* 39, *q.* 1–5, *n.* 45, 47.

[155] *Ibid. n.* 50.

[156] See *De caelo* 281b15–23.

[157] See also Hintikka, *Time and Necessity*, pp. 205–206.

[158] *Lect.* I, *d.* 39, *q.* 1–5, *n.* 50.

[159] *Ibid. n.* 51.

[160] *Ibid. n.* 55–57.

[161] *Ibid. n.* 58.

[162] R. Green has edited the text in his unpublished thesis *An Introduction to the Logical Treatise De obligationibus, with Critical Texts of William of Sherwood (?) and*

Walter Burley, Louvain 1963. The work is cited by C. L. Hamblin in *Fallacies* (University Paperbacks), London 1970, pp. 126–128; and by L. M. De Rijk in 'Some Thirteenth Century Tracts on the Game of Oblication', *Vivarium* **XII** (1974), 94.

[163] De Rijk, *op. cit.* pp. 94–96.

[164] *Ibid.* pp. 103–117.

[165] *Ibid.* pp. 112–113.

[166] The rule and the comment are published in *Ioannis Duns Scoti Opera omnia* (*editio Vaticana*), Vol. XVII, p. 498.

[167] Cf. also. *Lect.* I, *d.* 39, *q.* 1–5, *n.* 59.

[168] *Ibid.* 60.

[169] *Lect.* I, *d.* 39, *q.* 1–5, *n.* 69, 71.

[170] *Ord.* I, *d.* 2, *pars* 2, *q.* 1–4, *n.* 262, *Ord.* I, *d.* 7, *q.* 1, *n.* 27, *Lect.* I, *d.* 7, *q.u.*, *n.* 32–33, *d.* 39, *q.* 1–5, *n.* 49, 51, 54. The term *possibile logicum* does not occur in the literature before Scotus; see H. Deku, 'Possibile logicum', *Philosophisches Jahrbuch der Görres-Gesellschaft* **64** (1956), 15; and Faust, *op. cit.* pp. 247–259.

[171] *Ord.* I, *d.* 43, *q.u.*, *n.* 9, 14.

[172] *Ibid.* *n.* 16; *Lect.* I, *d.* 39, *q.* 1–5, *n.* 72.

[173] *Ord.* I, *d.* 43, *q.u.*, *n.* 14.

[174] *Lect.* I, *d.* 39, *q.* 1–5, *n.* 72.

[175] See H. Schwamm, *Das göttliche Vorherwissen bei Duns Scotus und seinen ersten Anhängern* (Philosophie und Grenzwissenschaften, V), Innsbruck 1934.

[176] See J. Owens, 'Common Nature: A Point of Comparison between Thomistic and Scotistic Metaphysics', *Inquires into Medieval Philosophy. A Collection in Honor of Francis P. Clarke*, by J. F. Ross (ed.), (Contributions in Philosophy 4), Westport, Connecticut 1971, pp. 186–191; S. H. Nasr, *An Introduction to Islamic Cosmological Doctrines*, Cambridge, Mass. 1964, pp. 197–199.

[177] See *The Metaphysica of Avicenna* (*ibn Sīnā*). A critical translation-commentary and analysis of the fundamental arguments in Avicenna's Metaphysica in the Dānish Nāmai'alā'ī (The Book of Scientific Knowledge) by P. Morewedge (Persian Heritage Series, 13), London 1973, pp. 55–56.

[178] The relevant texts from the works of Avicenna are translated by G. F. Hourani in 'Ibn Sīnā on Necessary and Possible Existence', *Philosophical Forum* **IV** (1972), 74–86. See also Nasr, *op. cit.* pp. 198–202.

[179] *Plotini opera* I–II, P. Henry and H.-R. Schwyzer (eds.), (Museum Lessianum, Series Philosophica 33–34), Paris 1951–1959; *Enn.* V, 2, 1.7–9. For Plotinus' modal concepts; see also H. Buchner, *Plotins Möglichkeitslehre* (Epimeleia), München 1968.

[180] *Enn.* V, 4, 1.34–36.

[181] Cf. also *Enn.* III, 8, 10.1–14; V, 1, 6.30–33; V, 4, 2.19–23 and 26–30.

[182] See *The Metaphysica of Avicenna*, transl. by P. Morewedge, pp. 76–79 and 108; Hourani, *op. cit.* p. 80.

[183] *The Metaphysica of Avicenna*, pp. 66–68.

[184] *Ibid.* p. 67, Hourani, *op. cit.* p. 80, and Nasr, *op. cit.* pp. 212–214.

[185] "Et ita dico quod necessitas repugnat omni respectui ad posterius, quia ex quo omne posterius est non-necessarium, primum non potest habere necessariam habitudinem ad aliquam eorum." *Ord.* I, *d.* 8, *pars* 2, *q.u.*, *n.* 302; cf. *n.* 253–256.

[186] *Tractatus de primo principio* IV, 4.

[187] See *Guillelmi de Ockham Summa logicae*, Ph. Boehner, G. Gál, and S. Brown (eds.),

(Editiones Instituti Franciscani Universitatis S. Bonaventurae), St. Bonaventure, N.Y. 1974, I, *esp.* 70–74, pp. 209–228. *Iohannis Buridani Tractatus de consequentiis*, H. Hubien (ed.), (Philosophes médiévaux, XVI), Louvain, Paris 1976, *lib.* I, *cap.* 6, pp. 26– 30; Pseudo-Scotus, *In librum primum Priorum Analyticorum Aristotelis quaestiones*, in *Ioannis Duns Scoti Opera omnia* I, Wadding (ed.), Lyon 1639, *q.* 26, pp. 310–313; *Ockham's Theory of Terms. Part I of the Summa logicae*, translated and introduced by M. J. Loux, Notre Dame, Indiana 1974, pp. 23–46.
[188] S. Knuuttila, 'Medieval Modal Logic', forthcoming in *The Cambridge History of Later Medieval Philosophy*, A. Kenny, N. Kretzmann, and J. Pinborg (eds.).
[189] For the new fourteenth century approach to modal logic, see Ockham, *op. cit.* II, *cap.* 24–29, pp. 327–345; III–1, *cap.* 20–64, pp. 411–497; III–3, *cap.* 10–16, pp. 631–649; Pseudo-Scotus, *op. cit. q.* 25–33, pp. 309–325; Buridan, *op. cit. lib.* II, *cap.* 1–7, pp. 56–78; *lib.* IV, *cap.* 1–3, pp. 111–133. Cf. also A. C. S. McDermott, 'Notes on the Assertoric and Modal Propositional Logic of the Pseudo-Scotus', *Journal of the History of Philosophy* 10 (1972), 273–306; C. G. Normore, *The Logic of Time and Modality in the Later Middle Ages: The Contribution of William of Ockham* (Ph.D. dissertation), University of Toronto 1975.

BIBLIOGRAPHY

1. Editions and Translations

Alain of Lille, *Anticlaudianus, Patrologia latina* 210, 485–576.

Alain of Lille, *Regulae de sacra theologia, Patrologia latina* 210, 621–684.

Albert the Great, *Opera omnia cura ac labore A. Borgnet*, Vol. II, L. Vivès, Paris 1890.

Albert the Great, *Opera omnia cura Inst. Alberti Magni Coloniense B. Geyer praeside*, Vol. XVI, 1–2, Verlag Aschendroff, Münster 1960–1964.

Alexander of Aphrodisias, *De fato*, ed. by I. Bruns (Commentaria in Aristotelem Graeca, Suppl. II, 2), G. Reimer, Berolini 1892.

Anselm of Canterbury, *Opera omnia*, ed. by F. S. Schmitt, T. Nelson, Edinburgh 1946–1951.

Aristoteles, *Categoriae et De interpretatione*, ed. by L. Minio-Paluello (Scriptorum Classicorum Bibliotheca Oxoniensis), Oxford University Press, Oxford 1949.

Aristoteles, *De caelo*, ed. by D. J. Allan (Scriptorum Classicorum Bibliotheca Oxoniensis), Oxford University Press, Oxford 1936.

Aristoteles, *Metaphysics*, a Revised Text with Introduction and Commentary by W. D. Ross, 2 Vols., Oxford University Press, Oxford 1924.

Aristoteles, *Prior and Posterior Analytics*, a Revised Text with Introduction and Commentary by W. D. Ross, Oxford University Press, Oxford 1949.

Aristoteles, *Topica et Sophistici Elenchi*, ed. by W. D. Ross (Scriptorum Classicorum Bibliotheca Oxoniensis), Oxford University Press, Oxford 1958.

Augustinus, *Confessionum libri XIII*, ed. by P. Knöll (Corpus Scriptorum Ecclesiasticorum Latinorum 33), F. Tempsky, Vindobonae 1896.

Augustinus, *De civitate dei*, ed. by B. Dombart and A. Kalb (Corpus Christianorum, Series Latina 47–48), Brebols, Turnholti 1955 (*Patrologia latina* 41, 13–804).

Augustinus, *De nuptiis et concupiscentia, Patrologia latina* 44, 413–474.

Augustinus, *De spiritu et littera*, ed. by C. F. Urba and I. Zycha (Corpus Scriptorum Ecclesiasticorum Latinorum 60), F. Tempsky, Vindobonae, and G. Freytag, Lipsiae 1913.

Augustinus, *In Ioannis euangelium tractatus*, ed. by R. Willems (Corpus Christianorum, Series Latina 36), Brebols, Turnholti 1954 (*Patrologia latina* 35, 1379–1976).

Averroes, *Aristotelis Opera cum Averrois Commentariis*, apud Junctas, Venetiis 1562–1574, Nachdruck Minerva, Frankfurt am Main 1962.

Avicenna, *The Metaphysica of Avicenna (ibn Sīnā)*. A critical translation-commentary and analysis of the fundamental arguments in Avicenna's Metaphysica in the Da̅n*ish* Nāma-i ʿalāʾī (*The Book of Scientific Knowledge*) by P. Morewedge (Persian Heritage Series 13), Routledge and Kegan Paul, London 1973.

Bacon, Roger, *Sumule dialectices*, ed. by R. Steele in *Opera hactenus inedita Rogeri Baconi XV*, Clarendon Press, Oxford 1940.

Balić, C., 'Une question inédite de J. Duns Scot sur la volonté', *Recherches de théologie ancienne et médiévale* 3 (1931), 191–208.

Baudry, L. (ed.), *La querelle des futurs contingents (Louvain 1465–1475)*, textes inédits (Études de philosophie médiévale 38), J. Vrin, Paris 1950.

Bernard of Clairvaux, *Apologia ad Guillelmum*, *Patrologia latina* 182, 895–918.

Boethius, *Commentarii in librum Aristotelis Perihermeneias I–II*, ed. by C. Meiser, Teubner, Lipsiae 1877–1880.

Boethius, *Introductio ad syllogismos categoricos*, *Patrologia latina* 64, 761–832.

Boethius, *Philosophiae consolatio*, ed. by L. Bieler (Corpus Christianorum, Series Latina 94), Brebols, Turnholti 1957.

Bonaventura, *Opera omnia*, Vol. I, Collegium S. Bonaventurae, Quaracchi 1883.

Buytaert, E. M. (ed.), 'The *Tractatus Logicae Minor* of Ockham', *Franciscan Studies* 24 (1964), 34–100.

Cicero, *De divinatione*, ed. by A. S. Pease (University of Illinois Studies in Language and Literature, Vol. VI, 2–3 and VIII, 2–3), University of Illinois Press, Urbana 1920–1923.

Cicero, *De fato*, Lateinisch-deutsch, hrsg. von K. Bayer (Tusculum-Bücherei), Heimeran-Verlag, München 1963.

De Rijk, L. M., *Logica Modernorum. A Contribution to the History of Early Terminist Logic. Vol. I: On the Twelfth Century Theories of Fallacy, Vol. II, 1–2: The Origin and Early Development of the Theory of Supposition* (Wijsgerige teksten en studies 6, 16), Van Gorcum, Assen 1962, 1967.

Duin, J. J., *La doctrine de la providence les écrits de Siger de Brabant* (Philosophes médiévaux 3), Publications Universitaires, Louvain 1954.

Dunlop, D. M., 'Averroes on the Modality of Propositions', *Islamic Studies* 1 (1962), pp. 23–34.

Green, R., *The Logical Treatise "De obligationibus": An Introduction with Critical Texts of William of Sherwood and Walter Burley*, The Franciscan Institute, St. Bonaventure (forthcoming).

Hieronymus, *Epistulae I*, ed. I. Hilberg (Corpus Scriptorum Ecclesiasticorum Latinorum 54), F. Tempsky, Vindobonae, G. Freytag, Lipsiae 1910.

Hugo de Sancto Victore, *De sacramentis christianae fidei*, *Patrologia latina* 176, 173–618.

John Buridan, *Tractatus de consequentiis*, ed. H. Hubien (Philosophes médiévaux 16), Publications Universitaires, Louvain 1976.

252   SIMO KNUUTTILA

John Duns Scotus, *Abhandlung über das Erste Prinzip*, hrsg. und übersetzt von W. Kluxen, Wissenschaftliche Buchgesellschaft, Darmstadt 1974.

John Duns Scotus, *Opera omnia*, Wadding (ed.), Lyon 1639.

John Duns Scotus, *Opera omnia studio et cura Commissionis Scotisticae*, Civitas Vaticana 1950 –.

John Duns Scotus, *Philosophical Writings*, a selection edited and translated by A. Wolter, T. Nelson, Edinburgh 1962.

John Duns Scotus, *The De Primo Principio of John Duns Scotus*, ed. by E. Roche, Franciscan Institute, St. Bonaventure 1949.

John Duns Scotus, *Tractatus de Primo Principio*, ed. by M. Müller, Herder, Freiburg 1941.

John Duns Scotus, *A Treatise on God as First Principle*, transl. and ed. by A. Wolter (Forum Books), Franciscan Herald Press, Chicago 1966.

John of Salisbury, *Metalogicon*, ed. by C. C. I. Webb, Clarendon Press, Oxford 1929.

John of St. Thomas, *Outlines of Formal Logic*, transl. F. C. Wade (Mediaeval Philosophical Texts in Translation 8), Marquette University Press, Milwaukee 1955.

Lambert of Auxerre, *Logica (Summa Lamberti)*, ed. by F. Alessio, La Nuova Italia Editrice, Firenze 1971.

Loux, M. J., *Ockham's Theory of Terms: Part I of the* Summa logicae, transl. and introd., University of Notre Dame Press, Notre Dame 1974.

Minio-Paluello, L., *Twelfth Century Logic: Texts and Studies II*, Edizioni di Storia e Letteratura, Roma 1958.

Moses Maimonides, *The Guide of the Perplexed I–II*, transl. with and introduction and notes by Sh. Pines, The University of Chicago Press, Chicago and London 1974.

O'Donnell, J. R. (ed.), *Nine Mediaeval Thinkers. A Collection of Hitherto Unedited Texts* (Studies and Texts 1), Pontifical Institute of Mediaeval Studies, Toronto 1955.

Peter Abaelard, *Dialectica*, ed. by L. M. De Rijk (Wijsgerige teksten en studies 1), Van Gorcum, Assen 1956.

Peter Abaelard, *Introductio ad theologiam*, ed. by V. Cousin in *Petri Abaelardi Opera II*, A. Durand, Parisiis 1859.

Peter Abaelard, *Logica 'Ingredientibus'*, ed. by B. Geyer in *Peter Abaelards Philosophische Schriften* (Beiträge zur Geschichte der Philosophie des Mittelalters XXI, 1–3), Verlag der Aschendorffschen Verlagsbuchhandlung, Münster 1919–1927.

Peter Abaelard, *Sic et non, Patrologia latina* 178, 1329–1610.

Peter Damian, *Lettre sur la Toute-Puissance Divine*, introduction, texte critique, traduction et notes par A. Cantin (Sources Chrétiennes 191), Les Éditions du Cerf, Paris 1972.

Peter Lombard, *Sententiarum libri quatuor, Patrologia latina* 192, 521–962.

Peter of Poitiers, *Sententiae*, ed. by P. S. Moore and M. Dulong (Publications in Medieval Studies 7), 2d ed., The University of Notre Dame Press, Notre Dame 1961.

Peter of Spain, *Tractatus called afterwards Summule logicales*, ed. by L. M. De Rijk (Wijsgerige teksten en studies 22), Van Gorcum, Assen 1972.

Platon, *Timée, Critias*, texte ét. et trad. par A. Rivaud, Société d'Edition "Les belles lettres", Paris 1925.

Plotinus, *Opera I–II*, ed. by P. Henry and H. R. Schwyzer (Museum Lessianum, Series philosophica 33–34), Desclée de Brouwer, Paris 1951–1959.

Robert Grosseteste, *Die philosophischen Werke des Robert Grosseteste*, ed. by L. Baur

(Beiträge zur Geschichte der Philosophie des Mittelalters 9), Verlag der aschendorff-schen Verlagsbuchhandlung, Münster 1912.

Siger of Brabant, *Quaestiones super librum De causis*, ed. by A. Marlasca (Philosophes médiévaux 12), Publications Universitaires, Louvain 1972.

Siger of Courtrai, *Les oeuvres de Siger de Courtrai* par G. Wallerand (Les Philosophes Belges 8), Louvain 1913.

Simon of Tournai, *Expositio super simbolum*, ed. by N. Haring, *Archives d'histoire doctrinale et littéraire du moyen age* **41** (1974), 39–112.

Tertullianus, *De cultu feminarum*, ed. by A. Kroymann (Corpus Scriptorum Ecclesiasticorum Latinorum 70), Hoelder-Pichler-Tempsky, Vindobonae, Becker & Erler, Lipsiae 1942.

Thomas Aquinas, *Opera omnia*, Fiaccadori, Parma 1852–73, reprinted Musurgia, New York 1948–1950.

Thomas Aquinas, *In duodecim libros Metaphysicorum Aristotelis expositio*, Marietti, Torino 1950.

Thomas Aquinas, *In libros Aristotelis De caelo et mundo expositio, Opera omnia III*, Leonina ed., Romae 1886.

Thomas Aquinas, *In libros Aristotelis Peri hermeneias et Posteriorum analyticorum expositio*, Marietti, Torino 1964.

Thomas Aquinas, *Quaestiones Disputatae I–II*, Marietti, Torino 1953.

Thomas Aquinas, *Summa contra gentiles*, Marietti, Torino 1961.

William of Auxerre, *Summa aurea in quatuor libros sententiarum*, Parisiis 1500.

William of Ockham, *Summa logicae*, ed. by Ph. Boehner, G. Gál, St. Brown in *Guillelmi de Ockham Opera philosophica et theologica, Opera philosophica I*, Editiones Instituti Franciscani Universitatis S. Bonaventure, St. Bonaventure, N.Y. 1974.

William of Ockham, *The Tractatus de praedestinatione et de praescientia dei et de futuris contingentibus*, edited with a Study on the Mediaeval Problem of a Three-valued Logic by Ph. Boehner (Franciscan Institute Publications 2), The Franciscan Institute, St. Bonaventure, N.Y. 1945.

William of Sherwood, *Introductiones in logicam*, ed. by M. Grabmann (Sitzungsberichte der Bayerischen Akademie der Wissenschaften, Phil. hist. Abteilung 1937, 10), Verlag der Bayerischen Akademie der Wissenschaften, München 1937.

William of Sherwood, *Syncategoremata*, ed. by J. R. O'Donnell, *Medieval Studies* **3** (1941), 46–93.

William of Sherwood, *William of Sherwood's Introduction to Logic*, transl. with an introduction and notes by N. Kretzmann, University of Minnesota Press, Minneapolis 1966.

William of Sherwood, *William of Sherwood's Treatise on Syncategorematic Words*, transl. with an introduction and notes by N. Kretzmann, University of Minnesota Press, Minneapolis 1968.

2. Modern Literature

Adams, M., 'Did Ockham Know of Material and Strict Implication? A Reconsideration', *Franciscan Studies* **33** (1973), 5–37.

Beonio-Brocchieri Fumagalli, M. T., *The Logic of Abelard* (Synthese Historical Library), D. Reidel, Dordrecht 1969.

Blumenberg, H., 'Nachahmung der Natur', *Studium Generale* **10** (1957), 266–283.

Bocheński, J. M., *Formale Logik* (Orbis Academicus III, 2), Karl Alber, Freiburg/
    München 1956.
Bonnette, D., *Aquinas' Proofs for God's Existence*, Martinus Nijhoff, The Hague 1972.
Bosley, R., 'In Support of an Interpretation of On Int. 9', *Ajatus* 37 (1978), 29–40.
Buchner, H., *Plotins Möglichkeitslehre* (Epimeleia 16), Anton Pustet, München und Salz-
    burg 1970.
Byrne, E. F., *Probability and Opinion. A study in the medieval presuppositions of post-
    medieval theories of probability*, Martinus Nijhoff, The Hague 1968.
Chenu, M.-D., 'Grammaire et theologie aux XIIe et XIIIe siècles', *Archives d'histoire
    doctrinale et littéraire du moyen age* 10 (1935–1936), 5–28.
Chenu, M.-D., 'Un essai de méthode théologique au XIIe siècle', *Revue des sciences
    philosophiques et théologiques* 24 (1935), 258–267.
Connellan, C., *Why Does Evil Exist*, Exposition Press, Hickswille, N.Y. 1974.
Copleston, F., *History of Philosophy II: Medieval Philosophy*, The Newman Press,
    Westminster, Maryland 1955.
Dawson, J. G., 'Necessity and Contingency in the *De libero arbitrio* of Grosseteste', in *La
    filosofia della natura nel medioevo. Atti del Terzo congresso internazionale di filosofia
    medioevale*, pp. 357–362, Società editrice Vita e pensiero, Milano 1966.
De Bruyne, E., *The Esthetics of the Middle Ages*, transl. E. Hennessy, F. Ungar, New
    York 1969.
Deku, H., 'Possibile logicum', *Philosophisches Jahrbuch der Görres-Gesellschaft* 64
    (1956), 1–21.
De Rijk, L. M., 'Some New Evidence on Twelfth Century Logic', *Vivarium* 4 (1966),
    1–57.
De Rijk, L. M., 'Some Thirteenth Century Tracts on the Game of Obligation', *Vivarium*
    12 (1974), 94–123.
Faust, A., *Der Möglichkeitsgedanke. Systemgeschichtliche Untersuchungen I–II*, Carl
    Winter, Heidelberg 1931–1932.
Finili, A., 'Recent Work on the Tertia Via', *Dominican Studies* VII (1954), 22–47.
Frede, D., *Aristoteles und die 'Seeschlacht'. Das Problem der Contingentia Futura in De
    interpretatione 9* (Hypomnemata 27), Vandenhoeck & Ruprecht, Göttingen 1970.
Frede, M., *Die stoische Logik* (Abhandlungen der Akademie der Wissenschaften in
    Göttingen, Phil. hist. Klasse, 3. Folge 88), Vandenhoeck & Ruprecht, Göttingen
    1974.
Gilson, E., *The Christian Philosophy of St. Thomas Aquinas*, Random House, New York
    1956.
Gilson, E., *History of Christian Philosophy in the Middle Ages*, Sheed & Ward, London
    1955.
Grabmann, M., *Die Geschichte der scholastischen Methode I–II*, Herdersche Verlags-
    handlung, Freiburg 1909–1911.
Grabmann, M., *Mittelalterliches Geistesleben III*, Max Hueber, München 1956.
Grabmann, M., *Die Sophismatenliteratur des 12. und 13 Jahrhunders* (Beiträge zur
    Geschichte der Philosophie und Theologie des Mittelalters 36, 1), Verlag der aschen-
    dorffschen Verlagsbuchhandlung, Münster 1940.
Hamblin, C. L., *Fallacies* (University Paperbacks), Methuen & Co., London 1970.
Henry, D. P., *The Logic of Saint Anselm*, Oxford University Press, Oxford 1967.
Hick, J., *Evil and the God of Love* (Fontana Library), Collins, London 1968.

Hintikka, J., 'The Once and Future Sea Fight', *Philosophical Review* 73 (1964), 461–492.

Hintikka, J., *Time and Necessity: Studies in Aristotle's Theory of Modality*, Oxford University Press, Oxford 1973.

Hintikka, J. with Remes, U. and Knuuttila, S., *Aristotle on Modality and Determinism* (Acta Philosophica Fennica 29, 1), North-Holland Publ. Co., Amsterdam 1977.

Hourani, G., 'Ibn Sīnā on Necessary and Possible Existence', *The Philosophical Forum* 4 (1972), 74–86.

Jacobi, K., 'Kontingente Naturgeschehnisse', *Studia Mediewistyczne* 18 (1977), 3–70.

Jalbert, G., *Nécessité et contingence chez Saint Thomas d'Aquin et chez ses prédécesseurs*, Editions de l'Université d'Ottawa, Ottawa 1961.

Jolivet, J., 'Eléments du concept de nature chez Abelard' in *La filosofia della natura nel medioevo. Atti del terzo congresso internazionale di filosofia medioevale*, Società editrice Vita e pensiero, Milano 1966, pp. 297–304.

Kenny, A., *The Five Ways* (Studies in Ethics and the Philosophy of Religion), Schocken Books, New York 1969.

Knuuttila, S., *Aika ja modaliteetti aristotelisessa skolastiikassa*, Missiologian ja ekumeniikan seura, Helsinki 1975.

Knuuttila, S., 'De servo arbitrio', in *Iustificatio impii: Juhlakirja professori Lauri Haikolan täyttäessä 60 vuotta*, Helsinki 1977, pp. 139–149.

Knuuttila, S., 'Medieval Modal Logic', forthcoming in A. Kenny, N. Kretzmann, and J. Pinborg (eds.), *The Cambridge History of Later Medieval Philosophy*, Cambridge University Press, Cambridge.

Knuuttila, S., 'The Statistical Interpretation of Modality in Averroes and Thomas Aquinas', *Ajatus* 37 (1978), 79–98.

Lang, A., 'Zur Entstehungsgeschichte der Brocardasammlungen', *Zeitschrift für Rechtsgeschichte* 62 (1942), Kan. Abt. 31, pp. 106–141.

Lang, A., *Die theologische Prinzipienlehre der mittelalterlichen Scholastik*, Herder, Freiburg im Breisgau 1964.

Lovejoy, A., *The Great Chain of Being: A Study of the History of an Idea*, Harvard University Press, Cambridge, Mass. 1936.

Luscombe, D. E., *The School of Peter Abelard*, Cambridge University Press, Cambridge 1970.

Maier, A., *Die Vorläufer Galileis im 14. Jahrhundert*, Edizioni di Storia e Letteratura, Roma 1949.

McDermott, A. C. S., 'Notes on the Assertoric and Modal Propositional Logic of the Pseudo-Scotus', *Journal of the History of Philosophy* 10 (1972), 273–306.

Moody, E. A., 'History of Logic: Medieval Logic', in P. Edwards (ed.), *The Encyclopedia of Philosophy IV*, Macmillan and The Free Press, New York 1967, pp. 528–534.

Moody, E. A., *Truth and Consequence in Medieval Logic* (Studies in Logic and the Foundations of Mathematics), North-Holland Publ. Co., Amsterdam 1953.

Nasr, S. H., *An Introduction to Islamic Cosmological Doctrines*, Harvard University Press, Cambridge, Mass. 1964.

Normore, C. G., *The Logic of Time and Modality in the Later Middle Ages: The Contribution of William of Ockham* (Ph.D. dissertation, University of Toronto 1975).

Nuchelmans, G., *Theories of the proposition: Ancient and medieval conceptions of the bearers of truth and falsity* (North-Holland Linguistic Series), North-Holland Publ. Co., Amsterdam 1973.

Owens, J., 'Common Nature: A Point of Comparison between Thomistic and Scotistic Metaphysics', in J. F. Ross (ed.), *Inquiries into Medieval Philosophy. A Collection in Honor of Francis P. Clarke*, Greenwood Publ. Co., Westport, Connecticut 1971, pp. 185–209.

Pape, I., *Tradition und Transformation der Modalität I: Möglichkeit-Unmöglichkeit*, Felix Meiner, Hamburg 1966.

Patch, H. R., 'Necessity in Boethius and the Neoplatonists', *Speculum* 10 (1935), 393–404.

Peirce, C. S., *Collected Papers II*, ed. by C. Hartshorne and P. Weiss, Harvard University Press, Cambridge, Mass. 1932.

Plantinga, A., *The Nature of Necessity* (Clarendon Library of Logic and Philosophy), Oxford University Press, Oxford 1974.

Randall, J. H., *Aristotle*, Columbia University Press, New York 1960.

Rescher, N., *Studies in the History of Arabic Logic*, University of Pittsburgh Press, Pittsburgh 1963.

Rescher, N., *Temporal Modalities in Arabic Logic* (Foundations of Language, Supplementary Series 2), D. Reidel, Dordrecht 1966.

Rist, J. M., *Plotinus: The Road to Reality*, Cambridge University Press, Cambridge 1967.

Roberts, L. D., 'Indeterminism in Duns Scotus' Doctrine of Human Freedom', *The Modern Schoolman* 51 (1973), 1–16.

Scapin, P., 'Il significato fondamentale della libertà divina secondo Giovanni Duns Scoto', in *De doctrina Ioannis Duns Scoti. Acta Congressus Scotistici Internationalis Oxonii et Edimburgi 11–17 sept. 1966 celebrati*, Vol. II, pp. 519–566, Roma 1968.

Schwamm, H., *Das göttliche Vorherwissen bei Duns Scotus und seinen ersten Anhängern* (Philosophie und Grenzwissenschaften V, 1–4), Felizian Rauch, Innsbruck 1934.

Sharp, E. D., *Franciscan Philosophy at Oxford in the Thirteenth Century*, 2nd ed., Oxford University Press, Oxford 1964.

Siedler, D., *Intellektualismus und Voluntarismus bei Albertus Magnus* (Beiträge zur Geschichte der Philosophie und Theologie des Mittelalters 36, 2), Verlag der aschendorffschen Verlagsbuchhandlung, Münster 1941.

Stallmach, J., *Dynamis und Energeia. Untersuchungen am Werk des Aristoteles zur Problemgeschichte von Möglichkeit und Wirklichkeit*, (Monographien zur philosophischen Forschung 21), Anton Hain, Meisenheim am Glan 1959.

Tweedale, M., 'Abailard and Non-Things', *Journal of the History of Philosophy* 5 (1967), 329–342.

Weimar, P., 'Argumenta Brocardica', *Studia Gratiana* 14 (1967), 91–119.

Weinberg, J. R., *Abstraction, Relation, and Induction. Three Essays in the History of Thought*, The University of Wisconsin Press, Madison & Milwaukee 1965.

Wieland, W., *Die aristotelische Physik*, Vandenhoeck & Ruprecht, Göttingen 1962.

Williams, C. J. F., 'Aristotle and Corruptibility', *Religious Studies* I (1965), 95–107, 203–215.

Wolfson, H. A., *The Philosophy of the Kalam*, Harvard University Press, Cambridge, Mass. 1976.

Wolfson, H. A., *Religious Philosophy*, Harvard University Press, Cambridge, Mass. 1961.

Zimmermann, A., 'Thomas von Aquin und Siger von Brabant im Licht neuer Quellentexte', in A. Önnerfors *et al.* (eds.), *Literatur und Sprache im europäischen Mittelalter. Festschrift für Karl Langosch zum 70. Geburtstag*, Wissenschaftliche Buchgesellschaft, Darmstadt 1973, pp. 417–447.

JAAKKO HINTIKKA

LEIBNIZ ON PLENITUDE, RELATIONS, AND THE 'REIGN OF LAW'

1. LEIBNIZ AS A CRITIC OF DESCARTES

In January 1680 Leibniz wrote to Philipp as follows: "I esteem Mr. Descartes almost as much as one can esteem any man, and, though there are among his opinions some which seem false to me, and even dangerous, this does not keep me from saying that we owe nearly as much to Galileo and to him in philosophical matters as to the whole of antiquity. At present I recall only one of the . . . dangerous propositions. . . . It is in the *Principles of Philosophy*, Part III, Article 47, in the following words:

And, after all, it makes very little difference what we assume in this respect, because it must later be changed in accordance to the laws of nature. Hardly anything can be assumed from which the same effects cannot be derived, though perhaps with greater trouble. For, due to these laws, matter takes on, successively, all the forms of which it is capable. Therefore if we considered these forms in order, we all could eventually arrive at that one which is our present world, so that in this respect no false hypothesis can lead us into error.

I do not believe that a more dangerous proposition than this could be formulated. For if matter takes on, successively, all possible forms, it follows that nothing can be imagined so absurd, so bizarre, so contrary to what we call justice, that it would not have happened and will not some day happen. These are precisely the opinions which Spinoza has expounded more clearly, namely, that justice, beauty, and order are things relative to us but that the perfection of God consists in the magnitude of his activity by virtue of which nothing is possible or conceivable which he does not actually produce. These are also the opinions of Mr. Hobbes, who asserts that everything that is possible is either past or present or future, and that there will be no place for trust in providence if God produces everything and makes no choice among possible beings. Mr. Descartes was careful not to speak so plainly, but he could not keep from revealing his opinions incidentally. . . . In my opinion, this is the 'first falsehood' and the basis of atheistic philosophy, though it always seems to say the most beautiful things about God." [1]

S. Knuuttila (ed.), *Reforging the Great Chain of Being*, 259–286.
Leibniz on Plenitude, Relations and the 'Reign of Law' by Jaakko Hintikka from Leibniz: A Collection of Critical Essays, edited by Harry G. Frankfurt.

2. THE "PRINCIPLE OF PLENITUDE"

The thesis Leibniz here brands "the first falsehood and the basis of atheistic philosophy" was not original with Descartes and Hobbes. It is a version of one of the most famous metaphysical principles in Western philosophy and speculative theology, somewhat misleadingly labeled by A. O. Lovejoy the "Principle of Plenitude". What the principle says is fairly accurately brought out by Leibniz's paraphrase of Hobbes. It says that no genuine possibility can remain unfulfilled through an infinite stretch of time. Other more or less equivalent formulations are: What holds always, holds necessarily; there are no eternal accidents; what never happens, is impossible. The equivalences between these are based on assumptions which are unproblematic for our present purposes. However, the principle has different forms according to how the 'genuine possibilities' mentioned in our first formulation are understood. Are they possibilities concerning kinds of individuals? Particular individuals? Kinds of events? Sequences of events? A couple of distinctions between different variants of the principle will be needed later.

Lovejoy studied the history of the Principle of Plenitude in his famous book *The Great Chain of Being.*[2] As far as the history of philosophy is concerned, however, Lovejoy's work has to be read with considerable caution. It contains important mistakes, and it concentrates largely on one aspect of the principle only, viz., on its role in philosophical and theological ideas of creation and of the perfection of the world.[3]

Leibniz was right about Descartes and Hobbes. The passage he quotes from Descartes is rather inconspicuous, and seems to be partly an insurance against ecclesiastic condemnation. However, we shall see that deeper issues were probably involved in Leibniz's disapproval. As to Hobbes, he assents in so many words to the Principle of Plenitude in *De Corpore.*[4] Undoubtedly, Leibniz would have found his judgment confirmed if he could have anticipated the use of what he called 'the basis of atheistic philosophy' by David Hume in the *Dialogues on Natural Religion*[5] or if he had known of its use by Lucretius in *De rerum natura.*[6] However, it is less obvious what he would have said had he been aware of the acceptance of the Principle of Plenitude by many — perhaps most — pious scholastics.[7]

3. POSSIBILITY VERSUS COMPOSSIBILITY

In view of this Protean role of the Principle of Plenitude in Western philosophy, Leibniz's uncharacteristically violent rejection requires an explanation.

Some of his reasons are apparent in our initial quotation. They are connected with his central logical, metaphysical, and theological views. What he emphasizes here is that God has not created all possible beings because then creation would not have been guided by His "striving for the good", i.e., striving for such *desiderata* as order, beauty, and justice. Rather, He has created the best, i.e., the richest, possible world. By the richest world Leibniz means the world containing the greatest variety of jointly possible or compossible individuals (substances).

Leibniz's criticism of Descartes is thus geared to his distinction between possibility and compossibility. Since "not all possibles are compossible",[8] the viability of this distinction implies the failure of the principle of plenitude, applied to all possible individuals or kinds of individuals. By the same token, Leibniz turns out to have a much more drastic reason than those noted above to hold that God has not created all possible beings. Since they are not compossible, even God could not have done so. This would be a metaphysical (we moderns would say 'logical') impossibility which even God is subject to.

Leibniz appears to invest his idea of compossibility with a certain novelty, while admitting that "it may be that Diodorus, Abelard, Wycliffe, and Hobbes had this idea in their heads without completely untangling it".[9] He explains the distinction by identifying the possible with what does not imply a contradiction and by identifying compossibility with the possibility of joint existence.

In view of the crucial role of this notion in Leibniz, it merits a few comments. Critics have occasionally complained that the notion of compossibility does not bring in anything new, but rather relies on the same idea of possibility as the unadorned notion of possibility *simpliciter*. They are of course right in a sense. Using 'M' for 'it is possible that' and otherwise employing an obvious symbolism, the distinction between possibility and compossibility is illustrated by the difference between

(1) $M(\exists x)Ax \ \& \ M(\exists x)Bx$

and

(2) $M((\exists x)Ax \ \& \ (\exists x)Bx)$.

The former is a double assertion of simple possibility: it says that individuals of the kind A are possible and that individuals of the kind B are also possible. The latter is an assertion of compossibility: it says that individuals of both kinds can co-exist.

The fact that one and the same operator 'M' can, and must, be used both in (1) and (2) shows that one and only one basic notion of possibility is involved in them. This does not show, however, that Leibniz's distinction is gratuitous. On the contrary, we see from (1)–(2) that what Leibniz has in mind is an instance of the most common, and most important, type of a conceptual distinction. What distinguishes (1) and (2) is an 'operator switch', i.e., the order in which the operations 'M' and '&' are applied. Leibniz is thus making a formally correct and interesting point.

This does not, however, answer the question of the importance of Leibniz's distinction. It is not immediately obvious whether, and in what circumstances, (1) and (2) are really different.

4. LEIBNIZ NEEDS RELATIONS

Here modern logic offers us an interesting answer. However 'M' can be interpreted, for Leibniz it clearly meant logical possibility (freedom from contradiction). Now if A and B are monadic (non-relational, purely qualitative) predicates, whether complex or not,

$$(3) \qquad (\exists x)Ax \,\&\, (\exists x)Bx$$

is satisfiable (logically possible) if and only if $(\exists x)Ax$ and $(\exists x)Bx$ are both separately satisfiable (logically possible). In this case, this distinction between (1) and (2) collapses (for logical possibility). In contrast, when A and B are complex in such a way as to contain relational concepts it frequently happens that $(\exists x)Ax$ and $(\exists x)Bx$ are both satisfiable while (3) is not. A simple example is the following pair of existential statements:

(4)   there exists everybody's master;
(5)   there exists nobody's slave;

where the relations 'master' and 'slave' are assumed to be converses. There is nothing logically impossible in the truth of either (4) or (5), and yet they are incompatible. This incompatibility may be seen by asking: What is the relation of the individuals mentioned in (4) and (5)? By (4), the former should be the latter's master, which is ruled out (5).

Thus Leibniz's distinction is without difference as long as relational concepts are not employed. This is a striking result in view of the often repeated claim that Leibniz wanted to dispense with relations in the last analysis, and to reduce them to non-relational concepts. If this were the case, Leibniz's system would be inconsistent in an ironic manner. His distinction between possibility and compossibility would be a viable one only if his attempted reduction of relations to non-relational predicates fails.[10]

There certainly are passages in Leibniz suggesting such an attempt. The best-known one is probably the following:

> You will not, I believe, admit an accident which is in two subjects at once. Thus I hold, as regards relations, that paternity in David is one thing, and filiation in Solomon is another, but the relation common to both is a merely mental thing, of which the modifications of singulars are the foundation.[11]

Benson Mates has offered an interesting though perhaps not entirely conclusive discussion of this passage.[12] The indications concerning Leibniz's intentions that we can garner from his writings are indeed few and far apart. However, what there is seems to point less to a reduction proper of relational *concepts* to non-relational ones than to an attempt to paraphrase relational *statements* (statements saying that a certain relation holds between two or more individuals) in terms of non-relational statements attributing complex predicates (possibly including relations) to these individuals. These predicates, as Mates rightly emphasizes, must not be defined in terms of the other individuals, for that would trivialize everything.

5. AN EXPLICATION OF *EO IPSO*

As Mates also points out, Leibniz explicitly mentions an operation by means of which he apparently proposed to effect this paraphrase or reduction. In trying to spell out what Leibniz's intentions amount to, it is thus important to see whether this reductive *eo ipso* operation can be made sense of in systematic terms. Needless to say, this operation cannot be truth-functional. Leibniz explains it only through examples, one of which involves the statement

(6)   Paris loves Helen

which he paraphrases as

(7)   Paris loves, and by that very fact (*eo ipso*)
        Helen is loved.

An obvious generalization would be to paraphrase Rab by

(8) $(\exists x)Rax$, eo ipso $(\exists y)Ryb$

Mates does not offer any explication of the non-truth-functional operator *eo ipso* occurring here. The problem is to define the operation.

(9) $P_1(a)$, eo ipso $P_2(b)$

for arbitrary (usually complex) predicates $P_1(x)$, $P_2(x)$ and not just for predicates of the special forms $(\exists x)Rax$, $(\exists y)Ryb$.

It may be assumed that, although the complex predicates $P_1(x)$, $P_2(x)$ may depend on individuals other than a and b, they do not depend on a or b. (Hence $P_1(a)$ does not depend on b nor $P_2(b)$ on a.) For simplicity, let us assume that they are of the same depth, i.e., have the same number of layers of quantifiers and that they contain the same free singular terms (apart from a and b). Then they can be represented as a disjunction of conjunctions of the form

(10) $(\exists x)Ct_{11}(x, a)$ & $(\exists x)Ct_{12}(x, a)$ & ... & $(\exists x)Ct_{1i}(x, a)$ &
               $(x)[Ct_{11}(x, a) \vee Ct_{12}(x, a) \vee ... \vee Ct_{1i}(x, a)]$,
(11) $(\exists x)Ct_{21}(x, b)$ & $(\exists x)Ct_{22}(x, b)$ & ... & $(\exists x)Ct_{2j}(x, b)$ &
               $(x)[Ct_{21}(x, b) \vee Ct_{22}(x, b) \vee ... \vee Ct_{2j}(x, b)]$,

respectively. Here the $Ct_{ij}(x, y)$ are drawn from a certain fixed store of complex predicates, each specifying one kind of individual y as fully as one can do by means of $d-1$ layers of quantifiers and by reference to x.

The point of the *eo ipso* operation is that somehow (10) and (11) are jointly supposed to determine the relation which holds between a and b. Now there is one and only one case in which this determinacy obtains. Clearly a must be one of the x's in (11) and b must be one of the x's of (10). We have unique determinacy if and only if we can thus 'fit in' (10) and (11) together in only one way, that is, if and only if there is only one k and only one l such that

(12) $Ct_{1k}(b, a)$ & $Ct_{2l}(a, b)$

is logically consistent. Thus we now know what to do. We can confine our attention to those pairs of disjuncts (10), (11) for which the unique determinacy holds, and define (9) as the disjunction of all the different expressions (12) obtained from such privileged pairs. (Restricting our attention to the privileged pairs is simply a reflection of the idea that the *eo ipso* operation presupposes that a's having the predicate P_1 and b's having the predicate P_2 jointly determine a unique relation between them. Here we are accordingly disregarding those cases in which this presupposition is not satisfied.) This yields an eminently natural definition of (9). Its naturalness is attested to by the fact that for all primitive predicates (and for many complex ones) $R(a, b)$ will be equivalent to (8), as we undoubtedly would like it to be.

6. AXIOM OF REDUCIBILITY IN LEIBNIZ?

Thus we can see — at least in rough outline — the probable logic of Leibniz's attempted reduction — in so far as it can be called a reduction. If what has been said is the whole story, Leibniz was not eliminating relational concepts, but rather relational statements. They can be rewritten by means of the *eo ipso* operation in a subject-predicate form, and usually only with a complex predicate involving relational notions. However, we can still raise the question whether Leibniz perhaps went further and tried to eliminate also relational concepts. Such an elimination presupposes some sort of 'axiom of reducibility' (as we can fairly accurately call it à la Bertrand Russell) to the effect that each complex monadic predicate (possibly containing relations) can be reduced to simple (non-relational) predicates. It is difficult to give a definitive answer to this question, and it is not completely certain that an unambiguous answer can be extracted from Leibniz's writings.

Some partial evidence against ascribing such a reducibility assumption to Leibniz may nevertheless be registered here. Hidé Ishiguro has argued [13] that Leibniz's theory of space and time (as systems of relations among existents) does not commit him — and was not taken by Leibniz as committing him — to a denial of the reality of spatial and temporal relations. An interesting though inconclusive item of evidence evoked by Dr. Ishiguro is the list of simplest terms Leibniz could find. [14] This list includes such relational concepts as 'the same', 'prior', 'posterior', 'number', 'position', and 'place'.

In any case, it seems to me that we can understand in a way different from the traditional one (denial of the reality of relations) those statements of Leibniz's in which he says that relations are 'grounded' on their relata so that there are no 'purely extrinsic denominations' (*denominata pure extrinseca*). [15] They can be understood not as denying the reality or the irreducibility of relational concepts, but rather as asserting their indispensability for characterizing individuals (individual substances). On this view, a relation holding between a and b cannot in the last analysis be purely extrinsic, for the full specification of the individuals a and b themselves would have to depend on this relationship. In fact, in the passage just referred to, Leibniz explains the denial of purely extrinsic determinations by saying that they are ruled out by "the real connection of all things". A little later he says that "there is no term so absolute or so loose as not to include relations and the perfect analysis of which does not lead to other things and even to all others; so that you can say that relative terms indicate expressly the relations they contain." [16] It is hard to think of a stronger affirmation of the indispensability of relations.

Few philosophers nevertheless seem to have found a satisfactory way of reconciling such statements with Leibniz's apparent denials of the irreducibility of relations. For instance, Nicholas Rescher ascribes to Leibniz the view that all relations among individual substances are reducible to and derivable from the predicates of the respective substances. Rescher acknowledges that these predicates must not be relational in the blatant sense of referring explicitly to other particular individuals.[17] However, he seems to me to miss the correct *via media* here. As we already noted, in his subsequent criticism of Leibniz, Rescher presupposes that all those predicates to which relations are reduced are monadic in the sense of not even containing implicitly relational components. This means overlooking an intermediate position. This position maintains that relational statements can be reduced to statements in each of which a complex predicate is ascribed to one and only one of its relata. These complex predicates may still involve relational concepts, although they do not refer to any particular individuals of the universe except the one to which they are attributed.

The main substantial assumption I have to resort to in order to make my interpretation stick is that according to Leibniz the substantial form of an individual substance could, and should, be characterized in terms of quantifiers ranging over all the individual substances. (Of course, it could not be specified by reference to any other particular individual substances). Obviously, it would be going too far to claim that Leibniz was fully explicit in this matter. Leibniz had neither a terminology nor an explicit logical theory which he could have relied on in making his point. Nevertheless, there are many passages that strongly suggest something like the view just proposed[18] and none that to my knowledge are incompatible with it.

One small but telling piece of evidence for attributing this idea to Leibniz is the locution *ratio generalis ad individuum* which he uses to characterize the complete concept of an individual.[19] It scarcely makes sense unless this complete concept involves generality which respect to individuals, i.e., (speaking with the moderns) involves quantification over other (ultimately, all) individuals.

In some of his most explicit pronouncements on the subject,[20] Leibniz in any case makes it clear that what he terms "a mere ideal thing" is a way of considering relations "without considering which is the antecedent or which the consequent, which the subject and which the object" − that is to say, a way of considering relations not from the point of view of one of the relata but somehow in abstraction from them. There is nothing in such pronouncements to contradict my interpretation, it seems to me.

In his excellent article, Mates attributes to Leibniz an attempted reduction of relations to *simple* properties.[21] I cannot find any mention of the simplicity of those properties which (*apud* Leibniz) constitute the substantial form of an individual substance in the references Mates gives, or for that matter anywhere else in Leibniz. Hence Mates provides no evidence against the point of view I am tentatively proposing here.

It is also salutary to keep in mind that the doctrine of the ideality of relations was almost a commonplace in Leibniz's time and before it.[22] If Leibniz is compared with his predecessors, he will appear much less to stress the unreality of relations than when he is compared with later writers.

Be this as it may, my line of interpretation seems to do much better justice to what Leibniz is actually doing (and saying) than any alternative interpretation I am familiar with. We have already seen how it can in principle be implemented by means of a reconstruction of Leibniz's *eo ipso* operation. It may also be that this interpretation partly vindicates Russell's emphasis on an attempted reduction of all propositions to the subject-predicate form as a source of Leibniz's opinions.

It is not quite clear that even the reducibility of relations to simple properties would necessarily make much difference anyway. Granting the reduction (discussed above) of relational propositions to subject-predicate propositions with a possibly complex predicate containing relations, does it matter much if these relational predicates are reduced further to simple monadic predicates? If these simple properties are somehow necessarily connected with those complex relational properties (complex monadic predicates) which reduce to them, the reduction makes little difference to the logic of the situation and might merely serve as a device by means of which Leibniz can keep his relational cake as a logician and scientist while eating it as a metaphysician. It may be the case, however, that Leibniz was more consistent than this, though a definitive answer is hard to extract from his writings.

7. INDIVIDUALS AS REFLECTING THE WHOLE UNIVERSE

Such clues as we have discovered thus strongly suggest that Leibniz was not trying to reduce relations to nonrelational predicates but rather to reduce relational statements to statements in which a complex predicate (possibly involving relations) is attributed to a single subject. The study of such reductions belongs naturally to modern quantification theory. It seems to me that the resources of this theory can in general be brought to bear on Leibniz to an extent larger than philosophers usually realize.

In any case, we can, by means of the results of quantification theory, appreciate one of Leibniz's most characteristic and most puzzling doctrines. This is his idea that each individual substance 'reflects' the whole world it belongs to. As a corollary, it follows that according to Leibniz no possible (kind of) individual (i.e., fully characterized individual or individual specified by a complete individual concept) can occur in more than one possible world, for in virtue of this reflection a full specification of this individual will entail a specification of the rest of the world, too.[23] It follows further that two possible individuals (complete individual concepts) are compossible only if they occur in one and the same fully specified possible world.

This doctrine, which *prima facie* may seem rather far-fetched, receives a natural explanation in terms of the distributive normal forms (of first-order logic). Such normal forms are relative to a fixed finite non-logical vocabulary and to a given fixed number of layers of quantifiers, called the 'depth' of these normal forms. Any sentence with these characteristics can be transformed into a normal form with the very same 'parameters' − or into one with a greater depth, for that matter. Assuming for simplicity that no individual constants and no free individual variables are present, these normal forms are disjunctions of certain mutually exclusive conjunctions called 'constituents'. A constituent may be thought of as describing a kind of possible world. It does so by specifying what kinds of individuals exist in the world in question. In other words, it is of the form

$$(13) \qquad (\exists x)Ct_{i1}(x) \; \& \; (\exists x)Ct_{i2}(x) \; \& \; \ldots \& \; (x)[Ct_{i1}(x) \lor Ct_{i2}(x) \lor \ldots]$$

where $Ct_{i1}(x)$, $Ct_{i2}(x)$, ... is a subset of the set of complex predicates listing all the different kinds of individuals x specifiable by means of $d-1$ layers of quantifiers. Each of them is specified by listing, in addition to the monadic predicates x has, all the different kinds of individuals there exist in relation to x. These kinds of individuals of course have to be specified by means of $d-2$ layers of quantifiers. This 'relative' list (relative to x) of all individuals that there are has to match the 'absolute' list (13). The match cannot be a complete one, however, for there are d layers of quantifiers in (13) and only $d-1$ in the corresponding relative list. The individual x in question, we may say in quasi-Leibnizian terms, thus reflects the possible world described by (13) somewhat less clearly than (13) itself. To be precise, it reflects the world down to $d-1$ layers of quantifiers. Each conjunct $(\exists x)Ct_{ij}(x)$ occurring in (13) is hence compatible with only one constituent of depth $d-1$, the same for all of them. Each possible kind of individual (individual concept) specifiable by means of $d-1$ layers of quantifiers is thus compatible with at most one constituent (description of a 'possible world') of depth $d-1$.

This is already strongly reminiscent of Leibniz. A reason for the difference between the situation we have found in first-order logic and Leibnizian doctrines is also obvious. Our individual concepts have not been fully analyzed, for they are relative to a fixed finite level of analysis (fixed finite depth). Leibniz, in contrast, is considering an idealized situation in which the analysis has been carried *ad infinitum*. In so far as this idealization is legitimate, Leibniz's idea receives in a sense a complete vindication. It is true that there are certain difficulties in the idea of an infinite constituent, which looks like the most straightforward reconstruction of the Leibnizian idealization. However, an infinite sequence of increasingly deeper but mutually compatible constituents — which to all practical purposes amounts to an arbitrary complete first-order theory — is close enough a reconstruction of Leibniz's idea to enable us to say that in this way one of his most characteristic ideas can be vindicated.

To return to Leibniz's idea of compossibility, we can now see how it can also be vindicated. If relational concepts are present, not all possible kinds of individuals are compossible. Unless God is above the laws of logic — which was Descartes's way out — even He could not create a world in which they are all realized. The Principle of Plenitude is thus bound to fail if the sense of possibility involved in it is logical possibility (freedom from contradiction).

8. THE PRINCIPLE OF PLENITUDE HOLDS FOR COMPOSSIBILITY

It is especially important to appreciate Leibniz's doctrine that a possible individual cannot belong to more than one possible world when one is studying Leibniz's attitude to the Principle of Plenitude. This doctrine gives us a key to the understanding of several pronouncements in which Leibniz seems to accept the principle, his violent assertions to the contrary notwithstanding. A case in point is found in the statement[24] *ita dici potest, omne possibile existiturire*. Leibniz is not here saying that all possibilities will be realized, but rather suggesting that every individual that could be realized as a member of that particular selection of possible individuals which characterizes the actual world is realized in it. In other words, Leibniz's *omne possibile* has here something of the force 'all compossibilities'. As Leibniz says explicitly in his letter to Louis Bourguet, "It is very true that what is not, never has been, an never will be is impossible, if we take possible in the sense of the compossible. . . . "[25] Hence the Principle of Plenitude in a sense holds (*apud* Leibniz) for the notion of compossibility instead of plain possibility, and for it only. In fact, the quoted passage continues (after two lines) as follows: *Verum hinc non sequitur omnia possibilia existere.* Leibniz even seems to attribute the acceptance of the Principle of Plenitude to a confusion between possibility and compossibility.[26]

What Rescher calls the 'Principle of Plenitude'[27] is the version which pertains to compossibility rather than to possibility. Since it goes together with the negation of the more common variants of the principle, Rescher's terminology is not without dangers.

9. MONADS AS REFLECTING EACH OTHER VERSUS MONADS AS WINDOWLESS

My reconstruction of Leibniz's doctrine that individual substances 'reflect' the whole world implies that the existence or non-existence of each possible individual is specified as soon as we have specified the full concept of any one individual existing in the same possible world. This may seem incompatible with those views of Leibniz's which are sometimes expressed by speaking of the 'windowlessness' of monads. These views may seem to presuppose that each monad (individual substance) can happily exist no matter what happens to the others.

It is important to notice at once that the typical way in which Leibniz expresses these views is not to say in so many words that monads can exist or fail to exist independently of one another, though occasionally he comes rather close to doing so. Often he says merely that the apparent interaction between a given monad and others can be considered *as if* nothing but this monad and God existed. For instance, in Leibniz's *New System*, he writes that "the perceptions or expressions of external things come into the soul at their appropriate time, in virtue of its own laws, as in a world by itself and as if there existed nothing but God and the soul. . . . "[28] Now such pronouncements may perhaps be taken to suggest that according to Leibniz monads (which include souls) can exist or fail to exist independently of each other. This interpretation cannot be deduced from the texts, however. For instance, the passage just quoted is unashamedly metaphorical, containing both the explicit qualification 'as if' and indeed a little later an attribution of the very locution to others. Moreover, such an interpretation is ruled out by Leibniz's explicit doctrine that a monad (individual substance) can exist only in one possible world. For if a monad could exist or fail to exist independently of others, it could exist in different combinations of monads, i.e., in several different possible worlds. This is ruled out by Leibniz in the very same sentence, for he writes there that "each of these substances accurately represents the whole universe in its own way and from a certain point of view." Surely, if any of the other monads in the universe were to disappear, the monad in question could no longer express the world as 'accurately' as it did before the removal.

It seems to me that the statements in Leibniz's work which have prompted the misinterpretation in question have to be understood as dealing with the interaction of several monads rather than with their possible failure to co-exist. One may perhaps put Leibniz's point by denying not that the concept of each monad involves the existence of all the other monads in its universe, but rather that it involves the *necessary* existence of any other monad, except God. Hence there cannot be any necessitating causal connections between monads.

It is nevertheless only fair to say that this windowlessness doctrine of Leibniz's shows how close he came to being seduced into assuming some kind of 'axiom of reducibility'. This is shown by the fact that Leibniz clearly presents the windowlessness of monads as a consequence of their reflecting the whole world. What the latter doctrine amounts to is that any statements concerning the interrelation of two monads can be reformulated in terms of statements attributing certain complex predicates to each of them separately. If these complex predicates could be replaced, in virtue of an 'axiom of reducibility', by simple ones (involving no relations), then whatever we can truly say of one monad would be logically independent of what we say of any other, which I take to be the gist of the windowlessness doctrine. The fact that Leibniz always seems to guard his apparent claims that monads can exist independently of each other is nevertheless a good reason for thinking that he never yield to the temptation, although he seems to do so in giving his readers more picturesque illustrations of his doctrine and although there may have been some obscurity in his own thinking on this point. His own view seems to have been quite clearly that the *eo ipso* reduction is strong enough to support whatever claims of windowlessness he made.

10. LEIBNIZ'S LAW – SPURIOUS AND GENUINE

An important qualification to what has so far been said is that in a sense the *eo ipso* operation does not effect a genuine reduction of relational propositions to non-relational ones. It may be the case that, given the relational proposition $R(a, b)$, propositions $M_1(a)$ and $M_2(b)$ can be found such that $R(a, b)$ is logically equivalent to

$$M_1(a), \text{eo ipso } M_2(b).$$

From this it does not follow that $R(a, b)$ should be logically equivalent to the conjunction $M_1(a)$ & $M_2(b)$ or for that matter any truth-function of $M_1(a)$ and $M_2(b)$, for any choice whatsoever of the complex monadic propositions $M_1(a), M_2(b)$.

It is not hard to see, however, that the idea of individuals as reflecting the whole universe also serves to indicate how a more striking reduction might be possible *apud* Leibniz, provided that his famous assumption of the identity of indiscernibles (the converse of the ill-named 'Leibniz's law' of contemporary logic) is also accepted.

Suppose, for the purpose of seeing this, that a pair of (hypothetical) infinitely deep expressions $D_1(a)$ and $D_2(b)$ express the full concepts of a and b, respectively. Assuming that they are compossible, then in the relative list of a, as specified by $D_1(a)$, there must occur at least one entry − specified, say, by $(\exists y)Ct_i(a, y)$ − which is compatible with b in the sense that

$$Ct_i(a, b) \text{ \& } D_2(b)$$

is consistent ('metaphysically possible').

On one possible construal of Leibniz's identity principle, there will be only one such entry, should a and b be actually existing individuals. Then it may be shown that $D_1(a)$ & $D_2(b)$ logically implies $Ct_i(a, b)$, and vice versa, which gives us the desired reduction.

In this line of thought, I have operated freely with the fiction of infinitely deep propositions, which needs a justification. Rather surprisingly, a ready-made justification is far from easy to find in the literature. Modern logic is only now catching up with Leibniz's vision. The first attempt to systematize 'Leibnizian', i.e., infinitely deep, logics was made as late as 1976.[28a] We can nevertheless appreciate the structure of Leibniz's ideas even apart from the details of their modern reconstructions.

11. PLENITUDE AND THE WIDENING OF THE RANGE OF POSSIBILITIES

This does not exhaust the reasons why Leibniz was anxious to deny the

Principle of Plenitude. Another interesting group of reasons was connected with the development of modern science and of scientific method. In this area, Lovejoy's point of view is somewhat one-sided. He discusses this aspect of the history of the Principle of Plenitude almost exclusively in a cosmological framework. It is to some extent true that the principle played a role in encouraging philosophers and scientists to widen their cosmological perspectives. In order to find room in the actual universe for the many possibilities that the principle asserts to be realized in it, people had to acknowledge the narrowness of their experience as compared with everything there is to be found in the universe.[29]

However, this development seems to have been less important for the history of philosophy proper than Lovejoy's book perhaps suggests, and in any case it was conditional on more basic developments that are largely left untouched by Lovejoy. It is important to realize that the very term 'Principle of Plenitude' is a misnomer. What it asserts is not the plenitude of the actual world but an equation between genuine possibilities and the possibilities realized in the world. This implies the richness of the actual universe only if the range of genuine possibilities is thought of as being fairly extensive. The reason for its adoption can thus be the paucity of genuine possibilities there are to be realized rather than the plenitude of the actually materialized ones. When Lucretius or Aristotle assented to the 'Principle of Plenitude', what they were expressing was as much the scarcity of possibilities as the multitude of their realizations.

This point is closely related to Leibniz's criticism of the principle. "It always seems to say the most beautiful things about God," Leibniz concedes, in that it seems to assert that God in His omnipotence has realized everything that there is to be realized (God as *actus purus*). However, this is to consider the principle in one particular context only, viz., in relation to God's creation of the world. (This is one of the few perspectives in which Lovejoy views the Principle of Plenitude.) As Leibniz emphasizes, in other conceptual contexts the principle must be viewed in an entirely different light.

The remarkable development during the late Middle Ages and the Renaissance was in the first place the gradual widening of what was thought of as possible. What factors were operative in this development lies beyond the purview of this paper to examine. Duhem and Moody may very well be right in suggesting that theological doctrines concerning God's possibilities encouraged this widening of the scope of what was admitted as possible. The condemnation of 1277 in any case made it *de fide* to assert many possibilities which from the proper Aristotelian point of view were more or less nonsensical.

By and large, this widening of the range of the conceivable discouraged philosophers from believing in the Principle of Plenitude, rather than encouraging them to assert that the 'new' possibilities are somehow, somewhere, sometimes realized in our actual world. The first step was to excuse God's possibilities from the scope of the principle, but gradually other possibilities began to follow suit. Philosophers like Bruno − perhaps also Descartes to some extent − who at one and the same time glorified the multiplicity of possibilities and accepted the Principle of Plenitude, were the exception rather than the rule. No wonder Lovejoy is led to admit that neither Brahe, Kepler, nor Galileo was enthusiastic about the consequences of the Principle of Plenitude.

Leibniz is poking fun at this type of enthused acceptance of the Principle of Plenitude when he writes: "It cannot be denied that many stories, especially those we call novels, may be regarded as possible, even if they do not actually take place in this particular sequence of events which God has chosen − unless someone imagines that there are certain poetic regions in the infinite extent of space and time where we might see wandering over the earth King Arthur of Great Britain, Amadis of Gaul, and the fabulous Dietrich von Bern invented by the Germans."[30] Leibniz's criticism has a serious address, however, for he continues: "A famous philosopher of our century does not seem to have been far from such an opinion, for he expressly affirms . . . that matter successively receives all the forms of which it is capable. . . . "

12. THE PRINCIPLE OF PLENITUDE IMPLIES THE FAILURE OF ALL NATURAL LAWS

But this is not yet the worst. Perhaps the sharpest conflict was between certain forms of the Principle of Plenitude and the idea of a realistically interpreted science of nature employing general but not analytically (conceptually) true regularities, in short, between the principle and the idea of a law of nature.

In order to see this, let us consider the kind of simple situation inductive logicians like to start from. Let us consider a finite classification scheme for observed − as well as unobserved − individuals. All cells of the partition which go together with the classification scheme are possible to instantiate, an each individual belongs to one and only one of them. Let us assume that we have observed a fairly large number of individuals which are found to belong to certain cells $Q_1, Q_2, \ldots, Q_c$ of the partition, and to leave the rest of the cells $Q_{c+1}, Q_{c+2}, \ldots, Q_k$ empty. What can we tell on this basis of the unobserved individuals? What generalization concerning the whole universe can we set up on the basis of our sample? There is no need to discuss these questions here in great detail from the point of view of modern inductive logic. One type of answer merits our special interest, however. It is Carnap's answer or, strictly speaking, the kind of answer found in his published writings so far. It says that in an infinite universe all cells are instantiated with probability one. Therefore the one general law concerning the whole world that one can assert, with any probability however minute, is here the tautological (logically or conceptually true) statement that all our individuals exemplify one of our cells or the other. This is the only generalization one can accept in an infinite universe concerning all the unobserved individuals.

This consequence of Carnap's inductive logic has not remained without its critics. It would nevertheless have won many supporters among earlier philosophers. If the instantiation of each cell is a genuine possibility in the sense appropriate to the Principle of Plenitude, Carnap's answer is precisely the one prescribed by the principle. If it is possible that a given cell should be non-empty, according to the Principle of Plenitude there will actually be found an individual in it in the long run.

All the numerous philosophers who in the course of history have assented to the Principle of Plenitude are therefore in an implicit agreement with Carnap. The most influential of these unwitting supporters of Carnap is undoubtedly Aristotle. His belief in the Principle of Plenitude is documented in my paper 'Necessity, Universality, and Time in Aristotle'.[31] Since Aristotle also believed that all genuine knowledge is universal, his acceptance of the Principle of Plenitude is thus seen to be part and parcel of his belief that all true knowledge is at bottom conceptual, for from the principle it was seen to follow (in the simple but representative example just sketched) that the only acceptable universal statements are those that are true for logical (conceptual) reasons. No wonder Aristotelian science is conceptual to the extent it in fact is.

13. PRINCIPLE OF PLENITUDE AND OCKHAM'S RAZOR. THE CRIME OF GALILEO

Against this background it is not surprising that Leibniz, who more than perhaps any other philosopher was impressed by the idea of a law of nature, should have objected to the Principle of Plenitude with its disastrous consequences to any general regularity not holding already in virtue of what Leibniz called 'metaphysical necessity'. A relatively simple and perhaps a

little simple-minded argument against the principle was offered to him by
the principle of parsimony ('Ockham's Razor'). In order to see how it can
apply here, we only need to recall the classification problem sketched in the
preceding section. Surely it is against any conceivable variant of any reasonable parsimony principle to say, after having observed a fairly large number of
individuals belonging to relatively few cells, that among the so far unobserved
individuals there exist objects belonging to each of the remaining cells, too.
A more literal "multiplication of (kinds of) entities without necessity" is hard
to think of.

Leibniz, in fact, registers repeatedly the incompatibility of the Principle of
Plenitude with the requirement of parsimony. For instance, see his 'Preface to
Nizolius' [32] and Section 5 of his *Discourse on Metaphysics*.

This is not the whole story, however, of Leibniz's opposition to the
Principle of Plenitude. A political reason which seems to have remained tacit,
but of which Leibniz can scarcely have been unaware, was that Galileo was
silenced by means of arguments which presupposed the principle. When
pressed, Galileo was perfectly willing to admit that he was only describing
how things in fact are, not how God could or could not have made them
happen. [33] Yet one of the gravest philosophical and dogmatic mistakes his
criticis found in his work was that he was "limiting God's power to particular
effects", that is, apparently, claiming that things could not happen in any
other way. If this charge is to be made to stick, the readily available premise
which would make it look respectable is obviously the Principle of Plenitude.
What effect this use of the principle might have had on Leibniz, who was
busy trying to have Galileo's works removed from the Index, is easy to
guess.

14. PRINCIPLE OF PLENITUDE APPLIED TO SEQUENCES OF
EVENTS

Leibniz had further methodological and scientific objections to the Principle
of Plenitude, however. This principle is in an especially sharp conflict not just
with the idea of a non-conceptual law of nature, but even more so with the
idea of a mathematically formulated law of nature. If the dependence of
one magnitude on another can be formulated in terms of one particular
mathematical function, any other function automatically also represents a
conceivable (and hence in a sense possible) mode of dependence. There is no
a priori reason why freely falling bodies should obey the law $v = gt$ (velocity
proportional to time) rather than, say, the law $v = gs$ (velocity proportional to

the distance fallen), as is vividly brought out by the fact that Galileo initially assumed the latter rather than the former regularity.

If each of these conceivable and hence at least 'metaphysically possible' laws is sometimes instantiated, as a sufficiently strong version of the Principle of Plenitude requires, no mathematically formulated law of nature holds without exceptions. Mathematical physics is in principle impossible or at best only approximately or hypothetically true.

Thus we can see why Leibniz the mathematical physicist had as much to object to in the Principle of Plenitude as Leibniz the metaphysician. No wonder he complained that the Cartesian acceptance of the principle "would obliterate all the beauty of the universe".[34] Elsewhere he speaks likewise of the loss of the order of the universe instead of its beauty.

15. LEIBNIZ'S CRITICISM OF DESCARTES EVALUATED

In order to bring the weight of the incipient mathematical physics to bear upon the Principle of Plenitude, Leibniz nevertheless had to change the interpretation of the principle in a natural but interesting way. This tacit shift of ground makes his strong objection to Descartes perhaps slightly less than accurate. As our initial quotation within quotation clearly brings out, in asserting what Leibniz called the 'dangerous proposition',[35] Descartes had primarily in mind possible states of affairs, possible configurations ('forms') of matter, or (as we might also call them in view of the use Descartes makes of them) possible initial conditions. The very same quotation mentions apparently immutable 'laws of nature', to which Descartes does not contemplate exceptions. It is the initial conditions that Descartes thinks of as varying, and in fact as being largely arbitrary. This was a rather typical way of looking at the Principle of Plenitude in the Middle Ages. One of the most characteristic applications of the principle was to temporary configurations of individuals or kinds of individuals, as, e.g., Thomas Aquinas' use of the principle in his *tertia via* illustrates.

Leibniz, in contrast, changes the emphasis of the principle from possible individuals, kinds of individuals, or even temporary configurations of individuals to possible sequences of events or of kinds of events. (I wonder whether he is perhaps misinterpreting Descartes's phrase 'successively' so as to fit Descartes's words better to his interpretation.) This he does quite explicitly and consistently. For instance in a letter to Coste in 1707, in which he discusses the notions of necessity and contingency, Leibniz discusses how "one fact follows another".[36] Further examples are offered by Couturat,[37] and by the passage quoted above concerning 'possible novels'.

Again, Leibniz is to some extent reflecting a more general shift of emphasis. The gradual extension of the Principle of Plenitude to sequences of events tended to discourage philosophers and scientists more and more from holding the principle. According to Anneliese Maier, the beginning of the shift can be placed in the fourteenth century.[38] At that time, the focus of the concepts of possibility and necessity changed from a merely 'statistical' comparison of what the state of affairs is at different moments of time to questions concerning the different successions of states of affairs. This change was particularly clear among the Parisian nominalists. It may not be an accident that some of them also seem to have been among the first to dissent explicitly and without qualifications from the Principle of Plenitude.

It does not seem to be the case, however, that such sequences of events or of states of affairs are what Descartes had in mind in the passage Leibniz quotes. Hence Leibniz's criticism may appear somewhat misplaced. However, in a deeper sense it was probably justified. Cartesian science was conceptual for reasons not unrelated to the principle. One of the clearest statements to this effects occurs in the corollary to Proposition III of the 'Arguments drawn up in geometrical fashion" which Descartes appended to his reply to the second set of objections to the *Meditations*: "But we possess the idea of a power so great that by Him, and Him alone, in whom this power is found, must heaven and earth be created, and a power such that likewise whatever else is apprehended by me as possible must be created by Him too."[39] (Cf. also Descartes's reply to the sixth set of objections, Sec. 6.) Leibniz was therefore right in attributing a form of the Principle of Plenitude to Descartes. To what extent Descartes conceived of it in the same way as Leibniz did remains unclear.

Leibniz's criticism of Descartes is somewhat inaccurate in another respect, too. He clearly assumes that Descartes should have applied his version of the Principle of Plenitude to God's possibilities ("nothing is possible or conceivable which he does not actually produce"). Yet Descartes in so many words denied such applicability, although Leibniz probably was unaware of the most explicit instances of such denials. (A case in point is found in Descartes's letter to Father Mesland, May 2, 1644.) Even so, Leibniz could have accused — and indeed did accuse — the Cartesian God of arbitrariness. Maybe it is after all a good *argumentum ad hominem* for Leibniz to argue against Descartes not on the basis of God's incapacity of realizing all possibles, but rather on the basis of the resulting disorder, arbitrariness, and injustice.

We already saw in fact that the one important aspect of Leibniz's criticism of Descartes was directed against what we would call the conceptual character of Cartesian sciences. This Cartesian conceptualism turned on an application of the Principle of Plenitude to what is humanly conceivable ('clearly and distinctly'), not on an application to God's possibilities. In this direction, the edge of Leibniz's criticism is not dulled by the qualification just made.

16. LOGICAL NECESSITY VERSUS NATURAL NECESSITY

Throughout much of the discussion above, a critical reader may have missed an important distinction. What we have been considering appears to have been logical possibility only. Should we not have discussed natural or physical possibility instead of the purely logical one? The answer is twofold. For one thing, many of Leibniz's formulations (such as those in terms of freedom from contradiction, conceivability, etc.) clearly refer to logical rather than physical possibility (from our point of view), as does much of the phraseology of his predecessors. For another, no sharp and unequivocal distinction between logical and natural necessity and possibility is likely to be found in most of Leibniz's predecessors. Rather, the purposes which this distinction serves were partly catered to by some suitable derivative distinction between absolute and relative possibility. (Both these notions presuppose the same sense of possibility.) I have argued for this earlier in the case of Aristotle,[40] and somewhat similar remarks apply to many of his medieval successors. In fact, it is the gradual weakening of the Principle of Plenitude that tends to make indispensable a distinction between logical and natural necessity. In Leibniz, no such distinction is usually made in an explicit form, although his distinction between what is true in virtue of metaphysical necessity and what is true in virtue of the principle of sufficient reason (or of the principle of perfection) is perhaps something of an approximation to it. Such distinctions are occasionally assimilated by Leibniz to the distinction between absolute and hypothetical necessity.[41]

In a brief note, 'De rerum originatione radicali', Leibniz operates in so many words with a distinction between 'metaphysical' and 'physical' necessity.[42] The two are not unrelated to each other, however, for Leibniz says that "we now have a physical necessity derived from a metaphysical one", and in so many words identifies physical with hypothetical and metaphysical with absolute necessity.

Leibniz is thus seen to stick to the letter of the traditional view. Yet he is unwittingly preparing the ground for breaking the tradition. The traditional idea of a hypothetical necessity was necessity relative to a certain times or relative to occasions on which certain conditions are satisfied. For Leibniz, the hypothetical or physical necessity of those natural laws which in fact hold is conditional necessity relative to the assumption of our world's being perfect, the 'best possible world'.[43] This assumption was for Leibniz guaranteed by God's goodness, omniscience, and omnipotence – and of course also by His existence. Knock out these theological underpinnings, and the Leibnizian tie between metaphysical (logical) necessity and the physical necessity of actually holding natural laws disappears.

Although no clear distinction between logical and physical necessity thus emerges from Leibniz's writings, his contrast between metaphysical and moral necessity nevertheless seems to have constituted a strong impetus towards developing such a distinction.

17. 'THE REIGN OF LAW' IN MODERN LOGIC AND IN LEIBNIZ

For one more important aspect of Leibniz's ideas we must return to the classificatory situation discussed above. As the perceptive reader has undoubtedly noticed already, it seems to belie Leibniz's idea that the richest possible selection of compossibles is realized in the actual world. For clearly the existence of one kind of individual does not preclude the realization of any other. Thus the richest selection of compossibles is the one in which each cell is exemplified. Hence we seem to have reduced Leibniz, if not *ad absurdum*, at least *ad Aristotelem et Carnapium*. However, saying this is but to repeat what we said above to the effect that Leibniz's ideas can only be done justice to when relations are present. What happens then in modern logic in fact beautifully confirms Leibniz's ideas, as ably summed up by Russell. Earlier, I pointed out that in the relational case the distinction between possibility and compossibility is indispensable: not all possibles can be realized in one and the same universe. Now we can see another doctrine of Leibniz's vindicated. In the nonrelational case, no purely universal laws (universal statements) are true in an Aristotelian (or Carnapian) world except those that are logically true. In contrast to this, if relations are present, there holds in each universe at least one 'general law' of the form

(14) $(x)[Ct_{i1}(x) \vee Ct_{i2}(x) \vee \ldots]$

(cf. Section 8 above for the notation) which is not true for purely logical (conceptual) reasons. (In order to see this, let $Ct_{i1}(x), Ct_{i2}(x), \ldots$ be simply all those kinds of individuals, in the sense of Section 7 above, that are exemplified in the universe in question. By what was just said, they cannot comprise all such kinds of individuals.)

Thus each possible world is characterized (at each given finite depth) by the strongest 'general law' (in the sense of a statement of form (14)) true in it. This is, as Russell says, what Leibniz's idea of the 'reign of law' really amounts to.[44] Because of this, Leibniz can say that God's choice between different possible worlds is really a choice between the different over-all laws governing these worlds. "There is an infinity of possible ways in which God could form, and . . . each possible world depends on certain principal designs or purposes of God which are distinctive of it, that is, certain primary free decrees (conceived *sub ratione possibilitatis*) or certain laws of the general order of this possible universe with which they are in accord and whose concept they determine, as they do also the concepts of all the individual substances which must enter into this same universe. Everything belongs to an order . . . "[45]

If the universe in question contains, moreover, a maximally rich selection of compossibles, we have precisely the kind of situation Leibniz envisaged. Although there is no logical ('metaphysical') necessity that precisely this collection of compossibles should have been realized, and although many other kinds of individuals could have been realized, it is nevertheless true in our contemporary logic – even when we restrict ourselves to what can be expressed at some given fixed depth – that no other kind of individual (specifiable by means of expressions of this fixed depth) could have been instantiated, given the instantiation of all actually existing individuals. Leibniz's adherence to the Principle of Plenitude for compossibles is thus justified, given his general metaphysical outlook.

18. PLENITUDE AND RECIPROCITY

There is at least one more context in which Leibniz was (wittingly or unwittingly) confronted with the Principle of Plenitude. This happened in formal logic, where Leibniz was led to consider the interrelations of the so-called intensional and extensional points of view. (He called them *methodus per notiones et per individua*.) Here the Principle of Plenitude is equivalent to what is sometimes called the 'law of reciprocity': relations of concept inclusion are inversely mirrored by the extensions of the concepts in question. For if the addition of a new element E to concept T makes a difference, so that it is possible that an individual should exemplify T but not $E + T$, then it would follow from the Principle of Plenitude that this possibility is sometimes realized, i.e., the extension of $E + T$ is a proper subset of the extension of T.

Leibniz apparently came upon the reciprocity law first is a purely logical context[46] and overlooked the problems connected with it. Later, he became aware of some of the problems, although I have not found any explicit statement by him where the particular difficulties he discusses are related to the other repugnant consequences of the Principle of Plenitude or to the principle itself. The difficulties Leibniz discusses still belong primarily to technical logic.[47] Perhaps it is nevertheless significant that in this area, too, Leibniz eventually opposed the consequences of the Aristotelian and Cartesian Principle of Plenitude.

In any case, Leibniz could not have taken the easy way out which some of his commentators have prescribed. He would not have tried to save the reciprocity law by including 'possible individuals' within the extensions of the concepts so as to instantiate all the requisite classes. It is true that he mentions (in the paper on 'some logical difficulties' just referred to) 'supposed men' (*homines suppositi*) serving purposes closely related to the reciprocity law. But they cannot save the law, for Leibniz realized clearly himself that not all possible kinds of individuals are compossible. No conceivable universe could therefore offer us a set of individuals from which all the necessary extensions can be carved, and the use of 'possible individuals' is reduced to well-deserved absurdity. I strongly suspect that these difficulties were the main reason why Leibniz's work in logic remained as inconclusive as it was and why he published so little of it. He needed *possibilia* in his syllogistic theory because of his rejection of the Principle of Plenitude, but such merely possible individuals could never be pooled together in one well-defined 'region of ideas'.

19. AN INCONCLUSIVE CONCLUSION: LOGIC AND METAPHYSICS IN LEIBNIZ

If there is a general conclusion to our observations, it surely is a reaffirmation of Bertrand Russell's thesis that Leibniz's philosophical doctrines were heavily conditioned by his logical insights. In fact, this dependency cuts deeper than Russell himself and other commentators have so far brought out.

It may also be of some interest to see the kind of logic we have been relying on: ordinary quantification theory plus a touch of inductive logic. Modal logic (intensional logic) has not been essentially resorted to.

I suspect that in so far as Leibniz can truly be said to have preferred the 'intensional point of view' in his logical theorizing, his reasons are essentially connected with the rejection of the Principle of Plenitude.[48] If so, we also see how gratuitous the contrast between the two points of view is. No modern logician has dreamt of reviving the Principle of Plenitude, and yet there has been no general need whatsoever to drag intensions or possible individuals into discussions of syllogistic or other parts of first-order logic.

What emerges from our discussion is therefore an almost ironic observation. Tremendous though Leibniz's contributions to logic were, they did not even come close to spelling out the (to my mind even more impressive) logical (structural) insights on which his metaphysics was based. The most important secret of modern logic is not its symbolism, but the general concept of quantification. This was left by Leibniz for Gottlob Frege to spell out, although some of his own basic insights were, at bottom, quantificational.[49]

Florida State University

NOTES

[1] C. I. Gerhardt (ed.), *G. W. Leibniz: Philosophische Schriften*, 7 Vols., Berlin 1875–90, Vol. 4, pp. 283–84; translation from L. E. Loemker (ed.), *G. W. Leibniz: Philosophical Papers and Letters* (Synthese Historical Library), Dordrecht 1969, p. 273. Herafter I shall abbreviate these as G. and L., respectively.

[2] Cambridge, Mass. 1936.

[3] I have shown in 'Necessity, Universality, and Time in Aristotle', *Ajatus* **20** (1957), 65-90 (also Philosophy-106, Bobbs-Merrill Reprints in Philosophy, Indianapolis 1969) and in 'A. O. Lovejoy on Plenitude in Aristotle', *Ajatus* **29** (1967), 5–11, that Lovejoy was mistaken in denying that Aristotle held the 'principle of plenitude.' It also appears that Lovejoy was not entirely correct in ascribing the principle to Plato; cf. Erkka Maula, 'Plato or Plenitude', *Ajatus* **29** (1967), 12-50. These mistakes of Lovejoy's are connected with his preoccupation with the idea of plenitude in the creation of the world. In such a context, Plato – but not Aristotle – might indeed be expected to opt for the principle. The strength of the other ingredients in the 'principle of plenitude' is shown by the fact that these expectations turn out to be misleading.

[4] II, 10, iv.

[5] Part VII, first paragraph.

[6] Book V, lines 422-30 (cf. Book I, lines 1024-30).

[7] For comments on the history of the principle in the late Middle Ages, see Risto Hilpinen, 'Runsauden periaate ja Jumalan mahdollisuudet' (with an English summary), *Ajatus* **31** (1970).

[8] Leibniz to Louis Bourguet, G., Vol. 3, p. 573; L., p. 662.

[9] G., Vol. 3, p. 572; L., p. 661.

[10] For an earlier statement of this putative criticism of Leibniz, see Nicholas Rescher, *The Philosophy of Leibniz*, Prentice-Hall 1967, pp. 77–78.

[11] G., Vol. 2, p. 486; L., p. 609, translated by B. Mates.

[12] See Mates's paper, 'Leibniz on Possible Worlds', in *Logic, Methodology and Philosophy of Science III, Proceedings of the 1967 International Congress*, B. van Rootselaar and J. F. Staal (eds.), Amsterdam 1968, pp. 507–27, especially pp. 519–21.

[13] See Hidé Ishiguro, 'Leibniz's Theory of the Ideality of Relations', in Harry G. Frankfurt (ed.), *Leibniz: A Collection of Criticial Essays*, Garden City, N.Y. 1972, pp. 191–213; 'Leibniz's Denial of the Reality of Space and Time', *Annals of the Japan Association for Philosophy of Science* 3 (1967), 33–36; *Leibniz's Philosophy of Logic and Language*, London 1972, pp. 88–97.

[14] See, e.g., G. Grua, *G. W. Leibniz: Textes inédits*, Paris, 1948, Vol. 2, p. 542; similar lists are given by Leibniz elsewhere.

[15] See *Nouveaux Essais* II, 25, v.

[16] *Nouveaux Essais* II, 25, x.

[17] Rescher, *op. cit.*, p. 74.

[18] See, e.g., the passages from *Nouveaux Essais* referred to above.

[19] E.g., in his correspondence with Arnauld: see G., Vol. 2, p. 54; L., p. 335.

[20] E.g., in his fifth paper to Samuel Clarke, Section 47.

[21] See Mates, *op. cit.*, p. 511.

[22] See, e.g., Julius Weinberg, *Abstraction, Relation, and Induction: Three Essays in the History of Thought*, Madison and Milwaukee 1965, pp. 86–119.

[23] See, e.g., Mates, *op. cit.*, pp. 511–12.

[24] G., Vol. 7, p. 289. In the *Monadology*, Sec. 54, we likewise read: " . . . each possible has a right to claim existence in proportion to the perfection it involves. Thus nothing is entirely arbitrary."

[25] G. Vol. 3, p. 572; L., p. 661.

[26] G. Vol. 3, pp. 572–73; L., pp. 661–62.

[27] Rescher, *op. cit*, pp. 50–51.

[28] R. Latta (ed.), *Leibniz: The Monadology and Other Philosophical Writings*, Oxford, 1898, p. 313.

[28a] See Jaakko Hintikka and Veikko Rantala, 'A New Approach to Infinitary Languages', *Annals of Mathematical Logic* 10 (1976), 95–115. One main stumbling-block in developing a theory of infinitely deep languages has been the impossibility of giving a recursive truth-definition for them.

[29] Cf. Lovejoy, *op. cit.*, ch. IV.

[30] Foucher de Careil, *Nouvelles lettres et opuscules inédits de Leibniz*, Paris, 1857, pp. 178–79; L., p. 263.

[31] *Op. cit.*, note 3 above.

[32] G., Vol. 4, p. 158; L., p. 128.

[33] See G. de Santillana, *The Crime of Galileo*, Chicago, 1955, p. 167.

[34] Foucher de Careil, *op. cit.*, p. 179; L., p. 263.

[35] Descartes, *Principles* III, art. 47.

[36] B. Erdmann, *Leibnitii Opera*, Berlin 1840, pp. 447–50; P. P. Wiener, *Leibniz Selections*, p. 481.

[37] Couturat, *Opuscules et Fragments*, pp. 529–30; L., pp. 168–69.

[38] See Anneliese Maier, *Die Vorläufer Galileis im 14. Jahrhundert: Studien zur Naturphilosophie der Spätscholastik*, Rome 1949, ch. 8.

[39] Norman Malcolm has called my attention to the fact that this piece of evidence is

somewhat ambiguous. I quoted the translation of E. Haldane and G. T. R. Ross who follow the French version of Descartes's replies. The Latin version, however, says only that whatever is apprehended by me as possible, God *can* create. Of course, the two versions are equivalent precisely when the principle of plenitude is being presupposed.

It looks as if Descartes restricted the principle of plenitude to general possibilities concerning the material world. Thus Descartes writes in the Sixth Meditation, "... we must at least admit that all things which I conceive in [corporeal things] clearly and distinctly, that is to say, all things which ... are comprehended in the object of pure mathematics are truly to be recognized as external objects." Here Descartes infers *truths* about external objects from their *possibility* (clear and distinct conceivability).

⁴⁰ Jaakko Hintikka, 'Aristotelian Infinity', *Philosophical Review* 75 (1966), 197–218.
⁴¹ See, e.g., Leibniz's fifth paper against Clarke, Sections 4–6; *Discourse on Metaphysics*, Section XIII.
⁴² G., Vol. 7, p. 304; L., pp. 487–88.
⁴³ Cf. G., Vol. 7, p. 304.
⁴⁴ *A Critical Exposition of the Philosophy of Leibniz*, London 1937, p. 67.
⁴⁵ G., Vol. 2, p. 51; L., p. 511.
⁴⁶ See, e.g., Couturat, *Opuscules et Fragments*, p. 235; R. Kauppi, *Über die Leibnizsche Logik* (Helsinki, 1960), p. 45.
⁴⁷ See, e.g., G., Vol. 7, pp. 211–17; G. H. R. Parkinson, *Leibniz: Logical Papers* (Oxford, 1966), pp. 115–21.
⁴⁸ As I have pointed out in my paper, 'Necessity, Universality, and Time in Aristotle', *Ajatus* 20 (1957), 65–90, it even is a little surprising to see a believer in plenitude develop a modal logic. This surprise is occasioned by the fact that for such a philosopher necessity is at least materially equivalent with omnitemporal truth and possibility with sometime truth. Hence for him the modal element is simply tantamount to quantification over time. Ordinary extensional logic (quantification theory) seems to be all he needs. Only when the principle of plenitude is given up is one driven to a sharp distinction between modal and non-modal logic.
⁴⁹ For valuable comments on and criticisms of earlier versions of this paper I am indebted to Professors Raili Kauppi and Risto Hilpinen, as well as to Dr. Lauri Routila.

BIBLIOGRAPHY

Couturat, L., *Opuscules et Fragments inédits de Leibniz*, Presses Universitaires de France, Paris 1903, Nachdruck G. Olms, Hildesheim 1961.
Erdmann, J. E., *Lebnitii Opera Philosophica quae extant*, G. Eichler, Berlin 1840.
Foucher de Careil, A., *Nouvelles lettres et opuscules inédits de Leibniz*, Aug. Durand, Paris 1857.
Gerhardt, C. I., *Die philosophischen Schriften von Gottfried Wilhelm Leibniz I–VII*, Berlin 1875–1890, Nachdruck G. Olms, Hildesheim 1960–1961.
Grua, G., *G. W. Leibniz: Textes inédits*, Presses Universitaires de France, Paris, 1948.
Hilpinen, R., 'Runsauden periaate ja Jumalan mahdollisuudet', *Ajatus* 31 (1969), 93–116.
Hintikka, J., 'Aristotelian Infinity', *Philosophical Review* 75 (1966), 197–218, reprinted in J. Hintikka, *Time and Necessity: Studies in Aristotle's Theory of Modality*, Clarendon Press, Oxford 1973, pp. 114–134.

Hintikka, J., 'A. O. Lovejoy on Plenitude in Aristotle', *Ajatus* 29 (1967), 5–11.

Hintikka, J., 'Necessity, Universality, and Time in Aristotle', *Ajatus* 20 (1957), 65–90.

Hintikka, J. and Rantala, V., 'A New Approach to Infinitary Languages', *Annals of Mathematical Logic* 10 (1976), 95–115.

Ishiguro, H., 'Leibniz's Denial of the Reality of Space and Time', *Annals of the Japan Association for Philosophy of Science* 3 (1967).

Ishiguro, H., *Leibniz's Philosophy of Logic and Language*, Duckworth, London 1972.

Ishiguro, H., 'Leibniz's Theory of the Ideality of Relations' in H. G. Frankfurt (ed.), *Leibniz: A Collection of Critical Essays*, Anchor Books, Doubleday, Garden City, N.Y. 1972, pp. 191–213.

Kauppi, R., *Ueber die Leibnizsche Logik* (Acta Philosophica Fennica 12), Societas Philosophica Fennica, Helsinki 1960.

Latta, R., *Leibniz: The Monadology and Other Philosophical Writings*, trans. with introduction and notes, Clarendon Press, Oxford 1898.

Leibniz, Gottfried Wilhelm, Sämtliche Schriften und Briefe, Reihe VI, Band 6: *Nouveaux Essais sur l'entendement humain*, ed. by A. Robinet und H. Schepers, Akademie-Verlag, Berlin 1962.

Loemker, L. E., *G. W. Leibniz: Philosophical Papers and Letters*, transl. and ed. with introduction, 2d ed. (Synthese Historical Library), D. Reidel, Dordrecht 1969.

Lovejoy, A., *The Great Chain of Being: A Study of the History of an Idea*, Harvard University Press, Cambridge, Mass. 1936.

Maier, A., *Die Vorläufer Galileis im 14. Jahrhundert*, Edizioni di Storia e Letteratura, Roma 1949.

Mates, B., 'Leibniz on Possible Worlds', in *Logic, Methodology and Philosophy of Science III, Proceedings of the Third International Congress*, ed. by B. van Rootselaar and J. F. Staal (Studies in Logic and the Foundations of Mathematics), North-Holland Publ. Co., Amsterdam 1968, pp. 507–529.

Maula, E., 'Plato on Plenitude', *Ajatus* 29 (1967), 12–50.

Parkinson, G. H. R., *Leibniz: Logical Papers*, transl. and ed. with introduction, Clarendon Press, Oxford 1966.

Rescher, N., *The Philosophy of Leibniz*, Prentice-Hall, Englewood Cliffs 1967.

Russell, B., *A Critical Exposition of the Philosophy of Leibniz*, Allen & Unwin, London 1937.

Santillana, G. de, *The Crime of Galileo*, University of Chicago Press, Chicago 1955.

Weinberg, J. R., *Abstraction, Relation, and Induction: Three Essays in the History of Thought*, The University of Wisconsin Press, Madison and Milwaukee 1965.

Wiener, P., *Leibniz: Selections* (Modern Student's Library), Scribner, New York 1951.

JAAKKO HINTIKKA AND HEIKKI KANNISTO

KANT ON 'THE GREAT CHAIN OF BEING' OR THE EVENTUAL REALIZATION OF ALL POSSIBILITIES: A COMPARATIVE STUDY

One of the most fascinating themes in the history of western thought — in any case one of the themes that have actually exerted strongest fascination on historians of ideas — is the assumption which in its crude form says that in the long run everything possible happens. In a slightly more guarded formulation, it says that no possibility can remain unfulfilled through an infinity of time. In this sense, every (permanent) possibility is sometimes realized. Conversely, what is never realized is impossible, and by the same token what holds always (omnitemporally) holds by necessity.

The long-range history of this assumption was studied by A. O. Lovejoy in his famous book *The Great Chain of Being*. He misleadingly dubbed the assumption the *Principle of Plenitude*. This is misleading because the principle only asserts an equation between possibilities and their realizations in time. It can therefore be as much or as little a Principle of Paucity of Possibilities as a Principle of the Plenitude of their Realizations.

Nor is this criticism of Lovejoy only a matter of systematic or 'architectonic' interest. It is directly relevant to the underlying reasons for the historical interest of the Principle of Plenitude (as we shall go on calling it in the absence of any other handy label). Because the Principle asserts the balance between possibilities and their temporal actualizations, it is sensitive not only to shifts in people's ideas of what there actually is in the world (i.e., in their ideas of the relative richness or poverty of our universe), but also to changes in thinkers' conceptions of what more or less hidden possibilities there perhaps lurk waiting to be realized. Since these conceptions are often highly important but difficult to approach directly, the Principle of Plenitude becomes a useful indicator of such partly or completely tacit assumptions concerning the range of ontological and physical options there are. The wider the purview of these possibilities grows, the harder it becomes for philosophers (and other speculative thinkers) to maintain the Principle. Conversely, every restriction in the scope of the contingencies one has to consider makes it easier *ceteris paribus* to uphold it.

For instance, the gradual disenchantment of late medieval thinkers with the Principle of Plenitude is one of the best symptoms of that important broadening of the store of possibilities which in the late Middle Ages served

S. Knuuttila (ed.), Reforging the Great Chain of Being, 287–308.

to push the examination of question into the field of what is logically possible. (For this trend see John Murdoch, 'From Social into Intellectual Factors: An Aspect of the Unitary Character of Late Medieval Learning', in J. E. Murdoch and E. D. Sylla (eds.), *The Cultural Context of Medieval Learning*, D. Reidel, Dordrecht 1975, pp. 271–348.)

It is characteristic of Lovejoy's approach that in dealing with the Renaissance period his main attention is attuned to the widening of the sphere of people's ideas about the actual universe. But this pertains only to one half of the equation that the Principle of Plenitude is, to realizations and not to possibilities. It is in this respect a sobering thought that in spite of the tremendous expansion of the intellectual boundaries of the actual world only such exceedingly speculative thinkers as of Bruno could find these boundaries wide enough to uphold the Principle. For all others, possibilities had multiplied even faster than their presumed realizations.

In Kant, we are confronted with an essentially different historical situation. What is even more important, the general direction of development is different in his case from what we find with the medievals. One way of looking at the overall impact of his philosophy is to say that by emphasizing the concept of possible experience and the limitation of legitimate human conceptual thought to this possible experience, Kant in effect carved out of the wealth of all absolute possibilities a much narrower range of options, the humanly or empirically possible ones. The way of looking at the upshot of Kant's philosophy is lent contemporary interest by Hintikka's recent arguments, modified and developed further from Quine's well-known attacks on quantified modal logic, that an unrestricted use of logical (analytical or conceptual) modalities is pragmatically impossible if we want to use them in conjunction with such staple concepts as individual, identity, and quantification. For if these arguments are well taken, it follows that the only way of saving logical modalities is to restrict somehow the realm of 'possible worlds' we are considering. And this is just what Kant is doing on the view here suggested. Hence it would appear that Kant's thinking offers us an interesting example of a pioneering foray into a direction which we are all just now being inexorably pushed by the development of the semantics and pragmatics of modal logic.

The purpose of this paper is to supply some indirect evidence for this way of looking at Kant's achievement. Again, the ill-named 'Principle of Plenitude' performs its symptomatic function extremely well, we shall argue. Already the overall development of Kant's relationship to the Principle matches the expectations which our general view of its role as an ontological equilibrium postulate naturally give rise.

Kant's early views are well in line with Lovejoy's main emphasis. Lovejoy considers the Principle of Plenitude well-nigh exclusively from the vantage point of the richness of the realizations of possibilities, not from the direction of the paucity of the set of these possibilities themselves. Furthermore, he has largely in mind only one possible source of this richness, viz. the plenitude of the creation of the universe. In general, the idea of creation is important for Lovejoy's outlook on the Principle of Plenitude. A corollary to this outlook is Lovejoy's inability to cope with the attitude of those thinkers for whom the notion of creation played a subordinate or negligible role. Thus he gets Plato's and Aristotle's views neatly upside down. He claims that Plato accepted the Principle but that Aristotle did not, whereas the truth is much closer to the opposite.

Furthermore, it may be expected on the basis of an accurate appraisal of the Principle as a mere equation that its applicability to a sufficiently omnipotent creator easily becomes problematic in that neither its attribution to nor its denial from God makes much sense. The reason for this is that the Principle presupposes an independently specifiable range of possibilities whose realizations are at stake. Leibniz's possible worlds are perhaps the clearest cases in point. However, as soon as a thinker conceives of the realm of possibilities as being themselves created by a Divine decree, it almost becomes a matter of intellectual and theological taste whether we say that *all* possibilities are thereby *ipso facto* 'realized', or whether we want to put the shoe on the other foot and to say that since God could have established a different set of possibilities, He was left something undone that He has the power to do. Yet this choice makes all the difference to the Principle of Plenitude as applied to God. This confusion can be found repeatedly in the actual historical material.

Be this as it may, the pre-critical Kant does Lovejoy proud in his emphasis on the connection between plenitude and creation. While still in his dogmatic slumbers Kant professed to something very much like the Principle of Plenitude. In his *Allgemeine Naturgeschichte und Theorie des Himmels* (1755) he adheres to this doctrine, and motivates it by reference to the idea of infinite creation. God's creation of the world is without limits. The primary matter he has (directly) created is so 'rich' that in the course of eternity it shall realize all possibilities.

And hence it may be laid down, with good reason, that the arragement and institution of the universe comes about gradually, as it arises out of the provision of the created matter of nature in the sequence of time. But the primitive matter itself, whose qualities and forces lie at the basis of all changes, is an immediate consequence of the Divine existence;

and that same matter must therefore be at once so rich and so complete, that the development of its combinations in the flow of eternity *may extend over a plane which includes in itself all that can be*, which accepts no limit, and, in short, which is infinite. (*Universal Natural History and Theory of the Heavens*, tr. by W. Hastie, Ann Arbor, Mich. 1969, p. 140, our italics.)

The same year 1755 Kant published his 'Habilitationsschrift' *Principiorum primorum cognitionis metaphysicae nova dilucidatio*. The upshot of his discussion of possibilities and their realizations there is the same as in *Allgemeine Naturgeschichte*, but the explicit motivation is somewhat more complicated. The central thesis of this dissertation is the so-called principle of sufficient reason or, as Kant preferred to call it, of determining reason. According to this principle everything has its determining reason; no contingent being can come to be without existence having an antecedent determining reason. Since there cannot be an infinite regress of these determining reasons, there has to exist a being whose existence precedes its possibility. This is the necessary being, God.

We are thus witnessing in these pre-critical writings of Kant's full-dress rehearsal of several of the grand metaphysical themes Lovejoy so lovingly described. Indeed, what Kant is worried about is but the venerable problem of theodicy. God has just been found to be the first determining reason for everything else, a necessary precondition for the possibility of all other beings. Since nothing therefore can come to being without its determining reason, so that in a sense only what happens can happen, and what doesn't happen cannot happen. God seems to bear the moral responsibility for everything that happens in the world. (For God cannot be imagined without the other main precondition of responsibility, knowledge of the effects of His work of creation.) How is it then to be understood that God has decided to create the world like this, when he must have been aware ahead of time that his act of creation already included all the undeniable future evils and defects in the outcome of His creative activity? How is this consistent with God's goodness which ought to make Him shy away from all evil? And Kant answers:

Die Unendliche Güte Gottes strebt nach der möglichst grossen Vollkommenheit der geschaffenen Dinge und nach dem Glück der Geisterwelt. In diesem unendlichen Streben, sich zu offenbaren, hat sie ihre Mühe nicht bloss auf die vollkommeneren Reihen ihrer Ergebnisse, welche sich dann der Reihe der Gründe gemäss weiter entwickeln sollten, verwendet, sondern damit nichts auch von den Gütern niederen Grades fehle, *damit die ganze Welt in ihrer Unermesslichkeit alles, von der höchsten dem Endlichen möglichen Stufe der Vollkommenheit bis zu allen niederen und bis auf sozusagen das Nichts umfasse* (our italics) hat er auch gestattet, dass Dinge in seinen Abriss sich einschlichen, die trotz der Beimischung überwiegender Übel wenigstens etwas Gutes, das Gottes Weisheit daraus hervorlockte, zur Offenfarung des göttlichen Ruhmes durch ihre unendliche Mannigfaltigkeit beitrugen. (Immanuel Kant, *Zur Logik und Metaphysik, Erste Abteilung: Die Schriften von 1755–65*. Ed. by Karl Vorländer, second ed., Leipzig 1921, pp. 32–33.)

In other words, the Principle of Plenitude is what Kant resorts to in order to "justify God's ways to men".

These pre-critical ideas of Kant's are scarcely original. However, we shall not examine here their background in eighteenth-century German thought except for pointing out that they are not Leibnizian in that Leibniz emphatically rejected the Principle of Plenitude. However, the Principle was prevalent both in the Wolffian tradition and outside it (it is for instance found in Herder), so that Kant had plenty of immediate precursors in these respects. His theodicy is likewise a variant of well-known themes whose genealogy is partly delineated by Lovejoy.

Anyway, the answer to the theodicy problem just indicated did not satisfy Kant for long. In his essay "Der einzig mögliche Beweisgrund zu einer Demonstration des Daseins Gottes" (1763) Kant still holds that there has to be a necessary being whose existence constitutes a ground for the possibilities of all other beings. This necessary being, God, is a "first real ground of absolute possibility" and includes in itself everything thinkable. But now Kant disengages himself from his former line of thought; he draws a distinction which makes sense only if there exist unrealized possibilities. Kant must have reconsidered the problem of God's responsibility, because he nows says:

Ich nenne diejenige Abhängigkeit eines Dinges von Gott, da er ein Grund desselben durch seinen Willen ist, *moralisch*, alle übrige aber ist *unmoralisch*. Wenn ich demnach behaupte, Gott enthalte den letzten Grund selbst der innern Möglichkeit der Dinge, so wird ein jeder leicht verstehen, dass diese Abhängigkeit nur unmoralisch sein kann; denn der Wille macht nichts möglich, sondern beschliesst nur, was als möglich schon vorausgesetzt ist. (*Werke II*, Ernst Cassirer (ed.), Berlin 1922, p. 106.)

In respect to 'inner' possibilities (i.e., those permanent possibilities in which we are here interested) Kant thus has as it were 'intellectualized' them; he has now located them in God's thought and separated them from God's will. (This is a distinction which Descartes, as we shall later see, did not make.) Possibilities now have their own mode of being independent of their realizations, and Kant finds no reason any more to maintain their unconditional realization.

In his demonstration of God's existence Kant makes another distinction that is going to remain a fixture of his thinking from then on. He separates in the concept of possibility logical and real 'aspects'. (Both of these concern inner possibilities.)

Ein Triangel, der einen rechten Winkel hat, ist an sich selber möglich. Der Triangel sowohl als der rechte Winkel sind die Data oder das Materiale in diesem Möglichen, die Übereinstimmung aber des einen mit dem andern nach dem Satze des Widerspruchs sind das Formale der Möglichkeit. Ich werde dieses letztere auch das Logische in der Möglichkeit nennen, weil die Vergleichung der Prädikate mit ihren Subjekten nach der Regel der Wahrheit nichts anders als eine logische Beiziehung ist: das Etwas oder was in dieser Übereinstimmung steht, wird bisweilen das Reale der Möglichkeit heissen. (*Werke II*, E. Cassirer (ed.), p. 82.)

Logical possibility is, according to Kant, only formal possibility, and without material for thinking it is bound to remain empty. Thus every possibility has to ground itself in something real. If nothing were to exist, there would not be anything to think about, and accordingly nothing would be possible and everything impossible.

In the year 1770, in the year of his dissertation *De Mundi sensibilis atque intelligibilis forma et principiis*, Kant already stands on the threshold of his critical philosophy. This work was intended as a propedeutic to metaphysics, and its chief aim was to draw a boundary between the sensible and the intellectual modes of knowledge. Metaphysics was to be a science that would yield the supreme principles of the use of pure understanding. Besides sensible knowledge (*cognitio sensitiva*) there is, Kant says, also rational or intellectual knowledge (*cognitio intellectualis rationalis*). This intellectual knowledge refers to the intelligible world, to its objective principles, and to its denizens, the things in themselves. In analogy to the distinction Kant had made in his proof of God's existence, he now distinguishes in the use of understanding two modes. The real use (*usus realis*) is the one through which concepts of things and relations are given to us, while the logical use (*usus logicus*) means comparing these concepts with one another according to the law of contradiction. The results of the real use of understanding, intellectual concepts, are pure ideas (*ideae pura*), i.e., they are given in pure reason. They are not abstracted from experience and hence owe nothing to it. Among these intellectual concepts Kant lists possibility, existence, necessity, substance, and cause, together with their opposites and correlates (§8).

From this intellectual world we have no intuition, only symbolic knowledge (*cognitio symbolica*). Pure reasoning proceeds always in terms of general concepts *in abstracto*, never in terms of singular representation *in concreto*. Intellectual concepts as such are empty of all intuitive content, at least for us human beings. But this is something we do not always grasp. Our reason is seduced by illusions and mixes the sensible with the intellectual. Kant calls 'deceitful axiom' (*axioma subrepticium*) a statement that attaches something sensible by necessity to everything intellectual. To refute this illusion Kant lays down his principle of reduction:

If of any intellectual concept whatsoever there is predicated generally anything which pertains to the relations of *space and time*, it must not be enunciated objectively and it only denotes the condition without which a given concept is not cognisable sensitively. (Translations from the 1770 *Dissertation* by G. B. Kerferd.) (§ 25).

If the subject of a proposition is a intellectual concept and the predicate a sensible one the proposition cannot be taken to be objectively valid. We cannot say: "Everything that exists, is somewhere (*quicquid existit, est alicubi*) because we are not allowed to restrict existence as such to conditions of our sensible knowledge, in the example at hand, space." But conversely we *can* say: "Everything that is somewhere, exists." In other words, our intellectual concepts 'cover' our sensible ones, but not vice versa (§ 24).

One mode of this illusion through which sensible cognition can steal into an intellectual concept is the following.

The same sensitive condition under which alone the *intuition* of an object is possible is the condition of the *possibility* itself of the object (§ 26).

The sensible conditions, according to which *we* decide if something belongs to the extension of given intellectual concept, are not the conditions on which a thing in itself belongs to the extension of that concept. That is why it is not true to say: Everything contingent sometimes fails to exist (*quicquid existit contingenter, aliquando non exstitit*) (§ 29).

Now the rejection by Kant of this proposition means a rejection of the Principle of Plenitude. The proposition is implied by the Principle of Plenitude. For contingence means precisely that for which it is possible not to exist. Hence the proposition claims that every possibility of that kind is sometimes realized. Kant does not accept the proposition, and accordingly rejects the Principle. This kind of proposition is a product of the 'poverty of reason' (*penuria intellectus*) (§ 29), he says. In it, a knowing subject has imposed his own limitations on the objects in themselves presuming that 'marks of identification' fetched from his experience are also those of the thing in itself. The best we can do is the following 'subjective statement'.

When it is not established that something had at some time not been in existence sufficients marks of its contingency are not given by common intelligence (§ 29).

From the possibility of a thing in itself (i.e., from its possibility as the intellectual concept that it is) we can say nothing that would limit it to the conditions of space and time. Our actual use of understanding (and of its products) does not reduce to our sensibility: What is given to us in understanding is often separated by a chasm from what is given to us in intuition.

For this lack of accord between the *sensitive* faculty . . . points only to the fact that the abstract ideas which the mind entertains when they have been received from the intellect very often cannot be followed up in the concrete and converted into intuitions (§ 1).

Here it is seen especially clearly how Kant's attitude to the Principle of Plenitude depends on, and is an indication of, his assumptions concerning the range of possibilities we have to keep an eye on. For his rejection of the Principle in 1770 is a consequence of extending the range of serious 'intelligible' possibilities far beyond what we can hope to find in experience.

These precritical views of Kant's are 'uncritical' in that they leave open a host of important questions. What is the abstract symbolic knowledge like which he postulates and which is not reducible to intuition? How does Kant for instance know, as he claims to know, that "this world, even though it exists contingently, is eternal" (§ 29)? What is the source of this knowledge and its non-intuitive criterion? Attempts to patch up these gaps led Kant gradually to his critical maturity. In doing so he adopts the Principle of Plenitude again, but now in a revised 'critical' form. Neither this double change of mind away from the Principle of Plenitude and back again to a qualified form of the Principle nor its connection with the general development of Kant's thought is registered neither by Schneeberger or by Pape.

In the *Critique of Pure Reason* Kant preserves his distinction between logical and real possibility. A *concept* is possible if it is not self-contradictory. This is the logical mark of possibility (B 625). But this logical possibility makes the concept possible only according to the analytical conditions of cognition. A logically possible concept can still remain 'empty', i.e., uninstantiated. Kant explicitly warns us not to confuse such a logical possibility of a concept with the real possibility of a thing.

For to substitute the logical possibility of the *concept* (namely, that the concept does not contradict itself) for the transcendental possibility of *things* (namely, that an object corresponds to the concept) can deceive and leave satisfied only the simple-minded (B 302).

It is scarcely surprising that after Kant has equated the transcendental (real) possibility of a thing with the fact that there really is a thing corresponding to the given object, he can indicate his regained qualified approval of the Principle of Plenitude with respect to *possibilities of experience*.

If, therefore, I represent to myself all existing objects of the senses in all time and in all places, I do not set them in space and time (as being here) prior to experience. This representation is nothing but the thought of a possible experience in its absolute completeness (B 523–524).

All spatio-temporally existing objects of senses thus make up all the possible objects of experience. Likewise after having asked whether "the field of possibility is larger than the field which contains all actuality" (B 282), Kant declares:

It does indeed seem as if we were justified in extending the number of possible things beyond that of the actual, on the ground that something must be added to the possible to constitute the actual. But this (alleged) process of adding to the possible I refuse to allow. For that which would have to be added to the possible, would be impossible (B 284).

How is this qualified return of Kant to the camp of the supporters of the Principle of Plenitude to be understood? What caused Kant to change his views about possibilities and their realizations so radically? What is involved is a fundamental revision of Kant's ideas about the distinction between sensibility and understanding. In the first *Critique* there is no longer the unbridgeable gap between them that Kant postulated in *De Mundi*. . . .

Objects are *given* to us by means of sensibility, and it alone yields us *intuitions*; they are *thought* through the understanding, and from the understanding arise *concepts*. But all thought must, directly or indirectly, by way of certain characters, relate ultimately to intuitions, and therefore, with us, to sensibility, because in no other way can an object be given to us (B 33).

When we are discussing the transcendental, real possibilities of things (objects) we therefore have to stay within the purview of sensibility, i.e., within the sphere of *empirical thinking*. According to Kant's postulate of empirical thought

that which agrees with the formal conditions of experience, that is, with the conditions of intuition and of concepts, is *possible* (B 265).

In a sense the concept of possibility has thus lost its earlier status of an intellectual concept and a pure idea. Admittedly it is still included among concepts of pure understanding. It is still a category. However, this 'purity' of the concept of possibility is only relative. At least indirectly all categories have to be related to sensibility. Categories are "a priori conditions upon which experience in general in its formal aspects rests". In this case the concept still belongs "to experience inasmuch as its object is to be met with only in experience" (B 267).

In another sense these categories are of course still 'pure'. They are given to us by 'pure synthesis' (B 104), not by the experientially grounded empirical synthesis through which empirical concepts are given (B 267). Therefore, since categories, "yielding knowledge of *things*, have no kind of application, save only in regard to things which may be objects of possible experience" (B 147–148), they have to be tied somehow to experience. This tie is accomplished by what Kant calls the 'transcendental schemata' of categories.

Now every concept has its own *schema*, i.e., a rule that make the content of the concept 'intuitive' through general representation. Pure concepts of understanding have their transcendental schemata. Since pure concepts of understanding are "quite heterogeneous from empirical intuitions" (B 176) there is a problem of how categories can be applied to appearances. Obviously, Kant says, there has to be 'some third thing' which is homogeneous on the one hand with categories and on the other hand with appearances, in order to make the application of the former to the latter possible. This 'third thing' is precisely the transcendental schema of the given category (B 177). These transcendental schemata in turn owe their ability to accomplish this connection completely to the form of inner intuition, which is for Kant *time*. In fact they are "nothing but a priori determinations of time in accordance with rules" (B 184). Kant likewise says that the real mediator between categories and appearances is the "transcendental determination of time" which is "so far homogeneous with the category ... in that it is universal and rests upon *a priori* rule" and homogeneous with appearance "in that time is contained in every empirical representation of the manifold" (B 177–178). In each schema time is determined differently. The schema of possibility is

the agreement of the synthesis of different representations with the conditions of time in general. Opposites, for instance, cannot exist in the same thing at the same time, but only the one after the other. The schema is therefore the determination of the representation of a thing at some time or other (B 184).

The difference between the schemata of possibility and actuality (which is: existence at some determinate time, B 184) does not lie in *whether* but in *how*, an object belongs to time. Since Kant, in his doctrine of transcendental idealism, had stated that

everything intuited in space or time, and therefore all objects of any experience possible to us, are nothing but appearances, that is, mere representations, which, in the manner in which they are represented, as extended beings, or as series of alterations, have no independent existence outside our thoughts (B 518–519),

it is clear that Kant's reference to "the representation *of a thing*" in the schema of possibility does not introduce any unintuited things in themselves. The difference between possibility and actuality does not lie in the objects, but merely in the character of their relationship to the knowing subject. What has to be added, according to Kant, to possibility in order for it to reach actuality "is only a relation to my understanding, that . . . there should be connection with some perception" (B 284). Because whatever is connected with perception *is* actual, the difference lies only in that whether this connection is acheived *now* or only sometimes.

A schema is a 'condition of judgement' (*Bedingung der Urteilskraft*) for the categories, without which we could not subsume anything under them (B 304). As such they obviously are restrictive conditions. Moreover, for Kant the 'tie' that connects these concepts of understanding to the conditions of sensibility, i.e., their schematization, is indispensable for them to have *any* significance whatsoever.

The schemata of the pure concepts of understanding are thus the true and sole conditions under which these concepts obtain relation to objects and so possess *significance*. In the end, therefore, the categories have no other possible employment than the empirical (B 185).

On the basis of these assumptions Kant asks, as if the question were addressed to his earlier self, what else could be understood by contingence than the possibility of non-being, and how else we could know this but from representing to ourselves a series of appearances which involve a change from being to non-being or conversely (B 301). His implicit answer is of course: from nothing else.

We can thus see how Kant's qualified re-adoption of the Principle of Plenitude flows from the same source as his introduction of the schemata. This common source is his restriction of the legitimate use of the concepts of understanding to possible experience. This is in keeping with the general outlook of Kant's critical philosophy mentioned above.

This appears indirectly also from the qualifications Kant makes in connection with the notion of real or empirical possibility. Kant warns us that, even though our concept of possibility is meaningful only in its schematized form, this is merely a consequence of *our* mode of cognition. For us humans the possible comprises only what is in accordance with the transcendental conditions of cognition, but in a series these conditions themselves are only possible. Thus

what is possible only under conditions which themselves are merely possible is not in *all* *respects* possible. But such (absolute) possibility is in question when it is asked whether the possibility of things extends further than experience can reach (B 284).

But this concept of absolute possibility (possibility in *all* respects) is to be firmly distinguished from the category of possibility. It "is no mere concept of understanding, and can never be employed empirically. It belongs exclusively to reason, which transcends all possible empirical employment of the understanding" (B 285).

This distinction is important also the other way round. Our category of possibility cannot refer to things in themselves. This is a mistake of the 'transcendental realism' and it is to be avoided. Hence even though sensibility has gained ground in Kant's thought since *De Mundi* . . . , it has to be prevented from getting too 'arrogant'. This is to be done by means of the concept of understanding and by means of the concept of *noumenon* – "that is, of a thing which is not to be thought as object of senses but as a thing in itself, solely through a pure understanding" (B 310).

The role of the concept of noumenon is mainly a negative one. It is a limiting concept, "the function of which is to curb the pretensions of sensibility" (B 311), i.e.,

to restrain the officious pretensions of understanding, which, presuming on its ability to supply *a priori* the conditions of the possibility of all things which it is capable of knowing, behaves as if it had thus determined these bounds as those of the possibility of all things generally . . . (*Critique of Judgement*, Preface 1790, tr. J. C. Meredith, Oxford 1952).

Noumena are not a special kind of objects (intelligible objects) for our understanding. By their means our understanding acquires only 'negative extension', Kant says (B 312). As such, they are indispensable to remind us that noumena are not accessible to our understanding, including our concepts of (empirical) possibility. Even though thus we cannot claim any validity for our concepts of noumena, we still can have an understanding of noumena 'problematically', Kant says (B 310). But positively speaking, for us humans noumena are neither possible nor impossible (B 343). They are simply beyond our categories. *A fortiori*, they cannot yield *for us* a genuine counter-example to the Principle of Plenitude.

Prima facie, Kant's attitude to the Principle of Plenitude might seem to resemble rather closely that of Thomas Aquinas. This saint had also held, according to the interpretation ably defended by Knuuttila (see 'Jumalan mahdollisuuksien lisääntyminen keskiajalla', *Teologinen Aikakauskirja* (1974), pp. 105–121) that the Principle is valid only for human possibilities but not for absolute (Divine) ones. Aquinas' viewpoint, like Kant's is basically epistemological. According to him (and here we follow Knuuttila rather closely), at the bottom of human epistemic possibilities there is always something real. Each and every universal is obtained from reality through sense-perception, and these abstract concepts are the elements of all our cognition. Knowledge consists in *compositio* and *divisio* carried out by the human intellect when it unites that which is united *in re* and separates that which is separated *in re*. *Possibilia secundum potentiam* are for Thomas natural possibilities, and with respect to them the Principle of Plenitude holds good, for we can obtain the concept (form) of such a possibility only in virtue of its having been realized in the world. These possibilities are the only possibilities *we* know.

But there is also another kind of possibility, absolute possibility, *possibile absolutum*, which is defined as freedom from contradiction. In the sphere of these absolute possibilities the Principle is no longer tenable according to Thomas.

In our human situation we can only form such compositions as are always (by necessity) or sometimes (possibly) actualized *in re*. The reason for this is of course the way in which our ideas of possibility are according to Aquinas derived from the actual *res* and which was just mentioned. For the same reason, our epistemic possibilities are inseparable from physical possibilities. Hence all examples Thomas can give us of epistemic possibilities should also be ontologically real possibilities. But absolute possibilities are also in another sense epistemic ones. They are in effect *God's* epistemic possibilities. (Hence the denial of the validity of the Principle of Plenitude by Aquinas with respect to absolute possibilities is probably calculated to uphold God's freedom from all necessity to actualize all *his* possibilities.) Although all the possibilities of nature are absolute possibilities, the converse does not hold. However, we cannot *know* any of those supernatural absolute possibilities. These are only known by God, and they relate to orders of being quite different from those of which a human mind can have any idea.

But although human beings cannot be acquainted by means of their natural epistemic capacities with these absolute possibilities which are known only by God, they can *know that* the range of absolute possibilities exceeds the created reality. It is possible to deduce from this real universe the existence of God and the independence of *His* possibilities from the possibilities of nature (and thus from the possibilities accessible to human cognition).

Thus there is a certain similarity between absolute possibilities according to Aquinas and according to Kant. Neither can be reached by the normal operations of the human understanding, and yet the idea of such possibilities is indispensable.

This similarity between Kant and Aquinas is in keeping with the fact that for Kant as for Aquinas absolute possibilities are in a certain sense humanly incomprehensible. This is vividly shown, in the case of Aquinas, by a quotation given by Knuuttila (p. 117) where St. Thomas speaks of the union of Christ's human and divine natures:

sed haec est quaedam unio singularis supra omnes modos unionis nobis notos ... et ideo, sicut virtus eius non est limitata ad istos modos bonitatis et esse qui sunt in creaturis, sed potest facere novos modis bonitatis et esse nobis incognitos, ita etiam per infinitatem suae virtutis potuit facere novum modum unionis .... (*De Unione Verbi Incarnati q. un., a. 1c.*).

Kant, on his part, likewise affirms that we cannot make to ourselves slightest representations of the possible objects of intellectual intuition. We are bound to our forms of intuition and understanding (B 311–312).

Other forms of intuition than space and time, other forms of understanding than the discursive forms of thought, or of knowledge through concepts, even if they should be possible, we cannot render in any way conceivable and comprehensible to ourselves; and even assuming that we could do so, they still would not belong to experience – the only kind of knowledge in which objects are given to us (B 283).

This similarity of Aquinas' view with Kant's can also be looked upon from the opposite direction. Kant based his belief in the Principle of Plenitude on the way in which time is schematized. Now Kant held that there could be rational beings other than us finite humans who unlike us could have intuitions not connected with sense-perception. Here Kant clearly has in mind the relation of the infinite being, i.e., God, to particulars. The direct relation to particulars which in His case corresponds to sense-perception is creativity or, as Kant calls it, spontaneity. God beholds individuals by creating them, while our perception can never create its objects, at best the framework (i.e., space and time) into which they are structured. But if so, God would not need any schematization, and Kant's reason for adopting the Principle of Plenitude for human thinking would fail to apply to God's possibilities. This indeed seems to be at least compatible with what he says.

But the opposite conclusion seems to be equally compatible with what Kant says one can make a case for an application of the Principle to God, although not for the same reasons as to us finite beings. If God really exhibits that complete spontaneity which characterizes intellectual intuition, every-thing that exists would be given to him by His own activity (B 68). Man, finite and sensible being is on his part dependent on his capacity for receiving representations (on his receptivity, see B 33). We shall return to this point below in discussing Descartes.

Man, with his spontaneity of understanding, can only *think* 'creatively'. For intuitions he must resort to the sense (B 135). In contrast, divine under-standing would by its creativity in representing something by the same time make this 'something' become existing (cf. B 139). God wouldn't have any need to remember, or to anticipate, what happens, for He lives in an eternal present. He would not have any relation to *time*, and thus to our schematized categories.

For were I to think an understanding which is itself intuitive (as, for example, a divine understanding which should not represent to itself given objects, but through whose representation the objects should themselves be given or produced), the categories would have no meaning whatsoever in respect of such a mode of knowledge (B 145).

Thus it seems to be a matter of opinion if we say either that in respect to God's possibilities the Principle of Plenitude holds good (everything in Him is 'actual') or that it does not hold good (our categories of actuality and possibility do not reach him). Perhaps we should rather ask to what extent the niche Kant left in his philosophy to the concept of God in the first place is to be taken very seriously. In the best case, God will be for Kant an idea which cannot be fully realized even in thinking.

Many similarities with Kant are thus in evidence in Aquinas. Among them there are the following.

(i)   Contrast between absolute and real possibilities.
(ii)   The unknowability of absolute possibilities.
(iii)   The need of nevertheless postulating these absolute possibilities.
(iv)   The equation of epistemic and natural possibilities.
(v)   Principle of Plenitude holds for real possibilities.
(vi)   The motivation of the Principle is in both cases epistemological rather than (say) ontological.

However, in spite of such similarities there obtains an important difference between Kant's views and the teachings of St. Thomas. The difference is in fact a neat corollary to Kant's often misunderstood 'Copernican Revolution'. Aquinas bases his belief in the applicability of the Principle to all humanly conceivable possibilities on the way we obtain our conceptions of all these sundry possibilities: we receive them for actualizations of the very corresponding possibilities. Small wonder, then, that they are all actually realized.

In contrast, Kant bases his qualified belief in the realization of all experiential possibilities on the way we humans actively represent a certain concept (that of time) in our experience. The principle does not apply by courtesy of the mind-independent sources of our conceptions, but in virtue of what we ourselves do to give them an experiential manifestation. And the gist of Kant's self-conscious 'Copernican Revolution' was just to emphasize the role of our own 'movements', that is, activities in all human knowledge.

Thus both Aquinas and Kant are basing their appraisal of the Principle of Plenitude on epistemological considerations. However, Aquinas' epistemology is in this respect an empiricist one. We receive our concepts from their actual instantiations in the world. In the contrast, Kant's epistemology is transcendental in his own sense of the word. It focuses on what we ourselves do to represent our concepts in experience, and sees in them the starting-point of 'critical' philosophy. In his preface to the second edition of the *Critique of Pure Reason* Kant, "proceeding precisely on the lines of Copernicus", rejects the view that knowledge must conform to objects. Rather, he says, objects or experience must conform to concepts. As Copernicus had made the spectators move, Kant transformed the knowing subject from a still-standing and passive receiver to a 'moving' or active contructor (B xvi–xvii). We shall return to the further repercussions of this difference.

On the basis of what has been said, it is clear that categories, as concepts of pure understanding, and their schemata are completely *a priori*. They are concepts to which all objects of experience must adjust themselves and with which they therefore must agree. And all objects of experience must do this because we make them to do so, because this is how our understanding operates. It is for this reason that we can be sure that all experience conforms to our categories. However, Kant's Copernican Revolution cuts even deeper than this. Even what he calls 'empirical concepts', although they are 'derived from existence' (B 267), are in a sense products of our own mind. They are also created by an act of synthesis, if now by an empirical one. Admittedly we *receive* representations, i.e., our mind must be *affected* in a certain way in order to prompt our creative apparatus into activity. We derive our empirical concepts from the representations of apprehension, but in fact we can so to speak *decide* what manifold of representations is united to an object. We have to lay down a rule – partly *a priori* in that we do not find this rule in representations, partly *a posteriori* in that it must be based on the received representations – which successions of representations make up an object.

... appearance, in contradistinction to the representations of apprehension, can be represented as an object distinct from them only if it stands under a rule which distinguishes it from every other apprehension and necessitates some one particular mode of connection of the manifold. The object is *that* in the appearance which contains the condition of this necessary rule of apprehension (B 236).

Concepts can thus be divided into three groups. First, there are the concepts of pure understanding, categories, secondly, there are concepts created by the 'objective reality of synthesis' (B 624), i.e., by synthesis contained in experience. Thirdly, there are empty concepts to which we also have given rise by our ability to think creatively but which do not find their counterpart in experience. These are accordingly not concepts of possible objects.

In short, according to Kant we combine successive representations of apprehension into a single object and thus derive the concept of this object. Then we state that objects that conform to such concepts are *possible* objects. To be able to decide whether a concept is an empty one or a concept of a possible object, it has to be shown that it really has been created by an objectively real synthesis. This Kant must have meant when he wrote:

But it (i.e., a concept) may none-the-less be an empty concept, unless the objective reality of the synthesis through which the concept is generated has been specifically proved; and such proof, as we have shown above, rests on principles of possible experience, and not on the principles of analysis (the law of contradiction). This is a warning against arguing directly from the logical possibility of concepts to the real possibility of things. (B 624, footnote.)

Thus what has happened is that Kant, in becoming 'critical' and in adopting again that once so sternly rejected Principle of Plenitude, has not so much widened the sphere of realizations to match the range of possibilities as reduced the field of possibilities and made them adjust themselves to actualities. What is especially noteworthy here, Kant's re-adopting of the Principle is a consequence of his 'Copernican' emphasis on the role of human activity (constructivity) in bringing about this adjustment of possibilities to actualities.

It is of course virtually impossible that the views of Aquinas on modality should have exerted any influence on Kant, by agreement or by disagreement. However, another thinker whose speculative ideas are in certain relevant respects not so far from Aquinas clearly did influence Kant. This philosopher is Descartes. He presents in fact interesting similarities and dissimilarities both with Kant and with Aquinas. If we look at the thinking of Descartes from the epistemic point of view, we find as his primary datum the famous 'clear and distinct ideas'. Descartes takes it to be a 'first principle' that there is "nothing in the effect that has not existed in a similar or in some higher form in the cause" (*The Philosophical Works of Descartes*, Vol. II, tr. by Haldane and Ross, Cambridge 1911, p. 34.) For this reason he can also say that "every perfection existing objectively in an idea must exist actually in something that causes that idea" (*ibid.*, p. 35). After demonstrating the existence of God, "who is all perfection and truth", Descartes see that "our ideas or notions, which to the extent of their being clear or distinct are idas of real things issuming from God, cannot but to that extent be true" (Vol. I, p. 105).

In view of our theme it is interesting to see that these clear and distinct ideas can also be understood as permanent possibilities. For in a sense we can apprehend as possible only that which we have a clear and distinct idea about. If so, we see that according to Descartes we can apprehend as possible only what is actual.

But we possess the idea of a power so great that by Him and Him alone, in whom this power is found, must heaven and earth be created, and a power such that likewise whatever else is apprehended by me as possible must be created by Him too (Vol. II, p. 59).

This 'must' which seems to be decreed by Descartes on God greatly offended Leibniz, who called Descartes' assumption "the first falsehood and the basis of atheistic philosophy". In reality, this assumption is but the good old Principle of Plenitude. (See Hintikka, 'Leibniz on Plenitude, Relations, and "the Reign of Law" ', above pp. 259–286.)

Like Aquinas (and later Kant) Descartes also saw that these possibilities available to human understanding by no means could be taken as exhausting the sphere of absolutely all possibilities. We must remember, he states as his principle xxiv of the *Principles of Philosophy*, that "our understanding is finite, and the power of God infinite." As a hint of those possibilities that we don't understand clearly God has revealed mysteries of incarnation and the Trinity, among others. We have to believe in them, although they surpass the range of our natural power of intelligence. "For we should not think it strange that in the immensity of His nature, as also in the objects of His creation, there are many things beyond the range of our comprehension" (Vol. I, p. 229).

Descartes' God is thus rather like the creatively and intellectually intuiting God of Kant's philosophy. For Him there is no distinction between possibility and actuality. In a letter to Mersenne (May 6, 1630) where Descartes speaks about God's relationship to truth, he uses the term 'possible' and 'true' alternatively.

As for the eternal truths, I say once more that *they are true or possible only because God knows them as true or possible. They are not known as true by God in any way which would imply that they are not true independently of Him (Philosophical Letters,* transl. and edited by Anthony Kenny, Oxford, 1970, p. 13.)

This is because God's will is in a position fundamentally different from ours. He does not have any pre-existing options to choose from. Nothing exists before God's act of will.

As to the freedom of will, a very different account must be given of it as it exists in God and as it exists in us. For it is self-contradictory that the will of God should not have been from eternity indifferent to all that has come to pass or that ever will occur, because we can form no conception of anything good or true, of anything to be believed or to be performed or to be omitted, the idea of which in the devine understanding before God's will determined Him so to act as to bring it to pass. (*Philosophical Works of Descartes*, Vol. II, p. 248.)

Descartes' God thinks 'creatively', i.e., thought cannot be separated from will in the case of God. We cannot speak of any universe of ideas of existing before the act of creation or "of ideally *pre*-existing "possible worlds'", as Ingetrud Pape aptly puts it in her *Tradition und Transformation der Modalität*, p. 75. God's cognition and His will are one and the same.

If men really understood the sense of their words they could never say without blasphemy that the truth of anything is prior to the knowledge which God has of it. In God willing and knowing are a single thing in such a way that *by the very fact of willing something he knows it and it is only for this reason that such a thing is true.* (*Philosophical Letters*, pp. 13—14.)

Not even the law of contradiction can bind this creatively thinking God. He would have done possible things he actually made to be impossible. He has *decided* what things stand in contradiction to each other; and even those contradicting relationships are necessary (to us) it must not be necessary for God to make it so.

I turn to the difficulty of conceiving how it was free and indifferent for God to make it not true that the three angles of a triangle were equal to two right angles, or in general that contradictories could not be true together. It is easy to dispel this difficulty by considering that the power of God cannot have any limits, and that our mind is finite and so created as to be able to conceive as possible things which God has wished to be in fact possible, but not to be able to conceive as possible things which God could have made possible, but which he has in fact wished to make impossible. . . . But if we would know the immensity of his power we should not put these thoughts before our minds, nor should we conceive any precedence or priority between his understanding and his will; for the idea which we have of God teaches us that there is in Him only a single activity, entirely simple and entirely pure. This is well expressed by the words of St. Augustine: *They are so because you see them to be so*; because in God *seeing* and *willing* are one and the same thing. (*Philosophical Letters*, p. 150–151.)

Now the law of contradiction presumably will never be actually violated. For it surely is based on most 'clear and distinct' ideas. Hence the realization of all possibilities cannot in some sense apply to God. The range of possibilities we saw Him realizing according to Descartes can only be the range of *natural* possibilities, which presumably is what our 'clear and distinct' ideas are all about anyway. As in Aquinas, so in Descartes the Principle of Plenitude apparently does not apply in any obvious sense to the characteristically *divine* possibilities.

However, here the problem mentioned earlier hits us (and Descartes) with vengeance. The Cartesian God is an *actus purus* in a peculiarly strong sense. He creates all possibilities, too, and not only their actualizations. Hence it sounds perfectly absurd for Descartes to speak of God's possibilities He has not realized. Yet we must at the same time say that He does this freely, which implies that there are "things which God could have made possible" but which He in fact has made impossible. These are of course humanly incomprehensible, but they come dangerously close to being nonsensical, too. This is an instance of the problems that come about in applying the Principle of Plenitude as soon as we cannot assume a neat pre-existing range of possibilities. Indeed, the collapse of possibility and actuality as well as of the notion of possibility of God, except in the qualified sense of natural possibilities. This is clearly reminiscent of Kant.

The most interesting partial analogy may nevertheless obtain, not between Descartes' and Kant's theological ideas, but between the Cartesian God and a Kantian man. In so far as the Principle of Plenitude applied to the Cartesian God, it is because He has through His own creative activity *defined* what counts as possible and impossible. Likewise, the reason why the Principle holds for a Kantian man was found to be that we ourselves as it were define what is and what isn't possible experience by imposing our own terms on all such experience. On different levels, these terms are embodied in the forms of sensibility, in the categories, and in their role in empirical synthesis, as well as in the schemata. Quite apart from the details of Kant's account, it thus looks as if Kant has stolen some of the creative liberty of the Cartesian God and awarded it to Man.

From the vantage point of this partial analogy we can at least understand what the main problem with Kant's theory of possibility was bound to be, and why. Ingetrud Pape has written:

Aus dieser Frage ergibt sich für Kant jene kühne 'Idee', die vielleicht das neuartigste Moment seiner gesamten Modaltheorie ausmacht. Am revolutionierendsten nämlich ist der Gedanke, dass die Modalitäten überhaupt *nur* Aspekte *unseres* Verstandes darstellen, d.h. dass sie weder der Sache an sich, noch einem anders strukturierten Verstande zukommen müssen. Sieht man das in dem ganzen Horisont seiner Folgen, so zeigt sich zuletzt das verblüffende Faktum, dass die Einsetzung der Modalität zum systematischen Thema, wie sie erstmalig in der Problemgeschichte bei Kant sich vollzog, *zugleich* und in selben Akt ihre Aufhebung als metaphysischer Thema bedeutet . . . . (*Pape*, p. 234.)

However, this 'Aufhebung' of the traditional conception of modality is but a corollary to the problem we discussed in connection with Descartes concerning God's primacy vis-à-vis the range of possibilities. When Kant puts man in the role of God in establishing himself what *counts as* possible, the same puzzles are bound to arise. Such a role assigned to human thinking is bound to eliminate to some extent the boundary of possibility and actuality, which is reflected by Kant's precarious readoption of the Principle of Plenitude. Perhaps even more importantly, it is also bound to make the very concept of possibility problematic, for we cannot in one and the same logical breath say that we humans have established what counts as possible, and that this *could* in principle be done differently, i.e., that it is *possible* that this decision should have been made otherwise. But this is precisely Descartes' predicament in speaking of his conceptually creative God.

This predicament is also reflected by such Kantian pronouncements as bear on the Principle of Plenitude. The reader has probably shared some of our frustration at not being able to produce a completely unequivocal avowal of the Principle from Kant's mature philosophy. What we have seen about the ambiguities of the very concept of possibility in Kant amply explains his hesitation, however. Once again, the Principle of Plenitude performs well its methodological function as a sensitive intellectual barometer.

Florida State University
University of Helsinki

BIBLIOGRAPHY

Descartes, *Philosophical Letters*, transl. and ed. by A. Kenny, Clarendon Press, Oxford 1970.
Descartes, *Philosophical Works*, transl. by E. S. Haldane and G. R. T. Ross, Cambridge University Press, Cambridge 1911.
Hintikka, J., 'Leibniz on Plenitude, Relations, and "the Reign of Law" ', in H. G. Frank-

furt (ed.), *Leibniz: A Collection of Critical Essays*, Anchor Books, Doubleday, Garden City, N.Y. 1972, pp. 155–190, reprinted in this volume.

Hintikka, J., *Time and Necessity: Studies in Aristotle's Theory of Modality*, Clarendon Press, Oxford 1973.

Kant, I., *Critique of Pure Reason*, transl. by N. K. Smith, Macmillan, London 1964.

Kant, I., *Schriften zur Logik und Metaphysik I: Die Schriften von 1755–1765, II: Die Schriften von 1766–1786*, ed. by K. Vorländer (Philosophische Bibliothek 46a–b), Felix Meiner, Leipzig 1921.

Kant, I., *Selected Pre-critical Writings* tr. and introduced by G. B. Kerferd and D. E. Walford, Manchester U.P., Manchester 1968.

Kant, I., *Universal Natural History and Theory of Heavens*, transl. by W. Hastie, The University of Michigan Press, Ann Arbor 1969.

Kant, I., *Werke I–XI*, ed. by E. Cassirer, Verlag Bruno Cassirer, Berlin 1912–1923.

Knuuttila, S., 'Jumalan mahdollisuuksien lisääntyminen keskiajalla', *Teologinen Aikakauskirja* (1974), pp. 105–121.

Lovejoy, A. O., *The Great Chain of Being: A Study of the History of an Idea*, Harvard University Press, Cambridge, Mass. 1936.

Murdoch, J. E., 'From Social into Intellectual Factors: An Aspect of the Unitary Character of Late Medieval Learning', in J. E. Murdoch and E. D. Sylla (eds.), *The Cultural Context of Medieval Learning*, D. Reidel, Dordrecht 1975, pp. 271–348.

Pape, I., *Tradition und Transformation der Modalität I: Möglichkeit-Unmöglichkeit*, Felix Meiner, Hamburg 1966.

Schneeberger, G., *Kants Konzeption der Modalbegriffe* (Philosophische Forschungen, N.S. 1), Verlag für Recht und Gesellschaft, Basel 1952.

INDEX OF NAMES

Mahdi, M. 15.
Maier, A. 72, 246–7, 255, 278, 284, 286.
Malcolm, N. 151, 162, 284.
Mansfield, J. 113.
Marcellinus 199.
Marlasca, A. 248, 253.
Marsh, R. C. viii.
Mates, B. 263–4, 267, 284, 286.
Matthews, G. B. 160, 162.
Maula, E. 8, 17, 44, 50–1, 55, 283, 286.
McDermott, A. C. S. 250, 255.
McKenzie, R. 162.
Meillet, A. 156, 161.
Meiser, C. 161, 240, 251.
Meredith, J. C. 298.
Mersenne, M. 304.
Mesland, D. 278.
Migne, J.-P. 155, 159.
Minio-Paluello, L. 96, 184, 241, 250, 252.
Moody, E. A. 163, 195, 238, 244, 255, 273.
Moore, G. E. 10, 11.
Moore, P. S. 244, 252.
Moreau, J. 108, 114.
Morewedge, P. 249, 251.
Moses Maimonides 207–8, 214, 245–6, 252.
Mourelatos, A. P. D. 53, 55.
Murdoch, J. E. 7, 16, 288, 308.
Müller, F. M. viii.
Müller, M. 247, 252.

Nagel, E. 114.
Nardi, B. 162.
Nasr, S. H. 249, 255.
Nehemas, A. 46, 55.
Newton, I. 111.
Normore, C. G. 250, 255.
Nuchelmans, G. 180, 241, 244, 255.
Nussbaum, M. C. 110, 114.

O'Donnell, J. R. 239, 243–4, 252–3.
Oehler, K. 108, 114.
Önnerfors, A. 257.
Owen, G. E. L. 44–7, 51–6, 67, 108, 114, 152, 162.
Owens, J. 108, 114, 249, 255.

Pape, I. 224, 240, 248, 255, 294, 305–8.
Parkinson, G. H. R. 285–6.
Patch, H. R. 175, 240, 255.
Pearson, A. C. 45.
Pease, A. S. 242, 251.
Peck, A. L. 110, 114.
Peirce, C. S. ix, 239, 255.
Penner, T. 110, 115.
Peter Damian 138, 155, 158, 162, 200–3, 245, 252.
Peter the Lombard 244, 252.
Peter of Poitiers 197–8, 205, 244, 252.
Peter of Spain 191–2, 243, 252.
Peters, F. E. 156, 162.
Philipp, C. 2, 259.
Philoponus 63.
Pilius 239.
Pinborg, J. 250, 255.
Pines, S. 245, 252.
Pitcher, G. 115.
Plantinga, A. 152, 162, 256.
Plato xi, 8, 17, 19–56, 61, 109, 111–2, 163, 242, 252, 289.
Plotinus 233–4, 242, 249, 252.
Porphyry 63.
Poser, H. viii.
Priscianus 152, 162.
Pseudo-Alexander 95, 101, 109, 111.
Pseudo-Cicero 154.
Pseudo-Scotus 250.
Putnam, H. 48, 56.

Quine, W. V. 11, 160, 288.

Randall, J. H. Jr, 241, 256.
Rankin, H. D. 45, 56.
Rantala, V. 284, 286.
Raven, J. E. 46–7, 56.
Remes, U. 114, 240, 254.
Rescher, N. 48, 56, 246, 255, 266, 270, 283–4, 286.
Rhodes, R. M. 155, 162.
Rist, J. M. 242, 255.

William of Sherwood 190–91, 193–4,
229–30, 243, 253.
Williams, C. J. F. 72, 215–7, 247.
Wilpert, P. 52, 56.
Wilson, C. 49.
Wolff, Ch. 291.
Wolfson, H. A. 207, 245, 256.
Wolter, A. B. 160, 247, 252.

Wood, O. P. 115.
Wright, G. H. von viii.
Wright, L. 110, 115.
Wycliffe, J. 261.
Wyttenbach, D. 49, 56.

Zimmermann, A. 248, 257.
Zycha, I. 244, 251.

INDEX OF SUBJECTS

Determinism, 4, 9, 72, 140–1, 164–5, 167–76, 184–5, 188, 199, 209, 212–3, 224, 235.
dictum, 180, 182, 196–7.
dictum de omni et nullo, 237.
Distributive normal form, 265, 268.
dynamis, 65, 77–8, 87, 90, 224, 234.
dynaton, 67, 99–100, 224.

Efficient cause, 84–5, 122, 139, 153, 208–12, 218–25, 228, 304.
Emanation, 233–4.
End (*telos*), 88–93.
energeia, 87, 89, 92, 98, 169.
Eponymy, 85–6, 95, 97, 109, 112.
Eternity: time *v.* eternity, 40, 140–1, 200, 205–6, 301; as omnitemporality, 59, 79–80; eternal things, 38–42, 61, 65–6, 75–6, 80, 91, 95–6, 98–9, 102–7 (*see also* God, eternity of); eternal motion, 61, 65, 75, 77–9, 83–4, 88, 101.
Excluded middle, the law of, 177, 180.
Existential dependence, 76, 91.
Existential equivalence, 76, 91, 94.

facere, Anselm's analysis of, 121–130.
Fallacies, 10–1, 68, 80, 164, 167, 172–3, 176, 178, 186, 189, 193, 198.
Forms: Plato on forms of relative characteristics of particulars, 26–8, 36, forms of non-relative characteristics of particulars, 30–36, forms instantiated by forms, 36–44, the form of the ideal city, 22–5, justice, 24–7, living creature, 31–3, 40, artifacts, 35–6, eternity, 40–1, stability, 41–2, motion, 41, being, 42–3, the Good, 43; Empty Forms Thesis criticized, 22–30, 36–44, 50–1; Aristotle's criticism of Plato's theory of forms, 37–40, 61, 77–78; forms in Aristotle, 83–5, 87, 89, 92–4, 96–7.
Freedom of the will, 117, 128, 133–5, 138–40, 144, 149, 175, 199–200, 218–20, 224–8, 233, 305.
Future contingents, 106, 140, 175–8, 184–6, 193–4, 205, 209–14, 225, 230, 232–3.
Future things, 120–1, 125–7, 133, 143, 149, 193–5, 212.

God: proofs for existence of, 74–8, 117–8, 130–1, 207, 218, 291, 304 (*see also* Ontological argument, *tertia via*); eternity and atemporality of, 140–1, 174, 198, 200, 301; freedom of, 138, 165, 201, 224–5, 229; goodness of, 30–2, 131–2, 187, 206, 234, 280, 290; justness of, 119, 128, 132, 206; necessary existence of, 117, 132–3, 144–7, 233, 290–1; God as First Principle, 218–20, 225, 233; Supreme Truth, 131, 143, 304; divine knowledge, 140–1, 174–5, 186, 197–8, 206, 213–4, 225, 230, 232–4, 280, 305; divine foreknowledge and providence, 2, 91, 140, 165, 170, 174–6, 184–6, 188, 203, 208, 213, 225, 230–2; divine omnipotence, 117, 119, 121, 128, 135, 138, 145, 199–207, 215, 219, 224–5, 232, 234, 236, 273, 280, 289, 304–5; divine will, 128–9, 138, 143, 200, 205, 218–20, 228, 232–4, 291, 305.

Homonymy, 37, 39, 85, 109.
Hyper-actuality, 74–6, 78, 94, 99, 104.

Impossibility: Aristotle, 58–9, 67–9, 80, 166–8, 170; Boethius, 171; Peter Damian, 200–1, 203; Abaelard, 182–4; Alain of Lille, 204; William of Auxerre, 204; Moses Maimonides, 207; Thomas Aquinas, 216–7; Duns Scotus, 231–2; Descartes, 305–6, Leibniz, 261, 270; Hume, 145; Kant, 292; divine impossibilities, 121, 128, 132, 138, 200, 231–2, 261; impossibility *per se v. per accidens*, 190, 195.
Incapacity, 65, 67, 69, 121, 127–8, 132, 138.
Incarnation, 117, 135–7, 304.
Incompossibility, 231–2.
Ideas, Platonic: *see* Forms.
Indestructible things, 64, 101–2, 104, 107.
Infinitely deep logics, 272, 284.
Infinity, 62, 275, 281, 289–90, 300, 304.
Instants of time, 196, 205–6, 222, 226–7, 229–30.

kinesis, 65, 77, 92, 169–70.

Laws of nature, 5, 223, 236, 274–7.
Leibniz's Law, 271–2.

Master argument of Diodrus, 9, 187.
Matter, 1, 5, 32, 34, 92–4, 97, 274, 289.
Megarians, 63–4, 80, 99, 166–70.
Metaphysics, 73, 218, 233–4, 279–83, 292.
Modal logic, 57, 71–2, 185, 215, 236–8, 282, 285, 288.
Modal syllogistic, 57, 80, 237–8.
modi significandi, 197.
Motion, 41–2, 75, 85, 88, 92, 166, 169–70, 219, 229. *See also* Eternity: eternal motion.

Nature, 35–6, 85, 88–9, 181–2, 199, 201, 203–4, 210, 217, 223.
Necessary beings, 96–7, 101–4, 233, 290. *See also* God, necessary existence of.
Necessary conditions as causes in Anselm, 122, 127, 143.
Necessitarianism, 221–2, 224.
Necessity: Aristotle, 59, 63–6, 79, 99, 101–5, 107, 166–7; Boethius, 140–1, 170–2, 174–8; Avicenna, 208, 233; Anselm, 117–22, 125–49; Abaelard, 181–6, Averroes, 209; Moses Maimonides, 207; *Dialectica Monacensis*, 190, 194; William of Sherwood, 193–4; Thomas Aquinas, 209–214, 216–7; Siger of Brabant, 209; Duns Scotus, 219–223, 229, 234; Leibniz, 278–81, Kant, 292; logical necessity, 131, 136–7, 234, 281; logical *v.* physical necessity, 139–40, 142, 223, 279–80; physical necessity, 218–9, 225; temporal necessity, 175–6, 178, 195, 221, 243; temporal *v.* simple necessity, 140–1, 171–2, 181, 184–6, 205, 209, 213; simple *v.* conditional necessity, 139–141, 174–5, 212–3, 279–80; preceding *v.* subsequent necessity, 138–43; necessity *per se v. per accidens*, 190, 194; metaphysical necessity, 219, 275, 279–81; proper *v.* improper necessity, 119, 125–6, 128–31, 134–5, 137–9, 141–6, 149. *See also* Consequence: necessity of the consequence *v.* necessity of the consequent.
Nominales, 165, 195–8.

INDEX OF SUBJECTS

319

Principle of Scarcity (partial denial of the Principle of Plenitude in Aristotle), 74, 77–80, 82, 87–8, 97, 100, 103–6.
Priority: kinds of priority in Aristotle, 73, 75–7, 81–99, 105, 107 (*see* actuality *v.* potentiality); ontological priority of Platonic forms, 20, 36; priority of causes in Duns Scotus, 228.
Probability, 275.
propositio, 180, 196–8.
Providence: *see* God: divine foreknowledge and providence.

Quantification, 264–8, 282–3.
quidditas, 231.

Reciprocity, the law of, 281–2.
Relations, 262–72, 280–1.

Sentences: temporally definite, ix, 9, 140–1, 167, 171, 173, 176, 178, 184–5, 196–8, 211–4, 221, 229, 235–6; temporally indefinite, ix, 9, 163, 167–9, 171–3, 175–6, 178, 180, 184–6, 188, 190, 192–3, 195–6, 211–4, 221–2, 230, 235.
Sophisms, 164–5, 185, 187–9, 193, 243.
Space, 148, 265, 293–6.
Species, 30–6, 83–5, 87–8, 91, 95, 182–3, 189, 235–6.
Statistical interpretation of modality: Aristotle, xi–xii, 9, 64–5, 166, 169, 211, 231; Boethius, 171–3, 176, 178; Abaelard, 180, 182–3, 186–7; Averroes, 246; Thomas Aquinas, 209, 211–4, 221–2, 224–5; Siger of Brabant, 209, 224; other medievals, 188, 190–1, 193–5, 198, 230; moderns, vii–viii, xi; not applied to divine possibilities by medievals, 224–5; criticized by Peter Damian, 201–2; Peter of Poitiers, 198, 205; Grosseteste, 205–6; Duns Scotus, 166, 218, 220–7, 231, 236.
Stoics, xii, 156, 194.
Substance, 75–6, 78, 88–9, 92, 94–8, 182, 189, 191, 261, 265–71, 281, 292.
Sufficient reason, 279, 290.
Supposition theory, 237.
Syncategorematic *v.* categorematic sense, 193–4.

Tense, 72, 194, 196, 200–1, 237.
Teleology, 90–1, 94.
tertia via, 1–2, 51, 74, 214, 277.
Time: Plato on, 40; Aristotle, 75, 77, 88, 94; Anselm, 148; Leibniz, 265; Kant, 293–7, 300–2; the interrelations of time and modality in Aristotle, 8–9, 57–72, 79–88, 99–106, 166–9; Boethius, 170–8; Abaelard, 179–181, 183–6; twelfth and thirteenth century logic, 188–195; Thomas Aquinas, 209–17; Kant, 296–7. *See also* Sentence, Eternity.
Truth: defined, 118–9; truth of statements, 75–6, 126, 139, 141, 143, 148, 163–4, 167, 171, 173, 175–81, 184–6, 188–98, 205, 210–13, 216, 229, 235, 237, 305. *See also* God: Supreme Truth.
Truth values, 138, 140, 142, 178; changing, 167, 171, 175, 177–8, 180–1, 190, 194–6, 211, 213, 221; not changing, 167, 176, 190, 194–7, 205.

SYNTHESE HISTORICAL LIBRARY

Texts and Studies in the History of Logic and Philosophy

Editors:

N. KRETZMANN (Cornell University)
G. NUCHELMANS (University of Leyden)
L. M. DE RIJK (University of Leyden)